Europe's Next Avoidable War

Europe's Next Avoidable War

Nagorno-Karabakh

Edited by

Michael Kambeck

and

Sargis Ghazaryan

First published 2013 by
PALGRAVE MACMILLAN

Palgrave Macmillan in the UK is an imprint of Macmillan Publishers Limited, registered in England, company number 785998, of Houndmills, Basingstoke, Hampshire RG21 6XS.

Palgrave Macmillan in the US is a division of St Martin's Press LLC, 175 Fifth Avenue, New York, NY 10010.

Palgrave Macmillan is the global academic imprint of the above companies and has companies and representatives throughout the world.

Palgrave® and Macmillan® are registered trademarks in the United States, the United Kingdom, Europe and other countries

ISBN: 978–0–230–30066–8

This book is printed on paper suitable for recycling and made from fully managed and sustained forest sources. Logging, pulping and manufacturing processes are expected to conform to the environmental regulations of the country of origin.

A catalogue record for this book is available from the British Library.

A catalog record for this book is available from the Library of Congress.

There was never a good war or a bad peace.
Benjamin Franklin in a letter addressed to
Sir Joseph Banks, 27 July 1783

Peace, progress, human rights – these three goals are insolubly linked to one another: it is impossible to achieve one of these goals if the other two are ignored.
Andrei Sakharov in his Nobel Lecture,
11 December 1975

Endlessly our people gathered their strength to face another day and they never stopped encouraging their leaders to find the courage to resolve this situation so that our children could look to the future with a smile of hope.
John Hume in his Nobel Lecture, Oslo,
10 December 1998

Contents

Introduction

Part I Approaching the Conflict: The Internal Rationale

Conclusion

List of Figures

List of Maps

Acknowledgements

The editors would like to thank all contributors and all the people who with their assistance and proof-reading helped us accomplish this volume, in particular Lidia Gromadzka, Diana Babayan and Claudia Kiso.

We thank the following for permission to reproduce the maps.

Map 1: Courtesy of the University Libraries, The University of Texas at Austin.

Maps 3 and 4: International Crisis Group (ICG). This map is for reference only and should not be taken to imply political endorsement of its content.

Notes on Contributors

Elmar Brok is an MEP (Member of the European Parliament) and one of the most renowned and influential foreign affairs experts among EU decision makers. An MEP since 1980, he is a member of the bureau of the group of the European People's Party (EPP). He is Chairman of the Foreign Affairs Committee of the European Parliament.

Andrew Cooper is Founder, Strategic Director and CEO of the UK-based opinion polling company Populus. He is a leading specialist in the field of opinion research and serves on the management committee of the British Polling Council, an organisation of which Populus is a founding member.

Bernard Coulie has been Honorary Rector of the Université catholique de Louvain (UCL, 2004–09). He is Professor of Armenian and Georgian studies at the Oriental Institute of the UCL, where he has also taught Greek and Byzantine studies. He has published many books and articles on these topics and served as editor of international journals and series. He also gives courses on European culture and identity at the Institute of European Studies of the UCL.

Caroline Cox (Baroness Cox) has been a member of the House of Lords since 1982 and has served numerous times as its Deputy Speaker. She is the founder and CEO of the Humanitarian Aid Relief Trust (HART). Besides being an active human rights activist, Baroness Cox is an eye witness of the conflict in Nagorno-Karabakh and is the author of a number of relevant publications in this field.

Frank Engel has been a Member of the European Parliament since 2009 and member of the bureau of the group of the European People's Party (EPP). He is Honorary Armenian Consul in Luxembourg.

Sargis Ghazaryan is Senior Research Fellow at European friends of Armenia (EuFoA), Brussels. He has taught Geopolitics at the School of International Relations and Diplomacy at the University of Trieste, Italy, where he was also Post-Doctoral Research Fellow in the Department of Political Science. He holds a PhD in Political Geography and Geopolitics and an MA in International Relations and Diplomacy, University of Trieste.

Richard Giragosian is the Director of the Center for Regional Studies. He is very well connected to the White House, a regular contributor to Radio Free Europe/Radio Liberty (RFE/RL) publications and a contributing analyst for the London-based Jane's Information Group, covering political, economic and security issues in the South Caucasus, Central Asia and the Asia-Pacific region.

Geysar Gurbanov is a blogger and youth activist from the Republic of Azerbaijan. He graduated from Baku State University with a Bachelor's in Law. In 2005–06, he studied Administration of Law and Justice in Washington, through a program of the Bureau of Educational and Cultural Affairs of the US Department of State. Before running for the 2009 municipal elections, he was employed as an executive director at the Euro-Atlantic Centre (NATO Information Centre). His professional portfolio includes work with OSCE-ODIHR, EPF-CRRC, British Council, and IREX. His personal blog, The South Caucasus Diary, discusses various aspects of political, economic and social life in the region, attracting around 3,000 readers from 47 countries.

Uwe Halbach is a researcher for the Russian Federation/CIS Department of the German Institute for International Affairs and Security (Stiftung Wissenschaft und Politik, SWP) in Berlin. His areas of expertise include the Caucasus and Central Asia, Russia and the CIS. He has been part of the EU's mission for the post-Georgian war report and is the author of numerous publications.

Paruyr Hovhannisyan is a Senior Counsellor with EuFoA (European Friends of Armenia) and an expert on Armenia's relations with the EU. He served as the Third, then Second Secretary of the Armenian Permanent Mission to the UN from 1998 to 2001. He was also Head of the International Economic Organisations Division with the MFA of Armenia from 2001 to 2005, and also served as a Counsellor and Deputy Head of the Armenian Mission to the EU from 2005 to 2009.

Michael Kambeck is co-founder of the NGO European Friends of Armenia and its Secretary General. He worked in the field of foreign affairs for many years, as Director for Government Relations at Burson-Marsteller and as Chief of Staff for the Chairman of the Foreign Affairs Committee in the European Parliament. He holds a PhD in Political Science from the University of Bonn and a Master's in European Studies from the University of Leeds.

Otto Luchterhandt is the Director of the division for Eastern Legal Studies at the University of Hamburg. He has conducted research in the fields of development of constitutional law, basic rights law, governmental regimes, the Church and the State and the enlargement of the EU. Professor Luchterhandt is an expert on the legal aspects of Nagorno-Karabakh's independence movement and the author of numerous publications.

Sergey Markedonov is currently a Visiting Fellow in the Russian and Eurasia Program at the Center for Strategic and International Studies (CSIS) in Washington, DC. He is an expert on the Caucasus. His publications include several books and reports, 50 academic articles, and more than 400 press pieces. From 2006 to 2010, he held teaching positions at the Russian State University for the Humanities, Moscow State University, and the Diplomatic Academy. From 2001 to 2010 he worked as head of the Interethnic Relations Group and deputy director at the Institute for Political and Military Analysis in Moscow. Markedonov graduated from Rostov-on-Don State University in 1995, where he also earned his doctorate in 1999.

Arpine Martirosyan, born in Yerevan, Armenia, currently resides in Sweden. She holds a BA in English and Italian Philology from Yerevan State University and recently completed a Euroculture Master's of Excellence, majoring in the EU policies of conflict prevention and resolution. Her thesis entitled "EU and Nagorno-Karabakh: rhetoric versus reality?" was published as a book in 2011.

Katherine Morris is an independent researcher, currently working at Safer World. She graduated from University College London with a BA in Russian and French, and from the College of Europe (Natolin Campus) with a Master's in European Interdisciplinary Studies.

Tevan Poghosyan is Executive Director of one of the best-known and most-active independent political NGOs in Armenia, the International Center for Human Development (ICHD). He is also editor on the South Caucasus region at the World Security Network Foundation. In 2001 he became the Executive of the Armenian Atlantic Association and in 2002 started lecturing on Conflict Management and Leadership at the Russian–Armenian (Slavonic) University.

Dirk Rochtus teaches International Relations and German History at Lessius University College in Antwerp. Since 2007 he has been a member of the Flemish Foreign Affairs Council. From 2005 to 2007 he was deputy chief of cabinet of the Flemish minister of Foreign Policy. Rochtus studied Germanic Philology and International Relations at the universities of Bonn and Antwerp. In 1996 he wrote his doctoral dissertation on "The Third Way in the German Democratic Republic 1989/90".

Dennis Sammut is Executive Director of the London Information Network on Conflicts and State-building (LINKS) and a long-time commentator on the Caucasus region and European security issues. From 2002 to 2007 he was co-ordinator of the South Caucasus Parliamentary Initiative. In 2007 he served as co-rapporteur of the Caucasus-Caspian Commission. Currently he is also the Chairman of the Consortium Initiative, a civil society platform supporting the Karabakh peace process.

Peter Semneby was the EU Special Representative for the South Caucasus from 2006 to 2011. From 1997 to 2000 he was responsible for the European Security and Defence Policy at the Swedish Ministry for Foreign Affairs; from 2000 to 2002 he was head of the OSCE mission to Latvia and from 2002 to 2005 he was head of the OSCE mission to Croatia.

Charles Tannock is an MEP (Member of the European Parliament) and the foreign affairs and human rights spokesman for the UK Conservative delegation. He was elected to the UK Conservative delegation bureau between 2005 and 2007. He is currently a member of the Foreign Affairs Committee, on which he is also the European Conservatives and Reformist Group co-ordinator (spokesman). He is also a member of the Human Rights Subcommittee.

List of Acronyms and Abbreviations

AP	Action Plans
ASSR	Autonomous Soviet Socialist Republic
BENELUX	Belgium, Netherlands, Luxembourg
BP	British Petroleum
BTC	Baku-Tbilisi-Ceyhan [crude oil pipeline]
CBMs	confidence-building measures
CIS	Commonwealth of Independent States
CSDP	Common Security and Defence Policy
CSOs	civil society organisations
CSTO	Collective Security Treaty Organization
EaP	Eastern Partnership
EC	European Commission
ECHO	European Community Humanitarian Aid Office
EEAS	European External Action Service
ENP	European Neighbourhood Policy
ENPI	European Neighbourhood and Partnership Instrument
EP	European Parliament
ESDP	European Security and Defence Policy
ESS	European Security Strategy
EU	European Union
EuFoA	European Friends of Armenia
EUSR	EU Special Representative to the South Caucasus
FDI	foreign direct investment
FEOGA	Fonds Europeen d'Orientation et de Garantie Agricole [European Agricultural Guidance and Guarantee Fund]
HALO Trust	Hazardous Area Life-Support Organization (HALO specialises in the removal of the hazardous debris of war)
HR/VP	High Representative of the Union for Foreign Affairs and Security Policy and Vice-President of the European Commission
ICAMOS	International Council on Monuments and Sites
ICHD	International Center for Human Development
ICJ	International Court of Justice
IDPs	internally displaced persons
IPA	Instrument for Pre-accession Assistance
IPSC	Institute for Political and Sociological Consulting
IRA	Irish Republican Army
ISAF	International Security Assistance Force

MEP	Member of the European Parliament
NATO	North Atlantic Treaty Organization
NGOs	non-governmental organisations
NK	Nagorno-Karabakh
NKAO	Nagorno-Karabakh Autonomous Oblast
NKR	Nagorno-Karabakh [de-facto] Republic
OIC	Organization of Islamic Conference
OSCE	Organization for Security and Co-operation in Europe
PCC	Parliamentary Cooperation Committee
PLO	Palestine Liberation Organization
SSR	Soviet Socialist Republic
TACIS	Technical Assistance to the Commonwealth of Independent States
TEAS	The European Azerbaijan Society
THM	town hall meetings
UN	United Nations
UNESCO	United Nations Educational, Scientific and Cultural Organization
UNOMIG	United Nations Observer Mission in Georgia
USA	United States of America
USSR	Union of Soviet Socialist Republics
YFD	Youth for Development

Ethnolinguistic Groups in the Caucasus Region

Ukraine • Rostov

Rostov

Sea of Azov

Krasnodar Kray

Krasnodar

Adygea

Maykop

Cherkessk

Kara Cher.

Black Sea

Sokhumi

Abkhazia

K'ut'aisi

Ajaria

Bat'umi

Elista

Kalmykia

Stavropol'

Stavropol' Kray

Kabar Bal

Nal'chik

Ingushetia

North Ossetia

Nazran'

Vladikavkaz

Chechnya

Grozny

South Ossetia

Ts'khinvali

Georgia

T'bilisi

Armenia

Yerevan

Turkey

Naxçıvan (Nakhichevan')

Naxçıvan

Azer.

Astrakhan'

Kazakhstan

Astrakhan'

Caspian Sea

Makhachkala

Dagestan

Azerbaijan

Baku

Xankändi (Stepanakert)

Nagorno-Karabakh

Iran

Legend

Caucasian Peoples

Abkhaz
1. Abkhaz

Circassian
2. A Adygey
3. Cherkess
4. Kabardin

Georgian
5. G Georgian

Dagestani
6. Agul
7. Avar
8. D Dargin
9. l Lak
10. L Lezgin
11. Rutul
12. Tabasaran
13. Tsakhur

Veinakh
14. Chechen
15. Ingush

Other

Indo-European Peoples

Armenian
16. a Armenian

Greek
17. Greek

Iranian
18. K Kurd
19. O Ossetian
20. Talysh

Slavic
21. R Russian

Altaic Peoples

Turkic
22. Z Azeri
23. Balkar
24. Karachay
25. Kumyk
26. Nogay
27. T Turkmen

Mongol
28. Kalmyk

Sparsely populated or uninhabited areas are shown in white.

Republic, oblast, or kray boundary

0   100 Kilometers
0   100 Miles

734538 (R00397) 1-95

Map 1 Ethnolinguistic groups in the Caucasus region

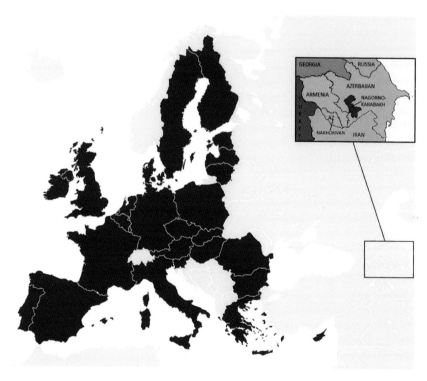

Map 2 Europe and South Caucasus

Map 3 Nagorno-Karabakh with adjacent territories

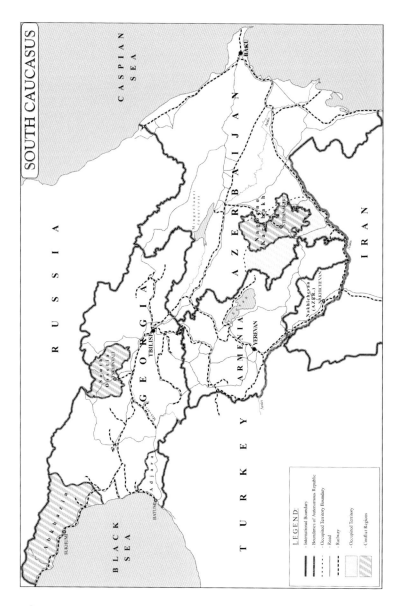

Map 4 The South Caucasus region with de facto entities

Introduction

1
Introduction

Sargis Ghazaryan

This volume was conceived as a response to the increased interest of the expert community, the scholars dealing with ethno-political conflicts in the European Union's (EU) neighbourhood and that of the general public. The decision to write such a book was all the more urgent given the likelihood of a renewed outbreak of war in and around Nagorno-Karabakh (NK), a small region of 4,400 sq. km,[1] with a population of roughly 130–140,000, and a contested status: de facto independent, but internationally recognised as part of Azerbaijan. Moreover, it is also our aim to contribute to filling a considerable gap in the area of research and policy analysis about the conflict in the current shifting geopolitical environment. Our purpose is to accompany the reader on an intricate, but fascinating journey which reflects the complex, tragic, yet still marvellous Caucasian patchwork. To that end, the conflict's timeline will surely be useful.[2]

"An arms race, escalating front-line clashes, vitriolic war rhetoric and a virtual breakdown in peace talks are increasing the chance Armenia and Azerbaijan will go back to war over Nagorno-Karabakh", as the International Crisis Group (ICG) puts it in its latest report,[3] exposes the need for such a volume now. In other words, by capitalising on the lessons learnt from the developments during the months leading to the August 2008 war in Georgia, we intend to shed light on the strategic significance of avoiding Europe's next war, for the security and foreign policy agendas of all actors directly or indirectly involved in the South Caucasus. The current overlap of interests of the major external actors involved in the Nagorno-Karabakh talks, France,

---

[1] *Encyclopaedia Britannica*, http://www.britannica.com/EBchecked/topic/401669/Nagorno-Karabakh (date accessed: 07 March 2011).

[2] See *Timeline 1918–2011*, pp. 24–32.

[3] International Crisis Group (2011) *Armenia and Azerbaijan: Preventing War*, ICG Report, 08 February 2011, Brussels, 5, http://www.crisisgroup.org/en/regions/europe/caucasus/B60-armenia-and-azerbaijan-preventing-war.aspx (date accessed: 07 March 2011).

United States and Russia is a distinctive feature for the prevention of war – unlike the pre-war situation in Georgia, where there was a clash of interests of the external actors. However, both the situation on the ground and the macro-regional security environment display so many variables and fragilities that the avoidance of military escalation is far from being guaranteed.

The book exposes the current situation in the Nagorno-Karabakh conflict and its implications, and has a strong interdisciplinary emphasis. By interdisciplinary emphasis we mean both the range of disciplines within the social sciences used to approach the general topic of the book and the combination of contributors who are both practitioners and scholars with a strong knowledge of this field, bringing a broad range of expertise to the volume. On the other hand, we have to acknowledge that, despite efforts, it was not possible to convince a larger number of Azerbaijani authors to contribute to the volume. The key reason for rejecting to contribute was assumably the fear for repression by the Azerbaijani state, inside and even outside of Azerbaijan. The editors addressed the issue of balance in five ways: (1) by inviting Azeri authors who are known to deliver an Azeri viewpoint independent of the prepositions from Baku (Gurbanov offers such a viewpoint); (2) by ensuring that several authors are invited, who are known to defend more pro-Azeri viewpoints, despite not being of Azeri origin (without sharp differentiation, just under one-third of the contributors fall into that group); (3) by limiting the number of contributors who are known to defend more pro-Armenian viewpoints (to roughly the same size as the aforementioned group); (4) by inviting a larger number of contributors who are explicitly neutral in their background and viewpoints (more than one-third); (5) most importantly, by verifying that all information provided in the contributions is factual and can be verified with the sources provided. This also counts for the Timeline and the Conclusion, where the editors sought to represent both viewpoints of the key issues indiscriminately. For example, our timeline includes information on the much disputed Khojaly killings of February 1992, representing that Azerbaijan views this as "Genocide", but also referring to relevant other sources – without making a conclusive judgement. Another example may be the much disputed meaning of the four UN resolutions of 1993 on the Karabakh war, both viewpoints of which are represented in the Conclusion chapter, and again leaving the conclusive judgement to the reader.

The volume collects contributions focusing not only on different aspects of the Nagorno-Karabakh conflict (particularly the EU's external actions related to conflict resolution) but also from the varied perspectives of legal studies, geopolitics, history, sociology, comparative politics, international affairs and EU foreign and security policy studies. In other words, our intention is to bridge academia with policy making in an effort which is not exclusively descriptive and analytical, but has the ambition of being prescriptive and providing policy proposals.

Our goal is to deliver a comprehensive picture by combining these diverse viewpoints on, and dimensions and narratives of the conflict as seen by different authors against the background of their respective specialities. For instance, when it comes to different narratives, the reader will find apparently diverging dates for the start of the military operations in Nagorno-Karabakh – some authors put it in the end of the 1980s, others in the beginning of the 1990s – that is, because of unusual fact of the absence of a declaration of war between Armenia and Azerbaijan, while several events between 1988 and 1992 were marked by the use of force or military hostilities. Besides, military operations were on-going between Azerbaijani and Armenian forces in NK, yet they also heavily affected the frontline communities along the Armenian–Azerbaijani border proper. In addition, our aim is to provide the reader with a thorough analysis of the conflict in Nagorno-Karabakh and of how it has evolved throughout the years, showing from a variety of angles how we got to where we are today and ultimately deriving concrete and more promising policy proposals than are otherwise currently debated. As the title suggests, the latter will focus on measures to reduce the heightened possibility of the outbreak of war. Overall, the book is intended to contribute to the debate in academia and among policy makers.

Until very recently, the conflict has mainly been analysed in the context of the Organization for Security and Co-operation in Europe (OSCE) Minsk Group activities, partly ignoring the fact that the powers concerned have evolved and that the EU as a new foreign policy actor is progressively appearing on the scene. In this context, the fact that the scope of the topic is located between the ethnic conflict in Nagorno-Karabakh and Common Foreign and Security Policy means that the theme can be perceived as part of the wider discourse on "conflict prevention and crisis management" and "state building and institutional transformation", which has been dominant in the EU ever since the fall of the Soviet Union.

Above all, the primary purpose of this volume is to explore the chances of war and peace in Nagorno-Karabakh amidst a rapidly evolving geopolitical environment, both regional and global, and to detect both a locus and a modus operandi for EU action, which may determine a breakthrough in the currently volatile and explosive situation around Nagorno-Karabakh.

Finally, the present volume offers a plurality of voices and perspectives, which by definition will in some cases be in contrast with each other. These analyses and their variety of perspectives are framed into a coherent framework, consisting of the introduction with the geopolitical setting and the timeline, the conclusion and in between the three parts: the internal rationale of the conflict; its external rationale; and the peace rationale, each focusing on the conflict from a particular angle. In Part I, we explore the internal rationale of the conflict, its genesis and evolution; its common features and differences with other ethno-political conflicts; the ways in which the involved societies perceive the conflict; and the place it has made in their collective consciousness for fears and expectations, assumptions and core beliefs, proximity and distance – in other words in their *mental maps*. In Part II, we analyse the external rationale by outlining the wider geopolitical visions of the EU, the United States, Russia and the regional actors who affect the conflict's dynamics. In Part III, final part of the book, we investigate the rationale for peace and try to answer the question: How can we avoid Europe's next war? In doing so, the authors explore the ways in which Europe can act to prevent another tragedy in the South Caucasus, or in other words, in Europe.

Part I   Approaching the conflict: the internal rationale

Prof. Bernard Coulie (Université Louvain la Neuve) approaches the conflict from historical, cultural and identity-oriented perspectives. By stating that the Caucasus is the "revolving door between East and West", and that the Nagorno-Karabakh conflict is "quintessential in that it confronts the observer with basic questions which exist more generally in today's world", he poses fundamental questions – from an innovative perspective – about war, the burden of history, cultural contamination, identity/otherness interplay and Europe's role in the region.

While comparing the conflict with other ethnic conflicts in Eastern Europe, **Uwe Halbach** (SWP, Berlin) reveals that the Nagorno-Karabakh conflict is arguably the most serious in terms of extra-regional implications. After outlining the distinctive traits of the conflict, he emphasises Azerbaijan's frustration with the status quo and Armenia's hopes to preserve the situation. The combined stagnation in the reconciliation process, and the urgency to resolve matters in order to avoid military escalation, constitute a significant challenge to the international community, according to the author. Moreover, the author argues that as with the 2008 war in Georgia, the international community will find itself similarly unprepared in the event of an outbreak of war in Nagorno-Karabakh.

Tevan Poghosyan (ICHD, Yerevan) and Arpine Martirosyan (independent expert, Uppsala) analyses the fascinating results of THMs (town hall meetings), which are informal public meetings conducted in Armenia, Azerbaijan and Nagorno-Karabakh. This unique format reveals important findings about the perceptions of war, security and social and economic development among different strata of the three societies. The author explains that solutions to the conflict are seen through one prism by the participants: their own position. Trust is regarded as a key to the solution of the conflict. Currently, however, the relationship between the parties is dominated by extreme distrust.

When it comes to the EU, the author exposes a mismatch between EU ambitions in the region and the way societies perceive the Union, a situation which the EU needs to take into account in order to adjust its tools to match its declared goals in the region.

Dirk Rochtus (Lessius University College, Antwerp) offers a unique analysis in which he draws comparisons between the independence movements of Flanders and Nagorno-Karabakh in order to highlight some surprisingly common features. After stating that neither Flanders nor Nagorno-Karabakh would tolerate the resurrection of a unitary, centralised state, he offers different policy options for the next stages in Nagorno-Karabakh conflict resolution.

Andrew Cooper (Populus, London) and **Katherine Morris** (independent expert, London) analyse the findings of the only internationally conducted comparative opinion poll to date in Armenia and Nagorno-Karabakh. The poll of October 2010 concerns the overall regional situation and the role of the international community. The results will surprise those who argue that the societies are not ready for peace. The findings highlight several important issues such as the threats perceived by the people and the need for specific confidence building measures; and the mismatch between the declared roles of international organisations and NGOs and how the people affected by the conflict perceive them.

The objective of **Baroness Cox's** (House of Lords, London) chapter is twofold. It describes, from the perspective of one of the very few Western eye witnesses on the ground, the political-military developments which led to the war in Nagorno-Karabakh between the collapse of the Soviet Union and the emergence of independent Armenia and Azerbaijan. However, the chapter is also devoted to the possible role of the UK in preventing a further escalation of tensions in the region. While the UK is not directly involved in the negotiation process, it is supporting current diplomatic efforts, and there is a certain potential to reinforce this policy.

Part II   The international community as foreign policy actor in NK: the external rationale

Having followed and promoted developments from within the EU's foreign affairs machinery, **Elmar Brok** (MEP, Brussels) provides an analysis of the transformation of the EU's non-role into a role in the South Caucasus, and in Nagorno-Karabakh in particular. He also sheds light on developments within the EU itself and its foreign and security policy toolkit. The leitmotiv of the chapter is the assumption that the "underlying basis for the EU's foreign policy remains the Union's common values of peace, achieved through economic and political integration, democracy and the rule of law – including international law". The author pledges an increased and more incisive role for the EU in addressing the conflict in Nagorno-Karabakh.

While outlining the shifting geopolitical environment in the region from a Euro-Atlantic perspective, **Richard Giragosian** (Regional Studies Centre, Yerevan) argues that two recent developments in the Southern Caucasus, namely the 2008 war in Georgia and the process of Armenian–Turkish rapprochement, have dramatically altered the regional security landscape, providing a window of opportunity to ensure durable security and lasting stability. The author suggests that in order to ensure lasting stability, there are two main sets of imperatives: firstly, a concerted international effort to ensure the immediate strengthening of a ceasefire regime in Nagorno-Karabakh and the participation of the latter at the negotiation table; and secondly, a firm enhancement of democratic and economic reforms throughout the region.

Sergey Markedonov (CSIS, Washington, D.C.) provides the reader with an extensive and comprehensive analysis of the shifting visions of Russia, the United States, Turkey and Iran regarding the South Caucasus in general and Nagorno-Karabakh in particular. Furthermore, he addresses both the recent conflict dynamic and the evolution of the peace process, highlighting cooperative, rather than competing, attitudes of Russia and the United States when it comes to the peace process in Nagorno-Karabakh. A consensus between Russia and the West regarding Nagorno-Karabakh is a significant exception compared to the situation surrounding Georgia in 2008 and can make a tangible difference while pushing for the final settlement of the conflict. Finally, he prioritises, in the current stage of the peace process, the prevention of the use of force by all sides through a legally binding document.

Paruyr Hovhannisyan (EuFoA, Brussels) presents a detailed analysis of the evolution of the EU position on the Nagorno-Karabakh conflict from the 1980s up to the present, and concludes by outlining anticipated future scenarios. He notes the importance of being mindful of recent history in order to ensure that current strategies remain consistent and sustained. While the chapter refers to all European Institutions and bodies, particular stress is made on the activities of the European Parliament, as the driver of EU new policies and innovative ideas vis-à-vis the region.

Part III Europe's next avoidable war: the peace rationale

By addressing the EU's potential to contribute to the resolution of the Nagorno-Karabakh conflict and to security in the region, **Peter Semneby** (former EUSR to the Southern Caucasus, Brussels) outlines the EU's policy in the region. He agrees that the situation around Nagorno-Karabakh, as one of the most dangerous conflicts in the EU neighbourhood, poses a serious danger for this volatile and strategically important region. According to the author, the peace process is being constantly threatened, and the EU could play a more assertive role.

Geysar Gurbanov (Azerbaijani blogger civic activist and former head of the NATO Information Centre in Baku, currently living in Seattle) reveals in a unique fashion the genesis and consequent evolution of the conflict: through the prism of the Greek myth of the Golden Apple of Discord, which led to the Trojan War. By furthering his analysis, based on genuinely innovative approaches to the conflict, the author applies the means of collective psychology to shed light on the conflict's societal dimension. Moreover, he applies this toolkit to the seemingly most insurmountable obstacles to the conflict's resolution. He argues that the solution to the conflict lies beyond the *realpolitik* of the state actors. In fact, he maintains that peace can be achieved only if larger parts of the societies affected participate, partially, through social media, and if democracy, tolerance and integration are enforced at a regional level.

In his mainly policy-oriented contribution, **Charles Tannock** (MEP, Brussels) seeks to answer the following question: "Since the conflict in and surrounding Nagorno-Karabakh is clearly an increasing security threat to the European Union (EU), what are the appropriate responses of the EU and its Member States to prevent and deter military escalation and a renewed outbreak of hostilities in the region and ultimately to resolve the conflict?" The author provides an uncommonly clear analysis of both threats and opportunities for the Union, which stem from regional instability in the South Caucasus, and he suggests truly innovative policy proposals, implying the use of the new foreign and security policy instruments in the EU's possession.

Dennis Sammut (LINKS, London) argues that at present, the positions of both Armenia and Azerbaijan are cemented and share diametrically opposite and mutually exclusive visions about ways out of the conflict. The 1988–94 war in Nagorno-Karabakh still has considerable influence on both countries' politics. The chapter urges political change whereby the political elites in both countries embrace a consensus for peace by overcoming their respective differences. He suggests building a broad foundation of those who believe that peace is the only way forward for a viable future.

According to **Frank Engel** (MEP, Brussels) the possibility of violent conflict is omnipresent in this region, as illustrated by the outbreak of war in Georgia in 2008. Arguments on both sides have the right to exist, but do not lead to the solution of the conflict. The author suggests that the Caucasus might follow the example set by the European Union which, after centuries of warfare in Europe, took the bold move of gradually rendering irrelevant the formerly contested borders of its Member States.

In his international law-focused analysis, **Prof. Otto Luchterhandt** (University of Hamburg) touches upon Azerbaijan's interpretation of the principle of self-defence. He compares Azerbaijan's position with that of Georgia before the 2008 war and suggests that conclusions need to be drawn from that experience and applied to Nagorno-Karabakh. The author strongly advocates for the urgency of an international, legally binding move resulting in Azerbaijan's compliance with the ceasefire for the entire duration of the Bishkek Ceasefire signed in 1994, which is indefinite.

Michael Kambeck (EuFoA, Brussels) draws conclusions from the volume by suggesting a set of recommendations for Europe on how to avoid the next war on the continent's soil – in Nagorno-Karabakh. As a basis for these proposals, the author coherently offers a comprehensive description of the status quo, derived from the contributions in this volume. Using the same methodology, he outlines scenarios of war and peace. Ultimately, he concludes that since the next war in Nagorno-Karabakh "can be avoided, it should be".

2

Background: Setting the Geopolitical Stage

Sargis Ghazaryan

This chapter provides background analysis on the conflict in Nagorno-Karabakh, the wider geographic region to which it belongs, and to the EU's role in the South Caucasus.[1]

The South Caucasus – a "non-region"?

Home to ancient civilisations, the South Caucasus has a history and identity largely shaped by Mesopotamian, Urartian, Ancient Greek, Roman, Byzantine, Persian, Arab, Ottoman, Tsarist Russian and Soviet legacies. While acting both as a filtering buffer and a *limes* between East and West, it has both imported and exported knowledge, iconographies and identity models throughout history, dispersed by merchants, philosophers, warriors and clergymen. Since Antiquity this small mountainous region has borne witness to multiple conflicting historical metaphors characterised by deep, multilayered segmentation of identity narratives. The definition by Friedrich Ratzel of borders as "scars of History"[2] illustrates brilliantly the state of affairs in the Caucasus, where borders combine reality with imagination, and history has left many open wounds. While ethnic Armenians and Georgians are indigenous to the Caucasus and form the oldest Christian nations, ethnic Azeris – mainly Shiite Muslims – are relatively new to the region.[3]

---

[1] By South Caucasus, we mean the region including Armenia, Azerbaijan and Georgia.

[2] F. Ratzel (1987) *Politische Geographie* (oder die Geographie der Staaten des Verkehres und des Kriegs – ed. 1902) (Munich: Oldenbourg).

[3] For a historical background and an analysis of nation-building processes in the South Caucasus see R.G. Suny (1993) *Looking toward Ararat: Armenia in Modern History* (Bloomington: Indiana University Press); T. Swietochowski (1985) *Russian Azerbaijan 1905–1920: The Shaping of National Identity in a Muslim Community* (Cambridge: Cambridge University Press); R.G. Suny (1994) *The Making of the Georgian Nation*

Many authors describe the current state of affairs in the Caucasus by using the metaphor of the "Great Game" – the nineteenth-century clash between the British and the Russian Empires for control of Central Asia. But the contemporary picture in the region is more complex, given the involvement of new actors and their competing interests, be those interests political, economic or ideological, on the one hand, and exclusively hegemonic or inclusively multilateral, on the other.

Another misleading geopolitical metaphor previously used to describe the regional geopolitical framework is that of two mutually exclusive geopolitical axes intersecting in the South Caucasus: North–South (Russia–Armenia–Iran) and East–West (Azerbaijan–Georgia–Turkey–United States). While conceived of as increasingly conflicting dividing lines and further strengthening zero-sum logic in the region, these axes are becoming outdated due to the rise of a certain degree of complementarity among the main international actors – Russia, the United States, the EU as a whole and its Member States, China, Turkey, Iran and others, are all engaged in the region and are apparently, or at least at a declaratory level, inclined to generate win-win situations after two decades of confrontation.

It is not surprising that a common feature of both the Great Game and the intersecting geopolitical axes metaphors, although purely descriptive, is their being exogenous, generated and managed by external actors and imposed upon the region.

The South Caucasus is entangled with frozen conflicts, which tend to suddenly de-freeze, yet the military spending of state actors is increasing, with the Azerbaijani military budget doubling year after year.[4] It is, in fact, unrealistic to speak about regional policies, since a regional identity is absent in the South Caucasus, and interstate relations are characterised mainly by contrasting, rather than cooperative, behaviours. Armenia, Georgia and Azerbaijan are still facing the challenges of statehood and sovereignty. Geographically speaking, the region displays two models in terms of sovereignty: a pre-Westphalian one, applied to the three de facto independent, but de jure non-state actors: Abkhazia, South Ossetia and Nagorno-Karabakh; and partly to Georgia and Azerbaijan, since they are still seeking to restore control over their formal, de jure, state territories; and a quasi-Westphalian

(Bloomington: Indiana University Press); R.G. Suny (ed.) (1983) *Transcaucasia, Nationalism and Social Change: Essays in the History of Armenia, Azerbaijan, and Georgia* (Ann Arbor: University of Michigan Press); B. Berberoglu (ed.) (1995) *The National Question: Nationalism, Ethnic Conflict, and Self-Determination in the 20th Century* (Philadelphia: Temple University Press).

[4] International Crisis Group (2011) *Armenia and Azerbaijan: Preventing War*, ICG Report, 8 February 2011, Brussels, 5, http://www.crisisgroup.org/en/regions/europe/caucasus/B60-armenia-and-azerbaijan-preventing-war.aspx (date accessed: 07 March 2011).

one, which better describes the state of affairs in Armenia. A common char-
acteristic of all de facto and de jure state actors in the region is that they
have missed a fully Westphalian experience of the nation-state when this
was a dominant tendency in the rest of Europe, largely subject to foreign
domination.[5] Currently, the local political elites are excessively devoted to
the idea of the nation-state, while Europe is becoming post-Westphalian.

There is a critical absence of security in the South Caucasus. At this point
one should define state security by offering a comprehensive theoretical framework. Barry Buzan's and Ole Waever's approaches are useful in this regard.
They argue that a comprehensive understanding of state security can no longer
ignore non-traditional challenges to states (i.e. social and economic turmoil,
democratic gaps, economic threats, environmental disasters, etc.) as well as
traditional external politico–military ones, dominant in Cold War studies.[6]
This theoretical shift is particularly important when analysing perceptions
surrounding security in South Caucasus countries. By stating that "security is
a relational phenomenon", based on mainly subjective threat assessments by
the actors or the "securitising agents" involved, Buzan and Waever argue that
both in the case of traditional and non-traditional challenges to state security,
the membership of a state to regional or sub-regional political and economic
groupings, or "regional security complexes", is extremely relevant.[7]

When it comes to the level of democratisation after almost two decades
since their independence, Armenia, Georgia and to a lesser extent Azerbaijan,
have managed to build up democratic institutional facades.[8] However, they
are still unable to stimulate and maintain fully participatory *polyarchies*,
in a Dahlian sense,[9] and fill the gap between the governments and their
electorates. This endemic state weakness can be understood to have several
components: a lack of institutional capacity; a lack of genuine legitimacy
and a constant polarisation of the political arena, combined with lack of
governance. Moreover, it can also be argued that South Caucasus societies
reflect a lack of state monopoly over the legitimate use of force, as defined
by Max Weber.[10] In fact, while some of the regional actors are displaying a

---

[5] Between the seventeenth and the end of the twentieth centuries the region was
divided under the domination of the Ottoman, Russian Tsarist, Soviet Empires and
Persia.

[6] B. Buzan, O. Wæver and J. De Wilde (1998) *Security: A New Framework for Analysis*
(Boulder: Lynne Rienner Publishers, London).

[7] Ibid.

[8] D. Lynch (2003) "A Regional Insecurity Dynamic", in D. Lynch (ed.) *The South
Caucasus: A Challenge for the EU*, Challiot Paper n. 65 (ISS-EU, Paris).

[9] See R.A. Dahl (1989) *Democracy and Its Critics* (New Haven: Yale University
Press).

[10] Y. Kalyuzhnova and D. Lynch (2000) "Euro-Asian Conflicts and Peace-keeping
Dilemmas", in Y. Kalyuzhnova and D. Lynch (eds) *The Euro-Asian World: A Period of
Transitions* (London: Macmillan Press).

certain degree of evolving democratisation, others are going down the road of autocracy.[11]

As far as non-military, economic security threats to the region are concerned, it is clear that economic development is very much dependent on the transport and communication networks of which a country is part. The inclusion of all the regional actors in macro-regional transport and communication networks is of vital importance for regional stability in order to avoid the rise of hegemonies. However, the current situation is not ideal from this perspective. In fact, in 1993 Turkey unilaterally closed its border with Armenia; the country is bypassed by the only pipeline delivering Azerbaijani oil to the Mediterranean and is also subject to similar isolation regarding new projects for energy transit routes and railroads. This can be seen as part of a wider Azerbaijani strategy of imposing a regime of maximum isolation on Armenia due to the unresolved status of the conflict in Nagorno-Karabakh.

The South Caucasus has no regional institutional structure. This critically low level of regional integration prevents local actors from defining common policies and jointly exploring ways to address regional insecurity and instability. Their efforts are directed more in the search for external support rather than on the establishment of a "Caucaso-centric" geopolitical discourse. The situation is further complicated by closed borders between Turkey and Armenia, Armenia and Azerbaijan and Georgia and Russia. It goes without saying that because the degree of regional integration in South Caucasus is critically low, the patterns of insecurity are extremely high, according to Buzan's and Waever's model.

Still, the mindset outlined above is gradually undergoing major changes. Arguably, we are witnessing epochal transformations in the geopolitics of

---

[11] See Nations in Transit 2001, The Freedom House (2011), 21 http://www.freedomhouse.org/images/File/nit/2011/NIT-2011-Release_Booklet.pdf (date accessed: 27 June 2011); see also Europa (2011) European Commission, High Representative of the European Union for Foreign Affairs and Security Policy, "Implementation of the European Neighbourhood Policy in 2010, Country report: Armenia", http://ec.europa.eu/world/enp/pdf/progress2011/sec_11_639_en.pdf (date accessed: 25 May 2011); Europa (2011) European Commission, High Representative of the European Union for Foreign Affairs and Security Policy, "Implementation of the European Neighbourhood Policy in 2010, Country report: Azerbaijan", http://ec.europa.eu/world/enp/pdf/progress2011/sec_11_640_en.pdf, (date accessed: 25 May 2011); Europa (2011) European Commission, High Representative of the European Union for Foreign Affairs and Security Policy, "Implementation of the European Neighbourhood Policy in 2010, Country report: Georgia", http://ec.europa.eu/world/enp/pdf/progress2011/sec_11_649_en.pdf, (date accessed: 25 May 2011); in the same issue see also the European Parliament Resolution of 12 May 2011 on Azerbaijan, http://www.europarl.europa.eu/sides/getDoc.do?pubRef=-//EP//TEXT+TA+P7-TA-2011-0243+0+DOC+XML+V0//EN (date accessed: 17 May 2011).

the region, due both to endogenous and exogenous developments, such as the August 2008 war in Georgia; the "reset" of US–Russian relations; the Turkish search for "actorness" in its neighbourhood; unprecedented societal movements in Iran; new projects for the exploitation and transit of hydrocarbons to European markets from the Caspian Sea and Central Asia;[12] and growing EU ambitions in the field of foreign and security policies, to name just a few. These developments have also led to important shifts in the rationale surrounding the Nagorno-Karabakh peace process.

Moreover, there is currently a process underway which is leading to some kind of "intermediary" regional identity. It is the case of the rise of European awareness in almost all strata of local societies and the growing impact of this awareness on the local political discourse. All the state actors are included in the European Neighbourhood Policy (ENP) and in the Eastern Partnership, and are negotiating Association Agreements with the EU. Furthermore, they are also members of the Organisation for Security and Cooperation in Europe (OSCE) and the Council of Europe (CoE). As such, there are already tentative efforts underway to dilute the patterns of mutual enmity within the countries of the South Caucasus into a wider European, and not exclusively EU, political space. The main obstacles to the transformation of transitional regional identity into strategic regional awareness, otherwise defined as process of regionalisation, are the unresolved ethnic conflicts – the Nagorno-Karabakh conflict at present having the most dangerous potential to reignite.

Both regionalisation (an exogenous process driven mainly by economic interests) and regionalism (an endogenous process leading to political integration) are of fundamental importance for the EU's action in the region, and nationalism and "frozen conflicts" are the main obstacles to this process. In this perspective, Jean Gottmann's circulation-iconography relation,[13] as outlined below, provides a very useful descriptive toolkit.

The current historical imperative for the South Caucasus is the need to transform the trauma of disaggregation, partition and ethnic wars into memory, cohabitation and intercultural dialogue at the regional level. Partitioning brings with it major political consequences: majorities become minorities and vice-versa, and the regional balance of powers undergoes deep alterations.

The political partitioning of geographical space is therefore an essential concept and a political issue of fundamental importance. The question asked by Gottmann in 1952 was: Why does mankind need to partition

[12] The Caspian basin emerges strategically as a non-OPEC, huge source of oil and natural gas situated between the Middle Eastern and Russian energy networks where, apart from Russia, all external actors are relative newcomers.

[13] See J. Gottmann (1952) *La politique des Etats et leur géographie* (Paris: Armand Collin).

geographical space; what leads to the fragmentation of mankind along territorial lines? The answer was: The interplay between *circulation* – meaning movement flows but also cultural contamination and integration – and *iconography* – meaning ancestral symbolic systems, new and old identity narratives and localism or nationalism. Circulation and iconography are, therefore, the two extremes between which geopolitics acts. When circulation increases, the geographical space becomes integrated. However, the rise of iconographies leads to additional or reinforced political partitioning of the geographic space. It is certainly a zero-sum relation.

The violent period, which led to the independence of the former Soviet republics of the South Caucasus and caused ethnic conflicts in the region, interrupted a sort of "Gottmannian" circulation, at least from socio-economic and cultural viewpoints. This process led to an immediate destruction of the supposed ethno-culturally emancipated model of the Soviet Union and brought about the dominance of *iconographies*, which still prevails in the region. This process resulted in increased partitioning.

Currently, iconographies seem to prevail in the whole region. This is, to some extent, understandable, because they act as self-defence mechanisms. However, the European institutions are better equipped to regenerate the potential that is necessary for an increase in circulation, which can lead to integrational political discourses, not least because the EU is a vivid example of such a transformation.

The strategic promise, in the long term, of a common European destiny for the South Caucasus, would certainly emerge as the main antidote against a re-proliferation of nationalism. As for incentives for both regionalism and regionalisation, given the importance of steel and coal in post-war European integration, hydrocarbons might have the same stabilising role in the post-Soviet Southern Caucasus, conflict-torn and segmented as the region has become. However, the abundance of hydrocarbons in the region has, to date, brought about patterns of destructive destabilisation. In fact, increased military spending is turning into a Cold War style arms race. Yet, unlike the bi-polar world, which was restrained by the nuclear deterrent, the Southern Caucasus is currently witnessing the procuring and stockpiling conventional weaponry at unprecedented levels.

The EU – a prominent absent or reluctant heavyweight appearing on the stage?

The EU is currently facing global and multi-dimensional security challenges, and it has to generate global and multi-dimensional responses jointly with other regional and international organisations. It aspires to become a security provider in the international arena. It develops pragmatic threat assessments and is gradually transforming words into deeds. We are currently witnessing efforts by the EU to transform its declared goals into

concrete policy through robust means in the sphere of its foreign and security policies.

At that time of the inclusion of the three South Caucasian countries into
the framework of the ENP in 2003, political analysts and scholars wondered
whether the far-reaching intentions of EU decision makers would result in
political substance during the years to come. The recent evolution of the
ENP and its upgrading to the Eastern Partnership is positively engaging the
South Caucasus and highlights the importance of EU efforts to "develop a
zone of prosperity and a friendly neighbourhood"[14] in the region by offering enhanced cooperation to neighbours who are not yet candidates.

EU–South Caucasus relations are increasingly becoming a strategic issue
for both sides, and a breakdown of this process could lead to a certain degree
of destabilisation in the South Caucasus. The EU position in the region is
determined by evolving threats and opportunities which still require deep
analysis. Initially, EU policies towards the region had to face both internal and external challenges. The EU had to act in an extremely polarised
geopolitical environment in which the influence of external power politics
such as the Russian Federation, the United States, Turkey and Iran clearly
prevailed over the EU's *normative power.*[15] It would not be incorrect to assert
that a clash between Hobbesian, hard-power oriented and Lockean, soft-
power oriented approaches to security in the South Caucasus was taking
place in the 1990s.

As regards the threat–opportunity dichotomy, all five key threats to the
Union identified in the European Security Strategy (ESS) – extremism, terrorism, state failure, regional conflicts and organised crime,[16] are either
present or can be potentially generated in the region. Opportunities include
the prospect of a stable, secure and democratic periphery, energy security
and diversification of energy corridors and the role of the region as a bridge
between the EU, Middle East and Central Asia. Moreover, the Union emphasises the importance of regional cooperation and regionalisation in the
South Caucasus – a public good which is badly needed by the local actors.

The impact of the threats to the Union stemming from the South Caucasus
were clearly exposed during the 2008 Georgian war and highlighted how

---

[14] Europa (2003) European Commission, *Wider Europe – Neighbourhood: A New
Framework for Relations with our Eastern and Southern Neighbours*, Brussels 11 March
2003, http://ec.europa.eu/world/enp/pdf/com03_104_en.pdf (date accessed: 03
March 2011).

[15] For an analysis of the EU normative power, see N. Tocci (ed.) (2008) *Who is a
Normative Foreign Policy Actor? The European Union and its Global Partners* (Brussels:
Centre for European Policy Studies (CEPS)).

[16] Europa (2003) European Council, *A Secure Europe in a Better World. European
Security Strategy*, Brussels, 12 December, http://www.consilium.europa.eu/uedocs/
cmsUpload/78367.pdf (date accessed: 03 March 2011).

"the EU's security begins outside our borders".[17] Unfortunately, the level of regional insecurity has not undergone significant change since 2008. Arguably, this situation lies at the heart of EU strategy regarding the South Caucasus, and can be seen in the *Report on the Implementation of the European Security Strategy*.[18] This report points to the relevance of the South Caucasus and its "frozen conflicts" on the one hand, and the potential of the region when it comes to the EU's energy security, on the other.

Finally, a perceived setback for the EU was the abolition of the post of EU Special Representative (EUSR) for the South Caucasus, in February 2011, amid a row to reorganise its external action tools and to set up the European External Action Service (EEAS). The post of the EUSR had been launched in 2003[19] and had a very broad mandate, including the promotion of regional cooperation, conflict prevention and settlement, and liaising with both internal and external stakeholders of the three South Caucasus countries.[20] Moreover, the EUSR's mission also entailed the need to display political proximity both to the EU leadership and the political elite, as well as to the civil societies of Armenia, Azerbaijan and Georgia. It was intended that EU–South Caucasus relations were subsequently less likely to drop off the political agendas of the actors involved.

Fortunately, a new EUSR mandate for the South Caucasus and the crisis in Georgia has been set up, entering into force on 1 November 2011. The French diplomat Philippe Lefort has been appointed to the post, replacing both Peter Semneby, the former EUSR for the South Caucasus, and Pierre Morel, the former EUSR for the crisis in Georgia. Ambassador Lefort has been given a broad mandate, including "the development of contacts with

---

[17] Europa (2011), European Union External Action, *Eastern Partnership*, http://eeas. europa.eu/eastern/index_en.htm (date accessed: 12 June 2011).

[18] Europa (2008) European Union External Action, Report on the Implementation of the European Security Strategy: Providing Security in a Changing World, Brussels, 11 December 2008, http://www.eu-un.europa.eu/documents/en/081211_EU%20 Security%20Strategy.pdf (date accessed: 03 March 2011).

[19] Europa, Council of the European Union, *Mission statement of Peter Semneby, EU Special Representative for the South Caucasus*, http://www.consilium.europa.eu/ policies/foreign-policy/eu-special-representatives/former-special-representatives/ peter-semneby.aspx?lang=en (date accessed: 05 March 2011). On the same issue, see also Europa (2003) Council Joint Action 2003/872/CFSP, *Extending and Amending the Mandate of the Special Representative of the European Union for the South Caucasus*, Official Journal of the European Union, 8 December 2003, http://www.consilium. europa.eu/uedocs/cmsUpload/L326–13.12.2003.pdf (date accessed: 05 March 2011).

[20] Europa (2010) Council of the European Union, *Council Decision 2010/109/CFSP, Extending the mandate of the European Union Special Representative in South Caucasus*, Official Journal of the European Union, 22 February 2010, http://eur-lex.europa.eu/ LexUriServ/LexUriServ.do?uri=OJ:L:2010:046:0016:0019:EN:PDF (date accessed: 05 March 2011).

governments, parliaments, other key political actors, the judiciary and civil society in the region; encouraging the countries in the region to cooperate on regional themes of common interest, such as common security threats, the fight against terrorism, illicit trafficking and organised crime; and contributing to the peaceful settlement of conflicts in accordance with the principles of international law and to facilitate the implementation of such settlement in close coordination with the United Nations, the OSCE and its Minsk Group".[21]

Given the challenges threatening the region, complementary rather than exclusive relations are necessary between the EU, Russia and the United States in order to determine their South Caucasian policies. Such a scenario does not seem to be out of reach at present, and it would be in line with the EU's declared goal to seek effective multilateralism when conducting its foreign and security policies.

As far as the conflict of Nagorno-Karabakh is concerned, unlike those over Abkhazia and South Ossetia, the EU has been quite reticent on the diplomatic stage. In fact, the peace talks are conducted in the framework of the OSCE Minsk Group by French, Russian and US Co-Chairs. However, the official EU position is supportive of the work of the Minsk Group, and it declares itself ready to implement confidence-building measures between the parties and to contribute actively to post-conflict rehabilitation.[22]

It remains to be seen whether the new EUSR will manage to perform effectively such a role together with the EEAS bodies dealing with the region.

Nagorno-Karabakh – tying and untying the Gordian Knot

Amidst the complex geopolitical equations outlined above, and given the polarised security environment, Nagorno-Karabakh must be seen as a specific case. On the one hand, it symbolises the Armenian state's legacy, as its Armenian rulers have managed to remain independent, or at least to maintain an autonomous status throughout the entire arch of history, especially from the fourteenth century on, when the last Armenian kingdom lost its sovereignty.[23] On the other hand, it embodies plurality

---

[21] Europa (2011) Council of the European Union, *New EU Special Representative for the South Caucasus and the crisis in Georgia*, Brussels, 26 August 2011, http://www.consilium.europa.eu/uedocs/cms_Data/docs/pressdata/EN/foraff/124436.pdf (date accessed: 26 August 2011).

[22] Azatutyun, *EU Ready to Financially Support Nagorno-Karabakh Settlement*, Commissioner Fule's interview with RFE/RL's Armenian Service, Prague, 22 June 2011 http://www.azatutyun.am/content/article/24273170.html (date accessed: 22 June 2011).

[23] R. Hovhannisyan (1988) "Nationalist Ferment in Armenia", *Freedom at Issue*, No. 105.

and multiculturalism, as in the case of Shushi, one of the most vibrant interethnic and interconfessional centres of the Caucasus throughout the nineteenth and the beginning of the twentieth centuries. This does not, however, imply that there were no cases of armed confrontations between Armenians and Azerbaijanis, which in particular occurred at the beginning of the twentieth century. Yet, these tensions were diluted to some extent by a supranational political actor, tsarist Russia.

With the conquest of the Caucasus in 1920 by the Bolsheviks, the Armenian populated region was annexed to the territory of the Socialist republic of Azerbaijan, thus enclosing the ethno-political tensions within the narrative of the "New Soviet Man" – a sui generis concept and artificial archetype of the Soviet citizen emancipated from any ethnic, linguistic or cultural kinship. This decision has continuously cast a shadow over the aspirations of the region's population which was subject to the Soviet centre–periphery "colonial" network of relations. In the 1940s, 1960s and 1970s, revolts and mass protests erupted, aiming to secure more social and cultural rights or unification with Armenia, but their message remained "unheard" by the Soviet leadership.[24]

However, the 1980s were the turning point for the "anti-colonial" aspirations of the Armenian majority[25] of Nagorno-Karabakh. The local leadership, together with the Armenian intelligentsia throughout the Soviet Union, used the new rights brought about by Gorbachev's *glasnost* to voice their aspirations for self-determination for the first time in Soviet history. The move caught Gorbachev unprepared, on the one hand, and inspired the advocates for self-determination in the Soviet Baltic republics, on the other. It also triggered ethnic hatred, arguably as an effect of the revival of pre-Soviet ultranationalist discourses and as a reaction to the Soviet imposition of the "New Soviet Man" metaphor. This resulted in a tragic chain of cause–effect actions in Azerbaijan and Armenia, such as the atrocious pogroms against the Armenian populations of Sumgait, Kirovabad and Baku and their forced expulsion from Azerbaijan; and in Armenia, resulting in the expulsion of the ethnic Azeris from southeastern Armenia by the end of 1989.[26]

Paradoxically, the central government in Moscow was completely unprepared for such developments, and its reaction either missed the target or was

---

[24] R.G. Suny (1993) *Looking toward Ararat: Armenia in Modern History* (Bloomington: Indiana University Press), 194–5.

[25] USSR Census (1989) *Itogi Vsesoiuznoy perepisi naseleniia 1989 goda* (Minneapolis: East View Publications), http://www.eastview.com/research-collections/product_view.asp?sku=IE00030&Russia/Russian/ (date accessed: 03 March 2011).

[26] Ethnic Azeris quitting their properties in Armenia were compensated by the Armenian SSR. H. Avetisyan et al. (eds) (2009) *The Republic of Nagorno-Karabakh: A Process of State Building at the Crossroad of Centuries* (Yerevan: IPR), 32–3.

exaggerated. Shortly afterwards, in 1991, the Nagorno-Karabakh authorities declared independence from Azerbaijan and subsequently conducted a referendum on independence, in accordance with the Soviet constitution.[27] The end of December that same year marked the collapse of the Soviet Union, and the local political elites in the Caucasus were influenced by extreme nationalist visions, again probably as a reaction to Soviet rule. The first days of 1992 marked another turning point in the Nagorno-Karabakh conflict – the moment when the conflict departed from political arena and entered its disastrous military stage, after Azerbaijan resorted to military means to impose control over Nagorno-Karabakh.[28] After having lost almost two thirds of the enclave's territory at the peak of the fighting in 1992, the outnumbered (but better organised and more strongly motivated) Armenian forces won control of Nagorno-Karabakh and the surrounding seven districts of Azerbaijan.[29] The war led to huge civilian casualties on both sides, as the front line fighting, with its heavy artillery and air force, ebbed and flowed through villages and towns.

The war in Nagorno-Karabakh ended in 1994 with a Russian-brokered tripartite ceasefire signed by Nagorno-Karabakh, Armenia and Azerbaijan. This resulted in Azerbaijan's loss of control over Nagorno-Karabakh and seven surrounding districts; the conflict cost the combatants 25,000 casualties[30] and created over a million internally displaced persons (IDPs) and refugees,[31] and an abundance of mines and cluster ammunition had been spread all over Nagorno-Karabakh. Moreover, the war resulted in Turkey's unilateral and unsanctioned embargo of Armenia in solidarity with Azerbaijan.[32]

---

[27] Nagorno-Karabakh was transferred under the direct rule of Moscow between 1988 and 1989, see T. de Waal (2010) *The Caucasus: An Introduction* (New York: Oxford University Press), 109–13.

[28] Ibid. 109–24.

[29] Ibid.

[30] M. Mooradian and D. Druckman (1999) "Hurting Stalemate or Mediation? The Conflict over Nagorno-Karabakh, 1990–95", *Journal of Peace Research*, Vol. 36, No. 6, 709–27.

[31] 450,000 Armenian and 586,000 Azeri IDPs and refugees, see ICG op. cit., 1.

[32] This embargo is still holding amid efforts by the international community to normalise bilateral relations between Armenia and Turkey, and to convince Turkey to reopen its border with Armenia. In fact, after signing protocols on the normalisation of relations with Armenia in October 2009, Turkey made their ratification conditional upon a settlement of the Nagorno-Karabakh conflict on Azerbaijan's terms. This move was triggered by Azerbaijan, and it backfired, as it stalled the embryonic relations between Armenia and Turkey, set against the backdrop of the 1915 Ottoman genocide of Armenians. Moreover, it limited the political resources required by the Armenian government to agree on a compromise deal with Azerbaijan over the final settlement of the Nagorno-Karabakh conflict, given the atmosphere of heightened war rhetoric and the increased pace of military spending in Azerbaijan.

The war in Nagorno-Karabakh went almost unnoticed by international public opinion, since in the early 1990s the eyes of the world were directed at the humanitarian disaster in the Balkans, and the Caucasus was still perceived to be a region in the Russian backyard. Stories about the conflict rarely appeared in the international media. The efforts of the Conference on Security and Co-operation in Europe (CSCE) and later the OSCE also went largely unnoticed, as they did not manage to produce any tangible effects during the war until the 1994 Bishkek ceasefire.

Today, after 17 years of confidential talks in the absence of the main interested party (Nagorno-Karabakh) and ups-and-downs, both in negotiations and along the line of contact, scepticism prevails among those directly affected by the conflict. Moreover, due to a recent unprecedented increase (both qualitative and quantitative) in ceasefire violations and the inflammatory political statements and war rhetoric coming mainly from the Azerbaijani leadership, the possibility of a new outbreak of war, either by accident or design, has become a dreadful but realistic scenario.

Some Armenian political forces take the view that a continuation of the status quo will guarantee the political results gained by the victory on the battleground in 1994, in the hope that a Kosovo-style approach which allows for the self-determination of the people of Nagorno-Karabakh will be applied sooner or later.[33] For its part, oil-exporting Azerbaijan spent $3.1 billion in 2011 on its military,[34] which is more than the entire state budget of Armenia. Moreover, the Azerbaijani leadership seems to be confident of its capacity to conquer Nagorno-Karabakh. It is clear that the best way out the current situation lies elsewhere.

The major peculiarity of the truce is that this is a self-regulated, precarious and vulnerable ceasefire without any inter-position force having been interposed between Nagorno-Karabakh and Azerbaijani troops. Thus, the current status of "no peace no war" along the line of contact is upheld by the overall geopolitical balance in the region and by a subtle politico–military game of deterrence. There are just six non-permanent OSCE monitors in charge of observing the ceasefire; they are basically a symbolic presence, given that there are more than 20,000 soldiers on each side pointing guns at each other along more than 200 km. of trenches. The weight of mediation largely falls on three OSCE MG Co-Chairs, who keep up the tortuous negotiations over a compromise document in a climate of distrust.

Besides, in the absence of a permanent observer mission on the ground, it is difficult to identify the initiator of any ceasefire violations. Under these conditions, it will be very easy for the parties involved to create a casus belli

---

[33] T. de Waal (2010) "Remaking the Nagorno-Karabakh Peace Process", *Survival: Global Politics and Strategy,* Vol. 52, No. 4, 159–76.

[34] ICG, op. cit., 1.

in the event of an outbreak of war. Such violations threaten the precarious balance which has held since 1994, when the ceasefire deal ended fighting. They lead to an overall hardening of bargaining positions on both sides.

To date, while the negotiations have led to a number of declaratory expressions of goodwill by the parties involved, they have not produced a legally binding comprehensive agreement on a final settlement.

A renewed armed conflict over Nagorno-Karabakh would be catastrophic for the whole region, not only for Armenia and Azerbaijan. Its effects would go well beyond the geopolitical unit these states belong to and would arguably affect US–EU–Russian relations as well as the threat perceptions of Iran and Turkey. Furthermore, such a scenario would have a major effect on current understandings of humanitarian crises and energy security. It is also clear that under current circumstances, both military and diplomatic, the consolidation of the ceasefire regime is paramount to a decisive diplomatic push, the intention of which is to reach a framework agreement for the settlement of the Nagorno-Karabakh conflict in line with the L'Aquila (2009),[35] Muskoka (2010)[36] and Deauville (2011)[37] G8 joint statements by the presidents of France, Russia and the United States.[38]

---

[35] The White House (2009) *Joint Statement on the Nagorno-Karabakh Conflict* by US President Obama, Russian President Medvedev, and French President Sarkozy at the L'Aquila Summit of the Eight, 10 July 2009, http://www.whitehouse.gov/the_press_office/Joint-Statement-on-the-Nagorno-Karabakh-Conflict/, (date accessed: 06 March 2011).

[36] The White House (2010) *G8 Summit: Joint Statement on the Nagorno-Karabakh Conflict* by Dmitry Medvedev, President of the Russian Federation, Barack Obama, President of the United States of America, and Nicolas Sarkozy, President of the French republic, Muskoka, 26 June 2010, http://www.whitehouse.gov/the-press-office/g8-summit-joint-statement-nagorno-karabakh-conflict-dmitry-medvedev-president-russi (date accessed: 06 March 2011).

[37] The White House (2011) *Joint Statement on the Nagorno-Karabakh Conflict* by Dmitry Medvedev, President of the Russian Federation, Barack Obama, President of the United States of America, and Nicolas Sarkozy, President of the French republic at the Deauville Summit of the Eight, 26 May 2011, http://www.whitehouse.gov/the-press-office/2011/05/26/joint-statement-nagorno-karabakh-conflict-dmitry-medvedev-president-russ, (date accessed: 28 May 2011).

[38] These are three high-profile joint statements by the Presidents of the Minsk Group Co-Chairing countries (France–Russia–United States), enumerating the basic principles governing the final solution of the conflict and currently negotiated by the parties involved. Commonly known as Basic Principles or Madrid Principles, they were put forward at the 2007 OSCE ministerial summit in Madrid, in line with the Helsinki Final Act, namely: the non-use of force or threat of force; territorial integrity and equal rights and self-determination of peoples; and six elements of the conflict's settlement. These six elements are: return of the territories surrounding Nagorno-Karabakh to Azerbaijani control; an interim status for Nagorno-Karabakh providing guarantees for security and self-governance; a corridor linking Armenia to Nagorno-Karabakh; future determination of the final legal status of Nagorno-Karabakh

To conclude, the region is at a turning point between either transformation into a cooperative hub anchored to the EU, generating the security, stability and prosperity badly needed both for itself and for the surrounding troubled geopolitical environment; or it will turn into an extremely volatile territory characterised by ultranationalist, hegemonic and confined societies reminiscent of the twenty-year-long European nightmare between the two World Wars.

---

through a legally binding expression of will; the right of all internally displaced persons and refugees to return to their former places of residence; and international security guarantees that would include a peacekeeping operation. Moreover, in the latest Deauville joint statement, the three presidents "reiterate that only a negotiated settlement can lead to peace, stability, and reconciliation" and that "the use of force [for the settlement of the conflict] would be condemned by the international community". The presidents conclude by stating: "Further delay would only call into question the commitment of the sides to reach an agreement".

3
Timeline 1918–2011

Michael Kambeck and Sargis Ghazaryan

1918   **28 May:** Armenia declares independence after the World War I Genocide and being subjected to attacks by Turkish Kemalist troops amid tensions with Azerbaijan over the historically Armenian regions of Nakhichevan, Zangezur and Nagorno-Karabakh.

1920   **28 April:** The Bolsheviks conquer Azerbaijan, then Karabakh in May and Armenia in November.

1921   **4–5 July:** The Kavburo (Caucasian Bureau of the Russian Communist Party), supervised by the Commissar for Nationalities, Joseph Stalin, votes to attach Nagorno-Karabakh to Soviet Armenia. One day later, on Stalin's initiative, this decision is reverted and Nagorno-Karabakh is annexed to Azerbaijan.

1963   After a petition is sent to Soviet premier, Nikita Khrushchev, protesting the cultural and economic marginalisation of Armenians in Nagorno-Karabakh, 18 Armenians are reportedly killed in Nagorno-Karabakh. Armenian villages in Nagorno-Karabakh suffer from infrastructural discrimination, especially regarding gas, water and electricity supply. Meanwhile Armenian protests continue throughout the 1960s and 1970s.

1981   **June:** Nagorno-Karabakh's autonomy is restricted by Soviet Azerbaijan's Constitution.

1987   **August:** A petition for the unification of Nagorno-Karabakh with Armenia, which has approximately 100,000 signatures, is sent from Nagorno-Karabakh and Armenia to Moscow.

1988   **February:** The Nagorno-Karabakh Soviet of People's Deputies appeals to the USSR Supreme Soviet to transfer the region from the Azerbaijani Soviet Socialist Republic (SSR) to the Armenian SSR. This appeal is accompanied by the first-ever mass demonstrations in the Soviet Union, in Stepanakert and Yerevan, involving hundreds of thousands of Armenians led by dissident intelligentsia.
27–29 February: Anti-Armenian pogroms take place in Sumgait (Azerbaijan), killing 32 people. Local Armenian residents are expelled to Armenia.
March: Mikhail Gorbachev rules out any changes to the borders between Soviet Republics. Moscow announces an aid and investment package for Nagorno-Karabakh.

September–November: Armenians are driven out of Shusha and Azerbaijanis out of Stepanakert, the two major urban centres of Nagorno-Karabakh.

November: Azeri villagers are expelled from Armenia, but offered compensation by the Armenian SSR. Mass demonstrations by Azerbaijani protesters break out in Baku.

December: The leadership of the Karabakh Committee, the Armenian anti-Soviet movement, is arrested and transferred to Moscow.

1989 **August:** Azerbaijan imposes a railway blockade on Armenia and Nagorno-Karabakh, abrogating fundamental principles of Soviet solidarity.

November: The leaders of the Karabakh Committee are released. They form the Armenian National Movement. Levon Ter-Petrosyan is elected its chairman.

1990 **13–15 January:** Anti-Armenian pogroms are organised in Baku, resulting in the deaths of approximately 90 people and the deportation of all Armenians from the city, Azerbaijan's capital. Moscow sends thousands of Soviet Interior Ministry troops into Baku.

19 January: The Soviet government declares a state of emergency in Baku as clashes between Azeri protesters and Soviet troops result in 133 civilian deaths there.

19 May: Ayaz Mutalibov is elected President of Azerbaijan.

4 August: Levon Ter-Petrosyan is elected Chairman of the Supreme Council of the Armenian SSR.

23 August: The Supreme Council of the Armenian SSR adopts a declaration of independence and renames the country the Republic of Armenia.

1991 **April–July:** "Operation Ring", a plan intended to "disarm illegal formations in Nagorno-Karabakh", coordinated by Baku and Moscow, is carried out by Soviet troops and Azerbaijani Interior Ministry special force units. The operation lasts four months and results in attacks on, and deportations of, civilians from 24 Armenian villages.

30 August: The Supreme Council of the Azerbaijani SSR starts the secession procedure by declaring its independence from the USSR, proclaiming itself the successor of the Azerbaijani Democratic Republic of 1918–20.

2 September: Nagorno-Karabakh Autonomous Oblast (NKAO) declares its independence from the Azerbaijani SSR under the relevant USSR legislation regulating the secession of Soviet Republics. Legally, Nagorno-Karabakh remains still subjected to the USSR.

21 September: A referendum of independence is held in Armenia, and the country is proclaimed an independent state by the parliament.

16 October: Levon Ter-Petrosyan is elected President of Armenia.

18 October: The Supreme Council of the Azerbaijani SSR adopts a constitutional act on the independence of Azerbaijan from the USSR.

26 November: Azerbaijan's new National Council votes to revoke Nagorno-Karabakh's autonomous status and declares it an ordinary province of Azerbaijan.

10 December: In a referendum under the relevant provisions of the Soviet Constitution, Nagorno-Karabakh's population votes for independence.

28 December: Parliamentary elections are held in Nagorno-Karabakh

29 December: Azerbaijan's declaration of independence is affirmed by a nationwide referendum.

31 December: The Soviet Union collapses.

1992 **6 January:** The newly elected parliament of Nagorno-Karabakh reaffirms the region's independence by adopting the "Declaration on the State Independence of the Nagorno-Karabakh Republic" and calls upon the UN to prevent a humanitarian crisis.

January: A full-fledged war breaks out, both on the territory of Nagorno-Karabakh and along the Armenian–Azerbaijani border. Stepanakert is under heavy Azerbaijani attack, employing cluster bombs and artillery.

25–26 February: An estimated 600 Azeri civilians are reported killed after an attack on the village of Khojaly. The village, in the southern proximity of Stepanakert, had been used as a key base for Azerbaijani artillery targeting Stepanakert. Azerbaijan, still today, campaigns for the recognition of this incident as genocide. However, Ayaz Mutalibov repeatedly links the killings to the militia of Abulfaz Elchibey's Popular Front, as an instrument to force him out of power. Several non-Armenian sources report the existence of pre-attack warnings, the escape of more than 2,000 civilians through a humanitarian corridor, as well as the discovery of most Khojaly casualties in an Azerbaijani-controlled sector outside Khojaly. The exact course of events remains contested.

6 March: After the Azerbaijani Supreme Council accuses President Mutalibov of failing to defend civilians fleeing Khojaly, he is forced to resign.

1–12 June: Negotiations led by the Conference on Security and Co-operation in Europe CSCE Minsk Group (a group of 11 countries mediating a solution to the conflict) open in Rome. The talks collapse as Azerbaijan launches an offensive against Nagorno-Karabakh, occupying the northern part and displacing around 40,000 ethnic Armenians.

7 June: The leader of the Popular Front, Abulfaz Elchibey, is elected President of Azerbaijan.

1993 **March and August:** Combined Armenian and Karabakhi forces launch a counter-attack, regain parts of eastern and northern Nagorno-Karabakh and move westward, eastward and southward, beyond the administrative borders of Nagorno-Karabakh. The goal is to control strategic places from where the key Azerbaijani attacks have originated in the past and to shorten the frontline.

15 June: Heydar Aliyev (the former Soviet leader of Azerbaijan, former head of the soviet intelligence agency in Azerbaijan – Committee for State Security (KGB) and former deputy-Chairman of the Soviet Council of Ministers) becomes speaker of the Azerbaijani parliament. Elchibey is forced to flee Baku.

August: Around 2,500 Afghan mercenaries from Gulbuddin Hekmatyar's forces begin fighting Armenians in Nagorno-Karabakh.

31 August: Russian envoy Vladimir Kazimirov mediates a temporary ceasefire, which holds until early November. An agreement to renounce a military solution to the conflict is reached between Azerbaijan and Nagorno-Karabakh in Moscow.

3 October: Heydar Aliyev is elected President of Azerbaijan.

November: Azerbaijan violates the ceasefire agreement by launching a new large-scale offensive. Nagorno-Karabakh's Armenian forces repel the attack and advance to the south. Their goal is now to gain a significantly shorter frontline in the shape of a simple rectangle touching Armenia in the west and Iran in the south. The new much shorter frontline faces "risks" only from the east and north and lies in more controllable lowland area.

April, July, October, November: The UN Security Council passes four resolutions, calling for an end to the fighting and explicitly underlining that "all occupying forces" must withdraw from the territories which they have occupied. While Armenia interprets this as referring also to the Azerbaijani forces in the Shahumyan region of northern NK, the resolutions name territories outside the core of Nagorno-Karabakh now controlled by NK Armenian forces as examples. The resolutions support Azerbaijan by mentioning the inadmissibility of the use of force for the acquisition of territory, while Armenia insists not to acquire any territory but to only protect the local ethnic Armenian population against ethnic cleansing exercised by Azerbaijan. Finally, the resolutions call for a lasting ceasefire to be established. While Azerbaijan still considers the calls in the resolutions to be valid today, they were arguably marked by the situation of the time, especially the heavy hostilities ongoing throughout the year. Armenia considers the withdrawal accomplishable in the context of the Minsk Group proposed peace package (Madrid Principles, see 2007).

1994   **12 May:** The so-called Bishkek Ceasefire, brokered by Russia, comes into force and remains valid until today. The document is signed by the three belligerents, Armenia, Azerbaijan and Nagorno-Karabakh, as well as Russia's representative to the CSCE Minsk Group, Vladimir Kazimirov, on 5 May 1994, in Bishkek, the capital of Kyrgyzstan.

20 September: Azerbaijan signs a contract with foreign companies to develop its offshore oilfields; these companies shortly afterwards form a consortium named the Azerbaijan International Operating Company (AIOC). The AIOC includes Amoco (US), BP (UK), Delta Nimir (now Amerada Hess of the US), LUKoil (Russia), McDermott (US), Pennzoil (now Devon of the US), Ramco (Scotland), SOCAR (Azerbaijan), Statoil (Norway), TPAO (Turkey), and UNOCAL (US).

22 December: Robert Kocharyan is elected de facto President of Nagorno-Karabakh.

1995   **Mid-May:** A new round of negotiations in Moscow fails as Azerbaijan refuses to negotiate with the Nagorno-Karabakh authorities.

1996   **23 September:** Ter-Petrosyan wins second-term presidential elections in Armenia.

1997   **May:** Armenia and Azerbaijan accept an OSCE "package" peace proposal as a basis for talks.

25 August: Nagorno-Karabakh rejects the peace plan submitted by the OSCE Minsk Group in late May, formerly agreed to by Azerbaijan and Armenia.

September: A "step-by-step" peace proposal is presented by the OSCE Minsk Group. Ter-Petrosyan supports the new approach. His move opens divisions within his cabinet.

October: Armenia and Azerbaijan accept the OSCE peace plan as a basis, with some reservations, whereas, Nagorno-Karabakh rejects them and demands a package approach.

1998   **3 February:** President Ter-Petrosyan resigns after failing to reach consensus with the members of Armenia's National Security Council regarding the latest OSCE peace plan.

March: Robert Kocharyan, the former de facto President of Nagorno-Karabakh wins the presidential elections in Armenia.

October: Heydar Aliyev is re-elected President of Azerbaijan.

November: A Minsk Group "common state" proposal envisaging a confederative model as the basis for the solution to the conflict, is rejected by Azerbaijan.

1999   **27 October:** Gunmen storm the Armenian National Assembly and kill eight high-ranking officials, including Prime Minister Vazgen Sargsyan and Speaker of the Parliament Karen Demirchyan.

2000   **June:** The ruling Democratic Artsakh Union prevails with a slim victory in the Nagorno-Karabakh parliamentary elections.

2001   **4–6 April:** OSCE-mediated peace talks are held in Key West, Florida, at the beginning of the George W. Bush Administration. The parties are at their closest to a breakthrough throughout the entire mediation process. The agreement is, however, rejected by the Azerbaijani political elite, and Heydar Aliyev publicly withdraws his support after his return to Baku.

2002   **September:** Construction of the US-backed Baku-Tbilisi-Ceyhan (BTC) oil pipeline begins. It is set to bypass Armenia in delivering Azeri oil to the Turkish Mediterranean port of Ceyhan.

2003   **March:** Kocharyan wins a second presidential term in Armenia.

May: A pro-presidential coalition of parties wins parliamentary elections in Armenia.

8 July: The defence ministers of Armenia and Azerbaijan agree to downgrade tensions between the armies of the two countries.

4 August: The Azerbaijani parliament approves the appointment of Aliyev's son, Ilham, as Prime Minister.

October: Ilham Aliyev wins the first round of presidential elections in Azerbaijan.

12 December: Heydar Aliyev's death is announced.

2004   **January:** In Paris, Ilham Aliyev toughens Azerbaijan's position by stating his refusal to ever accept Nagorno-Karabakh's independence.

16 April: A series of talks coined the "Prague Process" between Armenian and Azerbaijani foreign ministers starts in Prague.

May: The EU announces its intention to include the South Caucasus within its European Neighbourhood Policy.

15 September: Presidents Aliyev, Kocharyan and Putin meet in Astana, Kazakhstan. They reportedly work out a new idea – Armenian withdrawal from the occupied districts in return for a referendum on Nagorno-Karabakh's status. The security along the Line of Contact worsens amid increasingly frequent ceasefire violations.

2005   **February:** OSCE officials conclude that neither Armenia nor the Krarabakhi de facto administration have implemented any settlement programme in the security buffer zone around Nagorno-Karabakh.
May: The BTC pipeline is inaugurated.
June: Parliamentary elections in Nagorno-Karabakh are won by a pro-presidential coalition.
27 August: Presidents Kocharyan and Aliyev meet in Kazan. They instruct their foreign ministers to work on a deal combining "package" and "step-by-step" approaches to the withdrawal of Armenian forces and the future use of a referendum to determine Nagorno-Karabakh's status.
November: After parliamentary elections in Azerbaijan, a pro-Aliyev coalition dominates the parliament.

2006   **18–19 January:** Armenian and Azerbaijani foreign ministers work out a draft document in London on the principles of the final settlement of the conflict.
10–11 February: The presidents of Armenia and Azerbaijan meet at Rambouillet Castle near Paris, together with French President Jacques Chirac, but fail to register any progress.

2007   **12 May:** After the parliamentary elections in Armenia, former Defence Minister Serzh Sargsyan becomes Prime Minister.
July: Bako Sahakyan is elected de facto President of Nagorno-Karabakh.
29–30 November: On the sidelines of the OSCE Ministerial Council in Madrid, the Basic Principles for the final settlement of the conflict are introduced to the parties by the Minsk Group Co-Chairs. The document is based upon the Helsinki Final Act's principles of non-use or threat of force, territorial integrity and equal rights and self-determination of peoples.

2008   **20 February:** Serzh Sargsyan wins the presidential elections in Armenia. The opposition contests the results of the vote and takes to the streets. The protests culminate in mass clashes on 1–2 March, resulting in ten casualties. Kocharyan enacts a 20-day state of emergency.
4 March: Azerbaijan attacks and takes control of some Karabakhi positions. After failed OSCE mediation, the Nagorno-Karabakh armed forces launch a counter-offensive and regain control over the lost positions.
8 August: War breaks out between Georgia and Russia.
6 September: Upon the invitation of President Sargsyan, President Gul of Turkey arrives in Yerevan. The parties agree to work towards a normalisation of bilateral relations.
15 October: Ilham Aliyev wins a second term in Azerbaijjan's presidential elections. He officially gains 87 per cent of the vote, while the opposition parties boycott the election.
2 November: On the initiative of Russia's President, Dmitry Medvedev, Presidents Sargsyan and Aliyev sign a joint declaration in Moscow reaffirming the non-use of force and compliance with the norms of international law in the settlement of the conflict.

2009   **18 March:** The limits on presidential terms are abolished by a referendum in Azerbaijan, amid international criticism. Effectively, President Aliyev can now run for office indefinitely.

10 July: During the L'Aquila G8 Summit Minsk Group Co-Chair countries France, Russia and the United States release a joint statement on the Nagorno-Karabakh conflict. They call upon Armenia and Azerbaijan to endorse the Basic Principles outlined in the statement.

10 October: Two protocols on the establishment of diplomatic relations and on the development of bilateral relations are signed in Zurich by the foreign ministers of Armenia and Turkey. The EU, Russia and the United States welcome the move and call for the ratification of the protocols "without any precondition and in a reasonable timeframe". The Foreign Ministry of Azerbaijan issues a press release declaring that Turkey's decision "directly contradicts the national interests of Azerbaijan and overshadows the spirit of brotherly relations between Azerbaijan and Turkey built on deep historical roots."

11 October: Turkish Prime Minister Erdogan declares the ratification of the protocols conditional upon "significant progress" in the Nagorno-Karabakh issue, such as the withdrawal of Armenian troops.

21 November: A day before his meeting with Sargsyan in Munich, Aliyev states that if the meeting fails to produce results, he will have the right to use military means to resolve the conflict. No breakthrough is registered during the 22 November Munich summit.

2010

22 April: Armenia suspends the ratification of the Turkish–Armenian protocols, as Turkish officials, in solidarity with Azerbaijan, exclude the ratification, preconditioning it to progress in the Nagorno-Karabakh negotiations.

17 June: Presidents Sargsyan, Aliyev and Medvedev meet in St Petersburg to focus on the timeline of the withdrawal of Armenian forces from the territories beyond the administrative borders of Nagorno-Karabakh, referred to by Armenia as a security buffer zone, and on the deadline for a referendum over the final status of Nagorno-Karabakh. No progress is registered. Aliyev leaves abruptly before the conference is over.

18 June: An Azerbaijani incursion across the Line of Contact into Karabakh leaves one Azerbaijani and four Armenian soldiers dead. Bellicose statements from Azerbaijan become more frequent and stronger.

26 June: During the Muskoka G8 summit France, Russia and the United States reiterate the message of their previous year's L'Aquila statement and urge the parties to agree upon the Basic Principles.

June–September: The number of casualties on the Line of Contact grows due to sniper fire.

12 October: Azerbaijan announces that its military spending will hit $3.1 billion in 2011, which exceeds the entire Armenian state budget.

27 October: In Astrakhan, Medvedev facilitates an agreement between Sargsyan and Aliyev regarding the exchange of prisoners of war and remains of soldiers killed along the Line of Contact.

2011

14 January: Armenia's foreign minister states that Armenia accepts the Basic Principles for the settlement of the conflict "as an integrated whole", as proposed by the Minsk Group.

5 March: At the Sochi summit mediated by Russia, Armenia and Azerbaijan agree to conduct joint investigations of "possible incidents along the ceasefire line" together with the OSCE. They also agree on an exchange of prisoners of war.

17 March: An hour after the exchange of prisoners of war in the Agdam area, a sniper shooting incident kills a soldier of the NKR Defence Army near Askeran.

26 May: During the Deauville G8 summit, France, Russia and the United States urge Armenia and Azerbaijan to agree on the Basic Principles before Kazan summit set for 24 June.

1–23 June: In a marathon meeting between the OSCE Minsk Group Co-Chairs, Russian diplomats and the foreign ministers of the conflict parties, so much progress is reported, that the Kremlin publicly expects a breakthrough in Kazan.

24 June: Upon his arrival at the Kazan summit, mediated by President Medvedev and the OSCE Minsk Group, Ilham Aliyev presents a list of last-minute amendments, mostly to provisions of the Basic Principles document which were previously dealt with among the foreign ministers of both sides. The summit fails.

References

Chronologies

Conciliation resources, *Nagorny-Karabakh: Chronology*, http://www.c-r.org/our-work/accord/nagorny-karabakh/chronology.php

C. Kolter (2011) "Chronologie", in Parlamentarische Gruppe Schweiz–Armenien (ed.) *Berg-Karabach: Geopolitische, völkerrechtliche und menschenrechtliche Aspekte eines Konfliktes* (Merkur Druck AG, Langenthal).

RFE/RL (Radio Free Europe / Radio Liberty) , *Nagorno-Karabakh: Timeline of the Long Road to Peace*, http://www.rferl.org/content/article/1065626.html

Essential reading

L. Chorbajian (2001) *The Making of Nagorno-Karabagh: From Secession to Republic* (London: Palgrave).

B. Coppieters (ed.) (1996) *Contested Borders in the Caucasus* (Brussels: VUBPRESS).

T. de Waal (2003) *Black Garden: Armenia and Azerbaijan through Peace and War* (New York and London: New York University Press).

T. de Waal (2010) *The Caucasus: An Introduction* (New York: Oxford University Press).

R. Hovhannisyan (1988) "Nationalist Ferment in Armenia", *Freedom at Issue*, No. 105.

International Crisis Group (2011) *"Armenia and Azerbaijan: Preventing War"*, Europe Briefing 60, Brussels, http://www.crisisgroup.org/en/regions/europe/caucasus/B60-armenia-and-azerbaijan-preventing-war.aspx

International Crisis Group (2009) *"Nagorno-Karabakh: Getting to a Breakthrough"*, Europe Briefing 55, Brussels, http://www.crisisgroup.org/~/media/Files/europe/b55_nagorno_karabakh__getting_to_a_breakthrough.pdf

D.M. Lang (1981) *The Armenians: A People in Exile* (London: George Allen Unwin).

D.D. Laitin and R.G. Suny (1999) "Karabakh: Thinking a Way out", *Middle East Policy*, Vol. 7, No. 1, October.

D.E. Miller and L. Touryan-Miller (2003) *Armenia: Portraits of Survival and Hope* (Berkeley, Los Angeles, London: University of California Press).

R.G. Suny (1994) *Looking toward Ararat: Armenia in Modern History* (Bloomington: Indiana University Press).

R.G. Suny (ed.) (1983) *Transcaucasia, Nationalism and Social Change: Essays in the History of Armenia, Azerbaijan, and Georgia* (Ann Arbor: University of Michigan Press).

C.J. Walker (ed.) (1991) *Armenia and Karabagh: The Struggle for Unity* (London: Minority Rights Group Reports).

On the participation of Afghan mercenaries in the conflict in Nagorno-Karabakh, see:

J.K. Cooley (2000) *Unholy Wars: Afghanistan, America and International Terrorism: New Edition* (London and Sterling, Virginia: Pluto Press), p. 180.

On Stalin's decision to allocate Nagorno-Karabakh to Azerbaijan and the status of Nagorno-Karabakh throughout the Soviet period, see:

T. de Waal (2003) *Black Garden: Armenia and Azerbaijan through Peace and War* (New York and London: New York University Press), pp. 90, 129.

R.G. Suny (ed.) (1983) *Transcaucasia, Nationalism and Social Change: Essays in the History of Armenia, Azerbaijan, and Georgia* (Ann Arbor: University of Michigan Press).

On the situation of the Armenian population of Nagorno-Karabakh in the Soviet Union, see:

D.M. Lang (1981) *The Armenians: A People in Exile* (London: George Allen Unwin).

R.G. Suny (ed.) (1983) *Transcaucasia, Nationalism and Social Change: Essays in the History of Armenia, Azerbaijan, and Georgia* (Ann Arbor: University of Michigan Press).

On Khojaly civilian casualties, see:

Human Rights Watch, *Response to Armenian Government Letter on the Town of Khojaly, Nagorno-Karabakh*, 23 March 1997, http://www.hrw.org/en/news/1997/03/23/response-armenian-government-letter-town-khojaly-nagorno-karabakh

Final report of the Memorial NGO's fact-finding mission after the events of Khojaly, May 1992, http://www.memo.ru/hr/hotpoints/karabah/Hojaly/index.htm

Nezavisimaya Gazeta, "Interview with Mutalibov", Moscow, 2 April 1992.

Novoye Vremia Magazine, "Interview with Mutalibov", Moscow, 6 March 2001.

A. Zverev (1996) "Ethnic Conflicts in the Caucasus 1988–1994" in B. Coppieters (ed.) *Contested Borders in the Caucasus* (Brussels: VUBPRESS).

For the UN Security Council resolutions on the Nagorno-Karabakh conflict, see:

UNSC resolution 822 (1993) http://documents-dds-ny.un.org/doc/RESOLUTION/GEN/NR0/700/07/img/NR070007.pdf?OpenElement

UNSC resolution 853 (1993) http://documents-dds-ny.un.org/doc/RESOLUTION/GEN/NR0/700/38/img/NR070038.pdf?OpenElement

UNSC resolution 874 (1993) http://documents-dds-ny.un.org/doc/RESOLUTION/GEN/NR0/700/59/img/NR070059.pdf?OpenElement

UNSC resolution 884 (1993) http://documents-dds-ny.un.org/doc/RESOLUTION/GEN/NR0/700/69/img/NR070069.pdf?OpenElement

On the legal procedures leading to the independence of Nagorno-Karabakh, see:

H. Avetisyan et al. (eds) (2009) *The Republic of Nagorno-Karabakh: A Process of State Building at the Crossroad of Centuries* (Yerevan: IPR), http://www.armeniaforeignministry.com/fr/nk/nk.pdf

O. Luchterhandt (1993) *Nagorny Karabakh's Right to State Independence According to International Law* (Boston: Armenian Rights Council).

R.G. Suny (ed.) (1996) *Transcaucasia, Nationalism and Social Change: Essays in the History of Armenia, Azerbaijan, and Georgia* (University of Michigan Press).

The USSR law on the "Procedure of Secession of a Soviet Republic from the Union of Soviet Socialist Republics", 3 April 1990, http://www.c-r.org/our-work/accord/nagorny-karabakh/keytexts5.php

Part I

Approaching the Conflict:
The Internal Rationale

4
The Quintessential Conflict – A Cultural and Historical Analysis of Nagorno-Karabakh

Bernard Coulie

The motivations which underlie conflicts have long attracted the attention of analysts, political commentators, journalists and historians. Depending on the epoch, emphasis is laid on economic or social elements, on the control of trade routes, access to water or energy or on religious factors. This emphasis is often a mirror image of the fears of each historic period. As regards more ancient eras whose wars are related in literary form in great epics such as the *Iliad*, exploration of the economic and political realities behind the poetic fiction has become a much-prized field of study. It is known, for example, that the Trojan War was less motivated by the abduction of fair Helen than by the Greeks' (and especially the Mycenaeans') desire to control the trade route of the Dardanelles straits between the Mediterranean and the Black Sea by capturing the city of Troy. Recent conflicts are not immune to this process of revision, and the way in which such wars are sometimes related leads, at times, to a veritable rewriting of history which almost borders on mythical narrative.[1] History is complicated, or rather, people's lives are complicated because history is, after all, what people think they know about their past or the way in which they would like to view it. This explains why the reasons for conflicts are almost always multiple and become entangled with economic and political issues, territorial claims, religious, cultural and linguistic antagonisms – not forgetting the inevitable assertion of some bloated egos. Besides, it is not unusual to see any of these aspects exploited by one or another of the parties involved.

---

[1] This applies to the Caucasian conflicts; see study of V.A. Shnirelman (2001) *The Value of the Past: Myths, Identity and Politics in Transcaucasia* (Osaka: National Museum of Ethnology).

See, among others, the analysis of the book by V. Rouvinski and M. Matsuo (2003) "Clash of Myths", *Journal of International Development and Cooperation*, No. 9, 101–17.

When these conflicts occur in regions occupied by markedly distinct populations (distinct because they speak different languages, practise different religions, claim to represent different identities, assert different reference points and alliances), this complex combination of motives becomes increasingly rigid and the conflicts more inextricable. This is obviously what is happening today and has been happening for centuries in the Caucasus and more particularly in the South Caucasus.

The history of the South Caucasus, today comprising the three republics of Georgia, Armenia and Azerbaijan and the surrounding territories dotted with entities which are more or less politically independent, has been turbulent and directly reflects those difficulties which have always beset the meeting of West and East, namely Europe and Asia.

In the South Caucasus, the Karabakh conflict is quintessential in that it confronts the observer with basic questions which exist more generally in today's world. The answers to the Karabakh scenario transcend the boundaries of this small state because they potentially concern many other parts of the world, not least within Europe itself. These questions can be summed up as follows:

- When the weight of history is such a heavy burden, must solutions take history into consideration or brush it to one side?
- When the meeting of cultures creates problems, does the solution lie in each culture retreating from the other and focusing on itself?
- Lastly, is Europe distant solely in geographical terms or do other factors intervene?

History's burden: when history becomes too heavy to bear

The South Caucasian region belonged to Mesopotamia, which is said to have been the cradle of civilisation, at least according to Western tradition. In antiquity, the region formed (not including the conquests of Alexander the Great) the easternmost spearhead of Greek and Roman cultures, just as it was the westernmost outpost of the Persian world. From then onwards, the South Caucasus remained the meeting place and scene of strife between Byzantium and the Persian world, and witnessed religious conflict in the Middle Ages, given the opposition between Christianity and Islam. These clashes reappeared as rivalries between Russia, the Ottoman Empire and Persia. Even today, the South Caucasian regions are lands under Russian, Turkish and Iranian influence, whereas the West is trying to play a role through the Eastern Partnership within the East Neighbourhood Policy of the European Union.

Throughout its history, the South Caucasus has always been the meeting place of political, cultural and religious antagonisms, a factor which explains its current fragmentation and instability and explains, too, why the Caucasus may well become the stage where the quest for world peace will play out – perhaps more so than the Middle East.

To grasp the Karabakh conflict, it must be set against the much broader backcloth of a place where great powers – even civilisations – meet and often confront one another. It is not a mere question of opposition between Karabakh and Azerbaijan, nor even between the latter and Armenia, nor between Russia and Turkey acting through small proxy states. These antagonisms are genuine and influence the conflict. But this conflict cannot be reduced or limited to any of these dimensions, because they embrace much wider phenomena which affect the entire modern world. There is unlikely to be a solution to the Karabakh conflict if it does not take this broader context into consideration.

This is not the place to narrate the history of the entire region[2] called, in turn, Utik, Artsakh, Khachen, Arran, Karabakh; each of these names reflects a period or a particular domination. It is correct to state that the history of Karabakh is directly linked to that of Armenia, to which it has always belonged, but that is not enough to explain the special destiny of this small territory. Two characteristics distinguish Karabakh from the rest of Armenia and enable us to understand the roots of today's problems.

Firstly, Karabakh's vicissitudes are those inherent to any border region because Karabakh has always formed the eastern extremity of Armenia and so has always been a place of passage and encounter.

Secondly, the region has for centuries enjoyed a fairly autonomous political system, distinct to the rest of Armenia; this relative autonomy, combined with its geographic features, bred a strong feeling of identity among its inhabitants. The territory's political organisation is based on princely families going back to the origins of Armenia, and it was these families who led the resistance against the Arab occupantion in the ninth century, the Seljuk Turks in the eleventh and twelfth centuries, the Mongols in the thirteenth and fourteenth centuries, and their Turkmen successors, the Kara-Koyunlu and the Ak-Koyunlu, in the fifteenth century. When Karabakh was ruled by Safavid Persia, established in 1502, the traditional Armenian families maintained a degree of independence once again. From the fifteenth

---

[2] Detailed bibliography up to 1988 in the bilingual English-Italian publication *Gharabagh. Documents of Armenian Art (Documenti di Architettura Armena Series)* (Polytechnique and the Armenian Academy of Sciences, Milan, OEMME Edizioni), 24–31.

For a bibliography up to 1995, see: http://www.umd.umich.edu/dept/armenian/facts/k_books.html.

Some publications are seminal; in French: P. Donabedian and C. Mutafian (1991) *Artsakh: histoire du Karabakh* (Paris: Sevig Press).

In English: L. Chorbajian, P. Donabedian and C. Mutafian (1994) *The Caucasian Knot: The History and Geo-politics of Nagorno-Kharabagh* (London: Zed Books).

to the eighteenth centuries, these hereditary princes, the *Meliks*, were the only authority able to defend the Armenians from invaders and looters, to defend the faith and traditions, and to stand out, in the centuries which followed, as the initiators of the Armenian renewal.[3] Reference to the era of the Melikdoms is essential if we want to understand Karabakh today.

During the second half of the eighteenth century, the Russian empire spread to the Caucasus; Karabakh was invaded in 1805 and annexed to the Russian empire by the Treaty of Gulistan in 1813. It was then that political decisions began to break the historic link which united Karabakh to the rest of Armenia. Karabakh was separated from Armenia in 1868 and became part of the new province of Elizavetpol, combining in a single administrative structure populations and territories as different as the eastern highlands of the provinces of Tiflis and Erevan and the steppes of the Baku regions. Thus, an arbitrary political decision flung together two completely different peoples on the same territory and in the same organised structure – Armenians and Tartars, Christians and Muslims, sedentary communities and nomads and semi-nomads, mountain people and people from the plains, farmers and pastoralists. The result could only be explosive, and it did indeed lead to the bloody clashes of 1905–06 between Armenians and Azeris. The subsequent incorporation of Karabakh into the Soviet Socialist Republic of Azerbaijan ratified the borders fixed in the nineteenth century but did not resolve the conflicts.

Karabakh is a particularly eloquent example of the world's frontier regions, meeting places of different peoples and cultures. These border zones provide the terrain – and therein lies their peculiarity – for confrontation between opposing political powers which impose their domination in their turn and most often exclusively so, that is by seeking to eliminate their adversary's nationals. Karabakh, however, is a special case arising from the long tradition of autonomy, which was initiated and developed under the Armenian princely families and resulted in a strong sense of identity. The Armenians were not the only people on this territory, but their footprint was profound, and the Melikdoms legacy finds expression today in the Armenian claim.

The Karabakh question is also one of knowing how far conflict resolution should take history into account. If our point of reference is the situation in the twentieth century – we might call it the "Azeri solution" – the solution will be different to that echoing the days of the province of Elizavetpol, or to one based on more remote periods when the Meliks ruled the territory. We are not seeking to repeat history or to restore outdated situations but to realise that each actor in a conflict has its own points of reference,

[3] R.H. Hewsen (1972, 1973) "The Meliks of Eastern Armenia", *Revue des Etudes Arméniennes*, N.S. 9 (1972), 285–329, and N.S. 10 (1973), 281–303 [the paper was published in two parts].

particularly those from the past. Each party identifies a moment in history deemed emblematic and creates the model of an ideal situation to which one must try to return. However, no negotiation is possible without first comprehending the other's references.

When these references diverge, when history becomes such a heavy burden, and when history has been extensively used by each party in support of the cause, one should ideally be able to imagine solutions from a "clean sheet", that is, solutions liberated from the past. But people are historical and cultural beings who never allow themselves to be reduced to rationality alone; and because they are historical and cultural beings, they are never entirely free from the past. That said, any solution must necessarily take the past into account.

Autonomy or disengagement?

One of the difficulties of recourse to the past lies in the fact that each party clings to its own version of history. When tensions between communities become increasingly strained, each community has a natural tendency to fall back on its own history. This approach is particularly visible in the revision of teaching curricula and altered communication policies. Education is a public service tool and is often used by the powers involved to promote certain ideas, even in advanced European democracies. Communication and the media may also shrink people's horizons by not providing coverage of another community.[4] Such reflexes, however natural they may be, engender ignorance of the other party, ignorance which becomes an obstacle to conflict resolution because it prevents the interlocutors from appreciating each other's points of reference.

This disengagement dynamic rests on two main factors which are mutually reinforcing:

On the one hand, the emergence of nationalism in Europe gave birth to the idea of the nation state, and the global influence of Europe in the course of history generalised the concept well beyond the European continent. It is normal for a group to seek to form an identifiable togetherness and to give expression to this identity by various means, such as territory, language or religion or ethnic unity. This development fashioned Europe and it points to the positive aspect of nationalism, but its evolution has also been the source of conflicts and wars because any affirmation of identity is necessarily at the expense of the other: identity relies as much on the assertion of one's character as on the capacity to recognise others as different. In other words, to identify oneself, one must be able to distinguish others from

---

[4] Such developments are noticeable in Belgium, for example.

oneself, because they occupy another territory, speak another language or practise another religion. The margin between this distinction and exclusion is slender and often crossed. Thus, nationalism has often provided the seeds of wars which have bloodied Europe. This is the negative aspect of nationalism. With its qualities and faults, national affirmation is one of the dominant factors in the modern world: it is moreover the factor which makes the modern-day European project atypical and a real challenge.

On the other hand, since the second half of the twentieth century, the world has gone global. Globalisation and internationalisation are radically different. Internationalisation means making existing states work together; it is therefore linked to existing states or to nation states and is based on all their claims, as is voiced, for instance, in the common expression "internationalisation of conflicts". Globalisation, however, is not linked to states as it transcends the frontiers between states and nations; it is, so to speak, a process which ignores states' nationalities and may even appear inimical to them. Neither is globalisation linked to the past; in this sense, it appears to be a subversive process in relation to the established order.

In a globalised world, nation states which asserted their distinctiveness now see the very framework which legitimated such claims to independence as being threatened by globalisation itself, and are trying to express themselves at another level, one closer to the individual. Moreover, since globalisation itself casts doubt on traditional models of functioning and interrelations, it raises fears that citizens might find new appealing understandings of local or regional allegiances. This is a well-known phenomenon in Europe, as many people believe that local aspirations for regional and community solidarity contradict the European aspiration itself: why, for instance, split up Belgium when what is needed is more unity at the European level? The contradiction springs from a false interpretation of the issues at stake. In fact, there is a direct link between world globalisation and the multiplication of territorial, political, community and cultural claims on a smaller scale. This is evidenced through conflicts between communities, as in Belgium; claims for regional autonomy as in the United Kingdom; emergence of regional nationalist parties as in Italy; division of the former Czechoslovakia and Yugoslavia into new independent entities, such as Kosovo, without mentioning the break-up of the USSR. The model has spread beyond Europe: in September 2010, when Israel's Prime Minister, Benjamin Netanyahu, addressed the President of the Palestinian Authority, Mahmoud Abbas, Netanyahu demanded that Palestinians recognise Israel as the nation state of the Jewish people, an expression that leaves no room for ambiguity.

These claims are legitimate in themselves, and it is therefore not a question of either denying or criticising them. They will continue to be part of the modern world for a long time to come. What is important is to weigh up their consequences. The nationalist dynamic is at work in many places and, because of globalisation, it finds expression in smaller entities than in the past. The South Caucasus is no exception to this development; just think of Abkhazia, Ossetia, Chechnya or Karabakh.

The Karabakh conflict is neither typical nor isolated. While it has assumed distinctive characteristics due to its specific history, it also rises from processes widely shared in today's world. These considerations do not free us from asking whether the demand for self-determination, although a right, is not sometimes an escape mechanism or expression of a difficulty or failure to face up to a complex reality and realise that this complexity arises from the effects of globalisation and/or from tensions between different communities. Self-determination should not generate monocultural or monoethnic entities, because the loss of the riches of such entities in human terms would be greater than the gain in political terms.

Distant Europe

If Europe is to play a role in solving the Karabakh conflict, it must do so by simultaneously taking into account the respective references of the interlocutors and the stakes and possible consequences of both their nations' and communities' claims. These are issues which the EU, owing to its past, should be able to apprehend better than any political entity in the world. However, where Karabakh is concerned, geographical distance and ignorance regarding the playing field makes for additional problems.

We must always remember that frontiers are conventions because they are often the result of provisional arrangements, and perception of them owes more to the effect of a teaching tradition than a geographical reality. Therein lies the crux when it comes to defining the limits of Europe to the east: Do we choose the Urals, the Black Sea or the Caspian Sea, or the Dardanelles? Where does Europe end, where does Asia begin? Is the Caucasus in Europe?

Admittedly the Caucasus is not well-known in Europe and is not often considered to belong to the European world. Why? More than geographical distance, cultural remoteness has shaped the current state of affairs in the teaching on the region, as have representations of the region.

Islam is a key factor in this European vision of the Caucasus. In a world allegedly liberated from religion, laicised and rational, the religious factor has never weighed so much in the way people regard one another. European culture functions in oppositional dualities (the profane and the sacred; zero and infinity; the empty and the full; black and white and so on). Europe needs an opposite number to be able to define itself and, during much of its history, Islam has conveniently supplied it with that "other". Moreover, in the eyes of a European, Islam is the world of the "other". The Caucasus is a region conquered and long dominated by that other; one of the three republics, Azerbaijan, is predominantly Muslim, and, to crown it all, to the West, the Caucasus is separated from Europe by Turkey, another Muslim- dominated country. But yet another religious factor separates the Caucasus from Europe: Christianity, paradoxically. Christianity in the Caucasus belongs to the Orthodox world, that of the Oriental Churches, independent of Rome and heirs of Byzantium. For centuries, first Byzantium, then the Ottoman occupation and lastly the Iron Curtain, largely hid the existence of this Orthodox world from European eyes. Considerable progress has arisen in this context, from the integration of Greece into the EU, from German reunification and European Union enlargement. This progress is not merely political, although its cultural effects are not yet fully in effect. After all, we still refer to Central and Eastern Europe.

To Europeans, therefore, the Caucasus seems a land different to their own. Because it is different, it must therefore be oriental and, to Europeans, necessarily part of Asia. Political complexity and ethnic and linguistic diversity add to the "foreign" cachet of the Caucasus. Remember that the Caucasus encompasses as much diversity as the entire European Union.

In the European *imaginaire*, the Caucasus has often been perceived as a terra incognita, source of dangers and of the marvellous (don't the two go together?): It is the land of the Golden Fleece, which Jason stole as he carried off Medea, the magician, whom he ravished in the full meaning of the term. It is also the land of definitive exile for those who override the rules or defy the gods, such as Prometheus who was chained to a rock in the Caucasus for having passed the Olympian fire to mankind.

The Caucasus is the revolving door between East and West: it exists both in Europe and in Asia and cannot be reduced exclusively to either of these two components. The Caucasus' very richness lies in its complexity, even if these are the qualities which pose problems for Europeans who are heirs of nationalism and therefore eager to minimise difference. The Caucasus is a differentiation for Europe and Asia, and can also be an enrichment for both. That is why the Karabakh conflict should attract Europe's full attention. What is at stake in Karabakh is not "merely" the fate of a few million Armenians, Azerbaijanis and other regional inhabitants, but fundamental questions about the future of Europe and the modern world.

5

A Case Sui Generis: Nagorno-Karabakh in Comparison with Other Ethnic Conflicts in Eastern Europe

Uwe Halbach

Between 1992 and 1994 ceasefire agreements marked an end to open military clashes over contested territories in the South Caucasus. In the following years, the politically unresolved conflicts involving Abkhazia, South Ossetia and Nagorno-Karabakh have all been presented as "frozen conflicts". In August 2008, an escalation between the smallest of all separatist entities, South Ossetia, and its "parent state", Georgia, triggered a short war between Georgian and Russian troops. Such recent developments should warn the international community that the unresolved conflicts cannot be assumed, in reality, to be "frozen". This applies not least to the situation in Nagorno-Karabakh – the most significant conflict of this region. The negotiations around Nagorno-Karabakh gained fresh impetus from the "Georgian crisis" of 2008, with an increased number of meetings between the presidents of Armenia and Azerbaijan. In 2009, the presidents engaged in official talks on six occasions, and diplomatic activities by Russia and other external actors were also evident. However, repeated military threats, even after the "Georgian lesson" and a growing number of violent incidents at the Line of Contact between Nagorno-Karabakh and Azerbaijan in 2010 made it clear that the international community cannot afford to regard this conflict as being "frozen" in any real sense.

What is the distinctive nature of this conflict? What distinguishes it from other unresolved post-Soviet regional conflicts and from other separatist conflicts worldwide? This chapter will focus on some features of the Karabakh conflict which have wider implications for current perspectives surrounding conflict transformation and conflict resolution. Some elements of the situation in Nagorno-Karabakh are similar to other conflicts, but other features are not, pointing to its distinctive nature. The case of Kosovo provoked a discussion on the issue as to how far secessionist conflicts are comparable, or sui generis. On one hand, conflicts in the post-Soviet areas share historical and structural roots mainly derived from Soviet territorial and nationality policies with their construction of ethno-territorial entities on different hierarchical levels. On the other hand, they are distinct in terms of:

- the historical depth of the conflict;
- the degree of violence during phases of armed conflict;
- the options of the separatist parties in the conflict regarding independence as a distinct state or union with another state;
- the potential for the independence of de facto states, from Transnistria to Nagorno-Karabakh;
- the ethno-demographic composition of the "zones of conflict" before the outbreak of secessionist wars in the beginning of the 1990s;
- the role that Russia plays as an external actor towards the conflicts and other criteria.

How far is the conflict in Nagorno-Karabakh sui generis? And to what extent is it comparable to other "frozen conflicts" in the post-Soviet area?

The first and most relevant territorial conflict in the transition from the Soviet to the post-Soviet period

The conflict in Nagorno-Karabakh was the first and gravest interethnic troublemaker at the end of the Soviet era during the transitional period of *Perestroika* and *Glasnost*. Its actors, especially Armenian intellectuals, were among the first to use these new conditions to articulate national grievances and demands. From 1987 on, the Karabakh question was mobilised on the Armenian side more forcefully than earlier advances which had been made during the Soviet period. With the request by the regional Soviet[1] in Stepanakert for the transfer of the Nagorno-Karabakh Autonomous Region from the Azerbaijani to the Armenian Soviet Republic in February 1988, this conflict became known to a broader international public. It also foreshadowed a broader spectrum of further conflicts regarding borders and territories within the demise of the Soviet Empire. There is a thesis that the Soviet central power was instigating this conflict according to a strategy of *"Divide et Impera*. Contrary to this perspective, the escalation of tension around Nagorno-Karabakh in 1988 and the reaction to it by the Soviet central power revealed a considerable lack of control and also demonstrated a remarkable loss of capacity for managing developments in the non-Russian periphery of the multiethnic empire.

Key conflict in the region, main barrier for intraregional development

Given the tension between Armenia and Azerbaijan and the potential for a classic case of interstate conflict, the case of Nagorno-Karabakh is perceived

---

[1] The regional Soviet was the local, regional legislative body in the Soviet system.

to be the key problem for the region. One Western analyst presents it as the "gravest long-term problem for the South Caucasus and the whole area between the Black and Caspian seas".[2] With closed borders between Armenia and Azerbaijan as well as between Armenia and Turkey, this conflict erected high barriers in a region which is always presented as a land bridge and strategic transit corridor between the Caspian and the Black Sea regions and between Europe and Central Asia. This transit and landbridge-function is of special importance for the European Union's policy towards the region. In its new Eastern Partnership advance the EU launched flagship initiatives, such as integrated border management, diversification of energy supply and the concept of a southern corridor with the South Caucasus in its centre. All these initiatives require increased intraregional cooperation between the new partner states. The unresolved conflict in Nagorno-Karabakh is the central spoiler for intraregional cooperation which involves all three South Caucasian states.

Armenia remained isolated from projects having a landbridge-function, such as the oil pipeline from Baku to Ceyhan via Tbilisi, the railway project from Baku via Georgia to Kars or the currently disputed new projects like Nabucco. The Karabakh question has become the main factor responsible for blocking a process of deep historical significance, namely the diplomatic rapprochement between Armenia and Turkey. It will be profoundly problematic for Armenia that recent commentaries on the geopolitical importance of this unresolved conflict and its regional environment are increasingly focused on Azerbaijan and its growing economic significance.[3]

Deeper historical background

In the case of Nagorno-Karabakh, as with other ethno-territorial conflicts, the relationship between the parties involved does not reflect some kind of primordial "ancient hatred". It belongs much more to the category of "modern hatred".[4] Over long periods Armenians and Azeris have lived together peacefully, and even after the Karabakh war both communities coexisted as

---

[2] T. de Waal (2010) "Remaking the Nagorno-Karabakh Peace Process", *Survival*, Vol. 52, No. 4, p. 176.

[3] Thus, a recent paper for a panel "Reimagining Eurasia" is eager to "focus US policymakers' minds on Azerbaijan, the region's pivot point. Azerbaijan is the gateway to the Caspian basin, and Central, South, Inner, and East Asia. It sits astride the world's fastest-growing trade route developing overland across those regions to and from the European Union and the Middle East". S. Charap, A. Peterson (2010) "Reimagining Azerbaijan. Building an Azerbaijan Policy Based on Today's Strategic Realities", *Center for American Progress* http://www.americanprogress.org/issues/2010/08/reimagining_azerbaijan.html .

[4] S.J. Kaufman (2001) *Modern Hatreds. The Symbolic Politics of Ethnic War* (Ithaca and London: Cornell University Press), pp. 49–63.

neighbours in other parts of the region, such as Georgia. Nevertheless, the historical and psychological background of mutual hostility is even deeper than witnessed in a conflict such as Transnistria. The entire twentieth century (at the very least) provides the historical context. The Karabakh war of 1991–94 was another major military clash between Armenians and Azeris after armed conflicts regarding territorial issues and mutual violence in 1905–06 and 1918–20. With competing historical claims to the contested territory, each party involved in the conflict presents the territory as being either Armenian since primeval times, or an integral part of the territorial history of Azerbaijan. Since the end of the 1980s, a "Karabakhization" of historiography in both Azerbaijan and Armenia led to a simplification of history writing, presenting each nation "as constantly struggling for independence in its 'historical' territories, including Nagorno-Karabakh, but being overwhelmed by various empires or aggressors".[5]

Thus, history plays a crucial role as a tool in this conflict. The contest on the battlefield of historiography goes back to Soviet times when there was already a major dispute regarding the Caucasian Albania, to which Karabakh belonged in early times.[6] With the return of the Karabakh question since 1987, the dispute as to how far this Albania belonged to the history of the Christian Armenia or to the territorial heritage of Azerbaijan became highly politicised. The conflict over Nagorno-Karabakh has been largely ignited due to mutually exclusive historical interpretations and demonstrates the necessity for observers and mediators to analyse more carefully issues such as collective memory and historical perception. Conflicting parties not only have differing representations about the recent history of the Karabakh conflict, but virtually opposite historical representations about the region, even starting with their understanding of ancient history. "In the Armenian literature the contested territory is portrayed in exclusivist terms as a historical Armenian (therefore non-Azerbaijani) territory, excluding any possibility that Azerbaijanis might also have a legitimate sense of belonging to Nagorno-Karabakh. On the other side it is presented in an exclusivist way as a historical Azerbaijani (therefore non-Armenian) land, a birthplace of Azerbaijani culture and identity, excluding any possibility that Armenians also might have a legitimate sense of belonging to Nagorno-Karabakh".[7]

[5] S. Minasyan (2009) "Armenia's Attitude Towards its Past: History and Politics", *Caucasus Analytical Digest*, No. 8, p. 10.

[6] M.H. Kohrs (2005) "Geschichte als politisches Argument. Der 'Historikerstreit' um Berg-Karabach", in A. Fikret and B. Bonwetsch (eds) *Osmanismus, Nationalismus und der Kaukasus* (Reichert Verlag, Wiesbaden), 43–63.

F. Shafiev (2007) "Ethnic Myths and Perceptions as a Hurdle to Conflict Settlement. The Armenian-Azerbaijani Case", *The Caucasus and Globalization*, No. 2, pp. 57–70.

[7] P. Gamaghelyan (2010) "Literature Matters", Caucasus Edition. *Journal of Conflict Transformation*, July.

Many regional conflicts are linked to an active cultivation of "chosen glories" and "chosen traumas" in the historical narratives of the parties to the conflict. In the case of Karabakh, this mechanism plays an important role. Perhaps the most comparable case of historiographical debates which directly provoke conflict in the South Caucasus has been the dispute regarding how far Abkhazia is an integral part of Georgian history and to what extent it represents a subject of history in its own right.[8]

Memory wars

Even more significant as an identity-building factor in unresolved regional conflicts is the experience of mutual violence and the dimension of victimisation which are crucial for the mobilisation of "memory wars". They represent the highest psychological barrier for conflict transformation and confidence building. With its comparatively long period of war (1991–94) and the preceding intercommunal violence, (with victims on all sides of the conflict), the case of Karabakh is a special one. Together with the civil war in Tajikistan (1992–96) and the two Russian wars in Chechnya, it is one of the gravest periods of violence in post-Soviet history, creating hundreds of thousands of refugees and IDPs and some twenty to thirty thousand casualties. This scale of victimisation provokes the cultivation of "hate" and "fear narratives" on all sides of the conflict. Particularly relevant might be the deep psychological impact of the violence experienced by Armenians, given the earlier trauma of the Armenian community during the Genocide of 1915. This alignment of the two experiences was first cultivated in the Karabakh Movement of 1988–90 with slogans such as "Sumgait[9] is the sequel to the Genocide".[10]

On the other side, the massacre of the civilian population in Khojaly in February 1992, and other events, are presented in Azerbaijan as the "genocide" of Azeris by Armenians. Regional conflicts provoked an inflationary use of the unique term "genocide". Thus, the Georgian offensive on South Ossetia on 7–8 August 2008 was presented in Russian war propaganda as a Georgian "genocide" of Ossetians.[11] In the post-Soviet Azerbaijani

---

[8] A critical assessment of these debates is given by G. Maisuradze (2009) "Time Turned Back: On the Use of History in Georgia", *Caucasus Analytical Digest*, No. 8, pp. 13–14.

[9] To learn more about the Sumgait events: T. de Waal (2010) *The Caucasus: An Introduction* (Oxford University Press), p. 111.

[10] H. Marutyan (2007) "Iconography of Historical Memory and Armenian National Identity at the End of the 1980s", in T. Darieva, W. Kaschuba (eds) *Representations on the Margins of Europe. Politics and Identities in the Baltic and South Caucasian States* (Frankfurt and New York), 89–114.

[11] For a critical assessment of this allegation of "genocide" by the EU Fact-Finding Mission, see: *Independent International Fact-Finding Mission on the Conflict in Georgia*, Report, Vol. II, 421–28.

historiography this term is also applied very readily. More or less every invasion of enemies into Azerbaijan is presented as "soy qirğini" (genocide), whereas advances of the Azerbaijani army are "yürüş" (military campaigns).[12]

The versions of Karabakh history are particularly full of "victimisation" narratives used as tools for evoking collective forms of remembrance. The conflict exists not only as a geopolitical reality, but also as a mental and socio-psychological one, and resolution of the conflict is impossible without both significant changes in perception and "transformation of narratives".[13] These, however, are extremely difficult tasks, as both parties are convinced that only their version of history is authentic. However, a kind of "twitter diplomacy" between young people on both conflict sides is emerging.[14] On a platform such as the Caucasus Edition of the *Journal of Conflict Transformation* (http://caucasusedition.net), such discussion about the transformation of narratives has also started to open up. However, such changes in perception regarding the conflict and its varying narratives require patience. And patience is shrinking dramatically for one side of the conflict, at least. In Azerbaijan, withdrawal of Armenian troops from Azerbaijan's territory is currently being presented as the only means of securing a breakthrough in negotiations, or "conflict resolution" will be found via military means.

Religious dimension?

The parties involved in this conflict have different religious backgrounds. Can the conflict be interpreted as a clash between Christian and Muslim parts of the Caucasus? It is certainly not completely free of religious partisanship. In the Karabakh war some Muslim militants from the North Caucasus participated in the fight against Armenian troops. Azerbaijan is supported diplomatically in the conflict by the Organization of Islamic Conference (OIC). OIC members gave strong support to Azerbaijan in March 2008, when the UN General Assembly backed an Azerbaijani-drafted resolution which referred to Karabakh as an internationally recognised part of Azerbaijan and demanded the "immediate, complete, and unconditional withdrawal of Armenian forces" from occupied Azerbaijani lands. Only 39 Member States,

---

[12] V. Adam (2005) "Umdeutung der Geschichte im Zeichen des Nationalismus seit dem Ende der SU: das Beispiel Aserbaidschan", in F. Adanir, B. Bonwetsch (eds) *Osmanismus, Nationalismus und der Kaukasus* (Kaukasusstudien, Band 9, Wiesbaden), p. 38.

[13] R. Garagozov (2010) "Towards Conflict Transformation through the Transformation of Narratives (Preliminary considerations)", Caucasus Edition. *Journal of Conflict Transformation*, August.

[14] O. Krikorian (2010) "Twitter Diplomacy. Can New Media Help Break the Armenia-Azerbaijan Information Blockade?", *Transitions Online*, February.

most of them affiliated with the OIC, voted for it, while over 150 others abstained or voted against. Recently, an "Organization for Islamic Karabakh Resistance" was founded under the Islamic Party of Azerbaijan.[15]

Azerbaijan repeatedly complained of Western partisanship with Armenia in the Karabakh conflict due to religious solidarity. However, instead of a Christian-Muslim "clash of civilisations" the antagonism between the parties to the conflict is perceived to be more one of ethnicity – more precisely as a clash between Armenian and Turkish ethnicities. The Armenian side integrates the conflict into its narrative of "traumatic experience with Turks". Azerbaijan is cultivating a self-identification as the first Westernised secular republic of the Muslim world, a country where Islam is far from being a state religion, and where the enemy is primarily Armenian, not Christian. Thus, the conflict is not "Islamicised" and is clearly different to conflicts in the North Caucasus. It also differs from many separatist conflicts which involve a Muslim party, which have been transformed into "jihad" in a regional spectrum ranging from Chechnya to Kashmir to the Southern Philippines. In this case, religious leaders are far from being the key players in the conflict. On 26 April 2010, the head of the Armenian Apostolic Church, Catholicos Garegin II, and Azerbaijan's Muslim Leader, Sheikh-ul-Islam Allahshukur Pashazade, together with the Russian Orthodox patriarch, met in Baku for the first time and gave their commitments for peace. According to Arif Yunusov, an expert at Baku's non-governmental Institute for Peace and Democracy, such a summit of religious leaders can only play a role in societies where the majority are true believers, and neither the Armenian nor the Azerbaijani society can be defined as such. The authority of the religious leaders "is not on such a level that we can talk about their contribution to a resolution of the Nagorno-Karabakh conflict".[16] The religious dimension in the case of the Karabakh conflict is therefore of lesser importance.

Separation of the ethnic parties to the conflict

Since 1988, the conflict of Nagorno-Karabakh and the ensuing war divided Armenian and Azeri populations more effectively than the secessionist conflicts in Georgia divided ethnic Georgian, Abkhaz and Ossetian populations before the August war of 2008. Whereas the ceasefire lines between "Georgia proper" and its breakaway territories had been, to a certain degree, permeable to traffic and trade, Nagorno-Karabakh has been strongly separated

---

[15] "Azerbaijan: Islamic party sets up body for Karabakh", BBC Monitoring Global Newsline Former Soviet Union Political File, 2 August 2010.

[16] Quoted by Eurasia Net: M. Muradova "Azerbaijan, Armenia, Russia Using Faith to Find Karabakh Peace", 28 April 2010, http://www.eurasianet.org/node/60948 (date accessed: 10 November 2010).

from its former "parent state" since 1994. Within nearly two decades in the contested enclave a generation of Armenian Karabakhis has grown up who have no contact with Azerbaijan or Azeri peers. Against this background, the image of Nagorno-Karabakh's voluntary return to the jurisdiction of Azerbaijan is unrealistic.

"Occupied territories" or "security buffer"?

There is a striking peculiarity in the topography of this conflict which distinguishes it from other unresolved regional conflicts from Transnistria to South Ossetia. The territorial quarrel is not limited to the contested political status of Nagorno-Karabakh itself, but includes surrounding territories which without doubt belong legally to Azerbaijan, but are under the control of Armenian troops. From the perspective of Azerbaijan, these seven regions of Lachin (1 835 km²), Kelbajar (1 936 km²), Jebrail (1 059 km²), Kubatly (802 km²), Agdam (1 093 km²), Fizuli (1 386 km²) and Zangelan (707 km²) are occupied territories and targets for ethnic cleansing. From the Armenian point of view, they constitute a "buffer zone" for the security of Nagorno-Karabakh within the battlefields of the Karabakh war of 1992–93. Some Armenian commentaries define them as "liberated territories", contrary to their adversary's terminology of occupation. However, the question arises: Liberated from what? From the Azeri population? Here, the terminology of "liberation" is clearly questionable.

The Madrid Basic Principles for peaceful resolution of the conflict envisage a gradual withdrawal of Armenian troops from these territories, to be followed at some future stage by a referendum on Nagorno-Karabakh's future status. However, this aspect of the Basic Principles is contested in Armenia and particularly in Nagorno-Karabakh itself. In May 2009, two prominent military officials from Karabakh, former armed forces commander Samvel Babayan and Defence Minister General Moses Hakobian, argued that Armenian forces should not withdraw from the districts of Azerbaijan which they currently occupy before a firm agreement is reached on Nagorno-Karabakh's future status. Hakobian told journalists in Stepanakert that "all the territories that we had liberated required human victims, and every person here has memories related to them. ... It will be difficult to cede those territories to anyone".[17] Thus, he made a connection between the "liberation", a terminology used for the "occupied territories", and the "victimisation" as discussed above.

---

[17] Quoted by L. Fuller (2009) in "Is the Karabakh Peace Process in Jeopardy?", *Eurasianet-Eurasia Insight*, http://www.eurasianet.org/departments/insight/articles/pp051609.shtml (date accessed: 20 November 2010).

According to some Armenian perceptions, there has already been a certain withdrawal of their own side's military in these territories. "In 1997, the buffer zone was to be deployed on the northern and southern borders of a demilitarised Lachin region [not the corridor] after the retreat of Armenian troops, a no-fly zone over the surrounding territories and Nagorno-Karabakh was to be operated, and there was a clause mentioning demilitarisation and absence of heavy weaponry in all other territories around Nagorno-Karabakh. Thus, there has constantly been regress for the Armenian side in the proposals made by the mediators since 1997".[18] Armenian willingness to hand back this "buffer zone" is currently constrained by repeated military threats from Azerbaijan. Against this background, Armenian commentaries point to "the misconception that the transfer of some or all territories controlled by the Nagorno-Karabakh Republic to Azerbaijan will contribute to bringing the settlement process any closer. The transfer of at least one area or only a part of it to Azerbaijan will, on the contrary, significantly intensify the military rhetoric of Azerbaijan, encouraging it to ultimately seize control of the Nagorno-Karabakh Republic".[19] However, despite this perception, the international community is awaiting the start of an Armenian troop withdrawal from at least five of the seven "liberated" or "occupied" territories.

In early July 2010, President Ilham Aliyev told representatives of the displaced Azerbaijani population of Nagorno-Karabakh that Armenian troops will withdraw from the Aghdam, Fizuli, Jebrail, Zangelan, and Qubadly districts of Azerbaijan immediately after the peace agreement is signed and from the Lachin and Kelbajar districts over five years. "The Azerbaijani population will return to all districts, including Nagorno-Karabakh, and much more time will probably be required for this. Peacekeeping troops will be deployed on the border with Nagorno-Karabakh ..." Azerbaijani Foreign Minister Elmar Mammadyarov presented the five-year plan for the withdrawal of troops from Lachin and Kelbajar as a compromise, noting that the former Armenian President, Robert Kocharyan, insisted on ten years, while Azerbaijan demanded that troops be withdrawn in only one year. According to the foreign minister, the mediators suggested a five-year period to which Azerbaijan has already given its consent. These statements enraged official Yerevan, Armenia's capital: "The Armenian side has never discussed the issue of Lachin and Kelbajar's return to Azerbaijani jurisdiction", stated Armenian Foreign Minister Edward Nalbandian.[20]

---

[18] A. Ayunts (2010) "Madrid Principles: Basis for Conflict Settlement or War?", Caucasus Edition. *Journal of Conflict Transformation*.

[19] Institute of Political Research (2009) "Karabakh Conflict: 15 Years of Neither War Nor Peace", *Situation 15 Questions and Answers*, Yerevan, May 2009.

[20] M. Muradova (2010) "Stalement in Karabakh Peace Talks", CACI (Caucasus and Central Asia Institute) Analyst, http://www.cacianalyst.org/?q=node/5388 (date accessed: 20 November 2010).

Lack of peacekeeping

Another other striking feature of the Karabakh-case – when compared to the situation in Georgia before the August war in 2008 or in Moldova – is the absence of peacekeeping or real ceasefire-monitoring. A monitoring mandate of the Organization for Security and Cooperation in Europe (OSCE) in the highly significant case of Nagorno-Karabakh is extremely limited. OSCE Ambassador Andrzej Kasprzyk and five assistants monitor "a ceasefire in which in excess of 20,000 troops on either side face one another across a 175 km long line of trenches and dug-out".[21] OSCE presence there can be likened to that of a fig leaf. The interest in peacekeeping along the ceasefire line has varied between the sides in the conflict. Armenia was in favour of a ceasefire line which was as fixed as possible, allowing it to consolidate its conquests in its new "security zone" around Nagorno-Karabakh. Azerbaijan wanted the ceasefire line, which runs across its de jure territory, to remain as impermanent as possible, and therefore in 1994 blocked the deployment of a Russian peacekeeping force and opposed any moves to strengthen the OSCE monitoring mandate. Plans for security arrangements following any agreement are still very sketchy. The lack of any credible proposals makes the two presidents cautious about signing an agreement without knowing what kind of security arrangements will be put in place to underpin it.[22]

International security guarantees, including a peacekeeping operation, are part of the "Basic Principles" for a peace agreement for Nagorno-Karabakh, together with the Armenian troop withdrawal from the Azerbaijani districts around the enclave, a corridor linking Armenia to Nagorno-Karabakh (an interim status for this entity guaranteeing its self-governance and security), the final status of the contested region to be determined in the future by a legally binding expression of public will and the right of internally displaced persons and refugees to return. The demand for international peacekeeping along the Line of Contact becomes increasingly urgent. The three Minsk Group Co-Chairs have recently noted increased tension in the region, including armed incidents on the Line of Contact and "inflammatory" public statements.[23]

Interstate or interethnic conflict?

Most "frozen conflicts" are a mixture of intrastate and interstate conflict configuration. Not unlike Georgia's separatist conflicts which led to war with Russia in 2008, the Karabakh conflict has serious potential to become

[21] T. de Waal (2010), op.cit., p. 166.
[22] T. de Waal (2010), op. cit., p. 167.
[23] M. Muradova (2010), op. cit.

a classical military conflict between two sovereign states – Armenia and Azerbaijan. With regard to intrastate or interstate configurations, the perceptions of conflict are different in Armenia and Azerbaijan, as they had been for each side in the Georgian conflict. For Azerbaijan, this conflict is primarily an interstate affair – a conflict with Armenia, which is occupying Azerbaijani territory. For Armenia it is rather an intrastate conflict regarding national self-determination between a former autonomous entity of Azerbaijan with a clear Armenian majority population and its old "parent state" which has lost its legitimacy to control the contested region. This unresolved conflict has transformed relations between Armenia and Azerbaijan into the most precarious and most tense interstate relationship within the post-Soviet space.

This interstate configuration also impacted upon the negotiation agenda due to another striking peculiarity of the conflict – the exclusion of Nagorno-Karabakh from the negotiation table of the OSCE Minsk Group since 1997, despite being the main territory involved in the conflict. Azerbaijan refused to recognise Nagorno-Karabakh as a legitimate party in the negotiation, though Baku had concluded several agreements with it in the early 1990s.[24] Here, we have a unique case of negotiation without representation for the key party in the conflict. The parties most affected by the conflict – the Nagorno-Karabakh Republic and its Armenian community as well as its Azeri population group which fled to Azerbaijan in the violent phase of conflict – are grossly under-represented.[25]

This exclusion of Nagorno-Karabakh from the negotiating table is not only a bone of contention between the immediate conflict sides, the de facto state and its former "parent state". There also appear to be varying perceptions of the conflict within Nagorno-Karabakh and Armenia. Though the Armenian government is principally supportive of a re-inclusion of Nagorno-Karabakh in negotiations, it has firmly established itself as the main negotiator on the Armenian side of the conflict via the Minsk process. According to an opinion poll conducted in Karabakh in May 2010, 85 per cent of the respondents see the region as independent, and 90 per cent want Armenia to withdraw from the peace talks and let the region find common ground with Azerbaijan on its own.[26] Political voices from Karabakh, such as that of its Foreign Minister, Georgy Petrossyan, say that Nagorno-Karabakh "bears no responsibility for the Madrid Principles or any outcome

[24] V. Kazimirov (2008) "Is there a Way Out of the Karabakh Deadlock?", *Russian in Global Affairs*, Vol. 6, No. 1, p. 188.

[25] A. Alizada (2010) "Negotiation without (due) Representation", Caucasus Edition. *Journal of Conflict Transformation*.

[26] "Karabakh people want Armenia to withdraw from peace talks" – sociologist, BBC Monitoring Global Newsline Former Soviet Union Political File, 29 July 2010 (Public Television of Armenia, Yerevan, in Armenian 1600 gmt 29 July).

based on that framework, since the process does not include Nagorno-Karabakh".[27] According to an expert from the Republic of Armenia: "To increase or restore its position, Armenia needs to exert every effort to re-include Nagorno-Karabakh into the negotiations. This will involve, first of all, overcoming the intransigence of Azerbaijan. In order to achieve any progress, the major external actors must convince the Azerbaijani government that the direct participation of Nagorno-Karabakh in the negotiations is indispensable".[28] On the other side, Baku is demanding the inclusion of the expelled Azeri community of Nagorno-Karabakh in the negotiations. "Each side sees the inclusion of the other not as a means to reaching a peaceful solution, but as conceding to a solution they cannot accept. The government in Baku believes that including the Nagorno-Karabakh Armenians in the talks would legitimise their de facto independence and seal the fate of the negotiations. Meanwhile, Armenian officials (both in Yerevan and Nagorno-Karabakh) view the inclusion of Nagorno-Karabakh Azerbaijanis (as representatives in their own right) as legitimising the claims that they have the right to return to their homes and have a say in determining the final status of Nagorno-Karabakh".[29]

Dimension of international conflict diplomacy

Whereas the international peacekeeping presence is low, if not entirely absent, the level of international mediation and peace diplomacy in the Karabakh conflict since 1992 has been higher and more permanent than in other "frozen conflicts" in the post-Soviet space. Its forum is the Minsk Group of 13 OSCE Member States. Since 1997 it has been under the leadership of the three Co-Chairs – the United States, Russia and France. The tripartite co-chairmanship structure emerged because of the perceived need to balance the competing interests and suspicions of Russia and the Western nations in the Minsk Group. In practical terms it is a cumbersome institution.[30] Since 2001, with the meeting in Key West, Florida, it has repeatedly made the mistake of announcing an imminent breakthrough in the negotiations, an announcement which had to be denied after every high-level meeting. Within the Minsk format there are meetings between the presidents of both sides in the conflict. "If the two Presidents were more committed to a result, rather than to process for the sake of process, they would set

[27] Quoted by International Crisis Group (ICG) (2009) "Nagorno-Karabakh: Getting to a Breakthrough", *Europe Briefing*, No. 55.
[28] G. Novikova (2010) "Implications of the Russian-Georgian War in the Nagorno-Karabakh Conflict: Limited Maneuverability" Caucasus Edition. *Journal of Conflict Transformation*, 15 August.
[29] A. Alizada (2010), op. cit.
[30] T. de Waal (2010), op.cit., p. 164.

up a permanent channel for bilateral contact and discussion of the conflict rather than relying entirely on the Minsk Group Co-Chairs to be their go-betweens. There was briefly such a channel between trusted presidential advisers, but it was discontinued after the OSCE Lisbon Summit of 1996. In 2004 two deputy foreign ministers...were entrusted with a bilateral mechanism, but they transferred responsibility to their foreign ministers. The ministers, in turn, initiated the Prague Process in 2004, but then gave way to the two Presidents".[31]

In the international environment mediating in this conflict, the absence of the European Union is remarkable. There are EU members in the Minsk Group, and France is one of the Co-Chairs, but this engagement is not under any EU mandate. Until the time of writing, the EU remains largely absent from mediating in the Karabakh conflict and from rehabilitation projects in the zone of conflict. This absence is even more remarkable against the background of increased EU engagement in the Georgian case of unresolved conflicts. The EU was a main donor for rehabilitation projects in Abkhazia and South Ossetia before 2008 and the most engaged international actor in the Georgian crisis of August 2008. The EU reacted immediately to broker a ceasefire between Russia and Georgia, allocating humanitarian assistance to the refugees, deploying a 200-strong monitoring mission, chairing a donors' conference and initiating a fact-finding mission on the origins of the conflict. When asked how the EU could increase support for resolving the Karabakh conflict, the answer was: "It is the OSCE Minsk Group's role". "Without addressing here the usefulness of that format, the EU could give more support through programs which help to create a better environment for the negotiations but do not duplicate them".[32] Thus, the EU could assist non-governmental organisations to promote public debate on resolutions to the conflict within the societies of Armenia, Azerbaijan and Nagorno-Karabakh. This brings us to another peculiarity of this conflict.

Underdeveloped inclusion of civil society actors into conflict-mediation and transformation

The negotiations in the Nagorno-Karabakh conflict are located exclusively on a high diplomacy level with "some of the most secretive and least inclusive peace talks in the world. The mediators in the Track One process give no support to a complementary Track Two process".[33] This exclusive configuration differs from the conflict between Georgia and Abkhazia in which, at

---

[31] Ibid.

[32] A. Poghosyan (2010) "EU's Current and Possible Role in the Nagorno-Karabakh Conflict Resolution Process", Caucasus Edition. *Journal of Conflict Transformation*, August 15.

[33] T. de Waal (2010) op.cit, p. 168.

least for a while, civil society actors and international NGOs participated substantially in efforts towards confidence building and conflict transformation. Thomas de Waal identifies important differences on either side of the Nagorno-Karabakh conflict which prevent a Track Two process from developing. The Armenians, as the victorious side in the Karabakh war, can afford to take a "more magnanimous stance on the issue of people to people contacts" and sometimes invite Azerbaijani experts to Armenia and even to Nagorno-Karabakh. The Azerbaijani authorities are much more suspicious of such contacts, worrying that they legitimise what they regard as the unacceptable status quo. Civil society initiatives could include "the chief missing element in the Minsk Group talks", that is, representatives of the Armenian and Azerbaijani Karabakhis.[34]

Russia's role

Russian involvement in the Karabakh conflict is different from that of Georgia's conflicts with Abkhazia and South Ossetia as well as from Russian politics toward Moldova's conflict with the Dniestr region. In the Karabakh conflict, Russia was less directly involved and did not hold a dominant position as "peacekeeper" as it did with its troops in Abkhazia and South Ossetia until August 2008 and continues to do in Transnistria. Since 1997, together with the United States and France, it holds the co-chairmanship of the Minsk Group within the OSCE, which has been the main mediator in this conflict since 1992. Though Russia has a close security relationship with Armenia, it is not putting pressure on Azerbaijan or acting as a direct "party to the conflict" as in the case of Georgia, where it clearly supported the separatist governments against the Georgian government. In the Transnistrian conflict, Moscow also stood on the side of the separatist "party to the conflict" extending financial and political support to the Transnistrian authorities and keeping detachments of its Fourteenth Army (currently around 1,200 troops) stationed in the breakaway region. But with the Moldovan government's commitment to neutrality with regard to NATO membership (which marks a relevant difference to the Georgian foreign and security policy), Russia changed its stance and is supporting a peaceful settlement by reuniting the "parties to the conflict" in a kind of confederation.

Russia does not automatically support the Nagorno-Karabakh Republic, at least not if compared to its substantial diplomatic, economic and even military support for other de facto states from the Dniestr Republic to South Ossetia, which have become more or less Russian protectorates. In comparison to the geopolitical environment of the Georgian regional conflicts, the Karabakh conflict is, to a lesser degree, embedded in the rivalry between

---

[34] T. de Waal (2010) op. cit., p. 168.

Russia and Western powers. Russia is cooperating with the other Co-Chairs of the OSCE Minsk Group on the implementation of the Basic Principles for a peaceful resolution of the conflict. However, Russian diplomacy plays its own game within this framework, within certain limits. Shortly after its war in Georgia, Russia took an initiative of peace diplomacy in the Karabakh conflict in November 2008, inviting the presidents of Armenia and Azerbaijan to Moscow and persuaded them to commit to a (nonbinding) declaration on a peaceful conflict resolution on the basis of the Madrid Principles. During the presidents' face-to-face talks in St Petersburg on 17 June 2010, Moscow presented a peace plan which Armenian leaders labelled a "new version" of the Madrid document drawn up by the mediating troika. The Azeri foreign ministry qualified this plan as being single-handedly drawn up by Russia, not a Minsk Group document, and therefore unacceptable to Baku. There are differences in the Co-Chairs' statements. In their 27 June statement adopted during the G8 summit in Canada, the US, Russian and French presidents vaguely said that the Karabakh status issue should be settled through a "legally binding expression of will". A Russian translation of the statement released by the Kremlin spoke of "a legally binding expression of the will of Karabakh's population".[35]

How far are Russia's bilateral relationships with Armenia and Azerbaijan committed to neutrality in the conflict? In Armenia there is a remarkable economic and security dependence on Russia, which accounts for the lion's share of investment in Armenia. Telecommunications companies, the banking system, energy plants, gas suppliers, the metal industry and the railway system are completely or partially under Russian control.[36] Russia is Armenia's biggest source of imported goods. The Armenian diaspora is quite widespread, but 70 per cent of remittances sent to Armenia are from Russia. The Armenian security dependence on Russia became a big issue in the summer of 2010, with defence officials in Moscow and Yerevan planning to sign a new military agreement which would assign Russia and its troops a greater role in ensuring Armenia's security.

The two governments amended a 1995 treaty concerning a Russian military base in Armenia. The defence ministers of both countries signed a protocol on 20 August in Yerevan, which prolonged the term of the base. The protocol makes clear that the Russian base will not only protect Russia's interests but also contribute to Armenia's national security. Moscow has committed itself to providing Armenia with "modern and compatible weaponry and military

[35] www.day.az , 22 July 2010. Quoted by E. Danielyan "Armenia and Karabakh Encouraged by UN Court Ruling on Kosovo", http://www.jamestown.org/programs/edm/ (date accessed: 30 July 2010).

[36] Arka News Agency "Russia has Lion's Share in Investments in Armenia: Russian Trade Representative. Yerevan", 17 September 2008, www.arka.am/eng/economy/2008/09/17/11200.html (date accessed: 20 November 2010).

hardware". In the summer of 2010, Yerevan and Moscow announced plans to significantly boost cooperation between their defence industries within the framework of the Russian-led Collective Security Treaty Organization (CSTO).[37] Thus, the question arises as to whether a Russian military partisanship is emerging in the unresolved conflict on Nagorno-Karabakh in favour of Armenia, in a context of growing military threats from Azerbaijan. On 25 August, Armenian Defence Minister, Seyran Ohanyan, told Radio Free Europe/Radio Liberty he had "no doubts" that under the new agreement, Russia would openly support Armenia in the event of a new conflict with Azerbaijan over Nagorno-Karabakh. The Azerbaijani Defence Ministry press service dismissed that claim and called it "laughable": "This agreement is between two States, it is up to them. But this protocol cannot hinder or stop the Azerbaijani army". Azerbaijan had no choice but to upgrade its armed forces by acquiring new weaponry.[38] And Baku, too,, is acquiring new weaponry from Russia. Armenian commentators expressed serious concern at reports about a planned (in the meantime concluded) sale of Russian S-300 air-defence systems to Azerbaijan. They said Armenia should even consider pulling out of the CSTO if the deal goes through.[39]

Azerbaijan and Turkey underpinned their bilateral relationship with the new Agreement on Strategic Partnership and Mutual Support. Turkish President, Abdullah Gul, ended an official visit to Baku on 17 August 2010 with the signing of this agreement. Details remained a guessing game: In the opinion of one Azerbaijani analyst: "The deepening of military cooperation between Azerbaijan and Turkey is now especially important for Baku. It does not mean that Turkey will deploy a military base in Azerbaijan soon. But some steps could be taken". Gul and Aliyev most likely discussed what "adequate steps" Baku could take in response to Moscow's base deal with Armenia.[40]

Is an antagonistic military partisanship emerging between Russia and Turkey in the conflict over Nagorno-Karabakh? These historical regional players in the South Caucasus, who have triggered several wars in the nineteenth century, are cooperating over many issues today. They have largely expanded their economic relations, and within the last few years have also improved their bilateral foreign policy relationships. Russia, together with other international actors, supported the diplomatic process of Turkish–Armenian rapprochement. Russia's increased military engagement in Armenia fits into a much broader picture than that of a military

[37] Armenian Official: "Russian Troops in Armenia Set for Mission Upgrade", Radio Free Europe/Radio Liberty, 31 July 2010.

[38] Azartac news agency, Azerbaijan, 23 April 2010.

[39] "Armenian Opposition Party Concerned About New Deal with Russia", Radio Free Europe/Radio Liberty, 24 August 2010.

[40] S. Abasov (2010) "Turkey's Gul Visits Azerbaijan: A Case of Sound and Fury?", *Eurasia Insight*, 17 August 2010.

partisanship in the Karabakh conflict. After its five-day war with Georgia, Russia is expanding its military presence in the Caucasian and Black Sea region, with the prolongation of its Black Sea Fleet's basing rights in Ukraine, new military bases in Abkhazia and South Ossetia and the extension of the stationing of Russian forces in Armenia.[41]

Militarisation

Nevertheless, prolonging the terms surrounding Russian bases and broadening their functions has provoked critical comments, even in Armenia. Ruben Hakobyan, Deputy Chairman of the oppositional Heritage party, stated that this deal signifies the end of the multi-vector foreign policy of Armenia, and expressed concern at the fact that "the South Caucasus is becoming one of the most militarised zones in the world".[42] Indeed, in the context of "frozen conflicts" this region has, within a few years, become the stage for an alarming story of militarisation. Since 2004, Georgia and Azerbaijan have driven this armament spiral in the region with the multiplication of their military spending. In Georgia, this process was stopped, or at least interrupted by the war in 2008, whereas Russia has been enlarging its military presence in Abkhazia and South Ossetia since the war. The Karabakh conflict is deeply embedded in an environment of ever-increasing militarisation and war threats by Azerbaijan, which has by far the biggest military budget in the region.

Did the Georgian crisis provide any sustainable lesson with regard to the use of military rhetoric in the context of unresolved regional conflicts? At first, it seemed so. Military rhetoric around the Karabakh conflict diminished after August 2008. It was largely absent from the presidential election campaign in Azerbaijan in October 2008. However, it has returned. In April 2010, the Azerbaijani defence minister reported to his president that his country was able "to hit any target located in Armenia" and that by the end of 2009 the Azerbaijani army had received arms worth more than $1 billion.[43] In reaction to this statement Armenia's defence minister warned that Azerbaijan would find itself in a "disastrous" situation if it used military force to regain control of Nagorno-Karabakh and surrounding districts.

The beginning of the withdrawal of Armenian troops from the territories surrounding Nagorno-Karabakh, with parallel international security guarantees, could form the first major step towards a "road map" to peace, but is currently blocked by loud sabre-rattling in Baku.

---

[41] V. Socor (2010) "Russian Military Power Advancing in the Black Sea-South Caucasus Region", *Jamestown Foundation Eurasia Daily Monitor*, Vol. 7, No. 157.

[42] "Opposition official notes Armenian foreign policy change after deal with Russia", BBC Monitoring Global Newsline Former Soviet Union Political file, 24 August 2010.

[43] Azartac new agency, Azerbaijan, 23 April 2010.

Conclusion

Some factors discussed above, such as the lack of peacekeeping and cease-fire-monitoring, the non-representation of Karabakh as the main party to the conflict at the negotiation table, and the status of the surrounding Azerbaijani territories under Armenian troops' control – these all make the Nagorno-Karabakh conflict different from other "frozen conflicts". It has some elements in common with other unresolved conflicts, but with particularly distinctive features, such as its "memory wars", the mutually exclusive historical narratives of the conflict and the contested territory, and its highly militarised context. Some of these characteristics underpin the stagnation common to conflict resolution. Baku's frequent hints at a military solution to the conflict render its resolution increasingly urgent. The growing tension between stagnation and urgency characterises the current situation in the South Caucasus. In its position towards the war of August 2008 in Georgia, the report from the European Union's fact-finding mission made it clear that not only the use of force, but also threats of military force, are illegal instruments in unresolved conflicts: "Both Georgia and Russia violated the prohibition of threats of force under Art. 2 (4) of the UN Charter. The mutual threats created a climate of mutual distrust, which escalated over the years up to the foreseeable serious crisis".[44] International actors have to pay special attention to both the dangerousness and the illegality of military threats in the unresolved conflict over Nagorno-Karabakh, threats which come mainly from Azerbaijan. Such threats expose Azerbaijan's deep frustration with the status quo and its perceived ability to change the current situation via any means at its disposal. Both Azerbaijan's military escalation and Armenia's inclination towards preserving the status quo present serious challenges to the international community.

---

[44] *Independent International Fact-Finding Mission on the Conflict in Georgia*, Report Vol. II, September 2009, p. 238.

6
What the People Think: Town Hall Meetings Reveal the EU's Potential and Limits in the Nagorno-Karabakh Conflict

Tevan Poghosyan and Arpine Martirosyan

The vulnerable "no peace-no war" status quo in the Nagorno-Karabakh (NK) conflict does not seem to be favourable for either party in the conflict. Despite the 1994 ceasefire, there is a constant threat that war will break out. Therefore, it might be more urgent for the international community to try to prevent imminent war than to commit itself to the diplomatic resolution of the conflict. Regular ceasefire violations increase the number of casualties and loss of life. Despite the insistence of mediators and third parties on a solely peaceful resolution to the NK conflict, the military rhetoric of the Azerbaijani president (which only serves to arouse hatred in his people) threatens a renewed call to war. That a new war could provide the final resolution of the NK conflict is increasingly a belief held by all parties in the conflict. This has been stated (at times with particular vigour) during the town hall meetings (THM) organised and carried out by the International Center for Human Development (ICHD), Armenia, and its partner in Azerbaijan, Youth for Development (YFD).

Through 2008 and 2009 more than 2,000 Armenians and Azerbaijanis participated in THMs organised by ICHD and YFD in 23 cities of Nagorno-Karabakh, Armenia and Azerbaijan. The objective of the THMs was to shed light on what societies involved in the NK conflict think about possible ways of resolving the situation. Since it has been claimed that the NK conflict has been orchestrated by elites – thus marginalising ordinary citizens and depriving them of any chance to participate in any decision-making forum – the THMs have been of unique importance from this point of view. The parallel THMs have therefore provided a forum to discuss the NK conflict from different perspectives. People discussed the current situation, the possibility of a new war, the chances of resolving the conflict by peaceful

62 *Tevan Poghosyan and Arpine Martirosyan*

means, as well as debating the importance of international peacekeepers and the experiences of refugees and IDPs, and so forth.[1]

Many participants shared the conviction that war is inevitable and that it is the only alternative to the status quo. One of the Armenians interviewed argues that he would not exclude the possibility of the onset of war: "Azerbaijan talks about it (war) every day. They are getting ready for war, and we are getting ready for defence".[2]

Similar statements from the Armenian side are unsurprising. This is due to the constant aggressive military rhetoric from Azerbaijan. The following statement made by an Azerbaijani participant confirms this view: "We are always stating that Armenians are our enemies" so "the war will never end.[3] The discussants also expressed their opinion regarding third states, in which they had minimal confidence. The international mediators involved in the prevention/resolution process do not enjoy high levels of credibility or trust from either Armenians or Azerbaijanis. The idea of international peacekeepers has also been discussed with a certain level of scepticism. For many Armenians, who were supportive of the idea of deploying international peacekeepers, Russians were the preferred actors and Turks were the least welcome. Most of the Armenians taking part in this forum, however, were against international peacekeeping. Many participants were sceptical, citing the example of Kosovo's failed peacekeeping forces.[4] According to one Armenian participant, "We will have another Kosovo; calling the peacekeepers is not going to resolve anything".[5] Azerbaijanis were also pessimistic, and one referred to the terrible things happening in Afghanistan "under the peaceful forces".[6] It is interesting to observe that no major hopes were expressed regarding any external actor. Third parties are perceived to be unreliable, since it is believed that everyone pursues his own interests. Nevertheless, there are a few different answers as to the role and importance of different political actors who can mediate peace in the conflict. While Russia and Turkey are better known to ordinary people, the role of Europe is ambiguous. It is worth noting that, for many, there is no clear distinction between Europe and the European Union (EU). Europe as a geographical and cultural entity is at times confused with the European Union. This can be attributed to the lack of knowledge about what the EU is or does in the

---

[1] International Centre for Human Development (ICHD) (2010) *The Resolution of the Nagorno-Karabakh Issue: What Societies Say: Discussion results of Armenians and Azerbaijanis at the parallel Town Hall Meetings: Comparative analysis of the THM outputs* (Yerevan: ICHD).
[2] ICHD (2010), op. cit., p. 28.
[3] Ibid., p. 29.
[4] Ibid., p. 84.
[5] Ibid., p. 83.
[6] Ibid., p. 86.

region, but also to the lack of active involvement in regional matters on the part of the EU. While ordinary people are more or less comfortable discussing Russian or Turkish interests in the region, they lack adequate information about the objectives of the EU, why it should intervene, or how it could help. Moreover, several Armenian participants blamed Europe for not acting or helping in the past when war originally broke out. One Armenian participant asked, "What did Europe do fifteen years ago? Why are you anticipating that it will do something now?"[7]

Nevertheless, the EU could have a real opportunity to increase its involvement in the region and in the NK conflict resolution, since it is regarded as a relatively neutral actor by all parties involved.

The European Union's involvement in numerous unresolved South Caucasian conflicts is relatively new. Its full involvement in the region is hampered by Russia's dominating presence as a regional superpower. The United States is another power interested in the region, mainly because of the Caspian Basin. The presence of both a regional and international superpower complicates the EU's engagement in the region. It is noteworthy that when speaking of regional powers, none of the THM participants mentioned the EU as a political power in the region. The EU is, nevertheless, present in the region and is carrying out the "soft" diplomacy of long-term improvements by implementing its long-term conflict prevention instruments. The Union's engagement in the region's conflicts is often passive, and at times, invisible. Since it acts as an observer rather than a participant, this erodes the credibility of its conflict prevention/resolution policy objective. This invisibility leads to the assumption that there is no real need for Europe to even acknowledge NK's existence. As one Armenian stated, "the past 20 years have shown that we do not need Europe or any other region to acknowledge our independence. We can take care of ourselves quite alright".[8]

It has been widely argued that the EU is more an "economic superpower" than a political actor, or is simply a " 'political dwarf' unable to exert influence in international politics".[9] Over the past few years, however, the EU has managed to acquire an improved political status by increasing its engagement in preventive diplomacy in regions or countries which are experiencing, or are prone to, conflict. The THMs, however, showed that people are unconvinced by the EU's potential, or do not know how the EU might contribute. In fact, very little has been said about Europe or European intervention in regard to conflict prevention or resolution during the organised forums. Nevertheless, the EU is engaged in NK conflict prevention/resolution, despite

---

[7] Ibid., p. 202.

[8] Ibid., p. 205.

[9] R.H. Ginsberg (2001) *The European Union in International Politics* (New York: Rowman & Littlefield), p. 1.

its seemingly minimal involvement. Ordinary people know little about EU policies in regard to the NK conflict. Consequently, it is harder for them to assess or evaluate such policies. However, the EU's engagement in the NK conflict is far from direct. Conflict resolution is mentioned as a priority in some of its policy documents, but the EU has not included the conflict zone itself in any of its projects, fearing that this might be viewed (primarily by Azerbaijan) as de facto recognition of NK's independence. The fact that the second EU Special Representative to the Caucasus (EUSR) – the EU's most important conflict prevention and resolution instrument – has not visited Nagorno-Karabakh illustrates the weakness of the EU. In this way, the Union lets itself be manipulated by Azerbaijan. In the framework of the European Neighbourhood Policy (ENP) Armenia, EUSR's mandate is to "contribute to conflict prevention and assist the conflict settlement mechanisms in the region".[10] This implies that the EUSR should be directly involved in peace-building and violence-prevention in NK. How is the EU representative able to help the EU to promote its role as an international political actor if the representative has never been to the region or gained a real depth of understanding about this area, which is in the midst of serious conflict and can cause formidable problems to the EU's stability in the future? That said, the EUSR's activities, as defined in the official EU documents, seem to be hindered by the inconsistent policies practised by the Union.

The war of 2008 between Georgia and South Ossetia proved that the EU's stability is vulnerable and that instability in its neighbourhood causes immense economic damage to the EU. The 2008 war also demonstrated that Russia still maintains regional hegemony despite Georgia's clearly evident Western aspirations. Georgia has more than once asked for the EU's active involvement in its internal conflicts. The EU stressed its commitment to promoting European values as a means of conflict resolution in Georgia by helping to create a Georgian state, which could be more attractive than aspiring for independence or Russian supervision for South Ossetia and Abkhazia.[11] In light of the armed conflict between Georgia and South Ossetia, which rapidly turned into the devastating Russo–Georgian war in 2008, the project to make Georgia a "place to stay" for the people in the breakaway regions was not very successful. On the other hand, the EU was conscious of the ongoing tension between the Georgian state and the two autonomous regions, and could have used more effective means to prevent the conflict instead of trying to make Georgia a better place for the people of South Ossetia and Abkhazia. Georgia could have become a good opportunity to

---

[10] Europa (2005), http://ec.europa.eu/world/enp/pdf/country/armenia_country_report_2005_en.pdf (Brussels: Commission of the European Communities).

[11] P. Jaward (2006) *Europe's New Neighborhood on the Verge of War: What role for the EU in Georgia?* (Frankfurt: Peace Research Institute), p. 28.

demonstrate the Union's political ambitions if it had taken into account all early warnings and reacted effectively and in time. Instead, Georgia is often referred to as another lost opportunity for the EU. Nevertheless, the EU still seems to be more popular in Georgia than in Armenia or Azerbaijan.

Russia's presence in Armenia, on the other hand, is increasing steadily. The Russian military base in Armenia was extended for 49 years instead of the original 25, calculated from 1995.[12] This means the Russian presence makes it a key player in determining the stability or instability of the region. After the Armenian–Russian military agreement, Russia's long-time rival, Turkey, another regional power, started talking about the possibility of locating its military bases in the Azerbaijani enclave of Nakhichevan,[13] strategically situated at the Turkish–Armenian border. Given these developments, Russia and Turkey can easily assume all the political power in the region, leaving the EU behind. Russia is already perceived to be the only effective military power in the region. As THMs show, many Armenians express their hopes for the future in terms of Russian help if another war breaks out. Many Armenians said that only "Russian troops can protect us".[14] This is not to suggest that the EU should send troops to Armenia or Azerbaijan, even hypothetically. However, if the EU does not become seriously engaged in the conflict by implementing other than military measures, it will soon lose its importance as a political actor who can prevent, settle or resolve conflict. NK could become another missed opportunity for the EU to mediate peace or prevent another avoidable war.

The EU is largely perceived as a humanitarian donor and a provider of financial aid. Indeed, it is the largest humanitarian aid donor in the world and spends billions of Euros on post-conflict rehabilitation. This is another reason why the Union adopted conflict prevention as one of its main policies. It is much more profitable to prevent than to reconstruct later. Moreover, being the world's biggest trading bloc, the Union viewed peace as a necessary precondition for secure and stable trade among its partners.[15] At times, however, the EU's preventive instruments lose their original characteristics and become solely identified with financial aid, which is clearly damaging to the EU's reputation as a political actor. If the EU only wants to be a financial aid provider, its activities are then justified by, and fully correspond to, those intentions. However, if the EU wants to prove that it has

---

[12] Panorama.am (2010) *Armenia to Host Russian Military Base for 49 Years*, http://www.panorama.am/en/politics/2010/08/05/baxdasaryan-security/ (date accessed: 13 August 2010).

[13] News.az (2010) *Theoretically Placement of Turkish Military Bases "Possible in Nakhchivan"*, http://www.news.az/articles/21523 (date accessed 25 August 2010).

[14] ICHD (2010), op. cit., p. 66.

[15] V. Kronenberger and J. Wouters (2004) *The European Union and Conflict Prevention: Policy and Legal Aspects* (The Hague: T.M.C. Asser Press), p. xxv.

a genuine commitment to conflict prevention or resolution, it must implement other measures. It is true that the EU does not, and for the near future will not, possess Russia's military power and political strength in the region. Nevertheless, it must try to strengthen its position by using conditionality instruments and demonstrating that conflict prevention and resolution is of key concern to the EU.

The EU's image as a political actor capable of influencing the direction of the NK conflict is vague at best. The people who are most affected by the conflict – the Armenians of NK – are left in isolation and marginalised by the international community, including the EU. Nagorno-Karabakh is excluded from all regional initiatives which can in no way contribute to a peaceful resolution of the problem. Insufficient infrastructure, economic and political isolation, and lack of resources deny the people of Nagorno-Karabakh the right to basic human needs and the possibility their being met – the most important of which is *security*. People no longer have any hope in third parties. As one Armenian expressed himself in the THMs: "We have not learnt our lesson. The powerful states have always acted in their own benefit, but they have tried to assure us that they care for us. Nonetheless, we still stretch our hand out for help and expect that Europe will help us".[16]

In order to increase its role and profile in the resolution of the NK conflict, the EU should include the region and its people in its regional initiatives. By doing so, the EU will make itself known to the people of NK and, once it gains the trust of the local community, will have a chance to boost its influence. Choosing a truly neutral and impartial role, that is one that does not give in to Azerbaijani pressure any more than to Armenian, the EU has a real chance to become a more reliable mediator. But in order to achieve this, the EU needs to become directly engaged in the regions' problems, and a simple threat to put persons and institutions on "black lists" must not be enough reason to isolate NK, to avoid travel, aid and civil–society projects there. By marginalising the NK population, the EU contributes to the deterioration of the socio-economic situation. Believing that "peace depends on development and development depends on peace",[17] the EU thus tends to exclude the possibility of peace, because it itself contributes to the limits for the development process in Nagorno-Karabakh.

For the EU, the NK conflict resolution is seen as a priority in the Armenian and Azerbaijani European Neighbourhood Policies' (ENP) Action Plans (AP). Armenia, Georgia and Azerbaijan were included in the ENP in 2004. With future possible enlargement on the EU's agenda, the South Caucasus could

---

[16] ICHD (2010), op. cit., p. 199.

[17] E.J. Stewart (2006) *The European Union and Conflict Prevention: Policy Evolution and Outcome* (Berlin: LIT Verlag Münster), p. 103.

become a close neighbour to the EU. Instability in the neighbourhood could therefore threaten the Union's own future security. The EU has stressed its commitment to conflict resolution in the ENP, making it a priority which should be carried out in APs. However, since coherence in EU policies is constantly lacking, the EU has failed to attribute equal importance to conflict resolution in APs and, from policy to policy, from AP to AP, has defined each party involved in the conflict differently . For example, in the Armenian AP, NK conflict resolution is under priority area seven, whereas in the Azerbaijani AP it is priority area number one. Moreover, whereas in the Armenian AP the document mentions that EU dialogue should be intensified with the *parties* concerned, which includes NK as a party to the conflict,[18] the Azerbaijani AP for the same statement excludes NK by using the word *states*.[19] This can only mean that the EU has neither a coordinated approach to the problem, nor any coherent and fixed policy towards the NK as a party to the conflict. The EU has stressed more than once that it is eager and ready to support or assist the OSCE Minsk Group. However, it has not demonstrated any stronger intention to become more actively involved in the conflict. The EU should think beyond the existing strategic frameworks. By doing more than just *supporting* or *assisting* the OSCE Minsk Group, it should keep in balance the roles of a neutral mediator and a political actor who can achieve change. It should not be provoked or manipulated by any other parties in the conflict, and should not ignore those who are most vulnerable to security problems – those who most need support and protection. The EU should not put oil interests above human security and freedom, and it should think twice about gaining economic benefits now: If war does break out, the EU will spend twice its gains to rehabilitate the region in the aftermath. Buying oil and gas from Azerbaijan disregards the failure of democracy in the country, overlooks the absence of the rule of law, and ignores the fact that oil revenues are spent on enlarging the Azerbaijani military capacity. By trading with Azerbaijan for oil, the EU directly contributes to the Azerbaijani authorities' mission of becoming the most militarised state in the region, thus making war a real possibility.

The EU, not Azerbaijan, should use conditionality in matters regarding the inclusion of NK in regional activities. The EU should address this problem strictly: firstly by making EUSR's presence more visible. The EUSR should not only be encouraged to visit the region, but to speak directly with the local communities. The EU should bear in mind that had the NK not been a legitimate party in the conflict, it never could have signed the 1994 ceasefire.

---

[18] Europa (2006) *EU-Armenia ENP Action Plan* (Brussels: Commission of the European Communities), p. 9.

[19] Ibid., p. 3.

The Hague Court ruling on Kosovo confirmed the legitimacy of the right of peoples to self-determination, in line with international law. The EU should not wait for the conflict to be "resolved" before it addresses the NK people or to include the region in its regional initiatives as it has stated in the European Neighbourhood Policy Instrument (ENPI) Country Strategy Paper for Armenia.[20] The people of NK and the region should not be left in isolation, because this contradicts the EU values of human rights and democracy and it risks casting a shadow over the EU's humanitarian agenda. Moreover, the EU should neither ignore nor forget the historical precedents of including non-recognised entities in regional cooperation programs, as in the case of Northern Cyprus.

The EU should avoid triggering more tension by favouring one side over another, or by placing oil over security. Priorities must be well coordinated and agreed amongst all EU Member States. Early warnings and signals, such as hysterical military rhetoric and threats, need to be taken into serious consideration to prevent a new war from breaking out. By using all means at its disposal, the EU should pursue its objective by bringing all parties involved in the NK conflict to the table. By omitting or ignoring one party, the EU risks seriously hindering resolution of the conflict, since without the people of NK and its government, there will be no genuine agreement on any matters. It is high time that the EU understood this. The EU should restructure its own foreign policy and redefine its priorities and objectives. The Lisbon treaty could be a good opportunity to do so. The EU should propose the most effective measures to settle the NK conflict using the formidable number of tools at its disposal.

THM demonstrated that neither the people of Armenia, Nagorno-Karabakh, nor Azerbaijan view the EU as a powerful political actor in the region. The few words said about Europe or European States stressed the lack of knowledge about European involvement in the NK conflict. The EU is not mentioned as a powerful key player in any aspect, neither political nor economic. Political actors mentioned most frequently are Russia, Iran, Turkey, the UN and NATO. The EU is missing from this list. This should be of growing concern to the EU, in light of the constructive role it wants to play in the region. Boosting its authority and image in the region should become one of the Union's top priorities.

Only by engaging with those whose security is most jeopardised by the conflict, by trying to de-isolate them and showing a genuine interest in the peaceful resolution of the conflict, can the EU hope for a better political image, which could eventually gain credibility and win support from the local community.

---

[20] Europa (2007) *ENPI Armenia Country Strategy Paper 2007–2013* (Brussels: Commission of the European Communities).

7
What the People Think: Key Findings and Observations of a Town Hall Meeting Project in Azerbaijan, Armenia and Nagorno-Karabakh[1]

Tevan Poghosyan and Arpine Martirosyan

Introduction

A town hall meeting (THM) is a way to conduct an informal public meeting. It is usually organised within different communities (rural and urban) and is open to the public – everybody can attend and present their opinions, as well as hear responses from the authorities. In the context of the ICHD-led THMs, it provided a mechanism for people to voice their opinions on the resolution of the Nagorno-Karabakh conflict. These THMs were conducted in 2006–07 and financed by the UK embassy in Yerevan. The ICHD conducted them in Armenia and NK, and the Azerbaijani partner, Youth for Development (YFD), in Azerbaijan.

General observation

There is strong asymmetry in the kind of opinions expressed by residents of Armenia and NK and the residents of Azerbaijan. This asymmetry can be explained by the asymmetry of concerns: usually an issue which was of concern for one party in the conflict provokes numerous comments but barely gains the attention of the other party. In a nutshell, neither a deep dialogue nor meaningful debate occurred, since one party did not care much about the concerns of another. This difference in perspective was sometimes so significant that one could find specific issues and topics which were of major significance to one party in the conflict yet attracted zero attention

---

[1] International Center for Human Development (ICHD) (2010) *The Resolution of the Nagorno-Karabakh Issue: What Societies Say* (Yerevan: ICHD).

from the other. This is quite a contrast, given that that both Armenians and Azerbaijanis were discussing the same scenarios about Nagorno-Karabakh conflict resolution.

The key findings and observations are synthesised below in the most impartial language possible, and without reaching political conclusions. We have not assumed a role in which we find and judge the "truths" and "falsehoods" of people's opinions. One should read original transcripts to grasp the full depth and emotional nature of different people's perspectives.

Current situation

All parties in the conflict have exposed the entire diversity of attitudes and opinions about the current situation, termed status quo. Interestingly, in cases where the participants across borders expressed matching opinions and positions, the reasons behind taking these positions seem to differ as one can judge when looking at their justifications. Reasons for preserving the current situation are mainly based on two factors: the absence of war and/or of better alternatives. Besides, the prolongation of the status quo is also perceived as an opportunity for both sides, but in different ways. Armenians see it as a security guarantee "until oil ends in Azerbaijan", and Azerbaijanis consider it to be a pressure on Armenia in terms of isolation and blockade until "Armenia loses the race for economic development". Opinions against the current situation are a result of the uncertainty and, in some ways, the fragility of the status quo. The major argument that Azerbaijanis mentioned against the status quo was de facto Armenian rule in Nagorno-Karabakh. There are also other views about the status quo which reflect people's perception of it as something natural and/or based on a consensus or imposed by centres of global power and geopolitical players in the region, such as Russia and the United States.

War

The opinions of participants across the borders are largely the same when they speak of war. War is understood as a last option and a negative development, but in some cases it is perceived to be inevitable. There are also people who believe that war is impossible. It is noteworthy that the opinions of people across the borders are somewhat shared and often almost identical. Another group of people believes that war is inevitable despite the fact that many people across the borders do not favour it. Some people believe that war remains a last option and that compromise and peaceful solutions through negotiations are a viable alternative to war. Meanwhile, others do not have confidence in the negotiations and a peaceful solution, believing that there is no alternative to the status quo but war. The consequences of a possible future war are perceived differently by the parties, since Azerbaijanis in some sense take the view that a future war means war against Russia.

Security

Security is recognised as a basic human need and is of the utmost concern for people. This is absolutely true with regard to all key issues in the NK conflict, whether it is the issue of the return of refugees and internally displaced people (IDPs), economic development and communication, war, identity and culture and even the prospect of coexistence or any other issue. The perception of security is very diverse across the borders. It seems that this issue probably raises the most contrasting views among the parties. The key concerns that people have expressed regarding security can be grouped into several categories, as follows:

• Identity and coexistence

Armenians believe that Azerbaijan's rule is a major threat to Armenian identity and consider this threat to be at the heart of the conflict. They also recall Armenian collective memory to reinforce this position. Azerbaijanis' opinions vary on this matter: some consider the coexistence of Armenians and Azerbaijanis to be impossible, while others think that Armenians shall have the right to live in Azerbaijan but should not be entitled to any specific minority rights or regarding education, but simply language rights.

• Military security

The majority of participants consider the current status quo to be the result of the current military balance. Armenians and Azerbaijanis share the view that military security is very important and should be provided by their own military forces: Armenians want the status quo in terms of military security to remain the same, while Azerbaijanis want Azerbaijan military forces to be located in NK. Remarkably, both parties unanimously reject the option of peacekeepers (see the international peacekeepers section, below).

• Demography

Armenians consider demographic change to be one of the threats to their identity in Nagorno-Karabakh. The "demographic threat" is one of the key factors underlying attitudes towards the return of the refugees and IDPs. It seems that Azerbaijanis do not consider demography to be an issue at all.

• Threats and Fears

Other security issues can be summarised as fears and threats from different factors which are shown in the table below:

Armenians	Azerbaijanis
Time, legal claims, betrayal, historical memory, innate fear, fear of Turkey, possible war	Psychology, ecology, terrorism, legal, precedent for other ethnic groups, black market

• Politics and diplomacy

Most participants consider the South Caucasus as being subject to the crossfire of interests of the centres of global power. Many participants across the borders believe that their political leaders and governments do not have adequate capacities to face the challenges resulting from these interests or to respond in the interests of their citizens. The majority of Armenians are afraid of being outmanoeuvred by Azerbaijani diplomacy and through the "information war". Azerbaijanis see the NK conflict as an instrument in the hands of powerful players in the region and are afraid of being manipulated by those players.

• Economic and social development

People across the borders are also concerned about the economic and social development of their own societies and believe that the conflict has a major impact on this issue. There are also many corresponding opinions held by people who believe that the NK conflict will not have a decisive effect on economic development and prosperity. All parties to the conflict refer to economic and social development as being crucial for the NK conflict's resolution in the future. Thus, while Armenians consider strong economic development as the key to a favourable solution, many Azerbaijanis believe that the blockade of Armenia should be continued to leverage a favourable solution in the future.

Demilitarisation

One of the major issues beyond the possible resolution scenarios is the demilitarisation of the region. This is in line with the concept of returning surrounding territories and summoning an international peacekeeping mission to Nagorno-Karabakh. Despite various opinions regarding the surrounding territories and peacekeepers (see respective sections) almost all opinions on demilitarisation are negative. Armenians see the role of their own armed forces as being their only guarantee of security, while Azerbaijani participants will only consider unilateral Armenian demilitarisation. Both sides therefore reject the concept of a demilitarised zone.

International peacekeepers

All parties in the conflict hold a common attitude towards international peacekeepers and their possible future role in the region. The majority of participants rejects the very idea of a peacekeeping mission and provides different reasons for this position. Those who agree with summoning peace-keepers to the region also insist upon some conditionality. These conditions are usually mutually exclusive. However, it should be mentioned that the main driving force in determining the attitude towards peacekeepers is the political attitude towards other players, so that participants in discussions do not look at the "peacekeeping soldiers", but rather at the country/nation-ality they represent. It also seems that the concept of peacekeepers has a rather negative characterisation in this region.

Land communication

One of the issues discussed by the town hall meeting participants was a ret-rospective examination of the Key West plan, which was on the negotiation table and had previously been rejected by both parties. One of the elements of that plan was an immediate solution, giving independence to Nagorno-Karabakh in exchange for a sovereign corridor to Azerbaijan's enclave Nakhichevan via southern Armenia. The majority of opinions by partici-pants across the border reject this opportunity retrospectively. Armenians rejected it because of the fear of losing Meghri. Meanwhile, Azerbaijanis sim-ilarly reject this option but use the argument that such an "exchange" is not a compromise at all. Either they consider such an "exchange" to be unfair or they think that the current alternative of travelling to the exclave via Iran degrades this option. It should be mentioned that discussion of this issue among Armenians heightened emotions, which can be attributed to their historically burdened attitude towards Nakhichevan, which Azerbaijan eth-nically cleansed of its Armenian minority in the late 1980s and early 1990s.

Territories

The geography of the Nagorno-Karabakh conflict is somewhat complex and hence Armenians, Azerbaijanis, the international community and diplo-mats have all developed their own vocabularies when describing it. The vocabulary is quite varied and sometimes includes multiple definitions and terms: Nagorno-Karabakh, liberated territories, Nagorno-Karabakh Republic territory, occupied territories, adjacent territories, surrounding territories, buffer zone, security zone, seven regions, five regions, and so forth. It is not the task of this publication to unravel the geography of the conflict but rather, to expose Armenians' and Azerbaijanis' views about it in order to classify, consolidate and illustrate the entire range of people's opinions. There are many views and opinions which approach the entire geography of the conflict unilaterally and consider it as being indivisible. Such views can be classified into the subcategory of "all or nothing" representing the solution of the Nagorno-Karabakh conflict regarding the entire geography. This approach is very similar to the opinion "status quo or war", as explored above. From the Armenian side this view is articulated as "these are our lands only", while Azerbaijanis express this as "when we mention the return of the territories we mean Nagorno-Karabakh and all the surrounding territories".

Across the borders, there are also opinions which refer to the surrounding territories – approximate to the territories/regions surrounding the former Nagorno-Karabakh Autonomous Oblast (NKAO) administrative borders – as a part of the geography on the negotiating table. Meanwhile, even those who talk about surrounding territories mostly consider these territories to be part of NK. In this sense, many opinions are, in essence, similar to those behind the "all or nothing" position.

Armenians' views can be further sorted into "emotional" and "rational" types. The emotional attitudes towards surrounding territories revolve around deaths and bloodshed in these territories. The rational attitudes refer to guarantees for security, buffer zone or object for bargaining in the peace negotiations.

Lachin and Kelbajar (Berdzor and Qarvachar) are regions formerly connecting the NKAO and Armenia SSR and have been reportedly called the "Corridor". Reportedly, their status on the negotiation table is in terms of a guarantee to connect Nagorno-Karabakh and Armenia until the final status of NK is agreed. The views of Armenian and Azerbaijani THM participants are totally different – we observe an absolute contrast regarding this issue, with few exceptions. So the attitude of many people to the status of the "Corridor" is absolutely coherent with their perspective on the overall solution of the conflict.

A range of other options on surrounding territories take into consideration a broader geography in terms of the conflict and do not necessarily refer to formal statements and diplomatic views. Perceptions of the geography of the conflict vary dramatically, ranging from Shahumian and Getashen to Zangezur.

Refugees and IDPs

The perception of Armenians and Azerbaijanis regarding refugees and IDPs sometimes diverge dramatically. It can be difficult to consolidate the messages in one group as there are not necessarily corresponding opinions across the borders in regard to the concerns of one or the other parties to the conflict. In general, there are opinions from across the borders which agree with the return of refugees and IDPs. However, many messages which support the claim of refugees' return come with specific conditions.

The messages opposing the return of refugees mostly understand that the return refers only to Azerbaijani refugees or IDPs. Such considerations are the immediate reflection of the formal discourse to which the populations are exposed in their media. The majority of Armenians attending the THMs were against the return of Azerbaijani refugees and IDPs, while only two Azerbaijani participants were against it. The Armenian participants also expressed concerns related to such asymmetry and bias of the discourse regarding the return of refugees. There is a dramatic difference between the attitudes of the participants towards "our" and "their" refugees and IDPs.

There are opinions which do not directly demonstrate the position of the participants on the return of refugees and IDPs. The "we will not return/ they will not return" type of messages express the view from both sides that refugees and IDPs may not wish to return.

Attitudes of the participants towards refugees and IDPs and their return can, in some way, be viewed as arguments and justifications behind the positions. Each attitude is somewhat unique and represents concerns referring to demographic fears, justice, human rights, security and the new source of conflict.

Views that the return of refugees is mere political pretext which represents an externally driven process are only expressed by Armenians. In general, these messages approach the issue of the return of refugees and IDPs from the perspective of possible political interest and "manipulation" and regard the process as being externally driven or artificial.

Looking at the future and postponement of the resolution

The concept of time became a dominant factor in the NK conflict – "time passes, negotiations are held, there is a ceasefire agreement and the future is still unknown". The political processes on Track One undoubtedly affect the discourse of ordinary people on the resolution of the NK conflict. Participants' perspectives about the future of the conflict can be consolidated into several groups, as seen below:

• Future is uncertain and conflict is unsolved

These views resemble the opinions held regarding retaining the status quo. Perspectives are very varied but they expose the level of confidence among participants regarding the effectiveness of the political processes. It seems that the participants see the resolution of the conflict through only one prism – their own position. Thus, the participants' opinions provide a reality test for the resolution of the conflict, in our favour/for our gain. The alternative options inevitably result in frustration – "if it's not going to be solved in a way we expect, let it remain unresolved".

- Nagorno-Karabakh as independent state or part of Armenia

Many Armenians clearly see the future of Nagorno-Karabakh as independent or part of Armenia, while Azerbaijanis reject such a view.

- Nagorno-Karabakh is part of Azerbaijan

No clear details are reported on "NK within Azerbaijan with wider autonomy status", but the THM participants tried to imagine such a future. Remarkably, the majority of Armenian and Azerbaijani participants shares the view of the impossibility of their living together but have opposite views on the future status of Nagorno-Karabakh.

- Resolving refugees and surrounding territories' affairs and leaving the status for a future referendum

People seem to be largely concerned about the geography of the conflict. They raise the question: Which NK are we talking about when we consider its future status? Interestingly, the majority of Armenian and Azerbaijani THM participants consider the referendum rather from the perspective of risks than of opportunities. Fears of the outcome dominate. While Armenians say, "the status at first and the issue of territories and refugees later", the Azerbaijanis say, "the people of Nagorno-Karabakh can determine their future according to the territorial integrity of Azerbaijan and Constitution". The sole message which lies between these two poles was voiced by an Azerbaijani: "We should prove to them that it is good for them to stay as a part of Azerbaijan".

Trust

Remarkably, almost in every scenario the participants referred to the issue of trust as the major cross-cutting issue, despite the fact that the issue of trust has not been directly reflected in the scenarios. All opinions, concerns and messages voiced by the parties reiterate emotions, historical memory and personal experiences. These voices expose the current stereotypes and the critical challenge these stereotypes pose for the process of peaceful resolution of the conflict. Thus, the key to a transformation of these stereotypes is to address the justifications and explanations of the participants' attitudes towards the other conflicting parties, themselves, other players and processes. The messages of ordinary people provide the guide for any successful intervention in this area.

Generally speaking, people across borders believe that trust can be restored under certain conditions of, and/or, compromise – "there can be trust if" However, in the majority of cases such conditions are either unfeasible or require major concessions from the respective other side. The majority of opinions reflected Azerbaijanis' distrust of Armenians and Armenians' distrust of Azerbaijanis, while only very few opinions reflected mutual trust. Both Armenian and Azerbaijani THM participants also expressed their trust and distrust towards other key players in the conflict such as Russia, the United States, Turkey, Iran, the OSCE Minsk Group, Europe, the EU and so forth. THM participants across borders also express distrust towards other players.

8
Nagorno-Karabakh: Learning from the Flemish Experience within Belgium?

Dirk Rochtus

Introduction

The story of Nagorno-Karabakh is of a people struggling for more autonomy in order to maintain their culture and nationhood. It is also about opposition to this endeavour from the state of which it is a part, according to international law. In this sense, Nagorno-Karabakh could *mutatis mutandis* be compared to Flanders, which is officially a federated entity of Belgium, but considers itself to be a nation in pursuit of more autonomy and – as some observers believe – its independence. However, the major difference is that Flanders is free from war, physical threat and violence on a mass scale, while in NK people have suffered from often fatal traumata inflicted by the parent state over many years and on ethnic grounds; the motivations for independence in Flanders are much more mundane. Moreover, the international community is not (yet) involved in searching for a solution to "the Belgian problem". What the populations in Nagorno-Karabakh and Flanders do have in common, however, are strong sense of identity and the drive to shape this feeling into an adequate state structure.

Federalism in Belgium has come a long way over several decades but remains incomplete, as state reforms have followed a ten-year pattern since 1970. Each decade, more autonomy is asked for the federated entities and each time the panic-driven question is raised as to how long the Federal State of Belgium will still last. The search for more autonomy, especially by Flanders, has always been accompanied by the question as to what this autonomy should look like. Would it take the form of autonomy within the Belgian state, would it lead to an independent state or a confederacy with Wallonia, or could it even create the opportunity for Flanders and Wallonia to join the Netherlands and France respectively?

The comparison between Flanders and Nagorno-Karabakh is interesting because both entities consider themselves to be a nation respectively within or against a state which many or most of their inhabitants experience as respectively strange or hostile. Flanders has gained more autonomy through a process of dialogue and negotiation so that there may be less resistance if this autonomy eventually results in independence. It is the feeling of being physically threatened which brought Nagorno-Karabakh to declare its independence. This happened abruptly, compared to the Flemish case of slowly gaining autonomy – the result of which being that Azerbaijan is unwilling to acquiesce with it. The independence of Nagorno-Karabakh is not an option for Azerbaijan. Both parties are diametrically opposed. For that reason it is useful to explore other options which could apply to Flanders and in an analogous sense, also to Nagorno-Karabakh. In this respect, Nagorno-Karabakh might draw lessons from the Flemish experience in its search for the most suitable kind of statehood to save Flemish identity.

The following investigation consists of two sections: First deals with the main characteristics of Belgian federalism and how Belgium is handling centrifugal tendencies on its territory. The second investigates several options which are open to Flanders and whether similar options might exist for Nagorno-Karabakh, or more importantly, what Nagorno-Karabakh might have to learn from these experiences. In reality, Nagorno-Karabakh will only consider some of them to be acceptable, such as independence or eventual unification with Armenia, both of which are rejected by Azerbaijan. Some of these options might have been in any form the subject of previous discussions, but here the direct comparison between two autonomy-driven "national entities" is provided.

Problems and solutions for multi-ethnic states

Belgium: the growth of federalism

Once a centralised, unitary state, with French being the language of government, administration, justice, defence and higher education, nineteenth-century bourgeois Belgium disregarded the individual and collective rights of the Dutch-speaking Flemings who made up more than 50 per cent of the population. The rationale was that "Unilingualism was considered to be absolute necessary for national integration".[1] Only those Flemings who assimilated into French-speaking culture could dream of climbing the social ladder. This democratic deficit gave birth to the so-called *Vlaamse Beweging*, or Flemish Movement, which sought equality in the public sphere for the two main languages, French and Dutch. The Flemish Movement was led by Flemish intellectuals (many of whom were educated in the dominant French language) who wanted more rights for Flemish culture and their Dutch mother tongue. The movement developed a strong dynamic which

---

[1] R. Van Dijck (1996) "Divided We Stand: Regionalism, Federalism and Minority Rights in Belgium", *Res Publica*, No. 12, p. 430.

would eventually result in the dismantling of the unitary character of the Belgian state many decades later.

Belgium is characterised by three cleavages. The linguistic cleavage between Dutch-speaking Flemings and French-speaking Walloons remains the most visible. The other division is socio-economic in nature and which, until the 1950s, pitted agrarian Flanders against industrialised Wallonia. From then on, foreign direct investment (FDI) in the North of the country would reshape Flanders as a modern, services-based economy, whereas the waning of the coal-and-steel-based industry in Wallonia made the declining South dependent on financial transfers from the richer Flanders. Reinforcing these divisions was an ideological dimension. As for the philosophical cleavage, until the 1960s the Catholic Church was the dominating force in Flanders, which was originally an agrarian society, whereas the agnostic or even atheist traditions of the social-democratic labour movement played a major role in heavily industrialised Wallonia. So the political culture and discourse were, and still are, different in Flanders and Wallonia; their respective populations, living in well-defined territories went through distinct histories related to language, economics and politics. The year 1963 saw the official demarcation of the language border, laying the institutional base for four linguistic areas, namely Dutch-speaking Flanders in the North, French-speaking Wallonia in the South, a German-speaking area in the eastern part of Wallonia, and French-and Dutch-speaking Brussels, the only bilingual part of Belgium.

At the end of the sixties, the political class in Belgium had become aware of the need for reform of the constitution: they wanted an answer to the question as to whether the unitary, centralised state was still the adequate instrument to govern such a multifaceted society. With his famous words "the unitary state is *passé*", Prime Minister Gaston Eyskens fired the starting gun in 1970 for the reform process which would turn Belgium into a federal state. This sounded like a real revolution, bearing in mind that only a few years earlier for any statesman even to consider, let alone mention federalism (in effect the F-word) was taboo. But reality forced the political class to accept that this was the only way to break the impasse which threatened to undermine the state itself. Whereas the Flemings pursued their autonomy for largely cultural reasons, the Walloons did so to advance their economic autonomy. Both motivations would lead to the application of two concepts in Belgium as a whole: the "community", based on cultural autonomy (for the "person") and the "region", based on economic autonomy (for the "territory"). On one hand, the federated entities consist of the Flemish community, the French community, and the German-speaking community, and on the other the Flemish Region, the Walloon Region and the Brussels Capital Region.

The federalisation process in Belgium is a dynamic one. After 1970, subsequent state reforms changed the constitution in 1980, 1988, 1993 and 2001.

It is also open-ended, as the process is not yet complete. After the federal elections of 2007 and 2010, the building of a new government turned out to be incredibly problematic, as Flemish- and French-speaking parties held different opinions about the extension and depth of new state reform. The Flemish side not only wants more competences for the federated entities, but also more fiscal autonomy in order to ensure greater responsibility in this area.

The main characteristics of the federal system can be summarised as follows:

There are two kinds of federated entities: Communities and regions with their own competences and institutions (their own parliament and government). Competences of the community refer to the individual, such as education, culture and tourism, and regional competences refer to the territory, such as housing, environment, agriculture and external trade. Communities and regions do not match, as there is an incongruence between their respective borders: The person-bounded competences in the Brussels Capital Region are exerted by the Flemish community and the French community.

An asymmetrical feature: Powers are technically devolved in a similar way to similar entities, but these entities may organise their institutions differently. The Flemish region and the Flemish community merged their parliaments and governments into one Flemish parliament and one Flemish government. A similar arrangement did not occur on the French-speaking side.

The territoriality principle: The competences of the communities and regions are generally exclusive and always restricted to their territory. So the French-speaking community does not have competencies regarding French-speaking people living in the Flemish Region and vice versa.

Bipolarity: The two major language groups enjoy protective measures (parity in the ministerial council). There are as many French-speaking ministers as there are Dutch-speaking, although the Flemings constitute the numerical majority in the country. There also is an "alarm bell" system, which means that there must be an equal number of ministers from both linguistic groups in both parliamentary chambers when political decisions touch upon the interests of one of the two main linguistic groups.

Centrifugal feature: There is a tendency towards devolution. The federated entities are always striving for more competences, especially Flanders, which is asking for substantial fiscal autonomy.

Nagorno-Karabakh: hypotheses for finding a solution out of the impasse

The question at stake in both Nagorno-Karabakh and Flanders is: which factors are of any use to strengthen or develop the autonomy of these national communities? In this section, I investigate the different options which might be open for Flanders in its pursuit of autonomy. By asking whether Nagorno-Karabakh could draw lessons from these options, I put forward hypotheses which merely serve as a discussion in an attempt to overcome stereotypes and dogma. However, what is excluded from the outset, and not discussed, is the return of Nagorno-Karabakh to Azerbaijan as a unitary, centralised state, just as federalism in Belgium cannot be reversed. Neither the Karabakh Armenians nor the Flemings would ever be able or willing to relinquish their achieved autonomy, their *acquis identitaire*, so to speak. Armenians cannot accept a "vertical link" between Azerbaijan and Nagorno-Karabakh,[2] just as there is no hierarchy in Belgium whereby federal laws and regional decrees have the same validity. What is also excluded here as a possible solution is the exchange of territory between Armenia and Azerbaijan (Nagorno-Karabakh in exchange for the Meghri region) as proposed by the US politician Paul Goble in 1992.[3] Of course Karabakh Armenians are committed to their self-declared independence, but until this is internationally recognised, one must be open to other options, even if only for the sake of creative thinking. The comparison with the Flemish case might even shed new light on options which have been rejected so far.

1   More autonomy

Flanders's pursuit of more autonomy does not need to be viewed as separatism. It can also mean autonomy within the framework of the existing Belgian state. Broad autonomy already exists, but this is increasingly regarded as too limited by a growing number within Flanders's political and economical circles of influence. The underlying reason for this state of affairs is that Flanders feels like a nation, and every nation tends to be a state or to make nation and state coincide. Here, we limit ourselves to the option that the Flemish nation is satisfied with being a federated entity, having quite a lot of autonomous power.

Baku promises Nagorno-Karabakh the broadest autonomy possible, almost the position which Serbia used to take towards Kosovo: "Everything but membership of the United Nations". In the words of Baku this sounded as follows: "Our greatest concessions are security guarantees for Nagorno-Karabakh Armenians and our readiness to grant the highest degree of

---

[2] Foreign Minister of Armenia, V. Oskanian, "Statement in Armenian National Assembly hearings on Resolution of the Nagorno-Karabakh Issue", 29 March 2005, http://www.mfa.am/en/speeches/item/2005/03/29/vo/ (date accessed: 12 February 2011).

[3] P.A. Goble (1992) "Coping with the Nagorno-Karabakh Crisis", *The Fletcher Forum of World Affairs*, Vol. 16, No. 2.

autonomy that exists in the world".⁴ In 1997, the Minsk Group even proposed that Nagorno-Karabakh would become "a state and a territorial formation within the confines of Azerbaijan [with] the right to maintain direct
relations with foreign states and international organisations".⁵ Of course,
in this hypothesis the Armenians of Nagorno-Karabakh would have to be
convinced that autonomy corresponds to their longing for self-development
and protection. It is noteworthy that the Minsk Group's proposal included
the possibility that the federated entity might maintain international relations, as do the communities and regions of Belgium, which can conduct
their own foreign policy concerning their own competences at home. In
Belgium this principle is called *in foro interno, in foro externo*. The Treaty
of Vienna of 23 May 1969 recognises the *ius tractatis* of federated entities,
under the condition that the constitution of the national state allows for it.⁶
What is possible for the regions and communities in Belgium could also be
possible for an autonomous Nagorno-Karabakh within Azerbaijan.

2   The Brussels model

Although Brussels is a region on its own, the person-bounded competences
like culture and education fall under the responsibility of the Flemish community and the French community. This means external entities are responsible for schools and cultural institutions in Brussels. The inhabitants of the
Brussels Region do not have a sub-nationality, so French-speaking people in
Brussels can send their children to Dutch-speaking schools and vice versa.

The parallel with Nagorno-Karabakh is that it would be seen as its own
"region" (as a federated entity), possessing its own regional competences
within the framework of a decentralised Azerbaijan. Both states, Armenia
and Azerbaijan, would then fulfill the role of the Belgian communities
and take responsibility for person-bounded or "community-related" issues
which concern their respective ethnic kinfolk in Nagorno-Karabakh, such
as culture, education, media, and language policy. They would act as the
guardians of the people who consider themselves members of the cultural
community represented by the "mother state". This is reminiscent of the
proposed "dual Azerbaijan/Armenia protectorate", one of the many ideas

⁴ "Azerbaijan promises Nagorno-Karabakh vast autonomy", Interfax, 19 May
2005.
⁵ OSCE Minsk Group draft, "Comprehensive Agreement on the Resolution of the
Nagorno-Karabakh Conflict", Argument II, point 2, July 1997.
⁶ J. Velaers (2006) "'In foro interno, in foro externo': de international bevoegd-
heden van gemeenschappen en gewesten", in F. Judo and G. Geudens (eds),
Internationale betrekkingen en federalisme, Staatsrechtconferentie 2005 (Gent: Vlaamse
Juristenvereniging), p. 17.

and proposals which have been discussed by politicians and academics in the search for a status solution.[7]

This model would also enable the return of Azeri refugees. The Armenians of Nagorno-Karabakh would have a guarantee that their culture and language would be protected, whereas the Azeri (minority) would not have to fear cultural discrimination or repression. On the "regional" level, guarantees can be secured for adequate representation of the Azeri minority in Nagorno-Karabakh, just as the Flemings living in Brussels (also in the minority), enjoy parity in the Brussels regional government.

The difference is that the communities and regions in Belgium all are part of one and the same sovereign state. If this were the case in this context, the status of Nagono-Karabakh would have to be resolved; Baku would be required to accept that another state – Armenia –act as a guarantor for people living on what would be a federated entity de jure on the soil of Azerbaijan.

3 Independence

Both influential voices in Flanders and some political parties are advocating for the independence of Flanders as a member-state of the European Union (EU). The existence of the EU softens the fear of separatism because if Flanders and Wallonia took this step, they would still work together in a European context.

Stepanakert sticks to its self-declared independence, so we have to consider this option whereby hypotheses 1 and 2 might not gain success (they have always been rejected up to the present time). *In se* there is nothing wrong with independence for two reasons: (1) the right of self-determination is universal, and (2) the birth of a new state does not constitute a danger to anyone.

As far as the former is concerned, there is always a conflict between the right to self-determination and the principle of the territorial integrity, which is illustrated by the Nagorno-Karabakh issue.[8] As far as the second reason is concerned, one can pose the question: What is a state? It is, in fact, an administration receiving orders from a democratically elected government. If Nagorno-Karabakh becomes independent, it does not do anything else but govern and administrate itself. As long as the state respects the principles of democracy and human rights internally and externally, one cannot raise objections on a rational basis against its existence. What could

---

[7] Quoted in International Crisis Group (ICG) (2005) "Nagorno-Karabakh: A Plan for Peace", *Europe Report*, No. 167, p. 13.

[8] D. Rochtus (2009) "Kruitvat Nagorno-Kaukasus: Wordt Nagorno-Karabach volgend strijdtoneel?", *Internationale Spectator*, Vol. 2, p. 91. (Translated: "Powder-barrel Caucasus: Will Nagorno-Karabakh become the next battle-place? (Netherlands: Institute for International Relations Clingendael, The Hague).

be problematic for the original state is the loss of impact in the political and economic fields and potential insult to its own national pride. But a new state must be sustainable. One cannot doubt that Nagorno-Karabakh as a self-declared republic would owe its survival to the support it gets from Armenia and the Armenian diaspora. We must, however, take into consideration that the difficult and unclear situation in which Nagorno-Karabakh finds itself does not offer many opportunities for the republic to develop itself in the broadest sense of the word, and so demonstrate that it could be a viable state. Differing from the pursuit of autonomy (in which case compromises can be negotiated and concluded), the unilateral declaration of independence leads to antagonism, because what is acceptable for one party is not for the other: It is, at first sight, a lose-lose situation. Whereas Flemish independence would still be acceptable (despite reservations in international circles) because Flanders and Wallonia continue to be part of a bigger whole, this fallback option is missing for Azerbaijan and Nagorno-Karabakh. The latter could only be the case in the following hypothesis:

4   Position within a larger regional framework

Belgium, of which Flanders is a federated entity, is part of a larger regional framework which displays some cohesion due to historical, cultural, geographical and economic factors, namely Benelux (acronym of Belgium, Netherlands, Luxembourg). The modern acronym blurs the fact that four centuries ago there already existed a certain unity of what were then called "the Low Countries" or the *Zeventien Provinciën*. Striving for autonomy does not prevent more intense cooperation between Belgium, the Netherlands and Luxembourg. Bringing about a stronger regional cooperative framework, especially against the background of the EU, appears well-timed. Small states, tied together by cultural and economic links, should cooperate much more effectively no matter how one defines their cooperation and statehood according to international law. How the Flemish pursuit of more autonomy corresponds to this is a mere technical matter, as is the question of how to reach agreements about the representation of a federated entity within such a large regional framework. One also has to take into account the federal structure of Belgium and the sensitivities which lie at the heart of its origins. The advantage brought forward in this hypothetical case is that this cluster of small states gains more influence and power within the EU. The disadvantage might be that Flanders is less visible on the European stage.

Analogous to the Benelux framework, one could consider a form of regional cooperation among the three republics of the Southern Caucasus as it used to exist for a short while in the 1920s. Aside from this abortive attempt, one could also bear in mind that the lands of the Southern Caucasus were characterised by a common historical and – more or less – common cultural texture. The idea of the nation state with its stress on homogeneity and fixed borders – which fetishised the state – separated the peoples living in this region from each other. Closer cooperation which transcends borders, could give a boost to the economic situation and, also, at a later point lead to rapprochement between the peoples of the different republics. What would be the role of Nagorno-Karabakh in this framework? It would either be part of one of the Caucasian republics, just as Flanders is a federated entity of one of the three Benelux states, or it would become a state on its own, like Luxembourg. In the latter case, one would have a combination of hypotheses 3 and 4.

The idea of a "Caucasian Benelux" is not realistic at this point, given the enmity between Azeris and Armenians. However, we should not forget that relations between Belgium and the Netherlands[9] were chilly until World War II, almost one hundred years later. However, the need for economic cooperation in the South Caucasus, a part of the world which enjoys considerable geostrategic advantages and mineral resources, could stimulate the will for political change. If this does not work, there remains recourse to the last hypothesis:

5   Irredentism

According to this hypothesis, a certain region detaches itself from a state, not with the intention to be independent, but to associate itself with or to fuse with a bordering state where its inhabitants share the language and culture. The idea of *Groot-Nederland* (Greater Netherlands) was once influential amongst those Flemish intellectuals who dreamt about the emancipation of the Flemish people. Since World War II, – with the rise of the European Community/European Union, Benelux and Belgian federalism – this irredentist concept has become outdated (although in 1997 a famous Dutch politician referred to Flanders an "attractive bride" for the Netherlands[10]). But if Belgium ceased to exist, the idea of Flanders as a smaller entity joining the Netherlands on the basis of their cultural and linguistic ties could gain support again. Both the Netherlands and Flanders as a federated entity already constitute a confederation in the field of language policy: the *Nederlandse Taalunie* (Dutch Language Union) founded in 1980, is composed of Dutch and Flemish ministers taking decisions together with regard to the role of their shared language. Of course, speaking the same language is no guarantee for a successful a political union. The people in both state entities have distinct backgrounds and experiences within the economic, political and cultural fields. Moreover, the danger exists that the smaller entity which

---

[9] The Netherlands lost its sovereignty over Belgium with the Belgian insurrection of 1830 and officially with the Treaty of London of 19 April 1839, also known as the Treaty of the XXIV Articles.

[10] A. Postma (1997) "Vlaanderen is Nederlands natuurlijke bondgenoot", *De Standaard* (Translated: "Flanders is the Natural Ally of the Netherlands").

joins the larger would be discriminated against or be required to submit to the "mother state". In order to guarantee that members of the smaller entity did not become second-hand citizens, the creation of a federation or confederation – or at least the granting of a special statute or cultural autonomy – would be desirable. The advantage of such a union is that the new enlarged state gains more economic power and political impact in the region or even at a global level.

Does the same apply *mutatis mutandis* to Nagorno-Karabakh? Perhaps the cultural differences between the Armenians of Nagorno-Karabakh and those of Armenia itself might not be as considerable as those between Flemings and Dutch people. If that were the case, turning Nagorno-Karabakh into a federated entity of Armenia might not be necessary, and perhaps at the utmost, some kind of decentralisation based on geography and economic data would suffice. For the Azeri side, Armenian irredentism could only have been acceptable under the conditions reflected in the afore-mentioned Goble plan; this was supported by Azerbaijan's late President, Heydar Aliyev, who pushed for a territorial swap with Armenia before his death in 2003.[11]

Conclusion

Of the five options dealt with above, only that related to independence will be entertained by the Karabakh Armenians. This is understandable for historical and political reasons, but it remains unacceptable for Azerbaijan. So Azeris and Armenians are locked in a stalemate, as are Flemings and French-speaking Belgians who since 2007 have undergone the almost impossible task of government-building. The two sides do not make progress as they are both captivated by the fetishised nation state. In their pursuit for autonomy or more rights for their nation, the Flemings have also been considering other options such as its strengthening or other alternatives to independence. They did not pursue independence as the sole option, which enlarged their room for manoeuvre. Their pursuit of autonomy has always been characterised by dialogue and negotiation, not by violence, as seems to be the case in the non-relationship between Azeris and Karabakh Armenians. The Flemings stayed within the legal order of things, but of course it was easier for them to behave in such a way since they were not confronted with physical destruction (although Flemings do refer to the "Flemish character" of Flemish municipalities around Brussels being threatened by "French-speaking imperialism"). However, debates surrounding Flemish autonomy are embedded in the broader regional context of Benelux and the EU, and it is unfortunate that a similar context does not exist in the Southern

[11] http://yandunts.blogspot.com/2008/10/interview-with-paul-goble-georgia-war.html (date accessed: 30 November 2010).

Caucasus. This context of intrastate cooperation makes the Flemings aware that independence *pur sang* might not exist: independence also means interdependence. Genuine reconsideration of these options regarding Nagorno-Karabakh might challenge ideas steeped in prejudice and could also offer an incentive to move towards dialogue and cooperation. However, these options will come to nothing if the idea of a unified Southern Caucasus is abandoned.

9

The Nagorno-Karabakh Conflict in Light of Polls in Armenia and Nagorno-Karabakh

Andrew Cooper and Katherine Morris

Introduction

Ethno-territorial conflicts, such as the dispute over Nagorno-Karabakh, are deeply entrenched in society, rendering diplomacy at the state level insufficient. This is particularly true of the NK conflict, where the combination of ethnic, separatist and irredentist grievances renders the legitimate status of the disputed region a "deep-rooted and emotional source of suspicion, fear, and potential violence amongst the conflicting parties".[1] Accordingly, if the population is not engaged in the peace process, any agreement reached at the official level threatens to be derailed by a subsequent refusal from the population. Moreover, the Basic Principles that form the foundation for current peace negotiations stipulate that the enclave's final status will be determined through a "legally binding expression of will by the Nagorno-Karabakh people".[2] Resolving the conflict thus demands mediation on two levels, involving both official negotiations within the format of the OSCE Minsk Group and wider peace-building activity, involving all layers of society in order to engage the populations with the peace negotiations; build confidence between the conflicting parties; and foster a sense of ownership over the process.

Against this context, in October 2010, Populus, a UK-based opinion polling company, in collaboration with an Armenian partner, the IPSC (Institute for Political and Sociological Consulting) carried out research for a comparative opinion poll in Armenia and Nagorno-Karabakh.

---

[1] N. Milanova (2003) "The Territory-Identity Nexus in the Conflict over Nagorno Karabakh: Implications for OSCE Peace Efforts", *Human Rights Without Frontiers International*, No. 2, (ECMI: Flensburg), p. 3.

[2] Statement by the OSCE Minsk Group Co-Chair countries, L'Aquila, Italy, 10 July 2009, http://www.osce.org/item/51152 (date accessed 28 January 2011).

Despite the importance of public opinion, there had previously been no such independently conducted international comparative poll. At the same time, the common perception is that domestic opinion in all three parties to the conflict (Armenia, Azerbaijan and Nagorno-Karabakh) resolutely oppose a peace settlement.[3] The foremost goal of the poll was, thus, to provide accurate information about public opinion towards the conflict – information which could be used to formulate strategies for engaging with populations in the region in order to prepare the people for a final peace settlement.

The poll was conducted in the run-up to the 2010 OSCE Astana Summit and, given the hopes that the summit might see tangible progress in the NK negotiations, the poll sought to provide a better understanding of issues on the ground to complement high-level negotiations. While the much-desired progress did not occur during the Astana Summit, the poll nevertheless offers an opportunity to illustrate local opinion, and it is hoped it can be repeated at regular intervals to provide a mechanism for benchmarking popular attitudes towards the peace process.

The results of the opinion poll provide a further opportunity to understand which issues have been "securitised" in Nagorno-Karabakh and Armenia. According to the Copenhagen School, security threats are not always objective; on the contrary, they can be constructed by a securitising agent, such as a government, in order to legitimise extraordinary measures. Securitisation is the process by which a securitising agent constructs a discourse around a certain theme or object (the referent object), in order to present it as a security threat. If successful, the audience, usually the population, then perceives the referent object as a real threat to their security.[4] With regard to the conflict in NK, understanding which issues have been securitised has implications for understanding how the population will respond to measures aiming at conflict resolution. The findings of the poll can assist in understanding which issues have been securitised, and as such have implications for engagement with the populations in NK and Armenia.

---

[3] See, for example, T. de Waal (2009) "The Karabakh Trap: Dangers and dilemmas of the Nagorny Karabakh conflict", *Conciliation Resources*, http://www.c-r.org/ourwork/caucasus/documents/Karabakh_Trap_FINAL.pdf (date accessed: 15 January 2011).
International Crisis Group (ICG) (2009), "Nagorno-Karabakh: Getting to a Breakthrough", *Europe Briefing*, No. 55, October, http://www.crisisgroup.org/~/media/Files/europe/b55_nagorno_karabakh___getting_to_a_breakthrough.ashx   (date accessed: 15 January 2011).
[4] The thesis of securitisation was first published in B. Buzan, O. Waever and J. de Wilde (1998) *Security: A New Framework for Analysis* (Boulder: Lynne Rienner Publishers).

The results of the poll suggest that while many issues concerning the ongoing conflict are perceived as major threats to the populations' basic needs, the people in NK clearly want peace. At the same time, they have little faith in the ability of most international organisations and countries to deliver that peace. The findings of the poll, thus, have implications for mediation efforts in the region, signalling homework, not just for the OSCE and other European institutions, but also for national civil society organisations (CSOs) and the governments of Armenia, Azerbaijan and (de facto) Nagorno-Karabakh. In particular, there is a pressing need to build confidence between international mediators and the public.

Methodology and quality control

The Nagorno-Karabakh poll was composed of 804 face-to-face interviews conducted between 22–26 October 2010, producing data accurate to a margin of error of +/– 3.45 per cent at 95 per cent confidence. Interviews were conducted across Nagorno-Karabakh – in Stepanakert and in the regions of Askeran, Hadrut, Martakert, Martuni and Shushi. The sample was distributed proportionally to reflect the population distribution in Nagorno-Karabakh; accordingly, 40 per cent of the interviews were conducted in Stepanakert, while 60 per cent took place in the aforementioned regions.

The comparative poll conducted in Armenia consisted of 1,208 face-to-face interviews between 15–18 October 2010. Data is accurate to a margin of error of +/– 2.8 per cent at 95 per cent confidence. Interviews were conducted in all ten Armenian marzes and in all Yerevan communities. Again, the sample was distributed proportionally to reflect the population distribution in Armenia, with 37.5 per cent of interviews conducted in Yerevan and 62.5 per cent in marzes.

In both polls, interviewers used the random walking method to select households to approach, thereby avoiding selection bias and ensuring a representative sample of respondents. All data was subject to rigorous checking and quality control processes to ensure accuracy and consistency.[5]

Nagorno-Karabakh conflict resolution

The ongoing conflict is a cause of major concern for the Karabakhi population; when asked an open question about the most pressing problems facing NK, 69 per cent of interviewees cited concerns related to the conflict (Figure 9.1).

---

[5] For further information about methodology and quality control, see the full report of the poll, available at http://www.eufoa.org/uploads/Documents/NK%20 poll_%20full%20report.pdf.

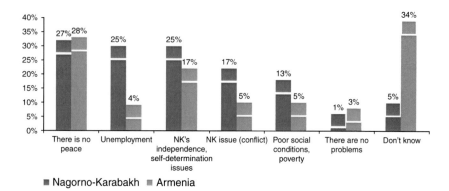

Figure 9.1   What people in NK and RA think are the most pressing problems facing Nagorno-Karabakh

Source: NK Poll (804); RA Poll (1208).

Regarding conflict resolution, people in Nagorno-Karabakh feel better informed about the current stage of the NK conflict resolution than do people in Armenia (68 per cent compared to 50 per cent); however, NK and Armenia residents express similar opinions concerning potential peace-deal components. Accordingly, residents in both countries strongly support measures they think will keep Nagorno-Karabakh closely associated with Armenia; they strongly oppose measures they think cede too much to Azerbaijan; and are moderately supportive of measures they believe may encourage peace but only if those measures do not compromise Nagorno-Karabakh's ties to Armenia.

Interviewees were presented with nine possible components for a potential peace deal, drawn from two measures being internationally debated and the seven options included in the "L'Aquila Declaration" of the OSCE Minsk Group Co-Chairs.[6] The options they were presented with follow (full answer options asked of respondents, and abbreviated answer options in chart):

- The implementation of confidence-building measures to create a better basis for further progress in the peace negotiations
- A ceasefire consolidation through the removal of snipers and installation of international observers along the Line of Contact

---

[6] Statement by the OSCE Minsk Group Co-Chair countries (2009), L'Aquila, Italy, http://www.osce.org/item/51152.

Included in the "L'Aquila Declaration" (to be considered as part of a comprehensive peace deal):

- International security guarantees, including a peacekeeping operation;
- An interim status for Nagorno-Karabakh providing guarantees for security and self-governance;
- Return of the territories surrounding Nagorno-Karabakh to Azerbaijani control;[7]
- Return of the territories surrounding Nagorno-Karabakh to Azerbaijani control, while banning Azerbaijani military from those territories;
- Presence of a corridor linking the RA to Nagorno-Karabakh;
- The right of all internally displaced persons and refugees to return to their former places of residence, mostly in the territories surrounding Nagorno-Karabakh; restoration of the USSR census of 1989;
- Future determination of the final legal status of Nagorno-Karabakh through a legally binding expression of will.

People in NK express a very high degree of approval toward the proposition for a corridor linking the two countries (8.5 on a 10-point scale), while the term "corridor" was generally interpreted in a broader way. They also support the determination of the legal status of NK (6.75). Interestingly, as in Armenia, people in NK would support a ceasefire consolidation through the removal of snipers and installation of international observers along the Line of Contact (6.35), even though removing their own snipers could be regarded as a security risk, and trusting international observers is not to be taken for granted. People strongly believe that if there were a ceasefire consolidation it would reduce casualties; make it easier for the OSCE to advance the peace negotiations; and reduce the risk of an outbreak of war. Half of NK residents also think it would make it easier to have trust-building measures between the conflicting parties. The populations in NK and Armenia rank the positive effects of a possible ceasefire consolidation in the same order, whereas Armenians are slightly more optimistic about their eventual effect (Figure 9.2). Conversely, people in NK overwhelmingly oppose measures they believe would involve ceding too much to Azerbaijan, especially returning territories surrounding Nagorno-Karabakh to Azerbaijani control (1.1 on a scale of agreement of 1 to 10), even if the Azerbaijani military were banned and this were part of a comprehensive peace deal (1.2 on the 1–10 scale). There are three potential peace-deal components which NK residents are noticeably less supportive of than Armenians. The NK residents express

---

[7] The "L'Aquila Declaration" is not precise about this point and, therefore, this option was presented in two variations.

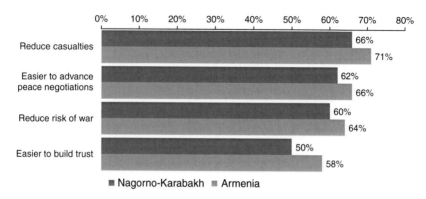

Figure 9.2   Effect of possible ceasefire consolidation (% who agree these would happen)

Source: NK Poll (804); RA Poll (1208).

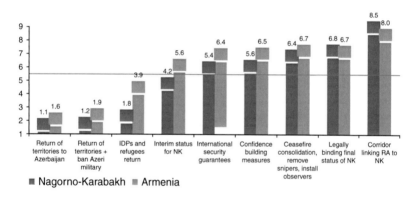

Figure 9.3   Attitude in NK and RA towards potential peace measures

Source: NK Poll (804); RA Poll (1208).

much stronger opposition to the proposal according internally displaced persons and refugees the right to return to their former places of residence, mostly in the territories surrounding Nagorno-Karabakh, and the restoration of the USSR census of 1989 (1.78 in NK and 3.73 in RA). They are also less supportive of international security guarantees, including a peacekeeping operation, as part of a comprehensive peace deal (5.44 to 6.43); the implementation of confidence-building measures to create a better basis for further progress in the peace negotiations (5.58 to 6.47); and an interim status for Nagorno-Karabakh providing guarantees for security and self-governance as part of a comprehensive peace deal (4.23 to 5.62) (Figure 9.3).

Attitudes to the OSCE Minsk Group

People in NK are poorly informed about the OSCE Minsk Group and do not express great optimism about its role and activities. One in two (51 per cent) people in NK say they feel informed about the OSCE Minsk Group's goals and activities, compared to 38 per cent in Armenia. Less than a quarter of NK residents say the OSCE Minsk Group is one of the organisations they trust the most – a strikingly lower level of trust even than in Armenia (38 per cent). Only a quarter of the NK population considers the OSCE Minsk Group to be one of the organisations most supportive of Armenia and Nagorno-Karabakh (Figure 9.3).

In NK, 43 per cent think the OSCE Minsk Group has a role to play in the conflict settlement – somewhat higher than in the poll in Armenia – but less than a third of people in Nagorno-Karabakh think the organisation is among those most interested in a peace deal. This has important implications for the OSCE, given that this is the express purpose of the Minsk Group. Conversely, Russia is seen extremely positively in Armenia and Nagorno-Karabakh, although it should be noted that this data may have been boosted by a recent visit to the region by Russian President Dmitry Medvedev. Much higher than the next best country or organisation (Figure 9.4) are levels of trust; supportiveness for NK and Armenia; a strong role in the NK conflict settlement; and interest in peace. These responses are similar to those found in Armenia, except for the fact that people in NK are 16 percentage points more likely to see a conflict settlement role for Russia.

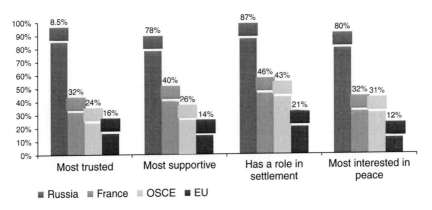

Figure 9.4 Opinions of countries and international organisations
Source: NK Poll (804).

Attitudes to other countries and international organisations

Turkey

Turkey's significant role in the region was reflected in the poll, with a clear majority of people in NK and Armenia expressing interest in developments in Armenian–Turkish relations; however, the findings make it clear that Turkey cannot be treated as a neutral player in the region. The populations in both NK and Armenia display a high degree of mistrust towards Ankara, rendering impossible the idea that Turkey could play a role in mediating the NK conflict.

After the events surrounding the Armenian–Turkish rapprochement over the last 12 months, people are doubtful of Turkey's commitment to reconciliation. Following the Armenian–Turkish protocols ratification problems in Turkey, they overwhelmingly approve (84 per cent to 11 per cent in NK; and 75 per cent to 19 per cent in Armenia) of the Armenian president's decision to suspend ratification of the protocols. Many believe it is very hard to conclude a rapprochement with Turkey at all, a sentiment they feel is reinforced by Turkey's problems ratifying the protocols. The vast majority of NK residents think Turkey's ratification difficulties are just a pretext to derail the rapprochement (7.91 on a 1–10 scale) and most, just as in Armenia, feel that they "always knew" that Turkey would never complete the rapprochement (8.4) (Figure 9.5). Even when prompted about the recently reduced role of the military and the appearance of other kinds of democratic progress in Turkey, they feel strongly that Turkey has not become a more reliable neighbour in the past five years (2.17), or that Turkish policy towards Armenia is more friendly than five years ago (3.72). Their responses are very similar to those expressed by the Armenian respondents.

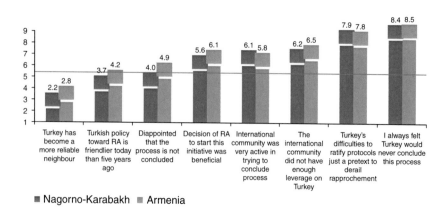

Figure 9.5 Opinions of developments in Armenia–Turkey rapprochement
Source: NK Poll (804); RA Poll (1208).

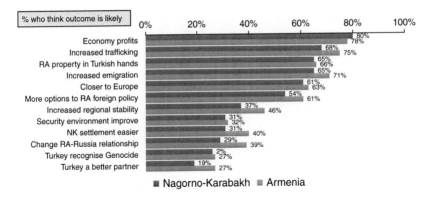

Figure 9.6 Expectation of outcomes from potential successful rapprochement (% who think outcome is likely)

Source: NK (804); RA (1208).

Nonetheless, NK residents do see that there would be genuine benefits from an Armenian–Turkish rapprochement. They feel strongly that the Armenian economy would profit from more international trade (80 per cent), and a majority think it would bring Armenia closer to Europe (61 per cent) and provide more options for Armenian foreign policy (54 per cent). As in Armenia, however, NK residents are very doubtful that it would encourage Turkey to recognise the Armenian Genocide or make Turkey a better regional player. Most also fear that it would increase illegal trafficking and emigration, and that there would be a problem with Armenian property falling into Turkish hands (Figure 9.6).

The EU

The EU's reputation in Nagorno-Karabakh is even lower than that of the OSCE. Only 16 per cent of people say it is one of the organisations they trust the most, and just 14 per cent see the EU as one of the most supportive of Armenia and NK. Only a fifth in NK – the same proportion as in Armenia – think the EU has a role in the conflict settlement process and barely one in ten think the EU is one of the organisations most interested in a peace deal, even lower than in Armenia (Figure 9.4).

Though most Nagorno-Karabakh residents do not regard the EU as having a role in the conflict settlement, as in Armenia, they nevertheless respond positively to some possible measures, indicating that the EU could in fact play a role. Of the possible EU initiatives, there is strong support for sending a permanent non-military EU observer mission to the region in order to avoid the outbreak of war "by accident". Equally, the NK population would

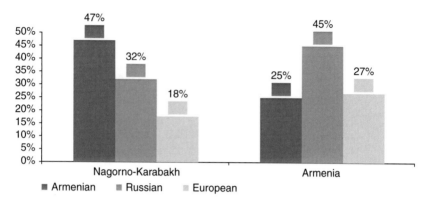

Figure 9.7   Which country's value system people wish NK/RA to be closest to
Source: NK Poll (804); RA Poll (1208).

like to see the EU upgrade its commitment to the peaceful settlement of the conflict by promoting democracy in the conflict-hit area. Residents also support the EU's brokering of a ceasefire consolidation agreement between Armenia and Azerbaijan, a measure they generally support, as outlined above. NK residents, like those living in Armenia, firmly oppose the EU ceasing its support of the ongoing OSCE Minsk Group-led negotiations and replacing them with a new EU format.

When asked whether their preferred value system is Russian, European or Middle Eastern, people in Nagorno-Karabakh are more likely (47 per cent) than even those in Armenia (25 per cent) to insist that their preferred value system is Armenian, even though this option was never read out during the interviews.[8] NK residents are less likely than Armenians to say that their preferred value system is Russian (32 per cent compared to 45 per cent). As in Armenia, virtually no one in NK wants their country's values to be closest to Middle Eastern values (Figure 9.7).

The domestic context

Outsiders have a tendency to view NK as an isolated, heavily militarised enclave; however, despite concerns about peace and security, people in NK are optimistic about their country's progress. Moreover, when faced with open questions, responses were fairly typical and interviewees did not offer militant or nationalistic responses. Indeed, the answers to questions concerning life in NK provide an image of a relatively calm and stable life.

---

[8] Reading out the option "Armenian" would not have produced any indicative data, hence this option was only recorded when respondents chose it despite being absent.

Accordingly, people in Nagorno-Karabakh are generally positive about the direction of their country – more so than Armenians – and 80 per cent of the Karabakhi people say their country is going in the right direction, compared to 50 per cent of Armenian respondents. Relatively, both figures are high compared to international standards, and while this is not a measure of happiness, it clearly demonstrates a feeling of progress.

A sense of progress is borne out by responses to further questions. People in NK believe the overall quality of life has improved noticeably over the last five years (on a 1–10 scale of how much NK has developed in the last five years, people rated the overall quality of life as 6.46). They consider the biggest improvements to have come in security (7.19); education (7.15); and infrastructure (7.14); but they display a less positive attitude toward the economy (6.13) and the fight against corruption (5.66). Interestingly, people in NK think Armenia has developed even more than NK in all areas over the past five years; people in Armenia, by contrast, think progress has been greater in NK than in Armenia. Despite the general optimism, there is thus a tendency in both countries to view the grass to be greener on the other side.

When asked about the problems facing their families, NK residents cited housing problems as the most pressing issue (31 per cent), followed by unemployment (21 per cent) and poor living conditions (19 per cent). At a state level, as already noted, the conflict is viewed as being the most pressing issue for NK, both among residents of NK and Armenia. However, NK residents also say that unemployment is a big issue, but one which people in Armenia do not perceive to be a key problem in NK. It is interesting that despite the close links between their countries, there is generally a lack of knowledge about the situation in Armenia amongst the Karabakhi population, and many people in NK do not know what the biggest issues facing

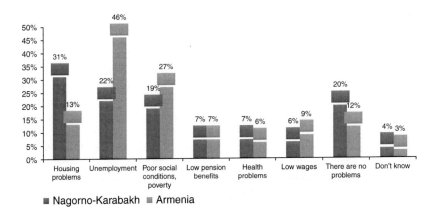

Figure 9.8 Most pressing problems facing people's families
Source: NK Poll (804); RA Poll (1208).

Armenia are; reciprocally, Armenians are not aware of the greatest issues facing NK.

Conclusion

The most striking finding of the poll is that people in both countries clearly desire peace but are mistrustful of current mechanisms in place to achieve it. There is widespread confusion regarding the mandate and mission of international organisations operating in the region, illustrating that international organisations need to develop their communications strategies regarding the region. This is particularly relevant for the OSCE; however, it also suggests that that there is a role for the EU to play, despite the fact that its relatively low regional profile is fostering mistrust. In both cases there is a strong case for stepping up engagement with civil society organisations (CSOs) as a means of facilitating understanding between the high-level negotiators and the wider public. Certainly, attempts to build confidence amongst the populations are likely to come up against resistance, particularly concerning attitudes towards the adversary, where negative representations of the enemy are deeply entrenched. Nevertheless, the overwhelming desire for peace suggests real room for progress, and engaging with civil society is thus an avenue worth pursuing.

With a view to assessing which reconciliation measures the population may consider as justifiable, the poll also sought to establish which threats have been successfully securitised in Armenia and Nagorno-Karabakh. Following Ankara's opposition to ratifying the rapprochement protocols, it is clear that the understanding of Turkey has been widely securitised. The low level of confidence displayed towards Turkey highlights the impossibility of Ankara playing a key role in mediating the conflict and, while in the long-term there is a clear need for confidence-building measures between Turkish society and the populations in Armenia and Nagorno Karabakh, it is apparent that for now the populations in NK and Armenia will not be able to treat Turkey as a non-partisan actor.

The main added-value of the poll was to provide the first internationally conducted opinion poll in Armenia and Nagorno-Karabakh. It is evident that, in NK and Armenia, neither governments nor international organisations are communicating effectively. However, peace can only be achieved if the people will ultimately support a deal. In order to avoid war in the first place, the people's options are key to determining which options are politically possible. By communicating more effectively or, in case of the EU and OSCE, by starting to communicate in the first place, the margins for manoeuvring could shift significantly towards more peaceful policies.

Part II

The International Community as Foreign Policy Actors in NK: The External Rationale

10
The EU's New Foreign Policy and Its Impact on the Nagorno-Karabakh Conflict

Elmar Brok

For many years, the EU has been working on the creation of a new and more effective foreign policy. Some Member States were more reluctant than others to create the instruments which we have today and which an EU of 27 needs in order to have an impact on the world scene. Europe was largely absent when the war in Nagorno-Karabakh broke out in 1991. This chapter analyses how Europe has changed and outlines the consequences for the South Caucasus and, more specifically, conflicts such as the one regarding Nagorno-Karabakh. Meanwhile, the chapter also explains that the underlying basis for the EU's foreign policy remains our common values of peace, achieved through economic and political integration, democracy and the rule of law – including international law.

Where was the EU during the Nagorno-Karabakh conflict?

In 1991, the EU was still called the European Community (EC) and had only 12 members. It was mainly an economic bloc which had spent many years working on the challenge to integrate Europe on the basis of common political and human values. It was at this moment that the Soviet Union finally collapsed, leaving a huge and dangerous vacuum to the east of what we had comfortably referred to as the Iron Curtain. Europe did speed up, rose to the challenge, managed to create the European Union, moved towards political integration and launched the largest ever programme for peace and prosperity: the EU's enlargement programme.

The EU's foreign policy was quickly adapted to look more towards the east. Many mistakes were made and there was no prior experience with the integration of so many countries. Which perspective to offer to whom? Who would pay for all the run-down economies? Who would manage to modernise so many pre-democratic systems? And what about the many ethnic conflicts?

103

The first half of the 1990s was a classic case of overstretch for the EU. While Europe rose to the challenge, we were bound to fail in some cases, simply because there was too much homework to be done and too many fires to be extinguished. If anyone today wonders whether the EU's enlargement represented good foreign policy, he should simply look at all the countries where the EU felt incapable of offering such a long-term EU perspective, such as those in the Balkans. "Enlargement or not?": This question could then seem like "peace or war?". However, it is also clear that the EU could not have offered an enlargement perspective to even more countries. And while the enlargement strategy proved to be very successful, the EU cannot be blamed for its limited resources. The responsibility to avoid ethnic conflicts or even wars always lay in the hands of the countries in question. Today, the Eastern Partnership (EaP) offers a European perspective comparable to that of the European Economic Area, allowing the participating countries to move as closely to Europe as Norway or Switzerland.

Seen entirely from their perspective, it seems a very weak excuse to the people in the South Caucasus that the EU was too busy with its imminent neighbourhood and internal reforms when the so-called "frozen conflicts" emerged. But we did not have much choice to act differently. Yes, there were numerous statements made about those conflicts by the European Council, by the Commissioner for External Affairs and by the European Parliament. But our priority had to be the Balkans, trying to avoid wars and later even enforce peace. Our televisions were showing victims every evening, in Bosnia–Herzegovina, Kosovo, Serbia and Montenegro, but virtually no camera went as far as the South Caucasus. The war in Nagorno-Karabakh was something very far away and abstract, while in front of our perceived house door the world required build-up programmes and UN peacekeeping troops. The EU was barely able to deal with those challenges in the early 1990s. While the EU's enlargement policy proved to become the biggest fast-track democratisation and stabilisation programme in world history, we failed to deal with Slobodan Milosevic, which was the EU's major concern at the time. Our foreign policy structures were too weak and not at all integrated between the EU members, to address frozen conflicts. Moreover, there was no clear EU strategy beyond enlargement during this period and, even if there had been, we would not have possessed the means to implement it. However, there were already common values among the EU Member States and this is what brought about change in the long run.

Aside from the tremendous challenges faced in the early 1990s, the nature of these conflicts also proved to overstrain the EU. Our common set of values dictates that, right until today, we must resolve conflicts such as the one in Nagorno-Karabakh in full accordance with international law. However, during the early phase of the Nagorno-Karabakh conflict, one breach of international law followed and created the next one. Without going into each one of them, the EU was not in a good position to assess the details of the conflict and its legal components, even though we always seek to base our actions on international law. There was an independence movement in Nagorno-Karabakh, which gave the Azerbaijani authorities the legal right to take measures to support their territorial integrity. But, there were also severe human-rights violations against the ethnic Armenian population in Nagorno-Karabakh and in other parts of Azerbaijan, including Baku and the region of Nakhichevan, which as a result gave the population the right to seek self-determination. The legal basis for the declaration of independence by Nagorno-Karabakh was enshrined in the Soviet constitution and, thus, was the same legal basis which the international community accepted for the recognition of the independence of Armenia, Azerbaijan and Georgia.[1] However, I believe that reviving the legal debate of the early phase of the conflict does not help its resolution today. The complex nature of that debate explains why it was very difficult for the EU to have a stronger position at the time. Today, the situation is very different in that we have used the recent years to upgrade our know-how and expertise regarding the EaP countries, not least due to the integration of so many countries from behind the Iron Curtain.

So, it is true that it took time – painfully long years – before the EU was ready to become a foreign policy player, especially in the South Caucasus. It is no secret that I would have preferred a faster development, particularly since we had the chance to establish a European foreign policy many years ago, at the latest with the Treaty of Nice[2] and the European Constitution.[3] But in Nice, the nation states were unable to agree to the real progress which would have prepared the EU's internal and foreign policy structures for 25 or more members. And later, when the EU already had 25 members, the nation states were unable to explain the constitution effectively to the

[1] Confer:
  - O. Luchterhandt (1993) *Das Recht Berg-Karabachs auf staatliche Unabhängigkeit aus völkerrechtlicher Sicht* (Archiv des Völkerrechts, Bd. 31), pp. 30–81.
  - A.L. Manutscharjan (2009) *Der Berg-Karabach-Konflikt nach der Unabhängigkeit des Kosovo* (Zentrum für Integrationsforschung, Diskussionspapier, Bonn): http://www.zei.de/download/zei_dp/dp_c193_Manutscharjan.pdf (date accessed: 4 October 2010).
  - O. Luchterhandt (2010) "Das Ausscheiden Berg-Karabachs aus Aserbeidschan durch Ausübung des vom sowjetischen Staatsrecht gewährten Selbstbestimmungsrechts", in V. Soghomonyan (ed.) *Lösungsansätze für Berg-Karabach/Arzach. Selbstbestimmung und der Weg zur Anerkennung* (Baden-Baden), 37–46.

[2] Treaty of Nice, signed 26 February 2001, 2001/C 80/01, http://eur-lex.europa.eu/en/treaties/dat/12001C/pdf/12001C_EN.pdf (date accessed: 20 November 2010).

[3] European Constitution, signed by all EU Member States on 29 October 2004, 2004/C 310/01, http://eur-lex.europa.eu/JOHtml.do?uri=OJ:C:2004:310:SOM:en:HTML (date accessed: 20 November 2010).

French and Dutch voters. Today, we have the Lisbon Treaty[4] and, while this change is less far-reaching and later than we hoped for, it does give the instruments to the EU which we badly need to exercise a more common foreign policy. These instruments are based on our common values. Currently, they are being used for the first time or just being created, as in the case of the European External Action Service. Today, we are a stronger Union of 27 members, representing 500 million people; and the voice of Europe has become pivotal in many foreign policy issues, not least where our political values are concerned.

How the EU has changed, and how this could influence conflicts like in Nagorno-Karabakh

The key difference between the early 1990s and today is not necessarily constitutional. I see the major transformation in the EU's strong and tangible commitment towards its eastern neighbourhood. When the successes and failures of the EU's policy towards the countries in Middle and Eastern Europe became apparent, we understood that we need to offer a European perspective to the countries who have not yet had such a perspective. This perspective had to be above the level of a simple association agreement with the EU but also below membership in the Union. The EU has in the last ten years clearly reached a saturation point of enlargement which makes the EU unready for further significant enlargements in the near future. Arguably, countries in an advanced state of readiness, such as Iceland or Croatia, could still join, but no large-scale enlargement could be digested by the EU at present. Unfortunately, this also means that ethnic or territorial conflicts to the east cannot be eased by the economic and political integration of their conflicting parties under the umbrella of the EU. If you think that this miracle would not work anyway, just take a look at the examples of Hungary, the Czech Republic and Slovakia, where especially ethnic tensions have long produced headaches for all observers of the fast-changing countries involved. But here was an EU perspective and strong pressure to resolve or at least contain the problems in a democratic way in line with international and, above all, European law. However, since such tools are and were not available for Belarus, the Ukraine, Moldova, Georgia, Armenia and Azerbaijan, we had to come up with something new.

The first result of such deliberations – the reply to the search for a perspective above the level of association and below EU membership – was

---

[4] Which only entered into force on 1 December 2009, http://eur-lex.europa.eu/ JOHtml.do?uri=OJ:C:2007:306:SOM:EN:HTML (date accessed: 20 November 2010).

the European Neighbourhood Policy (ENP).[5] Its aim is to create an area of stability, prosperity and democracy in the neighbourhood of the EU. The key tools are Association Agreements and the European Neighbourhood Policy Instrument (ENPI), a financial instrument at the disposal of the European Commission for the implementation of programmes in the ENP countries. While the EU follows a different and special track of association with Russia, the ENPI is also applicable there, underlining that it is an instrument for creating stability, not an instrument intended to create spheres of influence. The use of this instrument is determined by the performance of each country, especially regarding reforms for more democracy and European technical and legal standards, and so far the degree of ambition for these reforms has varied in countries such as Belarus or Azerbaijan, compared to Georgia or Armenia.

Since the ENP covers an area as diverse as the Mediterranean, parts of the Middle East and Russia, there was a certain frustration on the part of some countries in Eastern Europe. Ukraine and Georgia in particular feared that being in the same grouping as non-European nations from Northern African would not reflect their ambition to eventually join the EU or their clear European perspective as European countries. Besides, it became increasingly clear that today, those countries' biggest trading partner is the EU. The EU responded to the demand from those countries and in 2009 created the Eastern Partnership, a fast track of political association and integration, the speed of which is determined by the ambition and progress of each participating country. It envisages political institution building, as foreseen in the EURONEST assembly,[6] but in the long run also includes free trade and visa-free travel, as far as the participating countries are ready for this. Besides, it appropriately differentiates between, on the one hand, the Eastern European countries with their European perspective and, on the other hand, the non-European countries.

The ENP and the EaP are not just tools designed to demonstrate how friendly Europe and its eastern neighbours have become towards each other. They are an attempt to make a contribution towards increased stability, prosperity and democracy through economic and political integration. Those core values of the EU are important, since they have so often in the history of Europe been the only means to make war less likely or even unthinkable. This is why these tools are relevant for the Nagorno-Karabakh conflict. At the time of writing, the EU has begun to negotiate

---

[5] European Neighbourhood Policy (ENP), launched 12 May 2004, COM(2004) 373 final, http://ec.europa.eu/world/enp/pdf/strategy/strategy_paper_en.pdf (date accessed: 20 November 2010).

[6] EU-Neighbourhood East Parliamentary Assembly (EURONEST PA), 8435/09 (Presse 78), http://www.europarl.europa.eu/meetdocs/2009_2014/documents/depa/dv/200/200909/20090930_04en.pdf, (date accessed: 20 November 2010), p. 9.

a comprehensive Association Agreement with Armenia.[7] Azerbaijan has started the same process but may not have the same need for a very ambitious association as its economy draws heavily on the rich oil and gas revenues from the Caspian Sea. However, there is a certain group dynamic to be expected, especially since the third South Caucasus state, Georgia, has also started association talks. Integration of those countries with the EU is much easier for them than integrating with each other. As they align their trade laws, norms, customs, legal systems and even reach free-trade agreements with the EU, they automatically also integrate further with each other. In the case of Armenia, there is another often-overlooked factor: all states which associate themselves with the EU need to grant the same rights to other associated states. Concretely, this means that once there is a free-trade agreement between the EU and Armenia, Turkey could no longer treat Armenia differently from other EU markets and would have to eliminate trade barriers, such as the currently closed border between Armenia and Turkey. Such obligations could bring movement into otherwise blocked and confrontational situations. And if Turkey and Armenia celebrate a historic breakthrough in their relations, a solution for the Nagorno-Karabakh question will certainly become easier.

In the more distant future, similar scenarios are also imaginable between Armenia and Azerbaijan. Both would strongly profit from trade, but Azerbaijan would not agree at the present time to any direct trade, particularly with Nagorno-Karabakh, since this would consolidate the status quo. The most hope for improvements through the ENP and EaP can be found in democratisation effects. Progress in both conflicting countries would ease the key problem on the way to a solution of the conflict: the lack of trust. With a reference to the territorial integrity of Azerbaijan, the Azerbaijani government repeatedly and publicly plays with the idea of regaining control over Nagorno-Karabakh by military force.[8] This is tragic and underlines the mutual distrust between the two parties to the conflict. It is very difficult for both sides to agree to a peace deal which could then be communicated to their own populations, and such war rhetoric will make this task even more difficult. Besides, the war threats create deep mistrust on the side of Armenia and the international community. At the same time, the reflex-like reactions in Armenia and Nagorno-Karabakh, based on the principle of self-determination and underlining their readiness for war, do not help the negotiations either. In a more democratically mature environment, such behaviour would be questioned by the media and by a

---

[7] EU launches negotiations on Association Agreements with Armenia, Azerbaijan and Georgia, Europa – Press Release, 15 July 2010, IP/10/955, http://europa.eu/rapid/pressReleasesAction.do?reference=IP/10/955&format=HTML&aged=0&language=EN&guiLanguage=en (date accessed: 20 November 2010).

[8] For a collection of public quotations about this, please refer to http://www.eufoa.org/uploads/AliyevWarThreats.pdf (date accessed: 20 November 2010).

better organised political opposition. Both conflicting parties would tone down their pronouncements. The European Commission sees more room for improvement here on the side of Azerbaijan[9] but even if just one of the two conflicting parties creates an area visibly free, democratic and prosperous on their ground, the long-term pressure on the other will be strong. Azerbaijan needs to liberate its economy from the current dependency on oil and gas, while both countries know that their economic progress also affects the military balance between them. Both countries are therefore obliged to do everything possible for stability and progress, because otherwise one could outgrow the other. The EaP does not only focus on economic progress, but also very strongly on democratic development and strategies for regional integration and promoting mutual trust. All of these goals aim at regional stability and socio-economic progress. The EaP is not the only and maybe not even the most important factor for such progress, but it can definitely be a strong factor if the countries decide to want this. The EaP is therefore a tool which the two conflicting parties should make use of, while the economic progress which it seeks to provide will also contribute to the approval rates of the respective governments – or to the disapproval rates if the governments decide to disengage or fail to reap the fruits of this programme. But the best aspect of all this is that this tool can only help to bring peace, not war. Even if one country would – by its own choice – disproportionately profit from the EaP and the ENP, it could not use the economic fruits for aggression as this would immediately force the EU to roll back the cooperation as a painful sanction. But the countries could use their economic strength for non-aggressive defence measures, for a consolidation of their socio-economic situation and general internal stability.

In any case, the EU's new attention on Europe's East is based on its common values, which make it a reliable and foreseeable long-term foreign policy. This policy is based on international law and offers only opportunities for everyone interested in stability and progress in the region. It is supported by the EU at large and has strong advocates, especially among those Member States who joined the EU in 2004 and 2007. And it is today strongly embedded in the supranational structures, through the ENP and the EaP, and soon also with EURONEST.

The EU's new toolbox for foreign policy

As discussed above, the EU has fundamentally changed its perspective towards the South Caucasus. This changed approach and its embedding in

---

[9] European Neighbourhood Policy, Progress Report Azerbaijan, 12 May 2010, SEC(2010) 519, http://ec.europa.eu/world/enp/pdf/progress2010/sec10_519_en.pdf (date accessed: 20 November 2010).

the described new EU tools, the ENP and the EaP, have occurred simultaneously alongside the general reforms of the EU's foreign policy structures. Currently, the EU's foreign policy is still fundamentally based on the foreign policy of the large Member States. But, fortunately, this no longer remains our only tool in the toolbox. The arrival of the Lisbon Treaty brought about, amongst other things, three major changes to the EU's foreign policy setup: a permanent Chair to the European Council,[10] a common External Action Service[11] and a new "EU foreign minister": officially called the *High Representative for Foreign Affairs and Security Policy of the European Union and First-Vice-President of the European Commission, responsible for External Relations* – in short High Representative.[12] But before discussing the possible impact of these changes for the Nagorno-Karabakh conflict, it is necessary to take a look at the EU's handling of a comparable recent conflict before these changes – namely the war between Georgia and Russia in 2008.

When fights broke out in the Georgian breakaway region of South Ossetia during the night of 7 August 2008, the EU was taken by surprise. This was not because there were no warning signals or alarming developments beforehand. The EU had been following the gradual but visible escalation of tensions between Georgia and Russia in South Ossetia for quite a while.[13] But nonetheless, there was no real common strategy and no preparation for

---

[10] This is the summit typically made up of the EU's heads of states and governments. The post has been held by Herman Van Rompuy (European People's Party, Belgium) since December 2009.

[11] For more information see:
Press release and further links: http://elmarbrok.de/?p=350
EP report http://www.europarl.europa.eu/news/public/focus_page/008-76988-176-06-26-901-20100625FCS76850-25-06-2010-2010/default_p001c016_en.htm
Presidency report to the European Council on the European External Action Service, 23 October 2009, timeframe: http://register.consilium.europa.eu/pdf/en/09/st14/st14930.en09.pdf, p. 10.

[12] The post has been held by Catherine Ashton (Socialist, UK) since December 2009. The High Representative chairs the meetings of the Foreign Affairs Council, sometimes referred to as Council of the European Union. She is also responsible for the Council Secretariat, the European External Action Service and, where applicable, the EU's Special Representatives.

[13] Examples of the EU's communications about this conflict *before* the war started:
  • HR Javier Solana on the situation in Abkhazia and South Ossetia, Brussels, 11 July 2008, S250/08, http://www.consilium.europa.eu/uedocs/cms_data/docs/pressdata/en/declarations/101791.pdf.
  • EP-Resolution on the EU–Russia Summit of 26–27 June 2008, Strasbourg, 19 June 2008, P6_TA(2008)0309, http://www.europarl.europa.eu/sides/getDoc.do?type=TA&reference=P6-TA-2008–0309&language=EN.
  • EP-Resolution on the situation in Georgia, Brussels, 5 June 2008, P6_TA(2008)0253, http://www.europarl.europa.eu/sides/getDoc.do?type=TA&reference=P6-TA-2008–0253&language=EN.

a quick and unified response. The EU was mostly shocked that the Georgian government, as was later outlined in more detail in the EU's report on this conflict,[14] had apparently played a significant role in furthering or at least tolerating the military escalation and its consequences. The country had previously been regarded as a role model for the rest of Eastern Europe, as it voiced a clearly Western orientation. Now the EU had to deal with its own disappointment in Georgia's incapability to avoid this escalation, as much as in Russia's overreaction with force and its recognition of Abkhazia and South Ossetia, both of which violated international law.

While many in the EU were still chewing on this disappointingly bitter pill, and while half of Europe was on holiday, the recently started French EU presidency took the lead in handling the crisis. This responsibility was largely assumed by France's President, Nicholas Sarkozy. This is important to note, since one could imagine how this crisis might have been handled under the preceding and later presidencies of much smaller countries from new Member States with little EU experience – Slovenia and the Czech Republic. The latter was even partly without a firm national government during its EU presidency. Some may say it was pure luck that the French could easily take the lead because of their EU presidency. Others may argue that France or another large country would have assumed this leading role regardless. In any case, the EU had to assume a quick mediation role to contain the damage and avoid the worst scenarios in the South Caucasus. This task would not have been as quickly and clearly handled without the coincidence of the French presidency.

The case illustrates three things about the EU's policy towards the South Caucasus and the so-called frozen conflicts. First, as discussed, although the EU does follow the developments in the region closely, it often lags too much behind to be pro-active or even preventive. I hope strongly that this will never be the case as regards Nagorno-Karabakh, but if it should become necessary, we should not again be surprised and unprepared. Secondly, the Georgian war demonstrates that the EU is willing and able to play a positive role, refocusing conflicting parties on their obligations under international law and mediating between them. This does not mean, however, that the

---

• Declaration by the Presidency on behalf of the EU on the escalation of tension between Georgia and Russia, Brussels, 6 May 2008, PESC/08/59, http://europa.eu/ rapid/pressReleasesAction.do?reference=PESC/08/59&format=HTML&aged=0&lan guage=EN&guiLanguage=en,
• Declaration by the Presidency on behalf of the European Union on Georgia, Brussels, 21 April 2008, PESC/08/52, http://europa.eu/rapid/pressReleasesAction.do ?reference=PESC/08/52&format=HTML&aged=1&language=EN&guiLanguage=en.
[14] Independent International Fact-Finding Mission on the Conflict in Georgia, September 2009: http://www.ceiig.ch/Report.html (date accessed: 20 November 2010).

EU wishes to assume the mediating role in all conflicts. In the Nagorno-Karabakh case, we clearly support the lead of the OSCE,[15] as numerous Council communications, EP resolutions and a recent poll among MEPs have shown.[16] We believe that the OSCE, which has led the negotiations for Nagorno-Karabakh since 1992, is very experienced and no other negotiation format under international law would be able to find a solution very different to that found in the Madrid Principles proposed by the OSCE.[17] But, when necessary, the EU is and will be there. Thirdly, the EU was only able to play its role effectively in 2008 because of chance. Back then, our common foreign policy instruments were too weak to be strong at all times, and it was up to the ongoing French EU presidency to act. Today, we have taken the first step towards filling this void by creating the above-mentioned new EU foreign policy tools and positions. It is too early to assess their effectiveness, since they were put into place less than a year ago or are still being created. But their very existence shows that the EU has understood the problem and is tackling it.

The impact of the EU's new tools on the South Caucasus

So, how could the three new tools in the EU's external affairs toolbox impact upon the conflict of Nagorno-Karabakh? Firstly, they will influence situations which require the EU's attention and reaction. Such situations could be a new diplomatic initiative or the occurrence of a worrying event. In the past, the coordination of the EU's action or reaction depended strongly on the Member State currently holding the EU presidency, who was merely assisted by the Council Secretariat and the European Commission, with opinions from MEPs and most importantly from national governments on the sidelines of the debate. Today, it no longer matters much which country is running the EU presidency. However, the presiding country could still

---

[15] Organisation for Security and Co-operation in Europe, to which both conflicting countries are members.

[16] Examples:

• Statement by HR Catherine Ashton on Nagorno-Karabakh, Brussels, 21 May 2010, A 84/10, http://www.consilium.europa.eu/uedocs/cms_data/docs/pressdata/EN/foraff/114603.pdf

• EP resolution "A New EU Strategy for the Southern Caucasus", 23 April 2010, http://www.europarl.europa.eu/sides/getDoc.do?pubRef=-//EP//TEXT+REPORT+A7-2010-0123+0+DOC+XML+V0//EN&language=EN

• ComRes EP poll, August 2010, http://www.eufoa.org/uploads/Documents/documents/European%20Friends%20of%20Armenia%20Europoll%20Report%20Sept2010%282%29.pdf

[17] Only 17 per cent of MEPs support "Stopping the EU's support to the ongoing OSCE led negotiations and replacing it with a new EU format", ComRes EP poll, August 2010.

assume a bigger role than the other Member States, if it wishes to do so and if it has the capacity, know-how, history or special connection to the situation at hand as happened to be the case for France in the 2008 war in Georgia. But, generally, the Council's reaction will today be determined by the new functions presiding over meetings and summits, that is, the president of the European Council and the High Representative. Know-how and capacity will no longer depend predominantly on the size and particularity of the country holding the rotating EU presidency, but on the input from the European External Action Service. To sum up, the EU will be more prepared and capable at any time, irrespective of the country running the EU presidency or the personal interest of the large Member States' leaders. The EU will also be increasingly bound to its common values and strategies and in this regard become more predictable and reliable for its outside partners. There will be more continuity when actions or reactions are required or desired from the EU.

Secondly, let us explore the impact of the new functions on ongoing programmes of the EU, such as the ENP and the EaP, described above. Again, there will be more resources and increased continuity, since the key coordination will be driven by the new European External Action Service. As the European Parliament's negotiator for this service, I am pleased to say that the service has all the foundations to be very effective.[18] For us it was important to have a Service which is very closely connected to the Commission and of a supranational character, in order to ensure continuity and accountability. The EP has retained full rights over the budget and has even strengthened the accountability of the EEAS regarding human-rights actions and even peace enforcement actions – without infringing on the efficiency and reaction time of the service. It remains to be seen how the EU's leadership, above all the High Representative, will implement all this and conclude the construction of the service. However, it is likely that the EU's programmes, such as the EaP, will profit from it.

Thirdly, there is a growing understanding of the South Caucasus by the EU, followed by greater attention being given to Armenia, Azerbaijan and Georgia, and naturally also Nagorno-Karabakh. For this, some simple and concrete examples are worth considering. For many years, the Nagorno-Karabakh conflict has been marked by exchanges of gunfire along the Line of Contact, with recurring loss of life and a persistent danger of a military escalation. While the OSCE and the Minsk Group[19] Co-Chair

---

[18] Negotiators in the quadrilogue were Catherine Ashton, Elmar Brok, Roberto Gualtieri and Guy Verhofstadt. The agreement was reached in July 2010.

[19] OSCE Minsk Group was created in 1992 to encourage a peaceful, negotiated resolution to the conflict between Azerbaijan and Armenia over Nagorno-Karabakh. It is headed by the Co-Chairmanship consisting of France, Russia and the United States: http://www.osce.org/mg.

countries, France, Russia and the United States have traditionally reacted to such incidents, the EU has in the past largely remained silent. The High Representative has begun to change this practice and on various occasions has issued communications, making clear that the EU is increasingly concerned with the growing tensions over the last 12 months.[20] Regarding incidents such as skirmishes on the Line of Contact, it is unfortunate that at present, the EU does not possess sufficient observers on the ground to assess which of the conflicting parties has made the first step. This is something which will hopefully change over the coming months, and the EU Special Representative for the South Caucasus, Peter Semneby, initiated this debate at EU level in September 2010.[21] There is still a difference in the nature of our statements, as the EU "regrets" while the OSCE "strongly condemns"[22] – a significant distinction in international diplomacy. But the development is clear and it has to be welcomed that future incidents will surely not be met by the EU with passive tolerance, which could be interpreted by the guilty party as an encouragement.

Finally, the EU has begun a debate about more direct involvement in Nagorno-Karabakh on the basis of international law and with the full support of the ongoing OSCE lead peace negotiations. While the EU has, for many years, carried out programmes to aid the democratic, human-rights and socio-economic situation in disputed regions such as Transnistria, Abkhazia and South Ossetia, no such activities were implemented in Nagorno-Karabakh. In fact, EU officials are even barred from travelling to Nagorno-Karabakh and the EU Special Representative, Semneby, aborted a trip to Nagorno-Karabakh just before reaching the border, amid pressure from several countries inside and outside the EU. However, neither the conflicting parties, nor the peace negotiations, nor the population on the ground receive any benefit from such isolation. The European Commission has started to recognise this and is currently executing a 2 million Euro programme for confidence building in Nagorno-Karabakh, and implemented through international NGOs.[23] After the parliamentary elections in Nagorno-Karabakh in May 2010, the High Representative routinely issued

---

[20] Statement by HR Catherine Ashton on Nagorno-Karabakh, Brussels, 22 June 2010, A 110/10, http://www.consilium.europa.eu/uedocs/cms_Data/docs/pressdata/EN/foraff/115451.pdf.

[21] Reuters interview with EU Special Representative Peter Semneby about the need of international observers along the Line of Contact in Nagorno-Karabakh, 8 September 2010, M. Robinson, "Karabakh clashes risk escalation – EU envoy", http://www.alertnet.org/thenews/newsdesk/LDE6870BK.htm (date accessed: 20 November 2010).

[22] See Ashton statement of 22 June 2010 (source above) and OSCE statement of 21 June 2010, http://www.osce.org/item/44737.html.

[23] Mainly the NGO International Alert. The programme is at present not communicated publicly by the Commission.

a statement underlining that the EU cannot recognise the government in question, but also changing the entire tone of the declaration compared to earlier statements, because the EU does recognise the local attempts to administer Nagorno-Karabakh in an increasingly democratic way.[24] This is fully in line with the EU's approach of following international law while furthering our common values of human rights and democracy, values to which, by the way, the two conflicting countries, Armenia and Azerbaijan, have also committed themselves.

The EU's future role in Nagorno-Karabakh

With the described new foreign policy tools of the EU and its stronger engagement in the South Caucasus region, the EU's role in Nagorno-Karabakh is bound to grow. However, as noted earlier, the EU does not strive to substitute the OSCE in the negotiations for peace. Besides, such a development would be very unlikely, as neither the EU Member States nor the conflicting parties would benefit from it. However, the role of the EU is growing in order to present a supportive offer to the conflicting countries and the OSCE alike. Our message must be that we follow the process closely and whenever needed, we will be there. The EU focuses on our common values of peace, democracy and international law, including human rights. The ENP and EaP will play a vital role in creating more stability, democracy, economic progress and trade in Armenia and Azerbaijan, a key long-term contribution to peace. The stronger political involvement of the EU will pressure both conflicting parties to restrain all behaviour contradictory to international law, such as the threat of use of force, or the actual use of force, but also human-rights violations. The EU can play a role when more observers will be installed in and around Nagorno-Karabakh under the mandate of the OSCE. This measure is in the interests of all parties and should come sooner rather than later, not least to avoid an escalation or "war by accident". Azerbaijan, so far most sceptical about installing observers, needs them to ensure the absence of ethnic Armenian settlement programmes in the areas around Nagorno-Karabakh, currently controlled by Karabakhi or Armenian forces. Both sides need the observers to defend themselves against false accusations of military aggression – the classic "who shot first" question. And all parties involved need the presence of observers to ensure that such incidents become less likely, leading to a situation where the build-up of confidence becomes possible.

---

[24] The elections are no longer called "illegal" or described as a negative act, per se, since they do represent a democratic value for the people in Nagorno-Karabakh, Brussels, 21 May 2010, A 84/10, http://www.consilium.europa.eu/uedocs/cms_data/docs/pressdata/EN/foraff/114603.pdf.

The EU will soon have a stronger representation in these countries, as the EEAS replaces the Representations of the European Commission. It remains to be seen how this replacement covers for the discontinuation of the post of the Special Representative for the South Caucasus. In any case, actions and reactions by the European Union will become more frequent, intensive and coherent. Europe has a strong interest in peace and prosperity in the region, as much as do the conflicting parties and the mediating OSCE. We should not repeat the mistakes made before the war in Georgia. The threat of a regional escalation of the Nagorno-Karabakh conflict should act as a strong deterrent, so that all parties involved redouble their efforts to consolidate the ceasefire and by so doing allow for enough time to find a solution in accordance with international law. As the title of this book stipulates, this potential war is avoidable. The EU can and will play its particular and strengthened role to contribute to this aim.

11

Soft and Hard Security in the South Caucasus and Nagorno-Karabakh: A Euro-Atlantic Perspective

Richard Giragosian

Introduction

Historically, the South Caucasus region, comprising the former Soviet republics of Armenia, Azerbaijan and Georgia, has long served as an arena for competing powers and rival empires, hostage to the intense competition between much larger regional powers, as neighbouring Russia, Turkey and Iran have jockeyed for supremacy and influence. And those very same historic powers continue to exert influence today as dominant actors in the region, even as more distant world powers, such as the United States and the European Union, have each become more interested and engaged in the South Caucasus.

Since the collapse of the Soviet Union and the resulting abrupt onset of independence for each of the three states of the South Caucasus, the region has been viewed more as a "region at risk", as so-called "frozen conflicts", escalating tension and internal weakness have each contributed to a prevailing degree of instability and insecurity. Throughout this past decade of troubled transition, the course of democratic and economic reform in the region has also become hostage to unresolved conflicts and prisoner of political elites that rose to power in the wake of war and nationalism.

A new trajectory of shifting security

More recently, however, this traditional landscape of insecurity and instability has shifted along two very different trajectories. The first element of this regional shift was the brief but destructive war in August 2008 between Georgia and Russia, which triggered a new period of confrontation, with implications reaching well beyond the confines of the South Caucasus. Although initially centred on a conflict in Georgia's breakaway region of South Ossetia, the Georgian crisis expanded rapidly, sparking fresh tension between Moscow and Washington, seriously derailing Georgia's long-held aspirations to join the NATO alliance, and prompting Russia's rash and rather rushed decision to recognise the "independence" of the breakaway "proto-states" of Abkhazia and South Ossetia. The fallout from the Georgian conflict has been equally serious, with new doubts over the US commitment to the fledgling pro-Western Georgian democratic government. But even more troubling, the crisis further confirmed the inherent fragility of the strategically significant South Caucasus region.

For Armenia, the immediate effects of the August conflict in Georgia were serious, resulting in some $70 million in economic damage and losses and sparking a five-day nationwide shortage of gasoline after Georgian transport routes were closed. For Armenian national security, the conflict reaffirmed both the vulnerability of Armenia's dependence on Georgia as a key trade and transport route and reconfirmed the need for a new Armenian policy of strategic energy security.

In a broader context, the Georgian conflict with Russia also raised new doubts over Georgia's previous role as the regional "centre of gravity" for the West. Prior to the conflict, Georgia enjoyed a unique advantage as the focal point for Western security policy in the region. For the government of President Mikheil Saakashvili, Georgia's future was clearly tied to the West, reflecting a strategic vision that saw membership in NATO and the European Union as the ultimate guarantee to external security as a front-line state bordering a resurgent Russia. But new doubts over such a reliance on Georgia have also sparked new considerations of the necessity to secure a new regional "centre of gravity" in the South Caucasus. Western dissatisfaction with the Georgian leadership, although something that had started well before the August 2008 conflict, reached a turning point after Georgian leaders ignored Western cautions and concerns and proceeded to confront, or even provoke, Russian power directly.

War in Georgia: remaking the map

Aside from the damage, destruction and loss of life in the wake of the Russian–Georgian hostilities, one of the more significant longer-term results of the August 2008 war was its impact on the region. The Georgian crisis offered Russia an attractive opportunity to reassert its power and leverage throughout the region, an opportunity that was seized to virtually "remake the map" of the South Caucasus and to redraw the parameters of the region's strategic landscape. Although it was largely a Russian initiative that spurred the virtual redrawing of the regional landscape, the reaction and response to the new regional reality were equally as profound. From the Russian perspective, the new regional reality was marked by three distinct achievements: first, an abrupt end to NATO expansion in the South Caucasus, at least for the near-term, second, the demise of Georgian capabilities to fulfill its ambitions as a fully fledged Western anchor in the region; and, third, a serious escalation of tension and closer confrontation with the West as a whole. One of the broader lessons from the brief Georgian war was the revelation that it did not take much to trigger a return to open hostilities in the South Caucasus. Other lessons included a new recognition that so-called "frozen conflicts" were not very frozen after all, and could very rapidly thaw into "hot" confrontation – which underpins a related lesson that there is an unacceptably high risk in seeking to resolve essentially political conflicts through the application of military force. Nevertheless, some two years after the Georgian war, many in the region have failed to properly interpret the "lessons learnt" from that war or else they continue to adhere to a selective interpretation of those lessons. This misreading of the lessons from the Georgian war is most evident in Azerbaijan, where military officials in the Ministry of Defense in Baku stress that the only "mistakes" committed by the Georgian side were to overestimate their offensive capabilities while underestimating the Russian response.

Such a selective misinterpretation of the Georgian war has also tended to drive Azerbaijan closer to a much more deadly and assertive war strategy aimed at increasing its leverage by escalating tensions with Armenia and Nagorno-Karabakh. This new strategy, in part reflecting Baku's frustration with the peace process and its sense of betrayal by Turkey, has been marked by a serious spike in attacks on and military probes of Armenian defensive positions along the Line of Contact separating Nagorno-Karabakh from Azerbaijan. Given the steady escalation of military operations by the Azerbaijani side since June 2010, it seems clear that the Azerbaijanis seem to be making the same error in overestimating their own strength. Most distressing, however, these recent trends of escalation in the South Caucasus now reveal a fresh danger of renewed hostilities or even "war by accident", when limited skirmishes quickly spiral out of control and trigger larger operations based mainly on mutual "threat misperception".

Armenian–Turkish "football" diplomacy

The second, more promising, component of this regional shift was the start of fresh diplomacy between Armenia and Turkey, capped by the historic first-ever visit to Armenia by a Turkish head of state, when President Abdullah Gul arrived in Yerevan in September 2008 to attend an Armenian–Turkish soccer match. Marking the start of what later became known as "football diplomacy", Armenia and Turkey edged toward a groundbreaking agreement on normalising relations, including a possible reopening of the long-closed Turkish–Armenian border and the establishment of diplomatic relations. While the course of Turkish–Armenian diplomacy has since faltered since the signing of diplomatic "protocols" by the Turkish and Armenian foreign ministers in October 2009, there is, however, still a degree of optimism.

This optimistic hope for a breakthrough, most likely after Turkey's parliamentary election in June 2011, stems from two factors. First, the Armenian position of "no preconditions" toward Turkey has only encouraged the normally hesitant Turkish side to move much closer toward normalising relations with Armenia and modifying its long-standing blockade of Armenia. The same incentive will remain unaltered once there is an opportunity to restart the now-suspended policy of diplomatic engagement between Armenia and Turkey. Second, recent efforts to "sustain the momentum" of Armenian–Turkish engagement have increased in the wake of state-to-state talks. These efforts have included civil society cooperation, people-to-people contacts and exchanges, and Armenian–Turkish attempts at "track two" diplomacy.

The burden is on Turkey

But the real challenge, and the real burden, rests with the Turkish side. It was Turkey that closed its border with Armenia in 1993 and withheld diplomatic relations in support of Azerbaijan over its war for control of Nagorno-Karabakh. And, most crucially, it is Turkey that remains challenged by the need to face the historic legacy of the Armenian Genocide. At the same time, the normalisation of Turkish–Armenian relations also represents a strategic opportunity that Turkey may be in danger of missing, especially given a recent flurry of diplomatic threats and political posturing aimed at reassuring the nationalist camps within both Turkey and in Azerbaijan. But this issue of normalising must also be seen in the proper perspective, since any move by Turkey to reopen the border and extend diplomatic relations with Armenia represents only the bare minimum of expectations of normality between neighbouring countries.

In this way, even with an eventual Turkish adoption and implementation of this normalisation agreement, Turkey should not be overly praised or rewarded because such a decision would only be a first step in addressing more fundamental challenges facing Turkey, including the Kurdish and Cypriot issues and the imperative for significantly deeper reforms. Thus, for Turkey, the issue of normalising relations with Armenia also stands as a key test of Turkey's strategic future and as an indicator in the course of the Turkish bid for EU accession.

But it was the Georgian conflict that spurred a new breakthrough in talks, with an added impetus for at least opening the closed Armenian–Turkish border and offering both countries a potentially important economic and trade route as an alternative to the sole transit route through Georgia. Aside from the Georgian factor, another key to this new diplomatic opening, however, was Russia's support for such a breakthrough between Armenia and Turkey. More specifically, Russian policy had long been opposed to any significant improvement in relations between Armenia and Turkey, and the closed border was seen as a helpful way of maintaining Russian dominance over Armenia, as demonstrated by the continued presence of a Russian military base in the country (the only Russian base in the South Caucasus, if Russian military facilities in Abkhazia/South Ossetia are excluded) and Russian border guards policing Armenia's borders, as well as its economic dominance over the Armenian economy. But Russian policy shifted dramatically in the wake of the August 2008 Georgian crisis, with a possible Armenian–Turkish rapprochement only serving to bolster the Russian strategy to more completely isolate and marginalise Georgia. Nevertheless, Russia will only remain supportive as long as the future direction of Armenian–Turkish relations remains under its control.

There are also, however, added benefits for Russia from the issue, such as the possible sale of electricity to eastern Turkey from the Russian-owned energy network in Armenia. The breakthrough in Turkish–Armenian diplomacy was also a diplomatic coup by Moscow, with Russian officials virtually seizing a long-standing US foreign policy priority from the Americans. This was further demonstrated by the fact that the Armenian president publicly extended his official invitation to his Turkish counterpart to visit Armenia while on a state visit to Moscow and coordinated the opening closely with Russian officials. For Turkey, whose decline in power and influence in both the South Caucasus and Central Asia has never been fully reconciled with its vision and aspirations, the Georgian conflict prompted a new strategic diplomatic initiative. The so-called "Caucasus Stability and Cooperation Platform" is a Turkish initiative that seeks to forge a new cooperative attempt at conflict prevention, multilateral security and regional stability, but also reflects an effort to secure energy export routes.

But while this Turkish regional initiative is based on a new breakthrough with Armenia, including the opening of the border and an attempt to open a new chapter in relations, it also includes larger goals of engagement, with a broader strategic goal of Turkey as a leader in the region. And from this larger perspective, Turkey now views the unresolved Nagorno-Karabakh conflict as a central factor and impediment to regional stability. But there is a very important difference in Turkey's strategic view of Karabakh. Specifically, Turkey no longer seeks to merely support Azerbaijan, but is looking to expand its options in the region. Further, in terms of Turkish foreign policy this process of engagement, which was forged in the concept of "strategic depth" developed by Turkish Foreign Minister, Ahmet Davutoglu, represents an important policy modification. The scale and scope of the Turkish–Armenian breakthrough effectively overturns Azerbaijan's virtual veto power over significant aspects and options of Turkish foreign policy. In this way, the strategic concept of "one nation, two states", as the defining framework of Turkish–Azerbaijani relations, has been replaced by a more prudent policy of engagement that seeks to modify Turkey's failed policy of blockade and diplomatic isolation of Armenia. In this way, Turkey has corrected a failed course of its foreign policy, recognising that blockade and withholding diplomatic relations with Armenia has failed to result in anything except unifying and consolidating the people of Armenia.

Strategic opportunities

At the same time, the normalisation process between Turkey and Armenia offers several strategic opportunities. First, it enhances regional stability by seeking to resolve disputes by diplomacy rather than force, conforming to the deadly lesson from the Georgian war. A second opportunity stems from the possibility of leveraging Turkish–Armenian diplomacy to renew focus on the unresolved Nagorno-Karabakh conflict, which now stands as the last remaining "frozen conflict" in the South Caucasus.

A second opportunity centres on the broader impact of normalising relations with Turkey as an important mechanism to deepen democracy and bolster reform in each country, while also offering a new path toward regional reintegration and broader development once borders are opened and trade restored. And, finally, in a larger sense Turkey's diplomatic engagement of Armenia may also help advance Turkey's quest for eventual EU membership, and offers an important new mechanism for stabilising the restive Kurdish regions of eastern Turkey by stimulating commercial and economic activity, especially important in light of Turkey's recent launch of a new "Kurdish initiative". Moreover, for Turkey, opening its closed border with Armenia would constitute a new opportunity for galvanising economic activity in the impoverished eastern regions of the country, which could play a key role in the economic stabilisation of the already restive Kurdish-populated eastern regions and thus meet a significant national security imperative of countering the root causes of Kurdish terrorism and separatism with economic opportunity. This would also provide the Turkish military with an added economic measure to stabilise the East, with more promise than the traditional over-reliance on mere hard-line security responses to the Kurdish insurgency.

Likewise, an open border with Turkey would offer Armenia not only a way to overcome its regional isolation and marginalisation, but can also offer a bridge to larger markets crucial for longer-term economic growth and development. In addition, the commercial and economic activity resulting from the opening of the Armenian–Turkish border would foster subsequent trade ties between the two countries that, in turn, could lead to more formal cooperation in key areas, such as customs and border security, for only some examples. And with such a deepening of bilateral trade ties and cross-border cooperation, improved diplomatic relations would undoubtedly follow by necessity. Thus, the opening of the closed Armenian–Turkish border would not only bring about a crucial breakthrough in fostering trade links and economic relations, but may also serve as an impetus to bolstering broader stability and security throughout the conflict-prone South Caucasus.

The role of the West: the United States and the European Union

Another, and broader, shift in the regional geopolitical landscape can be seen in the changing nature of Western engagement. More specifically, both the United States and the European Union have instituted significant modifications to their strategic view of the South Caucasus, with a corresponding change in the scale and scope of their engagement in the region. For the United States, the South Caucasus returned to its more traditional role as a strategic subset of broader US–Russian relations, and mainly for two reasons. First, the Georgian war and the subsequent tension between Washington and Moscow tended to reinforce the view that the South Caucasus could not be treated as a region separate from the US relationship with Russia. This view inherently downgraded the region in terms of strategic significance and implied recognition of the more important calculus of a trade-off between accommodating a reassertive Russia with the geopolitical necessity of securing Russian cooperation over US needs in Afghanistan and Iran. In terms of Washington's "reset" of its bilateral relationship with Russia, this meant a veiled acceptance of Russian interests in the "near abroad", thereby reinforcing Moscow's view of the region as a "sphere of interest". This also translated into an American approach that sidelined Georgia as an issue about which Washington and Moscow would "agree to disagree", but which allowed both sides to move beyond the Georgia issue as an obstacle to broader and more strategic interests.

A second main factor tending to promote a higher priority for Russia over the region in US policy was the elevation of security-driven concerns and a US preference for stability over prior efforts at democracy-promotion and bolstering of sovereignty in the face of the region's vulnerability to Russian pressure or threats. For the United Sates, these new security priorities stemmed from the need for airspace access through the region, and through Russia, to facilitate operations in Afghanistan. Interestingly, this resulted in a shift from the previous decade, as the priority for secure energy pipelines and transit routes were replaced by a new need for transit routes and access through air corridors as the strategic imperative for the United States. The overall result of this shift in US policy was more of a strategic withdrawal from the region, however, with much less of a lead role for Washington in terms of being actively engaged in more local interests while focusing on broader strategic imperatives.

At the same time as this shift in US policy triggered a pullback from active and direct regional engagement, the European Union was faced with both a new opportunity and a pressing demand for greater, not less, engagement in the South Caucasus. After a difficult and trying test of its capabilities, it was, after all, European engagement in the Georgian war that resulted in a ceasefire. Although much of the diplomatic initiative was led by France, rather than the EU institutionally, the perception of effective European mediation marked an important test for the EU as a whole.

In order to sustain the success of greater engagement in the region, however, the EU needs to overcome the seemingly contradictory nature of EU strategy, as several leading EU Member States have tended to follow their own national policies, at times competing with, and diverging from, other EU states. Such divergence is most clearly evident in relations with Russia and over energy policy. Yet the EU holds an inherent advantage in both its EU Action Plans and its Eastern Partnership, which have each contributed to a steady accumulation of political capital in the region. Nevertheless, the future of EU engagement in the South Caucasus largely depends on the EU itself, which has already reached a crossroads, with a choice between the comfort of competing national policies and the challenge of forging a common policy for strategic engagement. And as a test, Brussels is already off to a disappointing start, as the looming decision to do away with the position of EU Special Envoy for the South Caucasus and to replace it with the still questionable capacity of its infant external diplomatic service, sends precisely the wrong message to the South Caucasus: that the region is, in fact, of lesser importance to the European Union. But there is still a sense of optimism that the EU will live up to its expectations for deeper engagement in the region, as it is no longer possible to ignore or downplay the imperative for the EU to assume a lead role in fostering greater security and stability in the South Caucasus, which remains very much a "region at risk".

Conclusion

In order to attain durable security and lasting stability in the South Caucasus, however, there are two main imperatives. First, as a short-term necessity, there needs to be a concerted effort to address mounting insecurity by strengthening the ceasefire regime between the Armenian/Karabakh and Azerbaijani sides. The necessity for diffusing tension over Nagorno-Karabakh stems from the escalation of hostilities through the latter part of 2010, as Azerbaijan has initiated a series of military operations probing Armenian defensive positions in and around Nagorno-Karabakh.

An additional approach to enhancing regional security may lie in charting a new course in mediating the Nagorno-Karabakh conflict. More specifically, within the larger context of the Karabakh peace process, there is an important lesson from the handling of Turkish–Armenian diplomacy. This lesson concerns the danger posed by the overall lack of transparency and inadequate public awareness of the details of the diplomatic process. In terms of the Karabakh peace process, for example, by its very nature, the closed and secretive process of mediation by the Organisation for Security and Cooperation in Europe's (OSCE) Minsk Group has tended only to foster misunderstanding and misinformation, especially as neither the Armenian nor the Azerbaijani governments are doing enough to prepare their constituencies for a possible peace deal – just as the Turkish and Armenian governments have done far too little to prepare their societies for the normalisation of their bilateral relations.

At the same time, there is no viable alternative to the OSCE Minsk Group as a mediator for the Karabakh conflict. The Minsk Group is the sole international body empowered to manage the mediation effort aimed at resolving the Nagorno-Karabakh conflict and has been long engaged in conducting delicate diplomacy toward that end. But the OSCE Minsk Group format is also structurally flawed by the absence of the democratically elected representatives of the Nagorno-Karabakh Republic (NKR) which, as an immediate party to the conflict, must be afforded a more direct and formal role in any peace process. Moreover, the failure to incorporate Nagorno-Karabakh in the peace talks as a party of equal standing only questions the viability of reaching a negotiated resolution capable of meeting the minimum standards of security and sustainability. Such a lesson has already been clearly demonstrated in other conflicts, ranging from the Palestinian to the Northern Ireland cases, affirming that mediation can only work when all parties to the conflict are directly included as interlocutors, such as the examples of the Palestine Liberation Organization (PLO) or the Irish republican Army (IRA). Only with the inclusion of the parties to the conflict can a viable and lasting settlement be reached and maintained.

The recognition of the vital and primary role of the OSCE Minsk Group as the mediator for the Karabakh is also based on acknowledgment of the fact that there is no viable alternative to the Minsk Group process. But the one most important factor missing from the peace process is that Karabakh itself has been denied a place at the negotiating table. Further, the real key to success for the peace process does not involve Russia or the United States, and certainly does not involve Turkey, due to its prior support for Azerbaijan. The real key to progress in the peace process is to include representatives of Nagorno-Karabakh as an equal party to the conflict and to grant them an equal seat at the peace table. Karabakh has been prevented from holding equal status with Yerevan and Baku for too long. Now is the time, especially after lessons from Georgia, to include Karabakh in the peace process, and to end Armenia's monopoly over negotiating on behalf of Karabakh, especially as the interests of Armenia and Karabakh are not necessarily the same.

But, equally important, a second imperative involving a longer-term need is to foster greater stability by enhancing democratic and economic reforms throughout the region. From this longer-term perspective, the real imperatives are internal in nature, stemming from several key challenges: the need to overcome the impediment of elections driven by power not politics, and leadership determined more by selection than election. In this way, legitimacy is the key determinant for durable security and stability, while the strategic reality of the region is defined less by geopolitics, and more by local politics and economics. But, most crucial for real democratisation is the lesson that institutions matter more than individuals. Consequently, it is the regimes themselves that hold the key to their future. And while external engagement is important, of course, real stability and security depend more on the legitimacy of regional governments and on local economics and politics than simply a reliance on grand geopolitics.

12
The Cold War Legacy in Nagorno-Karabakh: Visions from Russia, the United States and Regional Actors

Sergey Markedonov

At first glance, the situation regarding conflict resolution in Nagorno-Karabakh does not, at the time of this writing, seem fundamentally different from the situation one or two years previously. The substance of this discussion is well-known: arguments over the timeframe in which the five districts surrounding Nagorno-Karabakh are to be demilitarised; repatriation of refugees; the status of the disputed territory and various possible mechanisms which would ensure a prevention of the use of force. Endless talks are held within the framework of the OSCE Minsk Group and in the tripartite format, meaning with the presidents of Russia, Azerbaijan and Armenia, which was tested as early as 2008. Meanwhile, the negotiations themselves are held in an atmosphere of utter secrecy, and the text of the preamble has not been made available to either journalists or experts. At the same time, debates are under way about the possibility of compromise; the speedy establishment of peace; the "giving up" of two or three districts; how to protect the security of the unrecognised Nagorno-Karabakh Republic (NKR). Most importantly, the discussions have produced no concrete results, such as the signing of legally binding documents.

However, a closer look at the dynamics of the peace process in Nagorno-Karabakh reveals a number of important shifts, and these should be noted in order to gain a more accurate picture of the prospects of settling one of the oldest and most complex conflicts on former Soviet territory.

Rumours about approaching peace are followed by sharp outbursts of militarist rhetoric and violations of the ceasefire at the front line (this is how some people in Yerevan, Baku and Stepanakert – without any political correctness – refer to the Line of Contact of the parties involved in the conflict). In 2009 there were roughly 4,300 such infringements of varying degrees of severity (ranging from the firing of single shots to full-scale artillery duels). In 2008 the number of infringements equated to 3,500, with 1,400 in 2007. In 2006, in comparison to the succeeding years, the situation was relatively peaceful, with only 600 episodes registered.[1] In the context of the numerous changes occurring in the Greater Caucasus and its neighbouring regions, the increase in incidents taking place today demands the utmost attention. However, we will not focus on the simple geopolitical arithmetic, that is, the sharp increase in armed incidents we witnessed since the summer of 2010. It is far more productive to understand the processes by which such events, which tragically result in the loss of human lives, become possible.

A distinct conflict in the context of a new Caucasus status quo

This "hot spot" on the territory of the former Soviet Union is sharply distinguished from the others. The Nagorno-Karabakh conflict is the most intense of the armed confrontations in the post-Soviet Caucasus. It started in 1988 as a conflict between the Republics of Armenia and Azerbaijan and, in 1991, escalated into an international conflict, which continued for a further three years. The registered number of victims, refugees and internally displaced persons in Karabakh is greater than in Abkhazia, South Ossetia or Transnistria. In Karabakh, there is no peacekeeping operation in place to separate the parties involved in the conflict; everything depends on the Ceasefire Agreement, signed in May 1994, and the parties are divided by the front line. The only mediating force involved is the Minsk Group, which is famed for its inefficiency. The most effective mediatory achievement throughout this period has been the previously mentioned Ceasefire Agreement. The parties regularly test each other, but to some degree the arms race (not yet nuclear) within the region acts as a stabilising factor. People in Armenia, therefore, express concern about a possible deal between Azerbaijan and Russia, with the latter intending[2] to sell the S-300 "Favourite" anti-aircraft systems to the Caspian republic, which could seriously alter the security configuration in the region. To date, Armenia and the NKR compensated for their quantitative lag in aircraft with the quality of their own S-300 defences. However, provided that such a sale to Azerbaijan does not take place, and, bearing in mind that at present one cannot be sure of all the facts, it is likely that Baku does not have a definite advantage that would enable a decisive strike, such as a *blitzkrieg*.

In addition to human casualties, an escalation of violence could also damage the Azerbaijani government's reputation, which rests largely on the Karabakh factor. Consequently, any aggravation of the situation here could

---

[1] The Nagorno-Karabakh Ministry of Defense: on the Azerbaijani military post incident [Ministerstvo oborony Nagornogo Karabakha: na postu v. Azerbaijana proizohhel intsident s primineniem oruzhiya] The Caucasian knot [Kavkazskiy Uzel], http://karabakh.kavkaz-uzel.ru/articles/164575/ 2010 (date accessed: 21 January 2011).

[2] Note by the editors: after submitting this article, this arms deal has actually been concluded.

have much more serious repercussions for the Southern Caucasus and the CIS (Commonwealth of Independent States) as a whole. It should be noted that the growing number of armed incidents since the summer of 2010 is essentially a continuation of a trend that started several years ago, and can be understood as the "unfreezing" of the ethno-political conflicts. This "unfreezing" finally brought about the recognition of Abkhazia's and South Ossetia's independence, and with it, the formation of a new status quo in the Greater Caucasus.

The old status quo was established in the early 1990s with the collapse of the Soviet Union and a series of armed and latent conflicts caused by individual political entities, such as Abkhazia, Chechnya, Nagorno-Karabakh, South Ossetia and some ethnic and religious movements, and by the outcome of the "Belovezha division".[3] This division of the USSR was difficult to realise, as in many cases the borders between the Soviet republics were created without taking into consideration the opinions of the population but were instead constructed on the basis of ethno-political "engineering" adopted by the totalitarian state. By the mid-1990s, almost all the conflicts that had broken out following the collapse of the Soviet Union had been defined as "frozen". In some cases this was determined by the military and political balance (Nagorno-Karabakh), in others the use of force was supplemented by social, psychological and legal abuses (Chechnya, with its "delayed status" for five years). However, the "freezing" could only be sustained so long as the parties considering themselves to be losers were not interested in changing the balance of forces. The desire to change the established balance led to increased militarisation by those who wished for revenge.

However, not all countries have seen such an increase of resources (Georgia is in the worst situation here, Azerbaijan – a little better). That said, any claim that the old status quo in the Caucasus started to break down in August 2008 would be a major simplification of the situation. Before the "August war" in 2008 there were attempts to change the "frozen situations"; by Russia (Chechnya in 1999–2000) and by Georgia (in Abkhazia in 1998 and 2001 and in South Ossetia in 2004). Unlike Moscow and Tbilisi, Baku aimed to change the diplomatic format of the peace settlement and achieved quite positive results regarding the development of the Karabakh settlement into the negotiation process between Yerevan and Baku without Stepanakert.

---

[3] The Belavezha Accords is the agreement which declared the Soviet Union effectively dissolved and established the Commonwealth of Independent States in its place. It was signed at the state dacha near Viskuli in Belovezhskaya Pushcha on 8 December 1991, by the leaders of Belarus, Russia and Ukraine.

Nevertheless, August 2008 marked a qualitative break with the old status quo. Those five days in August challenged the principle of the inviolability of borders between entities of the former Soviet Union, which had remained intact for no less than 17 years. And this took place precisely in the Caucasus. This established a precedent for the recognition of new states among former Soviet autonomies on the Eurasian territory. One could argue that, to a certain extent, the period from August 2008 to the Kyrgyz events of June 2010 continues the transformation of the region which began at the moment the Soviet Union began to disintegrate. Ultimately, two partially recognised states – Abkhazia and South Ossetia, resembling Northern Cyprus or Western Sahara – have appeared in the Greater Caucasus.

After August 2008, Russia and Georgia departed to opposite sides of the barricades. It could be argued that, in the context of the twenty-first century, the total isolation of two countries from each other is impossible (and more importantly, illusory); however, the fact remains that, despite the preservation (and even consolidation) of Russian business interests in Georgia, political contacts between the two countries amount merely to the Geneva talks format, enabling both diplomatic communities to monitor the other side's position from time to time. One can exclude visits by (celebrity) Kseniya Sobchak or Mikhail Gorbachev (accompanied by other influential retirees) as serious political contacts. Similarly, the visits to Moscow by Zurab Nogaideli (former Georgian Prime Minister) and Nino Burjanadze (former parliamentary speaker) can hardly be perceived to be anything other than PR operations. By recognising Abkhazia and South Ossetia on 26 August 2008, Moscow made its choice concerning future prospects for relations with Georgia. But there are finer points to note here; Tbilisi made its own choice four years earlier, when it decided to "unfreeze the conflicts".[4]

Thus, the events of August 2008 left Russia without the tools it previously possessed for exerting pressure upon Georgia, and thereby pushed Tbilisi closer to the United States than it was before. This resulted in the signing of the charter on strategic partnership between Tbilisi and Washington in January 2009. Paradoxical as it seems at first sight, this pushed Abkhazia and South Ossetia even farther from Georgia and actually contributed to the consolidation of the new status quo. The United States and NATO have the resources to overwhelm Russia, and the Russian Federation does not have the ability to penetrate deep into Georgia. In military terms, Russia's potential is vastly greater than that of Georgia's, but it is not Moscow's aim to annihilate Georgia's statehood. If Russia

---

[4] See detailed observation of the Georgian attempts in C. Welt (2010) "The Thawing of a Frozen Conflict: The Internal Security Dilemma and the 2004 Prelude to the Russo-Georgian War", *Europe-Asia Studies*, pp. 63–97.

were to do so, it would encounter more serious resistance from the key international actors (United States, NATO and European Union) than was the case two years ago. At the same time it is extremely important for the Russian Federation to preserve its influence in the South Caucasus, in view of the multifaceted links between that part of the region and the North Caucasus.

But the development of a new status quo in the Caucasus is not limited to the recognition of Abkhazia and South Ossetia, and the severing of diplomatic relations between Russia and Georgia. The new status quo affected other countries in the region: Armenia and Azerbaijan. What did Yerevan and Baku derive from this war? Baku most likely realised that the "Serbian Krajina" scenario cannot be applied to the Caucasus.[5] The West (both the EU and the United States) wanted considerably less from the Caucasus than had sometimes been assumed. Thus, it was no accident that following the August war in 2008, Azerbaijan abstained from militaristic propaganda for several months.

In turn, Yerevan realised an unfortunate fact: for Armenia, Russia's victory over Georgia created many new problems, given that prior to the war logistics between the two allies[6] were conducted through Georgia. Having understood that the "Western factor" should not be overestimated (here Armenian and Azerbaijani diplomacy intersect), Yerevan began looking for ways to find compromises with neighbouring Turkey, whose claims to involvement – not only in Azerbaijani affairs but also in wider Caucasian geopolitics – became evident following the short-lived August war. Armenian–Turkish dialogue has become a serious factor influencing the regulation of the Karabakh process, although progress does not only depend on Turkish diplomacy. The effectiveness of the Azeri president, along with his diplomatic office, should also be recognised, for having managed to prevent the Karabakh problem from completely "detaching" itself from the process of Armenian–Turkish normalisation.

Thus, a geopolitical paradox has occurred! The absolute majority of zealots of Armenian–Turkish normalisation has spoken (and continues speaking) about the necessity of separating two problems: the peace process in Nagorno-Karabakh and reconciliation between Yerevan and Ankara. In reality, however, these two processes have merged. By means of multilateral pressure, especially from the United States, Turkey has been persuaded to

---

[5] In August 1995, the Croatian army swept into the Serbian Republic, Krajna, a small enclave which had been created by local Serbs in 1991. The international community's reaction was flaccid. Before this operation the United States provided one-sided technical and intelligence assistance to Croatia. As a result, Croatia restored its territorial integrity, but hundreds of Serbs were forced to flee.

[6] Armenia and Russia consider each other strategic allies, especially in military terms and in the context of the CSTO.

sign two protocols on the normalisation of relations with Armenia without any reference to Karabakh and the Armenian–Azerbaijani conflict. These protocols, signed in Zurich on 10 October 2009, were referred to by optimists as "historical" and a "breakthrough".[7] Certainly, the two protocols on the establishment of diplomatic relations and the opening of the Turkish–Armenian border became the first binding documents to be signed simultaneously by Yerevan and Ankara. However, without parliamentary ratification, these protocols will remain just paper. Indeed, after some consideration, at the end of 2009 and early 2010, Turkey linked once again the issue of reconciliation with the Armenian side with "progress" in the "Karabakh issue". As a result, the Armenian–Turkish rapprochement began to stagnate anew in 2010.

In contrast with the conflicts in Abkhazia, South Ossetia, Transnistria or the Balkans, during the Nagorno-Karabakh conflict neither Russia nor the United States have deviated significantly from their respective positions since the agreement of an indefinite ceasefire. Both sides (in their own way) have been interested in preserving the negotiations (despite the lack of concrete results) and avoiding an "unfreezing" of the conflict. Today, Moscow and Washington do not want to "raise the stakes" regarding Nagorno-Karabakh;. Moscow has enough problems in other places in the wider Caucasus region, while the United States currently faces major difficulties in the Greater Middle East from Iran, Iraq and Afghanistan to Turkey, Palestine and Israel. Those factors could theoretically offer an opportunity for positive conflict resolution in Nagorno-Karabakh. But at the same time, there are many existing nuances which would prevent the rapid finalisation of the process. In order to understand this better, one must consider the toolboxes of key stakeholders in this region.

Russian interests: caught between Armenia and Azerbaijan

Security issues in the Southern Caucasus have a particular resonance within Russian foreign policy. First and foremost, Russia is a Caucasian state, just like Armenia, Georgia and Azerbaijan. Seven constituent republics of the Russian Federation are located in the North Caucasus, and three neighbouring regions are situated in the Caucasian Steppe. The ethno-political tensions that have arisen in Russia's regions have been closely connected with the conflicts underway in the Caucasus. For example, Armenian refugees from Azerbaijan and Nagorno-Karabakh in the early 1990s seriously changed the

---

[7] Armenia's MFA promulgated the Armenian–Turkish Protocols: the full versions [MID Armenii obnarodoval Armyano-Turetskiye Protokoly: polnye versii] News of Armenia (Novosti Armenii) //http://news.am/ru/news/3438.html (date accessed: 23 January 2011).

ethno-demographic context both in the Krasnodar and Stavropol areas of Russia, provoking inter-ethnic tension.[8] Secondly, present-day Russia is a state with numerous diasporas, representing the various ethnic groups of the independent Southern Caucasus states. Thus, we can speak about "an internal Southern Caucasus" in Russia, which plays a significant role in the development of Russian business, as well as domestic and foreign policies. Russia's Armenian community is the largest diaspora from the South Caucasus. According to Russia's 2002 census, there are 1.13 million Armenians living in the country. This ethnic group is the fourth largest, following the Russians, Tatars and Ukrainians. In October 2003, the Union of Armenians of Russia helped establish the World Armenian Organization, which brings together representatives of Armenian diasporas in 52 countries. Ara Abramian, an influential Russian entrepreneur, was elected as president. Abramian helped renovate the Kremlin in 1994–99 and served as an official supporter during Putin's 2000 and 2004 presidential campaigns. The Novo-Nakhichevan and Russian diocese of the Armenian Apostolic Church, centered in Moscow, are active in Russia. Russia's Azerbaijani diaspora is the world's second largest, following that in Iran. The 2002 census listed 621,840 Azerbaijanis in Russia, spread among 55 regions. The largest groups are in Dagestan (111 700), Moscow (94 542), St. Petersburg (approximately 90 000), Volgograd region (14 000) and the Tver region (4 600). Azerbaijani businessmen, including Vagit Alekperov, Tel'man Ismailov and El'man Bairamov, have long worked at the highest levels in Russia. According to leaders of the diaspora organisations and representatives of law enforcement agencies, the Armenian and Azerbaijani presence inside Russia is significantly higher than official figures suggest. For example, the leaders of the All-Russian Azerbaijani Congress estimate that there are 1.5 to 2 million Azerbaijanis in Russia. Meanwhile, in 2001 Azerbaijani President, Heydar Aliyev, cited a figure of 1.2 million. Finally, Abramian claimed that there were 2 million Armenians living in Russia at the beginning of the 2000s.[9]

---

[8] Russian regions, such as Stavropol and Krasnodar; the Armenians became the second largest ethnic group, after the Russians, in the post-Soviet period. There are 350 200 Armenians in Stavropol, 274 600 in Krasnodar, and 230 000 in Rostov. See detailed observation in S. Markedonov (2009) "Russia's Internal South Caucasus: The Role and Importance of Caucasus Societies for Russia", *Caucasus Analytical Digest*, No. 4, pp. 11–14.

[9] See detailed observations in: A. Yunusov (2001) "Azeris in Russia: Change of Image and Social Roles" [Azerbaijantzy v Rossii: smena imidzha i sotsial'nyh rolei], *Diasporas [Diaspory]*, No. 1, p. 118, and: V. Dyatlov (2005) "New Diasporas of the Post-Soviet Epoch: Prerequisites and Mechanisms of Formation" [Novye diaspory postsovetskoy epohi: prichiny i mehanizmy formirovaniya] in V. I. Dyatlov, S.A. Panarin, M.Y. Rozhanskiy (2005) Baykalian Siberia: What is Stability Composed Of? (Irkutsk: Natalis).

Thirdly, having lost its influence in Georgia, Russia is interested in maintaining a balanced relationship with both Armenia and Azerbaijan. This is understandable as Russia maintains a military presence in Armenia, the military base in Gyumri, while Azerbaijan shares a common border with Russia, which lies through Dagestan – currently the most vulnerable and unstable republic of the Russian North Caucasus. Accordingly, increased attention has been paid to the intensification of making contacts with Yerevan and Baku. The loss of one of these partners would have serious consequences for Russia, as two out of the three entities recognised by the world community would be following an anti-Russian (at the very least, none too benevolent) course. It is no accident that the Russian approach to the Nagorno-Karabakh resolution is so different to the cases of Abkhazia and South Ossetia. Moscow, which is interested in developing a partnership with Azerbaijan, is extremely careful in its attitude toward the domestic events in de facto NKR. On 24 May 2010, the eve of the Nagorno-Karabakh Republic's parliamentary elections, the Official Representative of the Russian Foreign Ministry, Andrei Nesterenko, stated that Moscow supported the principle of Azerbaijan's territorial integrity as well as other fundamental norms and principles of international law. According to Nesterenko, the Russian Federation does not recognise NKR as an independent state.[10]

But the snag is that Russia's two potential partners in the Caucasus are locked in a confrontational relationship. The Karabakh conflict is perceived in both Armenia and Azerbaijan to be caught in a military–political stand-off and, moreover, one that has key significance for the two states' political identities. Furthermore, the conflicting sides are not only engaged in an arms race and information warfare within the region, but are also conducting a fierce struggle for external support. In this respect, Moscow is a crucial ally for both Baku and Yerevan. It is therefore no accident that in the summer of 2010 both Armenian and Azerbaijani political experts were in no hurry to comment on the August protocols between Moscow and Yerevan,[11] preferring to wait for September's signals from Dmitry Medvedev in Baku. Thus, Russian diplomacy faces a difficult task: to prevent itself from being drawn into this race or transforming into a player in this confrontation. We have seen that it is not uncommon for strong powers to become "dogs wagged by the tail" – as in the case of Russia with Chechnya, Abkhazia, and South Ossetia, and also in American–Georgian relations.

In August–September 2010 the Armenian–Azerbaijani geopolitical scales were balanced. Moscow made some fundamental steps outlining its

---

[10] RF recognised its support of Azerbaijan territorial integrity [RF podtverdila podderzhku territorial'noi tselostnosti Azerbaijana] http://www.rian.ru/politics/20100524/237860555.html (date accessed: 24 May 2010).

[11] See the full text of the Protocols' project on News of Armenia [Novosti Armenii] //http://news.am/rus/news/28027.html (date accessed: 17 August 2010).

principle position to Yerevan, Baku and the Nagorno-Karabakh resolution. On the one hand Moscow prolonged the presence of its base on Armenian territory,[12] thereby sending a signal to Baku that a violent solution of the Nagorno-Karabakh issue is unacceptable. While Azerbaijan has not received any tangible military–political "carrots," it cannot be totally ruled out that something like this will appear, in order to bring the scales into balance. However, no such incentive emerged following the Russian leader's visit to Baku. Nevertheless, it is important to note that in September 2010 Azerbaijan gained something no less important than tanks and guns: for the first time in post-Soviet history, it resolved the problem of delimitation and demarcation of the border with a neighbouring state, Russia. This problem has not yet been resolved with any of the other neighbouring countries. With Armenia, Azerbaijan has not so much a border as a front line. And even the border of the Nakhichevan exclave, which is much quieter than the Line of Contact in Nagorno-Karabakh, is closed and bristles with hostility. In the course of the Nagorno-Karabakh conflict, Armenian forces, occupying five districts neighbouring Karabakh entirely and two, partially, took control of the former USSR border with Iran on the River Araks. And despite a positive trend in relations between Tehran and Baku, the border between these two countries is a serious headache for Azerbaijani politicians (taking into account the growing ambitions of the Islamic Republic as a regional superpower).

Relations between Georgia and Azerbaijan are in many ways reminiscent of a "honeymoon" period; however the position of ethnic Azerbaijanis in Kvemo Kartli also creates considerable problems in bilateral relations between Baku and Tbilisi. As for the Caspian Sea border that Azerbaijan shares with Turkmenistan, the situation is similarly confused; the two republics have been arguing about oil and gas deposits in the Caspian Sea for many years. In the summer of 2009 Ashgabat even announced its intention of appealing to the International Court of Arbitration to uphold its rights to disputed fields.

The problem of delimitation and demarcation with Russia was also difficult to resolve. Talks on defining the 390 km state border have been ongoing, but in 14 years (beginning in 1996) the question still remained unresolved. From time to time the sides clashed over the problem of dividing the water resources of the Samur River, and there were discussions regarding the legal status of the border villages of Khrakhob and Uryanob. In 1954 these two villages in Azerbaijan's Khachmaz District were temporarily transferred to the Dagestani ASSR (Autonomous Soviet Socialist Republic) as pasture land, and 30 years later the Council of Ministers of the Azerbaijani SSR (Soviet Socialist Republic) extended the term of the previous document by a further

---

[12] The Russian military base in Armenia would stay in this country until 2044.

20 years (to 2004). The breakup of the USSR led to major adjustments to the former economic plans of the Communist Party. The situation was made more acute because the inhabitants were ethnic Lezgins, who also inhabit Dagestan. By the beginning of the 2000s many of them had acquired Russian passports. After August 2008 there was much speculation in the media on the subject of a repetition of the South Ossetian story in Azerbaijan. Today, all this idle theorising and speculation is left to the historians. Russia has become the first country after the breakup of the Soviet Union to sign a treaty with Azerbaijan on borders.[13] The presence of important officials in the Russian delegation responsible for administration in the North Caucasus (Aleksander Khloponin, Yunus-Bek Yevkurov) indicates that Moscow also considers the agreement with Baku to be advantageous. The Dagestani sector of the Russian border requires serious, and more importantly, effective cooperation with the southern neighbour.

But what did Moscow demand in exchange? In fact it did not ask for much – it is more a question of rhetoric. The Russian president, while in Baku, stated that he was personally interested in the peaceful resolution of the Nagorno-Karabakh conflict, and that Russian diplomacy would be used to implement this position. Moscow is prepared to continue to act as a mediator to seek solutions based on compromise. The signal has been sent, one can say. Following the Yerevan protocol, the Kremlin has been trying to draw the attention of its Azerbaijani partners to the fact that the Russian Federation is interested in any solution to the conflict except a military one. But is Russia fully capable of controlling its interests? The answer to that question is likely to be negative. Undoubtedly, some hotheads, both in Baku and in Yerevan, will be cooled by Moscow's position. But other considerations come into force, which even the staunchest admirers of the Kremlin in Armenia and Azerbaijan cannot ignore. Any Caucasian leader must resort to "patriotic rhetoric" in order to maintain his legitimacy. This becomes particularly relevant on the eve of elections. Therefore, a resumption of military rhetoric cannot be prevented, but this is not because politicians in Baku are more bloodthirsty. The loss of Karabakh is a national trauma that no one is ready to heal. Mentioning this maintains one's popularity. Thus, Russia's role in both Azerbaijan and Armenia should not be overestimated. However, the fact that Moscow is trying to play on several boards at once and attempting to pursue a balanced and pragmatic policy must be recognised.

---

[13] See more detailed observation of the Russian–Azerbaijani border issues in A. Yunusov (2007) *Azerbaijan in the Early 21st Century: Conflicts and Potential Threats* [Azerbaijan v nachale 21-go Veka: konflikty I potentsial'nye ugrozy] (Baku: Adyloglu edition); See information on Russian–Azerbaijani September: "2010 Agreement in Russia and Azerbaijan legalized the borders between each other" [Rossiya I Azerbaijan uzakonili granitsu mezhdu soboi] http://www.rtkorr.com/news/2010/09/03/168737. new?ref=rss (date accessed: 3 November 2010).

US approaches: the conflict seen through the prism of the Greater Middle East

The United States does not care as much as Russia (or Turkey and Iran) about the geopolitical dynamics surrounding the Caucasus. For Russia, any disruption in the Southern Caucasus could lead to a "defrosting" of the already unstable North Caucasus region, which would create internal political problems for Moscow. For Washington, however, the Caucasus is valuable as a testing ground where important political processes are developing which are not merely local. The United States is interested in the Caucasus, but this interest is not connected to any one place; it is part of larger external political projects, be they the "resetting" of its relations with Russia, a resolution of problems in the Middle East in general, or of the problems of Iran and Turkey in particular. In this sense it is possible to speak about certain asymmetrical perceptions of the Caucasus in Moscow, Tehran and Ankara on the one hand, and Washington on the other.

For example, what is Georgia? For American politicians, it is a "weak link" on the territory of the former Soviet Union, which Russia can use as a tool to establish a dominant role in the whole of Eurasia. In the United States this dominance is perceived to be part of a wider plan to reintegrate the former Soviet space. This reintegration is itself seen as a challenge to the United States and almost as a return to the times of the Cold War. Whether we like it or not, America's politicians and other experts link Moscow's increased geopolitical activity in the "near abroad" with solidifying authoritarian tendencies within Russia itself. According to this approach, the recognition of Abkhazia and South Ossetia is viewed not as the ethno-political self-identification of the small groups of peoples of the former Georgian Soviet Republic, but as a precedent for totally reconsidering the borders established between the former allied republics before 1991. Following the collapse of the Soviet Union, these borders became interstate. This leaves us with a paradox. While detesting Communism, Washington is prepared to defend those boundaries established by the Bolsheviks and authorised by Stalin personally. At the same time, an obvious notion is being ignored: Moscow's passivity in Eurasia could lead to increased nationalistic and anti-Western sentiments.

Another obvious notion is being ignored: Moscow's passivity in Eurasia could lead to increasingly nationalistic and anti-Western sentiments within Russia proper, while the United States' acquiescence to Russia's leading role in the CIS could actually advance the "reset" quite significantly. So what do Armenia and Azerbaijan mean to officials in Washington? Taking a step back from the traditional techniques of diplomatic rhetoric, it should be acknowledged that these two countries play a role in the larger context of American policy in the Middle East. Initially, the system of control over the macro region was conceptualised in Washington by strong interaction with its closest allies – Turkey and Israel. According to the authors of the "Greater Middle East" project, its realisation would successfully address a host of problems, from Israel's security concerns to the control of the region's main energy resources. The Southern Caucasus is the rear of the Greater Middle East, and, unlike the Line of Contact, it should be stable and quiet. In contrast to Russia, the United States considers the source of such stabilisation to lie in the building of "sustainable democracy" and market economies. Of course, the United States is not always deprived of its sense of realism. Besides being busy with the "democratisation" of Georgia, it has quite consistently criticised Armenia for "shortcomings in building democracy". At the same time, the United States has some reservations concerning the prospects of establishing "an open society" in Azerbaijan, as it probably realises that today nearly 60 per cent of the Azerbaijani population supports a military resolution of the Nagorno-Karabakh conflict.[14] Having an extremely low rating among the Islamic countries, Washington is extremely interested in strengthening its connections with Azerbaijan's elite. While it will certainly not replace Turkey (which in recent years has noticeably distanced itself from the United States), these connections can nevertheless be used to counterbalance Iran and as a successful ideological example. This is where the rhetoric that Secretary of State Hillary Clinton used in Baku for her July 2010 visit becomes relevant: the main priority is partnership in the energy and military-technological fields. As for human rights, Washington sees "enormous progress" in Azerbaijan by closing its eyes on the authoritarian trends in the country.

Today Washington views the Armenian factor as a way of applying pressure on stubborn Ankara, which has turned away from Israel and is watching Iran with interest. The loss of Turkey as a strategic ally (until recently, the United States has considered it the main "Muslim ally" and the outpost of the West in the Muslim world) would damage US interests. In this regard, Secretary Clinton's visit to the memorial of the victims of the Armenian genocide in Yerevan was hardly accidental. The relevant US State Department services could probably foresee the reaction of the Turkish authorities.

In contrast to the situation in Georgia, Washington sees extensive opportunities to cooperate with Moscow when addressing the entrenched Nagorno-Karabakh conflict between Baku and Yerevan. This is additionally advantageous for its larger-scale goals in Afghanistan and Iran, where Russia's support is quite important. Unlike the complex situation in Georgia, Russian policy in Nagorno-Karabakh is genuinely aimed at mediation, and not one-sided support of the unrecognised republic. Perceiving no threat of Soviet reintegration here, Washington is prepared to share the responsibility for resolving the Armenian–Azerbaijani standoff with Moscow.

---

[14] A. Yunusov (2007), op. cit., p. 187.

Moreover, the application by Azerbaijan of the "Georgian scenario" of "unfreezing conflicts" through a radical break in the status quo seems problematic. Two de facto states, supported by Moscow, struggled against Georgia. In this situation the interests of Abkhazia and South Ossetia and their aspirations of independence were either ignored by the United States or considered as not being worthy of attention. For the United States it was the conflict between Russia and Georgia, viewed through a whole complex of stereotypes (related to the young democracy and imperial schemes), which was significant. In this confrontation, Georgia was considered to be an agent of the West, whose acts of "conflict unfreezing" and divergences from democracy were forgiven. In the Nagorno-Karabakh case Azerbaijan not only fights against separatists, but is also in confrontation with Armenia, a recognised state with powerful support in the United States. It is possible to list numerous facts of such support, starting from the NKR social projects financed by the US Congress, and ending with Armenia–NATO projects. Neither Abkhazians nor Ossetians have such a powerful lobby in Washington. Baku also is beginning to obtain such lobbying resources, however. The United States has a serious interest in Azerbaijan, but at the same time Azerbaijan will be considered, like Georgia, as an "agent" of the West. For Baku, Moscow is an indirect opponent, Yerevan a strategic adversary. So, in the "unfreezing" game there will be no "bipolar model" here.

"Rediscovery" of the Caucasus: the implications of Turkish and Iranian influence regarding Nagorno-Karabakh[15]

The August war of 2008 increased Turkey's role in the Caucasus as whole. Ankara came across as a possible arbitrator and mediator for the settlement of the conflicts in the region, which raised the spectre of a revival of the Ottoman Empire, particularly in Armenia. The Turkish proposition for a "Caucasus Platform", alongside such projects as the "New European Neighbourhood", the "Black Sea Synergy" and the "Greater Middle East", aim at providing a conceptual framework which will serve region building. Almost simultaneously, the historic visit of Turkish President Abdullah Gul to Yerevan in September 2008 (sometimes called "football diplomacy") marked the beginning of Armenian–Turkish interstate dialogue.

Unlike the United States and the EU Member States, Turkey is not a "freshman" in the "big game" taking place in the Caucasus. During the sixteenth to eighteenth centuries, the Ottoman Empire, predecessor of the Turkish

---

[15] On Turkish and Iranian Caucasian policy, see M. Çelikpala (2010) "Turkey and the Caucasus: Transition from Reactive Foreign Policy to Proactive Rhythmic Diplomacy", *International Relations*, Spring Vol. 7, No. 25, pp. 93–126; and S. Markedonov (2009) "The Big Caucasus: Consequences of 'five day war', Threats and Political Prospects", Athens, *Xenophon Papers*, No. 7, pp. 63–65.

Republic, fought first with Persia, and later with the Russian Empire for domination of the Caucasus. During various periods of history, the great area of the Southern Caucasus used to belong to the Ottoman Empire or was moving in its military–political orbit. Today, Turkey features among the 20 biggest economies worldwide, while being one of the most economically advanced countries in the Islamic world, and Ankara stresses "soft power" in its diplomatic approach.

Prior to the Georgian war in 2008, when the geopolitical landscape of the Caucasus was defined by the old status quo, Turkish penetration in the region was out of the question. Today, however, Ankara is interested in actively taking part in the creation of a new security paradigm in the Greater Caucasus. Having declared European integration as one of its strategic goals, Turkey under Recep Tayyip Erdogan also tries to come across as an "outpost of the EU". But there is a general cooling in relations between both the United States and the EU with Turkey today. In the US context, this is due to the war in Iraq and their divergent approaches to the Kurdish question. Meanwhile, the cooling in relations with the EU is a result of the accession of the Republic of Cyprus to the EU and delays to Turkey's accession process. The change in relations with the United States and the EU objectively facilitates a new Turkish role in the region.

Ankara is interested in promoting a normalisation with Yerevan, which would meet its own interests. And among these interests, Azerbaijan's role is already significant. How is it possible to make Turkey more persistent in its dialogue with the United States and Russia? And how is it possible to insist that the partners, interested in relations with Turkey, are flexible in their negotiations with Ankara? The easiest way to achieve this is to make one's position known, and frequently so. Not only by means of military rhetoric (which is common), but also by military demonstrations. Remarkably, the representative of the Azerbaijani Foreign Ministry, Elhan Polukhov, commenting on the incident on the Line of Contact in Nagorno-Karabakh, which took place on the night of 19 June 2010, said quite clearly that "Azerbaijan will never accept the fact of occupation of its lands".[16] So Baku's tactic in holding talks will alternate between harsh militaristic statements and demonstrations of military force. And the main problem for Ankara is dependence, both domestic and external, on the Azerbaijani cause. Turkey is interested in enlarging its influence within the whole Greater Caucasus and in this way, the Azerbaijani factor must be minimised. But on the other

---

[16] Cited in "Azerbaijan recognized the fact of clash and victims in Nagorno-Karabakh" [Azerbaijan priznal fact boevogo stolknoveniya v Nagornom Karabakhe i nalichiye zhertv], *The Caucasian Knot* [Kavkazskiy Uzell] http://www.kavkaz-uzel.ru/articles/170417/ (date accessed: 19 June 2010).

hand, geopolitical traditions and the idea of Turkic solidarity push Ankara to play solely for Baku.

Thus, during negotiations with Washington and Moscow, Ankara can refer to Baku's stance as well as to Turkish unity, which it would like to ignore but cannot. As for the United States and Russia, both of these countries have their own reasons to take Turkey's opinion into account. For the United States, Turkey's military–political significance has not diminished despite their disagreements regarding Iraq in particular and over the Middle East in general. Given the current administration's plans in Afghanistan, the significance of the Indzherlik base should not be underestimated. For Russia, Turkey is turning into a primary economic partner. Last year, trade between the two countries grew by 49 per cent and reached the record high of $35 billion.[17] Thus, it is hardly accidental that the "escalation" in peace-making activities in Karabakh on behalf of both Russian and American politicians came soon after their meetings with the Turkish leaders, in December 2009 for the Americans and in January 2010 for the Russians. As a result, the stagnation regarding the Armenian–Turkish rapprochement has occurred due to the overlap of Ankara's and Baku's positions. At present, any possibility of encouraging parties to restart the process, aside from steps taken in the Nagorno-Karabakh issue, are viewed as problematic. The Turkish Prime Minister, Recep Erdogan, became seriously entangled in this issue, and Turkish decision makers place all the blame on Armenia. All the developments in 2009 also encourage Erdogan to remain indifferent. Azerbaijan's position is crucial for Ankara. Thus, without having any positive changes which satisfy Azerbaijan, it is unrealistic to expect any change in the Turkish–Armenian rapprochement.

Iran is also trying to nurture the formation of a new status quo in the Caucasus. Tehran finds it extremely painful to witness the appearance of various external actors in its neighbourhood. This accounts for Iran's desire to contribute to the settlement of the Nagorno-Karabakh conflict. In April 2010, the Iranian Foreign Minister, Manouchehr Mottaki, announced that Tehran would be ready to provide a three-sided forum (Iran–Armenia–Azerbaijan) and would play the role of mediator.[18] This statement was accompanied by several proposals from Iran which might be considered as alternatives to the "Updated Madrid Principles" (signed by the US, Russian

---

[17] "The Black Sea brought Russia and Turkey together" [Chernoe more cblizilo Posiyu I Turtsiyu] http://www.dni.ru/economy/2009/5/16/166399.html (date accessed: 16 May 2009).

[18] "Experts from Yerevan and Baku consider the Iranian and Turkish attempts to help the Karabakh conflict resolution as not serious" [Experty v Yerevane i v Baku schitayut popytki Irana I Turtsii pomoch' v reshenii karabakhskogo kobflikta neser'eznymi], *The Caucasian Knot* [Kavkazskiy Uzell], http://www.kavkaz-uzel.ru/articles/168296/ (date accessed: 30 April 2010).

and French presidents). Iran is not interested in a resolution to the conflict in Karabakh which would result in the engagement of international peace-keeping forces in the region, regardless under which flag (American, Swedish or German) such forces would be deployed. Tehran has already insisted that only regional forces should be present in the region. On the issue of Nagorno-Karabakh, the Islamic Republic has taken a distanced stance from all parties, and has advocated a political resolution of the conflict. Iran played a significant role as a mediator for the settlement of the Armenia–Azerbaijan confrontation in 1992–94. Given the blockade of Armenia by Azerbaijan and Turkey, Iran constitutes a corridor to the external world for this country. Thus, the Iranian mass media spread the news about the destruction of Armenian medieval monuments on the territory of the Azerbaijani exclave Nakhichevan (Old Julfa) in late 2005.[19]

Conclusion

Thus, a serious regrouping of forces is occurring in the Greater Caucasus. The old rules of the game, formats of talks and international missions (UN, OSCE in Georgia) either do not work at all or are not effective enough. Veterans such as Iran and Turkey are actively returning to the big geopolitical game, and Moscow's relations with its old allies (Armenia and the unrecognised republics) are changing (not simply worsening). In addition, one cannot rule out the appearance of new actors, for example, Israel, in the region. With regard to non-regional actors, in particular the United States, all of whom are attentively following the situation, there is a sense of apprehension related to further destabilisation or a possible "reintegration of the USSR". As a result, we are parting with the familiar Caucasus of 1990s and observing the creation of an altogether new Greater Caucasus.

This new geopolitical configuration creates positive conditions for a resolution of the Nagorno-Karabakh conflict and might prevent a new war. Unlike in Georgia, neither Russia nor the United States have an obvious desire to radically alter the Nagorno-Karabakh game. Both Moscow and Washington are rather satisfied with the negotiation process, and with their inevitably optimistic commentaries about the "coming peace". Paradoxically, the conflict-resolution process offers opportunities for cooperation between the West and Iran. Tehran also has no interest in the destabilisation of the disputed area. Nevertheless, from now on Turkey will play a much more significant role, particularly since it is playing its own independent game in

---

[19] Video-material: extermination of the Armenian khachraks (stone crosses) in Nakhichevan [Video-material: unichtozheniye Armyanskih khachkarov v Nakhichevane], Armenian Knowledge base, http://forum.armkb.com/news/ 21178-videomaterial-unichtozhenie-armyanskix-xachkarov-v-naxichevane.html (date accessed: 19 December 2005).

the Middle East on the Israeli-Palestinian, Syrian and Iranian fields, as well as in the Balkans. Furthermore, although both Moscow and Washington maintain that the Nagorno-Karabakh process and Armenian–Turkish reconciliation cannot happen simultaneously, they both quietly acknowledge a simple fact: in order to speed up Armenian–Turkish reconciliation, the resolution of the Nagorno-Karabakh problem should be pushed forward as well. There should be a negotiated document (this can be a protocol or a communiqué which is legally binding for both sides), which Recep Tayyip Erdogan or Abdullah Gul can present as a strategic advantage and as a result of establishing normal relations with Yerevan. This document would also help in their dialogue with the opposition and the political community of the country at large, because it would state the fact that the "fraternal Azerbaijani people" remain in the care of Ankara, while the reconciliation with Armenia did not come at a high political price.

Thus, the diplomatic bargaining continues. But the most important (even crucial) issue is to secure a compromise between Baku and Yerevan. What all parties need to do is to further the issue of security guarantees. A military conflict as complex as this, which is taking place in the vicinity of the Baku–Tbilisi–Ceyhan pipeline and the Iranian border (considering the bilateral Iranian-Azerbaijani problems); which is near Turkey (given the fact that the peace process between Ankara and Yerevan is not complete); and which has the involvement of a CSTO (Collective Security Treaty Organization) member (Armenia) and two NATO partners (Baku and Yerevan), as well as two members of the Council of Europe, will not be easily settled. Many parties will get dragged into it, and its resolution will be much more complex than in the case of Georgia.

Even if we cannot imagine an Azerbaijani military blitzkrieg, one must assume that guerrilla warfare, acts of terrorism and effective sabotage are also possible in Karabakh. Certainly, the recently strengthened Azerbaijani army is not comparable with the one which tried to quell Armenian resistance in Karabakh forcefully in the early 1990s. But even if the Azerbaijanis succeeded in completely or partially destroying the unrecognised Nagorno-Karabakh Republic's military–political infrastructure, Yerevan and the leaders of the NKR would not accept such a fate. And "appeasing" Yerevan would not avoid that groups outside the official government's control will act against the Azerbaijani armed forces. In this case, a situation reminiscent of the Middle East "intifadas" could arise. Thus, the potential for conflict will be doubled, if not tripled.

Today, one of the main issues in Russia's relations with the West, and firstly with the United States, is finding a basis for a new European and global security architecture. Common ground is being sought in settling the conflicts in the Balkans and in the Caucasus. Meanwhile, it is obvious that both Russia and the West are interested in stabilising the situation around Nagorno-Karabakh and, unlike in the Georgian case, there is consensus between them. Moreover, there are positive tendencies in the US–Turkish and Russian–Turkish bilateral relationships. It would therefore be easier to end the military rhetoric, whoever it comes from, with a unified voice. It is necessary to use negotiations as an opportunity to create real mechanisms for the prevention of force. But a major demonstration of power should and must force all parties to take the first steps in this direction. It makes sense to collectively impose legally binding documents banning the use of military force on all sides. Only once war has been rejected as the primary way of resolving the conflict will it be possible to discuss other issues. It is time to realise that until the battleaxe has been buried and the threat of renewed violence has ceased, there can be no compromise, either on status or on repatriating refugees. Not least because there is a real risk of the status quo being forcefully revised and of more refugees appearing.

13
An Eyewitness' View: Human Suffering in Nagorno-Karabakh and the Possible Role of the UK in Preventing New Violence

Caroline Cox

Introduction

The objective of this chapter is twofold. It aims at describing, from the perspective of one of the few Western eyewitnesses on the ground, the politico-military developments between the collapse of the Soviet Union and the emergence of independent Armenia and Azerbaijan which led to the war in Nagorno-Karabakh. The second part of the chapter is devoted to the possible role of the United Kingdom in preventing a further escalation of the tensions in the region. While the United Kingdom is not directly involved in the negotiation process, it is supporting the current diplomatic efforts, and there is a certain potential to reinforce this policy.

Humanitarian aspects of the NK conflict[1]

The Armenians suffered their greatest national tragedy at the hands of the Ottoman Empire during the massacres of 1894–96 and the genocide of 1915–16. Altogether, nearly 2 million Armenians perished, thus virtually eliminating Turkey's Armenian population. Most survivors of the genocide found refuge beyond the borders of present-day Turkey. Their descendants form the basis of the significant Armenian communities of North and South America, Western Europe and Australia. Hundreds of thousands of Armenians also live in Russia, Iran, Lebanon and Syria. Today the Republic of Armenia has a population of 3.6 million, 95 per cent of which is Armenian. In 1988, before pogroms and massacres were inflicted by the Azerbaijanis on Armenians

---

[1] Much of this chapter is drawn from C. Cox and J. Eibner (2003) *Ethnic Cleansing in Progress: War in Nagorno-Karabakh* (New Malden, Surrey: Christian Solidarity International).

146   *Caroline Cox*

living in Baku, Sumgait and Kirovabad, about 500,000 Armenians were living in the Soviet Republic of Azerbaijan. As many as 140,000 of these Armenians lived in the Autonomous Region of Nagorno-Karabakh, where they made up 75 per cent of the population, with Azerbaijanis, accounting for most of the remaining 25 per cent.[2]

Situation during the USSR collapse

The Armenian people living in the land known as Nagorno-Karabakh suffered greatly from Soviet policies of "divide and rule", when their land was cut off from Armenia by Stalin in the 1920s while he was deliberately setting up artificial ethnic patchworks through enclaves and exclaves in order to consolidate Bolshevik power in the region. Then, with the dissolution of the Soviet Union, the Armenians, who were a minority population in Azerbaijan's major cities (although they constituted a majority in Nagorno-Karabakh, itself),[3] suffered systematic and sustained policies of attempted ethnic cleansing by Azerbaijan, culminating in full-scale war when Azerbaijan began massive military offensives designed to eradicate any Armenian presence in the country.

This war raged from 1991 to 1994, causing immense suffering and large-scale displacement for both Armenians and Azeris. Eventually, it resulted in a ceasefire and a precarious "frozen conflict".

Subsequently, Azerbaijan is using its massive wealth from oil resources to promote a propaganda war, widely disseminating false and distorted versions of the history of Nagorno-Karabakh and of the war, denying the historically Armenian habitation of the land and portraying Armenians as the "aggressors" in the conflict.[4]

The decades-long Soviet policy of terror produced a precarious balance between the Armenians and Azeris. One of the key aspects of this policy was the campaign against religion. Marxist–Leninist ideology identified religion as one of the vital cultural roots of nationalism, which had to be severed. Both the Armenian and Azeri communities in Karabakh suffered grievously from the communists' atheist policies. During the Stalinist era the Armenian Church was obliterated. The Christians of Karabakh were left without a priest or bishop, all of whom been murdered, imprisoned, or sent

[2] 1989 USSR Census/Itogi Vsesoiuznoy perepisi naseleniia 1989 goda (Minneapolis: East View Publications), http://www.eastview.com/research-collections/product_view.asp?sku=IE00030&Russia/Russian/ (date accessed: 13 March 2011).
[3] 1979 USSR Census/Itogi Vsesoiuznoi perepisi naseleniia 1979 goda (Minneapolis: East View Publications), http://www.eastview.com/research-collections/product_view.asp?sku=RC000057&Russia/Russian/ (date accessed: 13 March 2011).
[4] News.Az, "Present-day Armenia Located in Ancient Azerbaijani Lands – Ilham Aliyev", 16 October 2010, http://www.news.az/articles/politics/24723

into exile.[5] All of the enclave's churches and monasteries were closed. Any public manifestation of the Christian faith became a punishable offense. The bravest of the faithful risked their lives and liberty by meeting in small groups in private homes. Official Islam likewise also ceased to exist in Nagorno-Karabakh. The closure of Shushi's three mosques left the enclave's Muslim minority without a public place of worship. The only option for Muslims wishing to practice their faith communally was to do so within the framework of semi-secret Sufi orders.[6]

Under Soviet rule, attempts to impose a Turkic hegemony over Nagorno-Karabakh continued. During the Soviet era the demographic balance shifted markedly in favour of the Azeris.[7] The main factors were the emigration of Armenians, the immigration of Azeris and the Azeris' high birth-rate. In 1921, when the enclave was awarded to Azerbaijan by a Stalin-backed decision of the Bolsheviks Caucasus Bureau, 94.4 per cent of the population was Armenian. Subsequently, the percentage of Armenians steadily diminished: by 1979, it was down to 75.9 per cent.[8]

There was a simultaneous depopulation of Armenians by Azeris in Nakhichevan – another disputed region wedged between Iran, Armenia and Turkey – which was granted to Azerbaijan by the Turkish–Russian Moscow treaty, also in 1921, and with which Azerbaijan has no common border. Armenians made up 40 per cent of Nakhichevan's population in 1917. Now, all the Armenians have been driven out. I was present during the final phase of the elimination, witnessing attacks by Azeri tanks on the few remaining villages.

Moreover, in Nakhichevan, the government of Azerbaijan has conducted a systematic campaign to completely demolish one of the largest cemeteries of medieval Armenian khachkars (cross stones), founded in the fifth century near the town of Julfa. Most of the original 10,000 khachkars, dating back to fifteenth and sixteenth centuries, were destroyed by the early twentieth century, leaving probably fewer than 3,000 by the late 1970s. According to the International Council on Monuments and Sites (ICOMOS), the Azerbaijani government removed 800 khachkars in 1998.[9] Though the destruction was halted following protests from UNESCO, it resumed four

---

[5] R.G. Suny (1996) Transcaucasia, Nationalism and Social Change: Essays in the History of Armenia, Azerbaijan, and Georgia (Ann Arbor: University of Michigan Press), p. 180.

[6] Ibid.

[7] Ibid. p. 195.

[8] 1979 USSR Census/Itogi Vsesoiuznoi perepisi naseleniia 1979 goda (Minneapolis: East View Publications), http://www.eastview.com/research-collections/product_view.asp?sku=RC000057&Russia/Russian/ (date accessed: 13 March 2011).

[9] The Independent, http://www.independent.co.uk/news/world/europe/azerbaijan-flattened-sacred-armenian-site-480272.html (date accessed: 15 March 2011).

years later. By January 2003 "the 1,500-year-old cemetery had completely been flattened", ICOMOS revealed.[10] In 2006, the European Parliament adopted a resolution condemning this act, yet later on the EP delegation was barred by the Azerbaijani government from inspecting the cemetery. Armenians inevitably feared that within a generation the Azeri authorities would succeed in a similar policy of extinction of their community in Nagorno-Karabakh. With the USSR collapse, the situation had further deteriorated, escalating into a full-scale war, with massive bloodshed on both sides.[11]

Although the primary focus of this chapter is not the detailed presentation of the various stages of the war and the atrocities committed against civilians, it is still necessary to shed light on at least the initial phase of the transformation of the political struggle into a bloody armed conflict. That turning point can be identified in the so-called "Operation Ring" carried out by Azeri and Soviet troops against Armenian civilians in Nagorno-Karabakh, and the consequent referendum for the independence of Nagorno-Karabakh.

"Operation Ring"[12]

In the spring of 1991, Azerbaijan embarked on a new type of offensive against the Armenians living in the Autonomous Region of Nagorno-Karabakh and in the Shahumyan district to the north. The code name given to this military assault was "Operation Ring".[13]

"Operation Ring" started in late April 1991 with the villages of Getashen and Martunashen. Together with the Azerbaijani Ministry of the Interior (OMON, or "black beret" forces), the troops of the 23rd Division of the Soviet Fourth Army stationed in Azerbaijan undertook systematic deportations of Armenians. The operations, carried out against vulnerable villagers, were notable for their brutality and cruelty. The assaults on Getashen and Martunashen established a pattern that was later used in villages of Shahumyan district and elsewhere in Nagorno-Karabakh. The deportation would typically begin with the Fourth Soviet Army troops surrounding the villages with tanks and armoured personnel carriers as military helicopters hovered low overhead. After the Soviet troops had surrounded the village, the Azerbaijani OMON would attack the villagers, harassing them on pretexts such as a "passport check".

[10] Ibid.

[11] For a detailed description of the human rights violations and atrocities committed during the war in Nagorno-Karabakh, see C. Cox and J. Eibner (2003), op. cit.

[12] The following two sub-chapters "Operation Ring" and "Referendum and Elections in Nagorno-Karabakh" are based on C. Cox and J. Eibner (2003), op. cit.

[13] R. Dember and R.K. Goldman (1992) Bloodshed in the Caucasus: Escalation of the Armed Conflict in Nagorno-Karabakh (New York: Helsinki Watch), p. 7.

The human rights abuses and the numerous acts of violence committed during "Operation Ring" are unspeakable: men were assaulted and killed; women were raped, children maltreated; civilians abducted as hostages. Azeri citizens from nearby villages would come with pickup trucks and cars and steal Armenian household goods and livestock, whereas Armenian villagers were driven off their land and had to live as displaced people, either elsewhere in Nagorno-Karabakh or in Armenia.[14]

Referendum and Elections in Nagorno-Karabakh

The "Operation Ring" carried out by Azerbaijan, and the intentions it bore, alarmed the Armenian majority of Nagorno-Karabakh. The spectre of the genocide in Turkey, the massacres in Transcaucasia and the "ethnic cleansing" in Nakhichevan revived the fear of Armenians for the loss of their ancient homeland. Perceiving the imminent threat to their autonomy and viable existence, they felt obliged to resort to measures for self-protection and survival.

The leaders of Nagorno-Karabakh, worried about the future of the autonomous enclave, came up with an idea to hold a referendum, with a view to declaring independence from Azerbaijan. Every citizen got a chance to vote. Although the vote was boycotted by Azerbaijan, the overwhelming majority of Armenians (over 90 per cent) voted in favour of independence. The referendum was followed by a general election for a parliament, which included proportional representation of seats for the Azeri population. The election was again boycotted by Azerbaijan, but the rest of the seats were filled and the parliament was opened in January 1992, with the blessing of the Orthodox Church Bishop of Karabakh, Parkev Martirosyan.

Angered by these developments, Azerbaijan proceeded to escalate military offensives in an attempt to quell the unilateral declaration of independence. By then, USSR President Boris Yeltsin had withdrawn the Soviet Army forces, which removed all the obstacles for the Azerbaijani armed forces and OMON to enter Nagorno-Karabakh. The latter became an open battlefield, with the civilians trapped inside, besieged, blockaded and bombarded.[15]

In the early days of the war, the people of Nagorno-Karabakh were fighting against seemingly impossible odds – relying on hunting rifles and home-made weapons to repel vastly superior ground forces and tanks. As the war escalated, Armenia sent reinforcements and Azerbaijan was aided by Turkey.[16]

---

[14] Ibid.

[15] C. Cox, J. Eibner and E. Bonnèr (1993) *Ethnic Cleansing in Progress: War in Nagorno Karabakh* (Binz: Institute for Religious Minorities in the Islamic World).

[16] G. Usher (1999), The Fate of Small Nations: The Karabakh Conflict Ten Years Later', *Middle East Report*, No. 213, pp. 19–22.

Situation after the ceasefire

In June 1994, a ceasefire was signed among Armenia, Azerbaijan and Nagorno-Karabakh. The attempts by Azerbaijan to impose a "military solution" to the "Karabakh problem" had failed, as the Armenians resisted the massive military offensives. The ceasefire has been maintained, precariously, with cross-border incidents often violating its provisions. However, Azerbaijan has been using its massive oil revenues to enlarge its extensive military capacity and has long been threatening resumption of hostilities, with increasing menace.

Azerbaijan frequently claims that about a million Azeris were displaced. However, Charles Blandy, Analyst of the UK defence academy estimates a maximum of 600,000.[17] Armenia suffered approximately the same number of people forced from their homes by Azeri massacres in Sumgait, Baku and Kirovabad (now Ganja) and by the war in Shahumyan and Nagorno-Karabakh.

For many years, Azerbaijan kept many of its displaced people in harsh conditions in camps, regularly taking visitors to see their plight. By contrast, Armenia worked hard to find some kind of accommodation for its displaced people. In the early days, this was often in tough, overcrowded conditions – but at least the displaced people were not forced to live in tents in camps.

These questions are apposite: Why did Azerbaijan, with massive oil revenues and funding from international aid agencies, force so many of its displaced people to live in these camps for so long, while Armenia, suffering from the after-effects of a catastrophic earthquake, an economic blockade by Azerbaijan and Turkey and with no oil revenues, managed to find some accommodation for its displaced people?

Inviolability of borders versus human rights

The peace initiatives of the international community have been hindered by an imbalance in the application of two principles: the inviolability of borders and respect for human rights. The Armenians of Nagorno-Karabakh are seen by the international community to have violated the principle of territorial integrity, to which international organisations are fundamentally committed. This commitment has been sustained despite the continuous and systematic violations of human rights, including crimes against humanity and attempted ethnic cleansing inflicted by Azerbaijan, as well as the economic blockade of Armenia by Turkey and Azerbaijan.

Some members of the international community have put a primacy on the inviolability of territorial borders, even if, as in our case, borders were

---

[17] C. Blandy (2008), "Azerbaijan: Is War Over Nagorny Karabakh a Realistic Option? Advanced Research and Assessment Group", *Defence Academy of the United Kingdom*, Caucasus Series 08/17, 12.

drawn arbitrarily or maliciously in the Stalin era. The application of this principle with regard to the case of Nagorno-Karabakh raises fundamental issues which, we suggest, will need to be considered in the longer term. Nagorno-Karabakh is not the only territory to suffer a tragic destiny as part of the aftermath of Stalin's cruel reign of terror, including his brutal policies of forced relocation of entire peoples to alien lands. There may therefore be a case for reconsideration of the balance between the sometimes conflicting principles of respect for territorial integrity and the right to self-determination. Elena Bonner Sakharov, among others, suggested that whereas the principle of respect for territorial integrity may appropriately command support in the longer-established states of Western Europe and North America, it may be less appropriate for the sometimes cruelly drawn boundaries of the former Soviet Empire.[18] She proposed that there may be a need for a period during which greater respect is given to the principle of self-determination, in some form, until some time has elapsed, allowing more congruence between ethnic, religious and territorial boundaries. In due course, when such boundaries have been established, then the principle of respect for territorial integrity may be more appropriately enforceable.

This consideration would be highly relevant for the Nagorno-Karabakh situation, in which Azeri policy – manifestly committed to the ethnic cleansing of the Armenians from Nagorno-Karabakh – would fulfil the criteria for the Armenians to make a strong case for self-determination based on the right to preserve their physical and cultural survival.

The doctrine of remedial secession emerged as a counterbalance to the internationally favoured principle of territorial integrity. It is described by a number of scholars as "a qualified right to unilateral secession", the legal basis for which stems from the right of self-determination.[19] States that are subjected to persistent and serious violations of human rights by the "parent states" often combine their argument to self-determination with a claim to a remedial secession. In the proclamation of the Nagorno-Karabakh Republic, the "policy of apartheid and discrimination pursued in Azerbaijan" was strongly emphasised.[20] However, self-determination and remedial secession claims combined with alleged human rights abuses still did not appear strong enough to strike the right balance with the principle of territorial integrity. This is where the concept of "earned sovereignty" has been of help. The concept assumes that once the entity claiming its

---

[18] A. Zverev (1996) "Ethnic Conflicts in the Caucasus 1988–1994", in B. Coppieters (ed.) *Contested Borders in the Caucasus* (Brussels: Vub Brussels University Press), http://poli.vub.ac.be/publi/ContBorders/eng/contents.htm (date accessed: 27 March 2011).

[19] D. Raic (2002) *Statehood and the Law of Self-Determination* (The Hague: Kluwer Law International).

[20] "Declaration on proclamation of the Nagorno-Karabakh Republic", 2 September 1991, http://www.nkr.am/en/declaration/10/ (date accessed: 11 March 2011)

right to self-determination also presents itself as an embodiment of democratic statehood, it can thereby "earn" its recognition.[21] Official Nagorno-Karabakh has, on many occasions, voiced and demonstrated its commitment to, and readiness for, self-government, the protection of human rights, and the promotion of regional security. "Today Nagorno-Karabakh continues to strengthen its statehood with democratically elected government, a court system, an independent foreign policy, and a commitment to educating its citizens".[22]

The Role of the United Kingdom in preventing a possible new wave of violence

The United Kingdom is one of the largest EU Member States with a strong foreign policy and conflict prevention history and experience. It is not by coincidence that the post of the High Representative of the EU for Foreign Affairs and Security Policy (HR) and Vice President of the European Commission is currently held by a British national – Baroness Ashton. The United Kingdom supports the general EU policy aimed at the endorsement of the OSCE Minsk Group Co-Chairs in the efforts to secure a peaceful settlement of the Nagorno-Karabakh conflict. Yet, there is certainly room for strengthening that policy on the bilateral level with Armenia and Azerbaijan.

In terms of UK priorities towards Armenia, the previous Labour government had three overarching themes: the NK conflict settlement, human rights/good governance and EU integration. Under the new coalition government, the latter theme has been somewhat weakened in order to make way for a new "economic prosperity" priority, with a British trade delegation to visit Armenia in spring 2011.[23] There have been a few high-level visits of Armenian delegations to the United Kingdom, the most significant of which was the official visit of President Sargsyan on 9–11 February 2010. However, the last visit to Yerevan by a UK cabinet member was by Foreign Secretary Rifkind in 1996, while Geoff Hoon and Baroness Scotland were the last Ministers of State to visit Armenia in 2006. Clearly, a high-level visit to the region, including to Armenia, is thus overdue. Meanwhile, the British Council is remarkably active in Armenia, providing support to the promotion of the English language and working with various organisations

[21] P.R. Williams and F. Jannotti Pecci (2004) "Earned Sovereignty: Bridging the Gap between Sovereignty and Self-Determination", *Stanford Journal of International Law*, 40(1), 1–40.

[22] C.B. Maloney (2005) "Commemorating the 17th Anniversary of the Nagorno-Karabakh Freedom Movement", *Congressional Record Proceedings and Debates of the 109th Congress*, First Session, Vol. 151, part 2, p. 2873.

[23] A. Hug (2011) "Spotlight on Armenia", The Foreign Policy Centre, http://fpc.org.uk/fsblob/1331.pdf (date accessed: 5 February 2011).

to give newly emerging Armenian political and intellectual elites UK-based opportunities. Besides, the British Alumni Association of Armenia has U.K.-educated members in several key positions, including in high-level political functions.[24]

Yet, the United Kingdom has more leverage on Azerbaijan than any other EU Member State. The United Kingdom is the largest foreign direct investor to Azerbaijan: in the last year, its foreign direct investments amounted to 49.1 per cent of the overall FDI in Azerbaijan.[25] BP, RAMCO and Monument Oil and Gas are the major investors. There are over 5,000 British expatriates, working mainly in Baku, and over 170 UK firms operate in Azerbaijan.[26]

Obviously, the UK government should be particularly concerned regarding gradually increasing chances of a war in Nagorno-Karabakh and the numerous war threats of the Azerbaijani government. Naturally, such threats also threaten UK investments in the region, especially in Azerbaijan. As was emphasised in the last International Crisis Group report (2011), titled *Armenia and Azerbaijan: Preventing War*, "greater efforts are needed to persuade Baku that such small steps (confidence-building measures [CBMs]) are directed not at its fundamental war-fighting capabilities, should it come to that, but rather at making the current situation more predictable and controllable and incidents more verifiable, so that an accident does not escalate out of proportion, against the interests of all".[27] Probably the UK government and the companies investing in the region are the best-positioned actors to deliver such messages to the Azerbaijani government. If Azerbaijan is interested in stable growth and investments, they need to provide a stable environment, that is, stopping threats of war and agreeing to CBMs, such as the removal of snipers from the Line of Contact. Increased support for confidence-building measures could be one of the most effective policy options for the UK government in the region.

It is believed that Nagorno-Karabakh has one of the world's highest per capita human accident rates caused by mines and cluster ammunition.[28] For this, it is worth looking at the case of the HALO Trust, a British NGO specialised in the removal of the hazardous debris of war. The HALO Trust is the only

---

[24] The British Alumni Association of Armenia official website, http://www.baa.am/membership/list.php (date accessed: 8 February 2011).

[25] News.az, "Foreign Investments in Azerbaijan grow 25.5% in April", http://www.news.az/articles/15951 (date accessed: 21 May 2010).

[26] The European Azerbaijan Society external public communication, Azerbaijan and the UK – "The Special Relationship", https://teas.eu/sites/default/files/UKAZ.pdf (date accessed: 8 February 2011).

[27] International Crisis Group (2011) "Armenia and Azerbaijan: Preventing War", *Policy Briefing* No. 60, 8 February 2011.

[28] http://www.halotrust.org/operational_areas/caucaus_balkans/nagorno_karabakh/problem.aspx (date accessed: 20 February 2011).

mine-clearance organisation operating in Nagorno-Karabakh; and development, reconstruction and other humanitarian aid there is dependent on the continuation of mine-clearance. Mine-clearance is also essential to reduce the number of accidents. HALO believes that with a 50 per cent expansion of the program, a mine-impact-free status can be reached by 2018 on the territory of Nagorno-Karabakh. However, this is largely dependent on the availability and provision of funds by various donors. Yet, the UK government has recently terminated all funding for the HALO Trust activities in the region. Insiders say that Azerbaijan has campaigned against humanitarian aid, mainly using leverage through BP, and arguing that such aid would predetermine the final status of NK. Incidentally, the Netherlands, another country with a strong BP presence, stopped their funding for this demining mission. This policy should be reversed before it becomes publicly questioned.

However, there are also positive examples of programs involving civil society. In order to make heard the voice of ordinary people from Armenia, Azerbaijan and Nagorno-Karabakh, as well as to engage the citizens in active discussion on this issue of high public importance, two non-governmental institutions – the International Center for Human Development (ICHD, Armenia) and Youth for Development (YFD, Azerbaijan) organised town hall meetings through 2008–09, on the possible scenarios for peaceful resolution of the NK conflict in Armenia, Azerbaijan and Nagorno-Karabakh. The project was actively supported by the British embassy in Yerevan and resulted in the publication of a unique analysis.[29] The British Council could also play an important role in bridging the civil societies.

There are certain indications that the UK government is considering undertaking more measures to this end. This line of approach was confirmed recently by the British Ambassador to Armenia, Charles Lonsdale, who said: "We attach importance to work with mass media and NGOs to develop dialogue in the region".[30] The so-called "Conflict Prevention Pool", established to enhance the effectiveness of the UK's contribution to conflict prevention and management, has been active in the South Caucasus since 2004, and its expenditure over 2010–11 amounted to almost £2.5 million.[31]

---

[29] ICHD (International Center for Human Development) (2010) The Resolution of the Nagorno-Karabakh Issue: What Societies Say: Discussion results of Armenians and Azerbaijanis at the Parallel Town Hall Meetings: Comparative analysis of the THM outputs (Yerevan: ICHD), www.ichd.org/download.php?f=533&fc=English%20 Book.pdf (date accessed: 22 February 2011).

[30] Panarmenian.net,   http://www.panarmenian.net/eng/society/news/63600/ British_Ambassador_to_Armenia_we_try_to_establish_dialogue_in_region_ through_media_NGOs, (date accessed: 9 March 2011).

[31] UN Embassy in Azerbaijan official site, http://ukinazerbaijan.fco.gov.uk/en/ about-us/working-with-azerbaijan1/funding-opportunities/020-CPP (date accessed: 3 March 2011).

Of particular interest are projects in and between Armenia and Azerbaijan, addressing the NK conflict, which will address the civil society, economic, international community and media objectives, namely:

- to build capacity and support for the civil society's collective contribution to conflict prevention initiatives at the local and national level,
- to raise awareness and understanding of the economic costs of conflict and benefits of peace and promote micro and macro economic cooperation,
- to build regional media networks and thus reduce the information isolation and false perceptions across the South Caucasus amongst communities divided by conflict and focus on neutral coverage by the media of the NK conflict for the local population
- to focus on youth with a view to overcoming stereotypes and uncovering myths, facilitating debate and enabling greater awareness of lives across the divide.

One could conclude that, though the United Kingdom is not a member of the OSCE Minsk Group and not directly involved in NK conflict mediation, still there is a room for the United Kingdom to contribute to the establishment of peace and stability in the region and, in fact, the British government has already initiated a number of measures to this end.

One should remember the words of William Gladstone, British Prime Minister and prominent statesman, reacting to the massacres of Armenians in the Ottoman Empire during the reign of sultan Abdul Hamid II: "I am silent only for fear of doing harm. The European mind wants plausible excuses to cover its disgrace. I do not wish to furnish them".[32] This quote could be considered as "a monument" to the Western powers' impotence to avert a humanitarian calamity at that time. I believe that today, principled proactive actions and increased pressure by the EU and its Member States, especially the United Kingdom – not prejudiced by narrow economic interests – would be more successful at preventing a possible new tragedy resulting from a new wave of violence in Nagorno-Karabakh.

Such a recommendation needs to be interpreted in the context of massive inequality between Azerbaijan and Armenia in resources for influencing the "international community". Azerbaijan has been investing its oil-based resources very effectively in disseminating to the international community its own versions of history and current events, combined with abundant invitations to foreign politicians and policymakers, as well as representatives of business and the media, to visit Azerbaijan and enjoy "red carpet" treatment. This "battle for the mind" as part of "the battle for peace" is

---

[32] "Gladstone on Armenia: he cannot find words to describe the guilt of the Turks", *The New York Times*, 26 June 1896.

also reflected in expensive initiatives and investment. Recently, the *London Evening Standard* revealed some interesting facts:

> In 2009 former Labour Prime Minister Tony Blair visited Azerbaijan, had a private meeting with Aliyev and is thought to have accepted £90,000 for a speaking engagement there. There is a Conservative Friends of Azerbaijan group to foster relations, and the Lib-Dems go even one step further. Last year the party received £11,500 in donations from The European Azerbaijan Society, a London based "non"-governmental organisation run by LSE-educated Tale Heydarov (son of a very controversial Azerbaijani Minister[33]), which promotes his country's interests in the world.[34]

The UK press also reported recently that Prince Andrew, third in line to the throne, had developed a "close friendship" with Azerbaijani authoritarian President, Ilham Aliyev, during at least seven visits over the course of five years. Apparently, at least two of the visits have been private, leading to speculation that the prince has personal business interests in Azerbaijan.[35]

The refraction of the United Kingdom's foreign policy in favour of Azerbaijan was once disturbingly reflected in an exchange between myself and the then-minister with particular responsibility for this part of the world. Having returned from Nagorno-Karabakh, where I had been deeply disturbed to see Armenian children killed by Azerbaijani cluster bombs,[36] I asked him if the British government would make representations to Azerbaijan, protesting against the use of cluster bombs against civilians. The response was a brief statement to the effect that no country has an interest in other countries; only interests – and the United Kingdom had oil interests in Azerbaijan.

However, as I pointed out in a subsequent debate: while I can understand our economic and financial interests, I do not believe it is in the long-term interests of any nation to allow such interests to undermine concern for fundamental human rights. Moreover, I do not believe the majority of British

---

[33] http://wikileaks.ch/cable/2010/02/10BAKU127.html (date accessed: 14 March 2011).

[34] "Andrew is only one of the many friends of Azerbaijan", *London Evening Standard: Londoner's Diary*, http://londonersdiary.standard.co.uk/2011/03/andrew-is-only-one-of-the-many-friends-of-azerbaijan.html (date accessed: 14 March 20011).

[35] "Britain's Prince Andrew Under Fire Over The Company He Keeps", *Radio Free Europe/Radio Liberty*, http://www.rferl.org/content/british_prince_andrew_under_fire/2333914.html (date accessed: 10 March 2011).

[36] On the use of cluster ammunition by Azerbaijan, see Z. Brzezinski, Z.K. Brzezinski, P. Sullivan (1996) *Russia and the Commonwealth of Independent States: Documents, Data, and Analysis* (Washington, D.C.: Center for Strategic and International Studies, M.E. Sharpe), p. 608.

people would support "oil business" at the price of "cluster bombs on children" – at least without saying something about it.[37]

But, now, there may be a more optimistic scenario, as economic interests may combine with the ethical case for recognition of the need for stability in the region. I firmly believe the Armenians have as strong a case for recognition of the right to self-determination as have other countries who have been granted this right, including East Timor (where I am also working) and southern Sudan (which I visited 30 times in their desperate war for survival from 1983–2005). But it should also be possible to persuade countries such as the United Kingdom to press for a peaceful solution to the current impasse in terms of self-interest, as a renewed war in the region could be disastrous for our own economic interests – and even worse for all the peoples who live there.

As a Briton, living in the country of Byron, who had such love for the Armenian people, and speaking in the same parliament as Lord Bryce, who spoke so honourably about the Armenian genocide, it is my fervent hope that my country will support an equally honourable solution for all people – Azeris, Armenians and other ethnic groups – who have suffered so much in the war, and who still suffer in its continuing aftermath.

---

[37] UK Parliament website, Hansard of the House of Lords Debate "Armenia and Nagorno-Karabakh", 15 December 1992, Vol. 541 cc516–50, http://hansard.millbanksystems.com/lords/1992/dec/15/armenia-and-nagorno-karabakh (date accessed: 11 March 2011).

14
Evolution of the EU Position vis-a-vis the Nagorno-Karabakh Conflict

Paruyr Hovhannisyan

Introduction

A common perception of EU policy concerning the Nagorno-Karabakh conflict is that Europe has no real interest in playing a decisive role and, even if it were to show the political will, would not have the adequate leverage to play a more active role. Yet, a closer analysis of EU policy since 1988 points to a different conclusion. The EU position can hardly be described as indifferent or unwilling. On the contrary, it has consistently aimed at a close follow-up of developments; has been supportive of efforts regarding a peaceful settlement; and, bearing in mind the fragile and sensitive situation in the region, has maintained a balanced policy of causing no harm.

It is not well-known that the European Parliament (EP) was actively following the escalation of the conflict in Nagorno-Karabakh from the outset, or that it adopted a number of resolutions addressed to the Soviet government, as well as to the governments of Soviet Azerbaijan and Armenia. However, from 1994 (after the signing of the Ceasefire Agreement between Azerbaijan, Armenia and Nagorno-Karabakh) until 2003 (establishment of the post of the EU Special Representative for the South Caucasus), EU policy could be described as rather limited. It was basically a reiteration of political support for the mediation efforts of the OSCE Minsk Group, and a promise of significant financial contribution to the economic rehabilitation of the region after the settlement of the conflict. The situation changed with the last EU enlargement in 2007, inclusion of the South Caucasus in the European Neighbourhood Policy (ENP), a strengthening of the EUSR mandate and the introduction of the Eastern Partnership initiative (EaP). At present, with the establishment of the European External Actions Service (EEAS) and the start of the EU–Armenia and EU–Azerbaijan negotiations on Association Agreements, it should be expected that the EU will conduct a more proactive policy in the South Caucasus and pursue its own initiatives in the context of Nagorno-Karabakh.

While the chapter refers to all European Institutions and bodies, particular stress is made on the activities of the European Parliament, as a locomotive of the EU's new policies and innovative ideas vis-a-vis the region.

European Parliament resolutions regarding the NK conflict during the Soviet period (1988–91)

The European Parliament closely followed developments in Nagorno-Karabakh from 1988 to 1991, and the region has been a subject of a series of resolutions.

The first resolution on "recent events in Soviet Armenia" was adopted on 10 March 1988 and referred to the mass demonstrations which had taken place in Soviet Armenia and the disturbances in Azerbaijan. The resolution qualified these protests as a "result from the past, from unresolved ethnic, cultural, religious and institutional problems and from repressions, in some cases brutal, with regard to both individual rights and at national level".[1] The movement in Nagorno-Karabakh was seen as one of the "attempts by various peoples in the Soviet Union to assert their identity, their culture and their autonomy".[2] A few months later, on 7 July 1988, the EP adopted another resolution "on the situation in Soviet Armenia" in which MEPs regarded "the historic status of the autonomous region of Nagorno-Karabakh (80% of whose present population is Armenian) as part of Armenia" and noted "the arbitrary inclusion of this area within Azerbaijan in 1923".[3] The resolution strongly condemned "the massacre of Armenians in the Azerbaijani town of Sumgait in 1988" and supported "the demand of the Armenian minority [ed: *referring to the whole of Azerbaijan*] for reunification with the Socialist Republic of Armenia".[4] The resolution also called upon "the Soviet authorities to ensure the safety of the 500,000 Armenians currently living in Soviet Azerbaijan and to ensure that those found guilty of having incited or taken part in the pogroms against the Armenians are punished according to Soviet law".[5]

A resolution "on repression in Soviet Armenia" was adopted by the European Parliament on 19 January 1989, after the devastating earthquake in Armenia in the end of 1988. While reiterating its position on "the reattachment of the

---

[1] Official journal of the European Communities, (1) Troubles in Armenia: Joint resolution replacing Docs. B2–39, 47 and 67/88 – On recent events in Soviet Armenia, No. C 94/117, 11 April 1988.

[2] Ibid.

[3] Official journal of the European Communities, (d) Joint resolution replacing Docs. B2–538 and 587 88 – On the situation in Soviet Armenia, No. C 94/117, July 1988.

[4] Ibid.

[5] Ibid.

autonomous region of Upper Karabakh to Soviet Armenia, it having been arbitrarily given by Stalin to Azerbaijan", the EP condemned the arrest of all the leaders of the Karabakh Committee by the Soviet authorities and called for their immediate release.[6] In the same resolution, the EP welcomed the decision of the USSR Supreme Soviet (of 12 January 1989) regarding the creation of a special status for the autonomous region of Nagorno-Karabakh under the direct control of Moscow and asked "the Soviet Government also to ensure the effective protection of Armenians living in Azerbaijan, where further acts of violence against the Armenians have occurred despite the earthquake".[7]

In the following resolutions on the situation in Armenia adopted on 18 January and 15 March 1990, the European Parliament reacted to the "resumption of anti-Armenian activities by the Azeris in Baku (an initial estimate talks of numerous victims, some of whom died in particularly horrific circumstances) and the attacks on Armenian villages outside Nagorno-Karabakh, such as Shahumyan and Getashen".[8] Once again, it was concluded that "the conflict now taking place is largely the result of the dividing up of the territory imposed by Lenin in Transcaucasia, and particularly the forced integration of the Autonomous Republic of Nagorno-Karabakh, mainly populated by Armenian Christians, into the Muslim republic of Azerbaijan in 1923".[9] Parliament called upon the European Commission and Council to "make representations" to the Soviet authorities, urging them to ensure the immediate lifting of the blockade imposed on Armenia and Nagorno-Karabakh by Azerbaijan; to guarantee real protection for the Armenians living in Azerbaijan by sending forces to intervene; and to make certain that the circumstances surrounding the pogroms perpetrated against the Armenians, in particular in Sumgait and Kirovabad (Azerbaijan), were brought fully to light. The parliament also expressed concern regarding the "human rights situation in Nagorno-Karabakh, which is administered by Azerbaijan against the will of the majority of its inhabitants, more than 75% of whom are Armenians, and at the continuing violence in Azerbaijan".[10] For the first time, the EP proposed "to send a small delegation to Armenia and Azerbaijan to report to Parliament and the European public on the situation of the Armenians".[11] The EP also called on "the Commission to grant

---

[6] Official journal of the European Communities, (b) Joint resolution replacing Docs. B2–1262, 1296 and 1304/88 – On repression in Soviet Armenia, No. C 12/146, 16 January 1989.

[7] Ibid.

[8] Official journal of the European Communities, (f) Joint resolution replacing Docs. B3–137, 139, 145, 156, 157 and 162/90 – On the situation in Armenia, No. C 38/81, 19 February 1990.

[9] Ibid., No. C 38/82

[10] Official journal of the European Communities, (g) Doc. B3–556/90 – Resolution on the situation in Armenia, No. C 96/260–261, 17 April 1990.

[11] Ibid.

substantial emergency aid to Armenia and Nagorno-Karabakh in the form of basic essentials".[12]

EU policy regarding the Nagorno-Karabakh conflict during 1992–2003

After the collapse of the USSR and declarations of independence in Armenia and Azerbaijan, the European Parliament adopted the last resolution directly referring to the Nagorno-Karabakh (NK) conflict on 21 January 1993. In that document, the EP called for an immediate ceasefire between the parties in the conflict. It was noted that "the economic blockade imposed by Azerbaijan and the resulting energy crisis were designed to draw Armenia into a direct armed conflict" and "the relentless blockade carried out by Azerbaijan constitutes a violation of international law".[13]

Afterwards the EP's general approach changed and, rather than adopting country-specific resolutions, the parliament started to issue resolutions on the regional situation. The first resolution of this kind was adopted on 27 May 1993 – the resolution on the situation in the republics of the former Soviet Union. The second part of the resolution was devoted to the "conflict between Armenia and Azerbaijan" and mainly called for "an immediate halt to hostilities, an end to the blockade of Nagorno-Karabakh and reopening of roads in order to enable emergency humanitarian aid to be sent to refugees".[14]

European Union interests in the South Caucasus during the 1990s remained largely in the economic sphere, focused especially on economic and technical aid offered to the region, thus reflecting a low political and strategic profile in the region. From 1991 to 2000 the EU allocated €280.33 million in grants to Armenia and €335.69 million to Azerbaijan through a range of instruments, such as the programme, Technical Assistance to the Commonwealth of Independent States (TACIS), ECHO Humanitarian Assistance, FEOGA Food Aid Operation, Food Security Programme and the Exceptional Humanitarian Aid.[15] Yet, contrary to the US policy of providing assistance to the population

---

[12] Official journal of the European Communities, (f) Joint resolution replacing Docs. B3–137, 139, 145, 156, 157 and 162/90 – On the situation in Armenia, No. C 38/82, 19 February 1990.

[13] Official journal of the European Communities, (f) Resolution B3–0049/93 – Resolution on Armenia, No. C 42/165, 15 February 1993.

[14] Official journal of the European Communities, (9) Republics of former Soviet Union – East-West relations in Europe, (a) B3–0540, 0551, 0554, 0565, 0605 and 0606/93, No. C 176/173, 28 June 1993.

[15] Commission of the European Communities, Country Strategy Paper 2002–2006 and National Indicative Programme 2002–2003 – Republic of Armenia, 27 December 2001, 26, http://eeas.europa.eu/armenia/csp/02_06_en.pdf (date accessed: 30 November 2010).

of Nagorno-Karabakh, no direct EU humanitarian aid was provided to NK. Meanwhile, Europe coordinated its national foreign policies on a case-by-case basis, without real collective coherence. Individual EU Member States were, and are, playing a significant role. After the establishment of the OSCE Minsk Group, Italy was elected as its Chair, replaced by Sweden in 1994 (not yet an EU member at the time) and then by Finland in 1995–1996 (jointly with Russia). The institution of the triple Co-Chairmanship was finally established in 1997, including Russia, France and the United States, and is currently carrying out the mediation efforts.

Since 1999, the European Parliament started to lobby to upgrade the South Caucasus on the EU agenda. In March 1999, the EP adopted a resolution "on support for the peace process in the Caucasus", largely endorsing the peace plan proposed by the OSCE Minsk Group. It is remarkable that in the same resolution it was admitted that "the autonomous region of Nagorno-Karabakh declared its independence following similar declarations by former Soviet Socialist Republics (SSRs) after the collapse of the USSR in September 1991".[16]

Signing the Partnership and Cooperation Agreement between the EU and three South Caucasus states on 22 June 1999 provided a formal basis for cooperation in all areas. For the first time, political dialogue was highlighted as an important issue, along with trade and economic cooperation. In the Joint Declaration of the EU and Armenia, Azerbaijan and Georgia, adopted during the signing ceremony, the presidents of the three countries and the EU leadership stated: "We emphasise the importance of the regional cooperation for the creation of amicable relations between the states of the region and for the sustainable development of their economies".[17] It was also stated that the conflicts in the South Caucasus were impeding the political and economic development of the region, and the EU stood ready to use its influence to underpin concrete progress in the peace processes.

On 28 February 2002, the European Parliament adopted a resolution on "EU relations with the South Caucasus" in which it noted "only limited progress has been achieved in attempts to resolve the conflicts" and regretted that "despite very promising results during the Armenia-Azerbaijan negotiations at Key West in April 2001, the follow-up talks planned for June 2001 in Geneva did not take place".[18] The parliament expressed its concern

---

[16] CA&CC Press, Resolution of the European Parliament on Nagorno-Karabakh, 11 March 1999, http://www.ca-c.org/dataeng/books/book-1/12.appendix-20.shtml (date accessed: 29 November 2010).

[17] Joint declaration of the European Union and the Republics of Armenia, Azerbaijan and Georgia, Europe – Press Release, 22 June 1999, http://europa.eu/rapid/pressReleasesAction.do?reference=PRES/99/202&format=HTML&aged=1&language=EN&guiLanguage=en (date accessed: 1 December 2010).

[18] European Parliament, Resolution on EU relations with South Caucasus: report on the communication from the Commission to the Council and the European Parliament

that "the risk of full-scale war involving the whole region still must be taken seriously" – a call that is still very relevant today.[19] In the same document, the EP strongly called upon the Council to appoint a Special Representative for the South Caucasus who would contribute to the peaceful resolution of ongoing conflicts, in collaboration with the UN and the OSCE. While reminding Armenia and Azerbaijan of their undertaking to step up efforts to find a solution to the NK conflict, the EP called "for the constructive engagement of the authorities in Stepanakert in the peace process".[20] In the same paragraph it called upon Armenia "to refrain from all measures in the occupied Azeri territories that might be interpreted as aiming to make the Armenian control permanent".

On 7 July 2003, the EU Council established the post of the EU Special Representative (EUSR) for the South Caucasus and appointed Ambassador Heikke Talvitie from Finland to this position. The mandate of the first EUSR was very broad, but only had a small budget and a few staff. The EUSR was supposed to "assist in conflict resolution" along with other tasks of enhancing the visibility of the Union in the region and to encourage cooperation between the South Caucasus states.

Strengthening of EU strategy towards the South Caucasus and current state of EU policy vis-à-vis the Nagorno-Karabakh conflict

Since 2004, the EP started to prepare regular resolutions/reports on "EU policy towards the South Caucasus". To date, three reports have been adopted. The first was drafted by Swedish rapporteur Per Gahrton (Greens Group) and adopted on 26 February 2004. The resolution noted that the South Caucasus continued to be excluded from the "Wider Europe – New Neighbourhood" initiative and called for a defined status for the South Caucasus region within the new EU policy. The resolution also called "upon all the countries in the region not to block efforts to bring the three states closer together by demanding a resolution of the Nagorno-Karabakh conflict as a precondition".[21] In the meantime, the EP requested "the Commission to set up twinning programmes between Nagorno-Karabakh, South Ossetia and Abkhazia from one side, and regions with special status in the EU countries

---

on the European Union's relations with the South Caucasus, under the partnership and cooperation agreements, 28 February 2001, p. 2, http://www.europarl.europa.eu/sides/getDoc.do?pubRef=-//EP//TEXT+TA+P5-TA-2002–0085+0+DOC+XML+V0//EN (date accessed: 1 December 2010).

[19] Ibid.

[20] Ibid. p. 3.

[21] Official journal of the European Communities, European Parliament resolution on EU policy towards South Caucasus, P5_TA (2004)0122, No. C 98 E/197, 23 April 2004.

from the other side so as to exchange experiences and find concrete solutions which respect the principle of territorial integrity of the countries concerned as well as right of self-rule for minorities".[22]

On 11 March 2003, the European Commission for the first time outlined the European Neighbourhood Policy (ENP) in its Communication to the Council and the European Parliament: "Wider Europe – Neighbourhood: A New Framework for Relations with our Eastern and Southern Neighbours".[23] Despite the above-mentioned call from the European Parliament, the South Caucasus countries were excluded from the initiative on geographical grounds. Yet, on 14 June 2004, the European Council decided to include Armenia, Azerbaijan and Georgia in the ENP and adopted a Strategy Paper on the European Neighbourhood Policy.[24]

On 20 February 2006, Ambassador Peter Semneby from Sweden was appointed Special Representative for the South Caucasus with a strengthened mandate. In accordance with the new mission, rather than merely assisting in conflict resolution, the EUSR should "contribute to the settlement of conflicts" and "facilitate the implementation of such settlement in close coordination with the United Nations Secretary General and the UN Mobile Team, the Organization for Security and Cooperation in Europe and its Minsk Group".[25] The EUSR should support the implementation of the EU's policy objectives, which include assisting the countries of the South Caucasus in carrying out political and economic reforms, preventing conflicts, promoting the return of refugees and internally displaced persons, engaging constructively with key national actors neighbouring the region, supporting intra-regional co-operation and ensuring co-ordination, consistency and effectiveness of EU actions in the South Caucasus. Despite different opinions about the effectiveness of the EUSR role, such a reinforcement of his mandate was definitely an important political signal.

After nearly one year of negotiations, the ENP Action Plan (AP) with Armenia (as well as Action Plans with Georgia and Azerbaijan) was signed in November 2006. The Action Plan for Armenia makes a few references

---

[22] Ibid. No. C 98 E/198.

[23] Commission of the European Communities, Communication from the Commission to the Council and the European Parliament "Wider Europe – Neighbourhood: A New Framework for Relations with our Eastern and Southern Neighbours", Com(2003)104 final, Brussels, 11 March 2003, http://ec.europa.eu/world/enp/pdf/com03_104_en.pdf (date accessed: 2 December 2010).

[24] 2590th Council Meeting – General affairs and External Relations, Europa – Press Release, 14 June 2004, C/04/195, p. 13, http://europa.eu/rapid/pressReleasesAction.do?reference=PRES/04/195&format=HTML&aged=0&lg=et&guiLanguage=en (date accessed: 2 December 2010).

[25] Official journal of the European Union, Council Decision 2010/109/CFSP extending the mandate of the European Union Special Representative for the South Caucasus, L. 46/16, 23 February 2010.

to the NK conflict. In the chapter on "New partnership perspectives", the EU confirmed its strong commitment to supporting the settlement of the conflict in "close consultation with the OSCE". Probably for the first time in such a bilateral document, the EU declared its readiness to "consider ways to strengthen further its engagement in conflict resolution and post conflict rehabilitation".[26] In the chapter on specific actions regarding the contribution to a peaceful solution of the NK conflict, the following measures are listed:

- Increase diplomatic efforts, including through the EUSR, and continue to support a peaceful solution of the Nagorno-Karabakh conflict;
- Increase political support to the OSCE Minsk Group conflict settlement efforts on the basis of international norms and principles, including the principle of self-determination of peoples;
- Encourage people to people contacts;
- Intensify the EU dialogue with the parties concerned with a view to the acceleration of the negotiations towards a political settlement.[27]

These measures were basically repeated under the chapter on general objectives and actions but also adjusted to the following concrete project proposals on the promotion of sustained efforts towards a peaceful resolution:

- Explore possibilities to provide EU support for humanitarian and de-mining initiatives;
- Promote measures to assist refugees and IDPs;
- Promote the active involvement of civil society;
- Reinforce the cooperation on these and other matters in support of conflict resolution with the EU Special Representative for the Southern Caucasus.[28]

The same measures had basically been listed in the ENP Action Plan for Azerbaijan. In contrast to the Action Plan for Armenia, though, NK conflict resolution is the number-one priority in the AP for Azerbaijan (number seven in the AP for Armenia). Besides, it is remarkable that in one of the measures on promoting a resolution of the conflict it states, "increase political support to the OSCE Minsk Group conflict settlement efforts on the basis of international norms and principles" – without reference to either the principle of self-determination of peoples or the principle of territorial

---

[26] European Neighbourhood Policy, EU/Armenia Action Plan, p. 3, http://ec.europa.eu/world/enp/pdf/action_plans/armenia_enp_ap_final_en.pdf (date accessed: 1 December 2010).

[27] Ibid. p. 9.

[28] Ibid. p.16.

integrity.[29] Instead, the latter is mentioned in the introductory part, referring to the mutual commitments of the EU and Azerbaijan to common values, "including the respect to and support for the sovereignty, territorial integrity and inviolability of internationally recognized borders of each other....".[30] The inclusion of this wording in the preamble of the document was largely the result of the dispute between Azerbaijan and Cyprus, provoked by the launch of direct regular flights from Baku to the Turkish-controlled part of Cyprus.

At the same time, cooperation for the settlement of the conflict over Nagorno-Karabakh was specified in Country Strategy Paper 2007–2013 for Armenia, adopted in the frame of the European Neighbourhood and Partnership Instrument (ENPI) – the ENP financial tool. In this document, the European Commission reiterated the continuation of its engagement in support of a peaceful settlement of the conflict over NK. "This involves in the first place supporting efforts of the EUSR and the OSCE Minsk Group, but also to encourage people to people contacts, to actively involve civil society in peaceful conflict solution efforts and to support humanitarian and de-mining initiatives. Depending on developments regarding the peaceful settlement of the conflict over Nagorno Karabagh, the EC will provide specific assistance related to all aspects of peaceful conflict settlement and settlement consolidation".[31]

In 2007 the European Parliament referred to the NK conflict on a few occasions. The EP position was expressed in the Final Statement and Recommendations of the EU–Armenia Parliamentary Cooperation Committee (PCC) Ninth Meeting, which took place on 29–30 January in Brussels. The EP reiterated "its full support for the peaceful settlement and fair resolution of the Nagorno Karabakh conflict in accordance with the principles of international law, which include the right to self-determination and respect for minority rights".[32] Furthermore, it was also stated that "the resolution of the Nagorno Karabakh conflict must include an agreement on the status of Nagorno Karabakh" and that "the people of Nagorno Karabakh should be involved in the negotiations to resolve the conflict".[33] It was also

[29] European Neighbourhood Policy, EU/ Azerbaijan Action Plan, p. 14, http://ec.europa.eu/world/enp/pdf/action_plans/azerbaijan_enp_ap_final_en.pdf (date accessed: 1 December 2010).

[30] Ibid. p. 1.

[31] European Neighbourhood and Partnership Instrument, Armenia: Country Strategy Paper 2007–2013, p. 17, http://ec.europa.eu/world/enp/pdf/country/enpi_csp_armenia_en.pdf (date accessed: 2 December 2010).

[32] EU–Armenia Parliamentary Cooperation Committee Ninth Meeting, Final Statement and Recommendations, http://www.europarl.europa.eu/meetdocs/2004_2009/documents/re/651/651470/651470en.pdf (date accessed: 3 December 2010).

[33] Ibid.

emphasised that further consolidation of democracy and progress on good governance in Nagorno-Karabakh would contribute towards a peaceful solution to the conflict.

The EU's commitment was also mentioned in the European Parliament resolution of 15 November 2007 on strengthening the European Neighbourhood Policy, which asked the Commission "to explore the possibility of providing assistance, in the form of local confidence-building and local economic rehabilitation projects, to Nagorno Karabakh, with a view to helping to resolve the conflict there".[34]

The European Parliament provided a number of recommendations and expressed its position on the NK conflict particularly extensively in its subsequent report on the South Caucasus – the resolution on "A more effective EU policy for the South Caucasus: from promises to actions" of 17 January 2008. Among the concrete proposals, the EP welcomed the Commission's "efforts to give aid and spread information to Abkhazia and South Ossetia", and "the initiative by the EU Special Representative for the South Caucasus, Mr. Peter Semneby, to open Information Offices in both regions", and asked the Commission and EUSR Semneby "to extend the same kind of aid and information dissemination to Nagorno-Karabakh".[35]

The analysis given in that document is actually applicable to most inter-ethnic conflicts. The resolution stated the following: "[T]he contradiction between the principles of self-determination and territorial integrity contributes to the perpetuation of the unresolved post-Soviet conflicts in the South Caucasus region; ... this problem can be overcome only through negotiations on the basis of the principles enshrined in the UN Charter and in the Helsinki Final Act and within the framework of regional integration; ... this process cannot take place without the support of the international community; ... the improvement in inter-ethnic relations, on the basis of European standards, and the enhancement of minorities' rights in such a way as to strengthen the civic cohesion of the states in the South Caucasus are essential in bringing about a negotiated solution to the conflicts in the region".[36]

The EP reiterated its respect and support for the territorial integrity of Azerbaijan, as well as for the right to self-determination and its strong

---

[34] EP – Resolution on strengthening the European Neighbourhood Policy, Strasbourg, 15 November 2007, A6–0414/2007, http://www.europarl.europa.eu/sides/getDoc.do?type=TA&reference=P6-TA-2007–0538&language=EN (date accessed: 3 December 2010).

[35] EP – Resolution on a more effective EU policy for the South Caucasus: from promises to actions, Strasbourg, 17 January 2008, A6–0516/2007, http://www.europarl.europa.eu/sides/getDoc.do?type=TA&reference=P6-TA-2008–0016&language=EN (date accessed: 3 December 2010).

[36] Ibid.

support for the OSCE Minsk Group. Nevertheless, the parliament regretted the lack of any substantial progress and warned "against any militant and provocative rhetoric that could undermine the negotiation process".[37]

The EP further called on "key actors in the region to play a constructive role in resolving unresolved post-Soviet conflicts in the region and to take steps to normalise its relations with neighbours".[38] In particular, Turkey was invited "to engage in serious and intensive efforts for the resolution of outstanding disputes with all its neighbours, in accordance with the UN Charter, relevant UN Security Council resolutions and other relevant international conventions, and including a frank and open discussion on past events" and "to start the process of reconciliation with Armenia for the present and the past".[39] In that context, the European Commission was encouraged to facilitate this process while taking advantage of the regional cooperation realised within the ENP and Black Sea Synergy policy. Meanwhile, both the Commission and the Council were asked to address the opening of the Turkish border with Armenia with the authorities of those two countries.

The EP's concerns regarding the situation around Nagorno-Karabakh were also reflected in the Final Statement and Recommendations of the EU–Armenia Parliamentary Cooperation Committee Tenth Meeting (7–8 April 2009, Yerevan). The "unacceptability of militaristic rhetoric and hate propaganda" was emphasised and "the importance of regional cooperation in order to improve the atmosphere for the solution of the conflict" was noted.[40] In this respect, the parliament welcomed the appeal of the OSCE Minsk Group Co-Chairs to develop confidence building measures and consolidate the ceasefire. The EP delegation called upon the parties to the conflict to withdraw snipers from the Line of Contact in accordance with the Joint Declaration of the Foreign Ministers of OSCE MG Co-Chair countries (4 December 2008, Helsinki). The OSCE proposal was supported by Armenia but rejected by Azerbaijan. It was probably for that reason that "the readiness of Armenia to develop confidence building measures" was commended in the Final Statement.[41] It was strongly reiterated that there was "no alternative to the peaceful resolution of the conflict" and "the military option as a solution to the Nagorno-Karabakh conflict should be excluded – parties should commit to political, peaceful settlement".[42] As in the case with the previous

---

[37] Ibid.

[38] Ibid.

[39] Ibid.

[40] EP – EU–Armenia Parliamentary Cooperation Committee Tenth Meeting: Final Statement and Recommendations, Yerevan, 7–8 April 2009, http://www. europarl.europa.eu/meetdocs/2009_2014/documents/dsca/dv/dsca20091006_04/ dsca20091006_04en.pdf (date accessed: 3 December 2010).

[41] Ibid.

[42] Ibid.

EP resolution, the PCC underlined the "importance of the involvement of representatives of Nagorno-Karabakh in the negotiations".[43]

In 2010, the European Parliament referred to the Nagorno-Karabakh issue in its last report on the South Caucasus – the resolution on the "Need for EU strategy on the South Caucasus" – adopted on 20 of May.

In general, the EP welcomed the pace of the negotiations on the Nagorno-Karabakh conflict, illustrated by the six meetings between the presidents of Armenia and Azerbaijan held over the course of 2009, and it fully supported the mediation efforts of the OSCE Minsk Group and the Basic Principles of the suggested settlement contained in the Madrid Document. Once again, the EP condemned "the idea of a military solution and the heavy consequences of military force already used" and called on "both parties to avoid any further breaches of the 1994 ceasefire".[44]

For the first time, the resolution stressed that "security for all is an indispensable element of any settlement" – a particularly sensible requirement for the population of Nagorno-Karabakh.[45]

The EP called on the Commission "to explore the possibility of providing humanitarian aid and assistance to the population in the Nagorno-Karabakh region as well as to the IDPs and refugees who fled the region" and asked the Commission and EUSR Semneby to "consider extending to Nagorno-Karabakh aid and information dissemination programmes as in Abkhazia and Ossetia".[46]

The resolution also mentioned the NK conflict in the context of relations with Turkey and stressed that the Armenia–Turkey rapprochement and the OSCE Minsk Group negotiations were separate processes that should move forward along their own rationales.

However, the resolution provoked controversial reactions in Brussels, but also in Yerevan and Baku. The Azerbaijani side, generally satisfied with the report, was not very happy that the resolution did not explicitly mention the support for the territorial integrity of Azerbaijan in the context of the NK conflict, as was the case with Georgia in the same document. In Armenia the report was received with much criticism because of the wording of paragraph 8, which called for "withdrawal of Armenian forces from the occupied territories of Azerbaijan" in the context of allowing the IDPs to return to their homes under the condition of providing international peacekeeping and security guarantees for the population of NK. Armenia's

---

[43] Ibid.

[44] EP – Resolution on the need for an EU strategy for the South Caucasus, Strasbourg, 20 May 2010, A7–0123/2010, http://www.europarl.europa.eu/sides/getDoc.do?pubRef=-//EP//TEXT+TA+P7-TA-2010–0193+0+DOC+XML+V0//EN (date accessed: 3 December 2010).

[45] Ibid.

[46] Ibid.

reaction was based on the argument that only some of the Basic Principles of the Nagorno-Karabakh conflict's settlement, being discussed in the frame of the OSCE Minsk Group, were mentioned, yet the most sensitive of them – the issue of the future status of Nagorno-Karabakh – was omitted.

As it is the case with other non-recognised entities, the EU generally reacted to the conduct of parliamentary and presidential elections in Nagorno-Karabakh by issuing statements on behalf of the EU presidency or High Representative for Foreign and Security Policy. The last statement was made by High Representative Catherine Ashton in reference to the elections in Nagorno-Karabakh on 23 May 2010. The statement reads: "I would like to recall that the European Union does not recognise the constitutional and legal framework within which the 'parliamentary elections' in Nagorno-Karabakh will be held this Sunday. This event should not prejudice the peaceful settlement of the Nagorno-Karabakh conflict. I reiterate our firm support to the OSCE Minsk Group, and the work of the three Co-chairs and their efforts towards a settlement of the conflict, and call on the parties to redouble their efforts to find a negotiated solution to the conflict. I recall the EU's readiness to offer further support to this end".[47]

It is remarkable that the language of the statements on Nagorno-Karabakh differ from the similar statements in case of *Transnistria*, Abkhazia or South Ossetia. Thus, the EU presidency made the following declaration regarding the presidential elections in Abkhazia in 2009: "The European Union has taken note of the 'presidential elections' held in the Georgian territory of Abkhazia on 12 December. The EU does not recognise the legal and constitutional frames in which the elections were held. EU continues the policy of upholding of territorial integrity of Georgia recognised by international law norms".[48]

In the same year another statement was issued by the presidency on South Ossetia: "The EU is aware that 'parliamentary elections' took place in the South Ossetian region of Georgia on 31 May 2009. The EU does not accept the legality of the 'elections', nor its results. The holding of such elections is illegitimate and represents a setback in the search for a peaceful and lasting settlement of the situation in Georgia. The EU reiterates its firm support for sovereignty and territorial integrity of Georgia within its internationally recognised borders".[49]

[47] Statement by High Representative Catherine Ashton on Nagorno-Karabakh, A 84/10, Brussels, 21 May 2010, http://www.consilium.europa.eu/uedocs/cmsUpload/114603.pdf (date accessed: 3 December 2010).

[48] Statement by the Presidency on behalf of the European Union at the OSCE Permanent Council on "presidential elections" in Abkhazia, Georgia, 12 December 2009, Vienna, 17 December 2009, http://www.se2009.eu/fr/reunions_actualites/2009/12/18/eu_statement_in_the_osce_on_presidential_elections_in_abkhazia_georgia_12_december_2009.html (date accessed: 3 December 2010).

[49] Delegation of the European Union to Georgia, Political and economic relations, http://eeas.europa.eu/delegations/georgia/eu_georgia/political_relations/index_en.htm (date accessed: 3 December 2010).

It is understandable that the EU avoids mentioning territorial integrity in the context of Nagorno-Karabakh so as not to contravene the road map for peaceful settlement of the NK conflict, based upon the Helsinki principles of non-use of force or the threat of force, territorial integrity, and the equal rights and self-determination of peoples. This approach is also in line with the position of the Minsk Group Co-Chairs, expressed in the Joint Statement by the Heads of Delegation of the Minsk Group Co-Chair countries (17 July 2010, Almaty): "These proposed elements have been conceived as an integrated whole, and any attempt to select some elements over others would make it impossible to achieve a balanced solution".[50]

The EU position was outlined for the last time in 2010 by the President of the European Council, Herman Van Rompuy, during the OSCE summit in Astana (1 December). While referring to the post-Soviet protracted conflicts, he mentioned the case of the NK as an example of the EU engagement in the effort to ensure long-lasting and peaceful solutions to these disputes: "We have re-emphasised the principles of peaceful settlement proposed by the Minsk Group as the best option to reach an agreement on Nagorno-Karabakh".[51]

Conclusion

The EU currently has no direct role in the Nagorno-Karabakh peace talks under the OSCE Minsk Group auspices but its stronger involvement is expected. Despite the European Parliament's traditional approach, largely reflected in the number of relevant resolutions condemning the isolation of Nagorno-Karabakh, NK remains the only case where the EU engagement is not visible. The EUSR Semneby was unable to visit the region, and there is no significant EC program aimed at assisting the population of Nagorno-Karabakh. One has to acknowledge that the EU-led initiatives for breaking the isolation of the populations of non-recognised territories would greatly contribute to an improved and safer regional environment in the South Caucasus.

First of all, as a privileged and trusted partner of both Armenia and Azerbaijan, and especially using the framework of the Association Agreement negotiations and the EaP, the EU could use its bilateral relations with each of them to contribute even more towards ensuring that the projects of reform, state-building and consolidation of the rule of law remain active. These will greatly contribute to a more secure regional environment and become an impetus to conflict settlement.

---

[50] Joint Statement by the Heads of Delegation of the Minsk Group Co-Chair countries, OSCE – Press Release, 17 July 2010, http://www.osce.org/press/72085 (date accessed: 4 December 2010).

[51] Remarks by Herman Van Rompuy at the OSCE Summit, Astana, 1 December 2010, PCE 288/10, http://www.consilium.europa.eu/uedocs/cms_Data/docs/pressdata/en/ec/118111.pdf (date accessed: 2 December 2010).

Secondly, the EU is the player best suited to support confidence-building measures in the region. Given the intensification of negotiations, the need has especially increased to support efforts to prepare the societies for a peaceful settlement and to dissolve negative imagery of the "enemy" side created over the years. The European Commission has already started some actions to this end. During the first half of 2010, a consortium of well-known EU-based NGOs presented a comprehensive package of confidence-building measures aimed at supporting efforts to create a positive environment in the context of the Nagorno-Karabakh conflict, preparing communities for a future peace settlement. The programme is funded under the Instrument for Stability (almost €2 million) and will mainly focus on the following areas: media initiatives, conflict affected groups and public policy.

The EU could play a key role in supporting OSCE efforts at consolidating the ceasefire regime in NK and the prevention of a new military escalation. Azerbaijan needs to be persuaded that it stands to lose far more than it would gain from any attempt to impose a military solution on the NK dispute. A hopeful move has been recently seen in June 2010. For the first time, High Representative Catherine Ashton made a statement on Nagorno-Karabakh, condemning a violent breach of the ceasefire on the northern border of Nagorno-Karabakh: "The High Representative regrets the armed incident resulting in the loss of human life that took place during the night between 18–19 June along the Line of Contact in the context of the Nagorno-Karabakh conflict. The High Representative calls on both sides to respect the ceasefire, restrain from the use of force or any threat thereof, and continue efforts for the peaceful resolution of the Nagorno-Karabakh conflict. The EU reiterates its full support to the efforts of the OSCE Minsk Group and the work of the three co-chairs".[52] To follow up the statement, EUSR Semneby was dispatched to the region in September to prevent any further escalation and also to ensure that the EU position, which rejects any attempt to use a military solution, is well-understood.

Finally, the EU is currently much better equipped to initiate and support regional cooperation in the South Caucasus. It is widely recognised that the EU has an important role to play in contributing to the culture of dialogue and understanding in the region. The multilateral track of the Eastern Partnership could be one of the best-suited mechanisms to achieve this aim.

---

[52] Statement by the spokesperson of High Representative Catherine Ashton on Nagorno-Karabakh, Brussels, 22 June 2010, A 110/10, http://www.consilium.europa.eu/uedocs/cms_data/docs/pressdata/EN/foraff/115451.pdf (date accessed: 4 December 2010).

Part III

Europe's Next Avoidable War:
The Peace Rationale

15

Conflict and Security in Nagorno-Karabakh: What Contribution from the EU?

Peter Semneby

It is clear that the European Union is now more intensively engaged in the South Caucasus than ever before. With the launch of the Eastern Partnership in May 2009 and the launch of the negotiations on the Association Agreements with the three countries, Georgia, Azerbaijan and Armenia of the South Caucasus, the EU has further signalled an increased level of ambition in this region. The Eastern Partnership is based on recognition of the level of interdependence between what we refer to as the "Eastern neighbours" and the EU, following the latest round of EU enlargement in 2005, as well as the importance of the region as a link to Asia and the Middle East.

Given recent history, none of us could have failed to notice that events in the Southern Caucasus directly affect the European Union. However, this new closeness is not just about geographical proximity – it is also one of values. In the past few years, we have seen an increasing convergence of values shared by the EU and the countries of our Eastern Neighbourhood.

The continued need to diversify energy resources and supply routes has also enhanced the interest and involvement of the European Union in the South Caucasus region. This only increases the interest of the EU in the region's stability and security, including addressing unresolved conflicts.

The EU maintains a fundamental interest in good, neighbourly relations and close cooperation between the countries in the region. Improving intra-regional relations generates mutual confidence and paves the way for sustainable progress in the region.

For its part, the EU stands ready – now more than ever – to provide assistance where it is needed in order to consolidate democratic institutions, good governance and respect for the rule of law. The Eastern Partnership is the EU's political answer to the challenges faced in the region today and a direct answer to the brutal war in Georgia in August 2008. Through this new partnership, and in recognition of the new situation faced in the region today, the EU is substantially upgrading its contractual relationship with each partner. However, we do so while recognising that our eastern partners do not have identical objectives in their relationship with the EU, but all of them, to varying degrees, are carrying out political, social and economic reforms.

In summary, the Eastern Partnership is at the core of the challenges faced in the region. A new security crisis in our Eastern Neighbourhood would have serious implications for our neighbours and also for the EU.

Nagorno-Karabakh is one of the least known and most dangerous of the conflicts in Europe's neighbourhood. A self-regulating ceasefire between deeply hostile parties poses serious danger for a volatile and strategically important region. With a growing role for the EU in the region as a whole, it is also justifiable to expect that the EU should pay greater attention to the conflict.

Broadly speaking, the EU – through the Eastern Partnership – believes that a contribution can be made to improving security in the region by effectively bringing our eastern partners closer to the EU. As with the European Neighbourhood Policy, the Eastern Partnership aims to contribute to stability and security on the EU's borders while enhancing good neighbourly relations and effective cooperation among partners. The Eastern Partnership will also seek to promote confidence in the region by increasing political contacts between partners (including among administrations, members of parliaments, NGOs and citizens) as well as by reducing trade barriers.

We foresee more cooperation on specific issues within the EU's Common Foreign Security Policy and European Security Defence Policy. Security-related early-warning systems will be enhanced, with particular focus on conflict areas. Closer cooperation on arms-export practices and non-proliferation is also envisaged.

The need for more stability in the South Caucasus

It is clear that the unresolved conflicts in the South Caucasus are the most important obstacles to the region's stability, security and prosperity. The current status quo, with the ongoing conflicts in the region, is unacceptable and unsustainable since it bears the constant risk of an escalation of tensions and a resumption of armed hostilities. The region, already so badly scarred by conflict, hardly needs a return to the tragic situation witnessed in the early 1990s.

In this regard, we continue to urge all sides to actively engage to achieve stability and peace. The war in Georgia clearly demonstrated that unresolved conflicts have the potential to negatively affect the EU's own security through their impact on energy supplies and trade routes. The protracted conflicts also undermine our efforts to promote political reform and economic development in the Eastern Neighbourhood. Furthermore, closed borders between Armenia and Azerbaijan, Armenia and Turkey severely hamper the full potential of the region, as does the absence of full-fledged relations between Russia and Georgia. The Georgian war demonstrated that "frozen" – unresolved – conflicts carry the danger of escalation and violence. The stalemate around Nagorno-Karabakh is also a precarious one, where 15 years of an uneasy ceasefire may have led both parties and their partners to complacency. If there was any lesson from the Georgia war, however, it was that frozen does not mean safe.

* * *

Regarding Nagorno-Karabakh, the EU's increased engagement in the region suggests that the Union could play a much more assertive role. Though formally not part of the Minsk Group, the EU can still make an important contribution to the resolution of this protracted conflict. The EU stands ready to step up its engagement in the settlement process, within the framework of supporting the work of the Minsk Group.

It is clear to most observers that serious efforts are still needed to pave the way for a lasting peace for Nagorno-Karabakh. In my contacts with the leadership in Armenia and Azerbaijan, I continually stress the need to avoid provocative statements and to work towards a settlement, to have the courage to make the difficult decisions needed, and to begin to prepare the ground to ensure that the public understands the benefits of a comprehensive settlement, and to gradually establish trust. Given that trust-building is a long process, security is an indispensable element of any settlement. Ultimately this will involve peacekeeping arrangements in line with international human rights standards that involve both military and civilian aspects.

Efforts to find a settlement for the conflict has seen some positive movement of late. Let us recall that in July 2009 the three Presidents, Obama, Medvedev and Sarkozy, issued for the first time a declaration in L'Aquila, setting out the main elements of the Basic Principles: this was significant in itself. These elements include:

- return of the territories surrounding Nagorno-Karabakh to Azerbaijani control;
- an interim status for Nagorno-Karabakh providing guarantees for security and self-governance;
- a corridor linking Armenia to Nagorno-Karabakh;
- future determination of the final legal status of Nagorno-Karabakh through a legally binding expression of will;
- the right of all internally displaced persons and refugees to return to their former places of residence; and
- international security guarantees which would include a peacekeeping operation.

But the peace process is also being constantly threatened by many factors outside the scope of the negotiators. Domestic political factors have led to changing attitudes to the Basic Principles, as have extended factors, such as the Turkish–Armenian normalisation process. It is important that efforts are made to ensure that these factors do not lead to a loss of momentum in the negotiations. Greater international attention to Nagorno-Karabakh may be necessary to ensure this.

There is a clear need to support efforts to prepare the societies for a peaceful settlement; in this regard, the EU has committed funding to civil society projects supporting people-to-people contacts, media development, and public awareness in Armenia and Azerbaijan, including Nagorno-Karabakh. These projects build on the EU's vast experience of peace-building in many other parts of the world. It is clear that the EU is in a unique position to make a contribution.

But there still remains a particular need to work with the populations of the two countries. We see a disconnect today between the highest levels – those conducting the negotiations, and the two populations still very much entrenched in their positions, relying on old stereotypes of the enemy. Without a shift in perspectives in these societies, it will be exceedingly difficult for the respective leaders to sell an eventual peace deal to their respective electorates. And the more time that passes, the more difficult it will become.

16

Nagorno-Karabakh Conflict: The Golden Apple of Discord or a Toy That Two Have Failed to Share

Geysar Gurbanov

History repeats itself. And many ancient legends find their reflections in real life. One of these stories that explains the complicated nature of the Nagorno-Karabakh conflict is the ancient Greek myth about the Golden Apple of Discord that led to the Trojan War. According to the legend, "Zeus had a banquet in celebration of the marriage of Peleus and Thetis; left off the guest list was Eris, the goddess of discord, and upon turning up uninvited, she threw a golden apple into the ceremony, with an inscription that reads, 'to the fairest'".

With some differences though, the recent history of Nagorno-Karabakh, a small enclave between two countries, resembles the same myth. When by the late 1980s the collapse of the Soviet Union was increasingly on the agenda of certain interest groups in Moscow, the wise of the Politburo did their best to save the dying empire and create crowbars that would preserve their political control over Soviet territories even after the collapse.

Divide et impera, the political conquest method, was applied all along the Soviet borders. For Armenia and Azerbaijan, the Nagorno-Karabakh became the *golden apple* thrown by Moscow to provoke ethnic discord that could slow down the collapse and underline once again the supremacy, omnipresence and almightiness of the *centre*. The conflict assured the political vulnerability of both states and, hence, allowed Russia to keep its political influence as a key facilitator between the two. As a result, two nations that failed to learn from the past engaged in a brutal and bloody conflict over who was "the fairest" to claim ownership over the apple, a piece of land that witnessed a lot of tears, casualties and shattered destinies.

While the conflict was triggered in Moscow, it was further fuelled by political and ideological leaders in Baku and Yerevan seeking inspiration in separatism and nationalism. Both Zori Balayan (Armenian) and Ziya Bunyatov (Azerbaijani), who claimed historical ownership over the Nagorno-Karabakh territories, each in favour of his own nation, failed to explain what to do

179

with people whom each government did not want in those territories. In this ideological collision, ethnic cleansing became the ultimate solution.

If the conflict itself resembles the story of the golden apple, after two decades of non-resolution the behaviour of Armenian and Azerbaijani sides recall a struggle over a toy that two have failed to share. While children usually tend to fight over a toy, in world affairs adults leading various groups – states, nations, elites, corporations – fight for power, income, lands and resources.

In fact, there is a strong psychological rationale behind the Nagorno-Karabakh conflict. Even over time, core human behavioural patterns do not change, but rather evolve to find their new reflections in different dimensions. Thus, a childish fight over a toy develops from the point of infants wrestling into academic and professional discourses, national referendums and armed conflicts over who owns this or another "toy". As human behaviour matures, a toy undergoes a metamorphosis from being an object of amusement to being labelled with terms such as territory, political office and money.

And just as every other human being has his own unique psychological state of mind, nations and political regimes have their own psychologies, which define their perception of life and find their reflections in their ideologies, traditions, culture and laws. Therefore, the conflict between two kids grows into a conflict between two groups – for example, genders, nations, political parties, this list is not exhaustive.

Studying the Armenian and Azerbaijani nations, one finds that apart from a few key differences such as religion and language, both have many more things in common. The two cultures have affected each other interchangeably. The influence is so strong that if you removed the "Armenian" and "Azerbaijani" labels from the discourse, the two would easily blend.

This common historical experience shared for many centuries can be further projected onto a psychological dimension. Mutual abuse over dominance and ownership led to a syndrome called *post-traumatic stress disorder*. It does not only occur on an individual level, it also happens with various groups. In this case it happened on a national level and defined each one's future behaviour. Eventually it is a chain of reactions between two children, Azerbaijan and Armenia, which underwent the following stages:

1. Azerbaijan had a toy it was enjoying over period of time;
2. Armenia saw the toy and decided to be a part of the game and claim ownership over it (in the 1980s this process was triggered by Moscow as described above);
3. Armenia went to take the toy from Azerbaijan and started playing with it.

Those who know the story are aware that throughout history players in this game exchanged their roles many times, leading to a situation when it became very easy to lose track of the scenarios and speculate on who started the fight first, that is, who was the owner and who was the envious one.

The Armenian side has its own well-documented and evidenced story that proves Azerbaijan being wrong, and the Azerbaijani side also has its own counter arguments supported with numerous historical facts that, at the same time, prove the Armenian story to be wrong. Usually discussions between the two on this topic can take an incalculable amount of time until another conflict breaks out. And anyone who offers a 50/50 formula, an impartial or balanced approach towards the story, is accused of bias and of taking sides.

In reality, it is a "chicken-and-egg" story when academic, ideological and political minds fight over the "truth", occasionally speculating, manipulating and taking advantage of it, while simple people who see both products on a market shelve do not care about this question as much as about the product's price and quality, which, in other words, are the peace and stability that both the Armenian and Azerbaijani nations want to have.

Armenia and Azerbaijan currently go through stage four of this process with the following possible scenarios:

1. The child Azerbaijan takes the toy back from child Armenia, that is, the parties engage in another brutal and devastating war. This option will likely lead towards the situation when elders, either in collective form – for example, OSCE, NATO, the UN – or, more dangerously as individual actors – for example, Russia, the United States, Iran or Turkey, who might show up to set these children apart and teach them at a very high cost some lessons on how to behave. This development scenario can potentially destabilise the entire region between the Black Sea and the Caspian Sea with unpredictable and irreversible consequences for global security and more far-reaching and devastating results than the 2008 Georgian war in the South Caucasus. Considering current militarisation trends, deadlocks in the negotiation process, a deteriorating state of democracy in both countries, the growing foreign ambitions of Azerbaijan and the impaired economic situation in Armenia, this scenario raises increasing concerns;

2. Both children, Armenia and Azerbaijan, realise their inability to settle the conflict on their own and call for the parents to decide who is wrong and who is right. Currently, this role is carried out by the OSCE Minsk Group. For a variety of reasons (some are described below) the Minsk Group failed to take substantial steps to achieve progress in the Nagorno-Karabakh negotiation process. Therefore, this parental role is then mistakenly shifted towards Russia, which plays a rather destructive role. But if this scenario should ever succeed, Armenia and Azerbaijan will be under permanent international supervision, and the parents will be supervising the ownership over the "toy";

3. The two children keep complaining to the parents about the situation and blaming them in double standards and bias while enjoying all the corrupted benefits of the status quo and delegating the responsibility to regional players. Unfortunately, regimes in Baku and Yerevan feel more comfortable with this scenario, which confirms their existing views and shifts the blame away towards a third party. The status quo allows leaders on both sides to draw attention away as much as possible from domestic problems, for example, omnipresent corruption, human rights abuses, democracy setbacks and a chronic lack of transparency.

4. The two children mature after twenty years of conflict and find a win-win solution that helps establish a power-sharing ownership over the toy. They understand that playing together might be much more fun and have more benefits. With the existing political regimes, this scenario is unlikely ever to occur because it requires much stronger transparency and democracy. To achieve this goal, current leaders in Baku and Yerevan have to be literally removed from the negotiation process and replaced with alternative political players, such as emerging oppositional youth groups that are more sympathetic towards each other than to their governments. This assumes that semi-authoritarian regimes in both countries have to leave the political scene. The cost of this peace will be very high, as it is hard to imagine both political elites giving up their powers in a non-violent manner;

5. The two children find another toy, that is, they identify another common idea or goal which will automatically exclude the Nagorno-Karabakh conflict from the political agenda and foster mutual trust and a peaceful coexistence in the South Caucasus. And, again, presumably with current political leaders both in power and in the classical opposition, this scenario is unlikely to occur.

The most important thing to realise is that it will not be up to the political regimes in Baku and Yerevan to decide positively on the future of the Nagorno-Karabakh conflict. Two decades have demonstrated that both tend to take advantage of the status quo to preserve their political power and wealth. Without any doubts, leaders in Armenia and Azerbaijan go for option 3, pretending to be loyal to option 2, and threatening with option 1.

It is not by chance that the conflict parties are referred to as "regimes". In both countries, with political power concentrated in the hands of corrupted elites, the term "nation" has little decisive power over the conflict. Unfortunately, the two nations fall under the influence of their state propaganda machines; they fail to participate in peace building and the negotiation process, and they rather believe that war is the best solution for this conflict.

Regretfully, both nations victimise themselves and see no light at the end of the tunnel. They blame political realities and historical circumstances. And, as in psychology, they tend to identify themselves as a product of their environments. But this deadlock is nothing but myth, as psychologists have discovered that thinking habits can be changed on both individual and group levels. Eventually, it becomes possible to choose how they think and how they perceive reality.

In the twenty-first century, when communication barriers between nations are lifted with the introduction of Internet-based social media tools, it is possible, as never before, to connect all the dots in the Nagorno-Karabakh conflict, to overcome mutual hatred, break through the state propaganda and agree upon the future.

While a corrupted environment of *realpolitik* has a strong influence, at the end it is the two nations that have the power of choosing to stand against their leaders and to demand peace. It will be up to the Armenian and Azerbaijani youth to utilise all available resources and suppress all traumatic memories to enforce either option 4 or 5.

Meanwhile, the Western allies of Armenia and Azerbaijan should slowly but effectively switch their attention and resources towards interest groups in the South Caucasus region that strive towards regional integration, democratic reforms and peaceful coexistence. An integrated and democratic South Caucasus will help avoid any regional military conflict that can carry security threats to the West. To achieve this goal and avoid a potential war between the two countries the following steps have to be taken:

1. Cross-regional and bipartisan projects should be established and promoted on public diplomacy, nongovernmental and professional levels;
2. Youth organisations and political movements which promote peace between the two countries and strive for regional integration should be funded and supported;
3. A new political ideology beyond Armenian and Azerbaijani nationalism should be created and propagated;
4. Stronger pressures should be applied on both the Armenian and Azerbaijani governments to allow greater freedom for political and social activism;
5. The inability of Armenian and Azerbaijani leaders to resolve the Nagorno-Karabakh problem should be exposed and criticised publicly;
6. The OSCE Minsk Group should take a more active role in the negotiation process and prevent Russia from taking a lead in conflict resolution;
7. Peacemaking through information, that is, greater access to Internet-based social media tools, should be provided and encouraged;
8. Peacemaking through personal involvement, that is people-to-people diplomacy, should be propagated through all available resources;

9. Research, training and educational projects and programs which defend the aforementioned positions should be launched and sponsored.

Peace in Nagorno-Karabakh goes hand in hand with democratic development in the South Caucasus. It is time for decision makers in Europe and the United States to realise that, currently, the two governments are interested in the status quo of the ongoing conflict and no positive change is likely to happen. It is time to initiate, and invest in, the creation of a new and more responsible political elite, headed by young political leaders in both countries, who will have stronger incentives to solve the conflict and bring about positive political change. A timely solution of the Nagorno-Karabakh conflict will foster the integration of Armenia and Azerbaijan into European political, security and economic structures, and will allow the West to expand its influence further in the South Caucasus and have a better and safer access to the energy resources of the Caspian Sea.

17
The EU's Commitment in Nagorno-Karabakh and the Required Steps Ahead

Charles Tannock

Introduction

The main policy question this chapter aims to answer is the following: since the conflict in and surrounding Nagorno-Karabakh is clearly an increasing security threat to the European Union (EU), what are the appropriate responses of the EU and its Member States to prevent and deter military escalation and a renewed outbreak of hostilities in the region and ultimately to resolve the conflict?

This chapter provides a brief description of the root causes of the conflict in Nagorno-Karabakh, its transformation from a political to a military confrontation in the last days of the Soviet Union and the current situation on the ground. The opinions are entirely personal to the author and do not necessarily reflect the views of his political party, European parliamentary group or the current Conservative-led UK coalition government.

This chapter also aims to analyse threats to the EU stemming from the fragile security environment in the South Caucasus, with a focus on Nagorno-Karabakh. It describes current and past EU involvement in the South Caucasus and proposes a set of possible policy options to be considered by the Union in its potential role in resolving the Nagorno-Karabakh conflict and helping to stabilise the region.

In light of the new mechanisms and tools for conflict resolution provided by the new Lisbon treaty, the policy options considered in this chapter concern three sets of instruments: declaratory politics and preventive diplomacy; wider socialisation through supporting civil society in the framework of the European Neighbourhood Policy (ENP) and its financial instrument, the European Neighbourhood and Partnership Instrument (ENPI); and the possible eventual deployment of Common Security and Defence Policy (CSDP) instruments. In other words, this chapter proposes an option to transform the current rather passive engagement of the EU in the South

Caucasus into a more proactive, effective and sustainable stance focused on conflict resolution.

The locus of the South Caucasus in the EU's security architecture

It is crucial that the South Caucasus is given serious consideration when examining armed conflict in Europe's greater neighbourhood. The EU enlargements of 2004 and 2007 extended the Union's borders further east and geographically closer to the South Caucasus. Since 2006 the three countries of the South Caucasus – Georgia, Armenia and Azerbaijan – have been formally designated by the EU as part of the "eastern dimension" of the ENP. Since that time these countries have also benefited from resources made available under the accompanying European Neighbourhood and Partnership Financial Instrument; and, more recently, under a Swedish/ Polish 2008 EU Council initiative, they have been branded as part of the six-country "Eastern Partnership", which formally embraces Ukraine, Moldova, Belarus, Georgia, Armenia, and Azerbaijan.

The "vulnerability" of the South Caucus region was clearly exposed during the August 2008 Georgian conflict, and illustrated how "the EU's security begins outside our borders".[1] However, aside from the Russia–Georgia war, this area is largely identified by its "frozen conflicts". It is not only European sources which refer to the region as being volatile; the US intelligence community also notes that any attempts at estimation of the duration of the ceasefire in Nagorno-Karabakh remain problematic.[2]

Despite numerous declarations by the European Council, which brings together the governments of the 27 Member States of the EU, the Union has done little proactively to promote conflict resolution in the South Caucasus, and particularly in Nagorno-Karabakh. Although frequently referred to as a "frozen conflict" given the difficulties in the negotiating process, Nagorno-Karabakh has conflict dynamics that are constantly shifting, according to expert analysts.[3] The risk of conflict escalation in the region thus remains high. As the 2008 war in Georgia showed, the costs to the EU of prolonged diplomatic inactivity can be tremendous in terms of both human suffering and lasting economic impact. The gravity of this situation poses difficult

---

[1] European Commission: The EU and Eastern Partnership, http://ec.europa.eu/ external_relations/eastern/index_en.html.

[2] Annual Threat Assessment of the US Intelligence Community for the Senate Select Committee on Intelligence, 2 February 2010, 37–9, http://www.dni.gov/testimonies/20100202_testimony.pdf.

[3] E.J. Stewart (2008) *The EU as an Actor in Conflict Resolution: Out of its Depth?* (University of Bath, United Kingdom), p. 3, http://www.research.plymouth.ac.uk/ pisc/PIP/ConflictResolution.pdf (date accessed: 17 May 2010).

strategic questions for the EU. Can the various instruments at its disposal be used successfully to meet the EU's principles of effective multilateralism, conflict prevention and comprehensive engagement? Is the EU able to single-handedly manage conflicts in neighbouring regions without the long-term carrot of EU membership as its incentive?

In light of the conflicts in Georgia and that between Azerbaijan and Armenia over the independence of the breakaway region of Nagorno-Karabakh, it is reasonable to believe that armed conflict could easily return to the South Caucasus region. Within this framework of a potential for renewed hostilities, one should also consider the current stalemate in the Armenia–Turkey rapprochement. The reason for this disappointing renewed recent impasse after so much initial positive publicity about the improved relations between Armenia and Turkey is the latter's insistence on two key preconditions, added after the signature of the protocols for the ratification in Ankara by the Turkish parliament of the protocols on the establishment of diplomatic relations between both countries: the withdrawal of Armenian forces from Nagorno-Karabakh and the demand to end the international campaign for the recognition of the Armenian Genocide. These preconditions are unacceptable to Armenia. The suspension of the Armenia–Turkey protocols will do nothing to reduce the volatility of this long-standing conflict in the South Caucasus, and has now placed Nagorno-Karabakh again at the heart of the dispute. Therefore Armenia–Turkey rapprochement is unlikely to resume until a solution is found to Armenia's conflict with Azerbaijan (Turkey's ethnically close ally and energy trading partner) over the Nagorno-Karabakh region.

The Nagorno-Karabakh conflict – war and stalemate

Nagorno-Karabakh is located on territory claimed by Azerbaijan and, since the early 1990s, has been a self-governing autonomous territory, albeit one not recognised by the international community as a sovereign state. After the collapse of the Soviet Union, Armenians living in Nagorno-Karabakh voted by a large majority in a referendum in favour of independence. The subsequent declaration of independence was followed by war between Azerbaijan and Nagorno-Karabakh. During this war, which lasted from 1988 to 1994, Armenia unsurprisingly sided with Nagorno-Karabakh, an overwhelming majority of whose population has always been Armenian. There have been numerous peace negotiations to determine the status of the region since a ceasefire was agreed in 1994, but recurring tension and periodic outbreaks of violence have still been witnessed during this time.

The roots of the conflict are primarily to be found in ethnic tensions within the region. Numerous refugees and internally displaced persons resulting from the war still shape today's conflict dynamics. Thirty-five thousand people have tragically died as a result of the conflict. Azerbaijan and Armenia both claim they have the right to use force to resolve the conflict: Azerbaijan to restore its territorial integrity, Armenia to protect Nagorno-Karabakh's Armenian population.[4]

Currently, especially in the context of the suspended protocols between Armenia and Turkey, one can observe a rise in bellicose rhetoric between Armenia and Azerbaijan. Furthermore, in recent years military spending has risen dramatically in Azerbaijan, whose coffers are swelled by petrodollars from the country's large oil and gas fields in the Caspian Sea. In the past few years, Azerbaijan has spent four times as much as Armenia on weapons, and Azerbaijani commanders are increasingly confident in their military superiority and that they would emerge victorious in a putative war.

However, Armenia's defence spending has itself doubled in the same period and the country is also taking steps to enhance its security. Recently the government in Yerevan agreed to extend the length of the lease of Russia's military base in Gyumri (Armenia's second largest city, near the border with Turkey), from 25 to 49 years, expiring in 2044. Russia, traditionally the guarantor of Armenia's security, further agreed that the base's remit would be extended specifically to protect Armenia's security, rather than just to manage Russia's military interests in the region. The Kremlin also agreed to upgrade Armenia's ageing arsenal with modern Russian weapons, in particular MiG-29 fighters and the latest S-300 anti-aircraft missiles – a move undoubtedly intended to galvanise bilateral ties and dissuade Azerbaijan from launching any pre-emptive military action against Armenia. Certainly if the two countries go to war, intervention by Russian forces in favour of Armenia could tip the balance decisively in Armenia's favour, though to what extent Turkey would directly come to the military aid of its ally Azerbaijan is unclear.

It is widely accepted that the "frozen conflict" in Nagorno-Karabakh remains one of the main obstacles for the peaceful economic development of the region. There are, however, legitimate questions about how frozen the conflict really is. Ceasefire violations are now common, with more than ten violations reported on average every day in 2009, three times as many as in 2007. Soldiers on both sides were killed in the spring/summer of 2010. The possible internationalisation of the conflict, with Russia, the United States and the European Union becoming increasingly engaged in the South Caucasus, only adds to the importance of an urgent settlement of this regional conflict. Neighbouring countries, such as Turkey and Iran, also take a major interest in the issue. Iran rather curiously sides with Christian-majority Armenia instead of with Muslim-majority Azerbaijan, as there are

[4] International Crisis Group (ICG) (2005) "Nagorno-Karabakh: A Plan for Peace", *Europe Report No. 167*, p. 6, http://www.crisisgroup.org/~/media/Files/europe/167_nagorno_karabakh_a_plan_for_peace.ashx (date accessed: 17 May 2010).

large Azeri minorities in Iran and Azerbaijani nationalists periodically make irredentist calls for a greater Azerbaijan, a desire that would potentially undermine the territorial integrity of the Islamic Republic of Iran. The European Security Strategy (ESS) notes that regional conflict areas are likely to involve "extremism, terrorism, state failure and organized crime".[5] Moreover, the South Caucasus is "strategically important in oil and gas production and transit",[6] which is of major concern to the EU. It is clear, therefore, that both EU interests and security are threatened by the conflict in the South Caucasus. The increasing significance of the South Caucasus region for the EU is also emphasised in the "Report on the Implementation of the European Security Strategy".[7] This report clearly points to the importance of the South Caucasus and its "frozen conflicts", but also notes the region's potential impact on other issues, such as the EU's external energy security policy.

Why involve the European Union?

Given the ongoing volatility and risk of conflict in the South Caucasus, it is important to understand why the EU has a responsibility to become actively involved in this neighbouring region. As noted above, due its geographical proximity and the region's significance for EU energy supply (oil and gas from the Caspian fields), the conflict poses a serious security threat to the EU. One of the EU's stated goals is to establish a secure, stable and prosperous ring of "well-governed states" in its neighbourhood. In light of the various hostile relationships in the region (Russia–Georgia, Armenia–Azerbaijan, Turkey–Armenia, Iran–Azerbaijan), it is therefore in the EU's interests to respond effectively and speedily to this kind of threat. To this end, the EU regards its European Neighbourhood Policy as one which "will reinforce stability and security and contribute to efforts at conflict resolution".[8]

Amidst such important security considerations, it is also clear that any military conflict likely will have an immediate economic impact – through disruption of energy corridors (oil and gas pipelines) and large flows of refugees. One should also emphasise that promoting peace, democracy and the

---

[5] European Council (2003) *A Secure Europe in a Better World. European Security Strategy*, Brussels, 12 December 2003, p. 5.

[6] E.J. Stewart (2008) op. cit., p. 3, http://www.research.plymouth.ac.uk/pisc/PIP/ConflictResolution.pdf (date accessed: 17 May 2010).

[7] Ibid. p. 6.

[8] Commission of the European Communities (2004) "European Neighbourhood Policy", *Strategy Paper*, Brussels, 12 May 2004, COM (2004) 373 final, 9, http://ec.europa.eu/world/enp/pdf/strategy/strategy_paper_en.pdf (date accessed: 18 May 2010).

rule of law are the EU's key values and therefore, irrespective of important security implications, are important in their own right.

Furthermore, to become a global player, the EU must demonstrate its capability to respond to conflicts in its own backyard and prove that it has learnt its lesson from the conflicts in the Balkans in the 1990s. By managing the current volatile situation in the South Caucasus through applying an effective multilateralism[9] with the US and Russia, the two other major players in the region, the EU could regain foreign policy credibility in the wider international community. Another important point is the presence in certain Member States (e.g., France, Germany, the Netherlands, Poland) of large diaspora populations of both Turkish and Armenian descent who, not unnaturally, wish for more economic and political stability in their countries of origin, and who lobby EU elected politicians with these ends in mind.

The need to act now

Although the conflict in Nagorno-Karabakh poses a growing threat to the EU, the Union should also consider its new ability to act. The new instruments and mechanisms provided by the Lisbon treaty have created a new setting. The treaty, which is now in force and thus a legal and political reality whatever one's opinions on its merits, therefore potentially represents a new window of opportunity for the EU to engage in the South Caucasus more effectively.

Every EU player must learn its new role and explore its room for manoeuvre during the implementation of the Lisbon treaty. It is important, particularly in the Common Foreign Security Policy (CFSP), to make constructive use of the new mechanisms provided by the treaty. The new improved combined office of a High Representative of the Union for Foreign Affairs and Security Policy and Vice-President of the European Commission (HR/VP), forming a lynchpin between the Commission and the Council, offer the opportunity to conceptualise and plan EU external relations more coherently and with less inter-institutional conflict, at least in principle. Another new facilitator body provided by the Lisbon treaty is the European External Action Service (EEAS) – the EU diplomatic service supporting the HR/VP. The EEAS supplies the EU with a well-resourced tool to also implement foreign policy more coherently, or at least that is the hope of its architects and supporters.

The need for increased EU involvement in the region was articulated as long ago as 2003, when the EU stated that it should "take a stronger and more active interest in the problems of the Southern Caucasus, which will

---

[9] European Council (2003), op. cit., p. 9.

in due course also be a neighbouring region".[10] However, in 2008, the EU did little to prevent the Georgian war. In light of current developments in the region, the outbreak of fresh hostilities and the major risk of escalating military action, it is clear the EU needs to act now. By adhering to a policy of precaution and prevention, the EU should be able to fend off armed conflict with a significantly lower financial and political burden (not to mention the avoiding of terrible human suffering) than if intervening only after military escalation. In the Implementation Report of 2008, the EU declares that it aspires to be "more active, coherent and capable".[11] But if we are to measure the EU according to its own principles and goals, it should surely be more proactive and preventive instead of reactive. The entry into force of the Lisbon treaty has brought fresh challenges for the EU, and in particular for the credibility of the CFSP, because the new permanent president of the European Council (currently former Belgian Prime Minister Herman van Rompuy), High Representative (currently the UK's Baroness Ashton), and the EEAS (the major CFSP innovations of the treaty), are struggling to establish a clearly defined role due primarily to inter-institutional wrangles between the parliament, Commission and Council and the EU national capitals.

Thus, by preventing or containing a possible military escalation in the South Caucasus in a timely, effective, coherent and proactive manner, the EU could create the good news story it desperately needs. At a time when the EU's Eastern neighbours are starting to lose confidence in their partnership with the EU, it is vital to demonstrate a serious commitment to their future stability and prosperity.

Future required steps for EU policy in the South Caucasus

Regardless of its various statements of concern, to date the EU has done little with regard to conflict resolution in the South Caucasus. As noted earlier, the term "frozen conflict" is misleading in this context, as the situation is constantly changing and the risk of increasing and sustained violence is high.[12] As was clearly evident during the Georgian war, the costs of prolonged passivity can be severe.

If the EU is to move forward effectively, it must strengthen and develop all available instruments. These instruments can be divided into three categories: (a). declaratory politics and preventive diplomacy; (b) wider socialisation in the framework of the ENP/ENPI and Eastern Partnership; and (c) possible eventual deployment of various CSDP instruments.

---

[10] European Council (2003), op. cit., p. 8.
[11] Ibidem p. 2.
[12] E.J. Stewart (2008), op. cit.

Declaratory politics and preventive diplomacy

For much of the past decade the EU has engaged in introspection while the outside world has waited for the Union to turn its dreams of a leading role on the global stage into reality. With various procedural and institutional changes in progress due to the Lisbon treaty, the EU is currently experiencing a process of change and adaptation. It is, therefore, to be expected that the EU should take time to reorganise and redefine competences and responsibilities. Meanwhile, the EU should continue to play to its strengths and deploy "soft" power using its existing and new means of declaratory Council resolutions and common positions.

Part of the old instruments which remain in the EU's toolkit are Common Positions and Presidency Conclusions. Another instrument relevant to the portfolio of declaratory politics are statements by the HR/VP and now, under the Lisbon treaty, the HR/VP's new right of initiative to propose CFSP positions to the Council for acceptance. These tools provide the EU with a relatively inexpensive means of demonstrating continued commitment to the region, while also sending an important signal to all those involved in or observing the conflict.

To progress further, the EU could increase direct high-level diplomatic engagement. In the aftermath of the Russian-Georgian war in 2008, the trio of the EU presidency-in-office (then President Nicolas Sarkozy of France) the European Commission (Commission President, José Manuel Barroso) and the High Representative (then Javier Solana) demonstrated that the EU can be a strong, fair and effective negotiator when its members and institutions act in concert to speak with one voice. The situation in the South Caucasus offers an opportunity for the EU to present a new image to the world, proving that it is an effective negotiator in the region and can take care of its (new) backyard. The South Caucasus, therefore, presents a chance for the EU to manage the crisis effectively and create a successful precedent for future conflict resolution.

It is also important to increase the budget, staff and political standing of the EU Special Representative to the South Caucasus (EUSR) for the South Caucasus in order to support diplomatic efforts in the region and to bolster the EU's profile in the region. The mandate of the EUSR, Peter Semneby, a Swedish diplomat, was very broad.[13] In 2008, after the breakout of armed conflict in Georgia, the EU had to appoint an additional

---

[13] Apart from promoting regional cooperation, contributing to conflict prevention and conflict settlement, liaising with the UN and the OSCE, providing the heads of the EU Monitoring Mission in Georgia (EUMM Georgia) with political guidance, and leading the dialogue with the main external actors concerned with the region, he is mandated to develop contacts with governments, parliaments, the judiciary and civil society in the three countries of the South Caucasus (Council of the European Union

Special Representative for the crisis in Georgia and to monitor the peace agreements with Russia (currently Pierre Morel of France). This was clearly a result of overstretching of the role of the EUSR for the South Caucasus. It is now possible for the EUSR for the South Caucasus to focus more effectively on the conflict in Nagorno-Karabakh due to the overlapping appointment of the EUSR for the crisis in Georgia. Given the lessons learnt from recent events in Georgia, the EU could consider providing the EUSR for the South Caucasus with an increased budget and support staff in order for the Special Representative to be able to prevent military escalation in and around Nagorno-Karabakh. Additionally, the political standing of the EUSR should be bolstered. This could be achieved through greater participation in the ongoing negotiations. The Special Representative could be invited to participate as an official observer in the negotiations of the Organisation for Security and Cooperation in Europe (OSCE) Minsk Group, for example.[14] The political profile of the EUSR could also be reinforced by the appointment of a more prominent heavyweight political figure (e.g., a former foreign minister or prime minister). However, as of 1 March 2011, the post of EUSR for South Caucasus was abolished by the EU Council. Currently there are discussions about creation of the new EUSR post for the frozen conflicts in the Eastern Partnership countries.

The European Parliament (EP), which by agreement with the HR/VP has acquired the new right under the Lisbon treaty to hold hearings with appointed EUSRs in order to monitor their effectiveness and value for taxpayers money, should also call for such changes above in its own resolutions on the South Caucasus and also from its dedicated EP delegation to the region.

Finally, within the framework of declaratory politics and preventative diplomacy, the EU could:

• actively support multilateral negotiations led by the OSCE in the Nagorno-Karabakh conflict;
• provide confidence-building measures;
• facilitate communication between the parties involved.

Although "effective multilateralism" is one of the self-declared principles of the EU's external action, there is little evidence that multilateral frameworks such as the OSCE have made significant progress. This is particularly relevant to its Minsk Group, set up in 1992 in order to address the

---

(2010), "Council Decision 2010/109/CFSP of 22 February 2010, extending the mandate of the European Union Special Representative in South Caucasus, Brussels).

[14] S. Freizer (2006) "Responding to South Caucasus Conflicts in the European Neighborhood", *European Parliament, Committee on Foreign Affairs, Hearing on the South Caucasus*, Brussels.

Nagorno-Karabakh question, and more broadly to resolve the other stalled conflicts in the South Caucasus. The EU has the opportunity to adopt the role of an "honest broker" in the conflict mediation, since it is not involved in political power struggles, as some of the Minsk Group Co-Chairing countries are.[15] The EU is a neutral mediator likely to be accepted by both sides of the conflict and is in a good position to work on confidence-building measures, while the Minsk Group continues to handle the negotiations, supported by the new EEAS diplomatic staff of the EU delegations in Baku and Yerevan. The EU could also endeavour to facilitate communication between the various parties involved in the conflict – including the de facto Nagorno-Karabakh authorities – with the intention of to some extent integrating them into the negotiation process.[16] France has allegedly been reluctant in the EU Council of Ministers to countenance relinquishing its key role in the Minsk Group and involving the EU to a greater extent in the peace negotiations, an anomalous policy that needs to be reconsidered.

Wider socialisation in the framework of the ENP/ENPI and Eastern Partnership

While enabling increased diplomatic efforts, the EU should also consider working on mid- to longer-term socialising civil society measures.

The EU could offer via the ENPI clear incentives, especially in the field of cross-party and transnational political association, and prioritise the use of these tools to advance conflict resolution. Currently elected representatives from Armenia and Azerbaijan meet regularly through the very large Parliamentary Assemblies of the Council of Europe, Black Sea Economic Cooperation Council and OSCE but there is scope to extend this with the smaller, newly proposed EURONEST Parliamentary Assembly for the six ENP Eastern Partnership countries, (although at the time of writing this is having problems due to the non-recognition of the Belarus parliament by the European Parliament). Affiliating the conflict countries' national MPs to organised transnational political family groupings could mean that peer pressure from other parliamentarians might be conducive to less intransigent views and more meaningful solutions for peace and resolution.

The ENP was designed with the intention of creating a peaceful and prosperous circle of friends around the EU's borders. It was modelled on the enlargement process, and it aims to use financial instruments similar to the Instrument for Pre-accession (IPA), for EU candidate countries, in the form

---

[15] E.J. Stewart (2007) "EU Conflict Management in the South Caucasus: A Preliminary Analysis", British Academy, Specialist Group EthnoPolitics, Nottingham, p. 11.

[16] International Crisis Group (ICG) (2009) "Nagorno-Karabakh: Getting to a Breakthrough", *Europe Briefing No. 55*, Baku/Yerevan/Tbilisi/Brussels, p. 2.

of the ENPI. However, it does not offer the incentive of eventual EU accession and thus the power of encouraging serious reform that led to the positive socialisation process and building of a robust civil society undergone by new EU Member States and currently underway in candidate states for EU membership. No country in the South Caucasus region has been given an EU membership perspective, nor is this likely for the foreseeable future, unlike in the Western Balkans, where the countries of the region are all formally designated as "potential candidates".

Given this situation, the EU should consider other concrete and tangible positive alternative incentives for these countries of the South Caucasus. While economic partnership is gaining more substance through the negotiation of free-trade agreements, and advancements are foreseen in the field of visa facilitation and possible eventual visa liberalisation (i.e., visa-free travel to the EU), the perspective of political association in existing and new multilateral parliamentary assemblies has to be defined and linked proactively to efforts in conflict resolution. These efforts could also be channelled through stronger horizontal economic and political cooperation resulting in the desired regional integration around the EU. However, at present the South Caucasus states are resistant and regard the ENP as a means of achieving better bilateral relations with the EU rather than multilaterally with their immediate neighbours. Without these more positive approaches the ENP and its Eastern Partnership will remain ineffectual and the EU will lose both its credibility and power in the eyes of the South Caucasus countries.

In order to implement its goals and to increase its visibility in the region, the EU should consider increasing the ENPI budget. Although the budget for the eastern dimension of the ENP was supposed to be €600 million for the period 2010–13, in the document presented on 3 December 2008, only €350 million is mentioned for this period. This amount could be increased for the EU's coming budgetary period, with the European Parliament using its budgetary power to influence this goal. However, the current atmosphere of austerity and budgetary cuts is an impediment, and therefore a shift in spending of resources is the obvious solution.

The EU should ensure that full use is made of the new instruments created by the Lisbon treaty in order to increase coherence in the planning and implementation of conflict resolution in Nagorno-Karabakh. New Action Plans will be negotiated in 2011. The former Action Plans were preceded by inter-institutional power struggles between the Commission and the Council. Failures in effective inter-institutional coordination made subsequent policy implementation even more problematic. The post of the HR/VP, straddling Commission and Council, should in theory facilitate coordination in the key planning phase. The newly created crisis management department would support this process, as it is part of the EEAS and is placed under the direct responsibility and authority of the HR/VP. With the new provisions, the EU delegations (formerly Commission delegations) will also be involved in conflict prevention and crisis management, and will be able to streamline the dynamics on the ground.

ESDP/CSDP instruments

Established in 1999 following the Western Balkan conflicts, the European Security and Defence Policy (ESDP) was designed to enable the EU to become a more credible actor in promoting international peace and to guarantee peace and security in its greater neighbourhood. The EU has grown considerably since 1999 and some of the Balkan countries are now EU members or candidates. With the entry into force of the Lisbon treaty the ESDP was renamed as the Common Security and Defence Policy (CSDP). CSDP missions encompass a wide range of actions, including military peacekeeping (e.g., ATALANTA, the naval mission off the Horn of Africa), rule of law (e.g., EULEX in Kosovo) and border assistance missions (e.g., EUBAM, the EU Border Assistance Mission to Moldova and Ukraine).

Considering the recent grave developments in the field, the EU could send a civilian observation mission to Nagorno-Karabakh, with the intention of reaching a common threat assessment. This would enable the EU to speak with one voice in the EU Council of Ministers. Unfortunately, however, disputes and disagreements were generally the defining characteristics of the CSDP and its predecessor, the ESDP. The NATO (ISAF) and EU (EUPOL) engagement in Afghanistan provide good examples of how problematic the deployment and coordination of military and civilian personnel outside of the EU's borders can be – not least when different organisations are involved on the ground. However, NATO is fully cognisant that it now must work more closely with the EU. In most cases these difficulties have not been caused by a lack of capacity but rather by the lack of consensus on how to use CSDP instruments on the one hand and of the lack of agreement between the Member States over the deployment of CSDP missions to particular geographic areas on the other hand. In order to overcome these problems of internal disagreement and the subsequent multiple positions in the Council, it is important to prepare the ground for a common threat assessment by sending a civilian observation mission to Nagorno-Karabakh.

The EU could also deploy a sizeable civilian rule-of-law mission to Nagorno-Karabakh. Rule-of-law missions are among the most effective CSDP tools and provide a means through which European values of rule of law and democracy can be promoted effectively beyond EU borders. As such, they also represent a move in the right direction towards cooperation, training and interoperability of the judiciary, police and border controls between the EU and its neighbouring states.

A rule-of-law mission would be particularly useful in the context of the Nagorno-Karabakh conflict. Sending such a civilian mission could enable the EU to provide confidence in the democratic process and the rule of law, promote legal reforms through assisted training of the judiciary and help to de-escalate the conflict by facilitating the negotiation process. Moreover, EU-led rule-of-law missions have so far demonstrated how they can make a contribution to stabilisation without having a common stance on the political finality of the negotiating process.[17] In Nagorno-Karabakh it is crucial that the EU should clearly communicate from the beginning that it acts as a neutral *super partes* power and that the deployment of the mission does not predetermine the final status of the region.

Finally, the EU should consider sending a small military peacekeeping CSDP mission. If the EU Member States are able to reach unanimous agreement, it is clear that Armenia, in particular, might find the presence of a small military peacekeeping CSDP mission very reassuring in guaranteeing the final negotiated settlement over Nagorno-Karabakh. It is crucial that the EU use all the instruments at hand to show commitment to peace in its neighbourhood. The EU must play an active role, especially since in the South Caucasus its role is more disputed by other regional actors, such as Russia, the United States, Iran and Turkey than it was (or is) in the Balkans. The proactive and creative use of declaratory politics, more effective wider socialisation measures (ENPI) and the deployment of civilian and possibly even military peacekeeping CSDP missions would help the EU to show presence in the region and to promote itself as an active and reliable partner and, moreover, have direct positive implications for security within EU borders. EU military missions are always controversial because they are perceived as threatening the role of NATO, though the previous ESDP experience to date from areas such as Aceh and the Democratic Republic of Congo to the ongoing CSDP operations in Bosnia–Herzegovina give grounds for optimism. One possible CSDP option in Nagorno-Karabakh, after a peaceful outcome is negotiated, might be on a basis of a coalition of the willing known in the Lisbon treaty as "permanent structured cooperation", enabling only those EU states strongly committed to this region and its stability to participate, allowing others to stay out.

Conclusion

Resolving the post-Soviet, so-called "frozen conflicts" from Transnistria in Moldova, ranging through Abkhazia and South Ossetia in Georgia to Nagorno-Karabakh, remains a major policy challenge to the CFSP. It is clear that there is a real risk for a return to violence in the South Caucasus and, in particular, over Nagorno-Karabakh. This chapter, drawing on the author's

---

[17] S. Ghazaryan, U.E. Franke, N. Koenig, J. Münch and S. Rothenpieler (2010) "Armed Conflicts in Europe's Greater Neighbourhood" in *Towards a Safer Europe*, European Values Network, europeanvalues.net, Prague, p. 64.

firsthand experience of the region as a parliamentarian and in the workings of the EU institutions, makes some suggestions as to what can be most easily done to reduce this risk. Even though some of these measures bear additional costs, these are much lower in all likelihood than the potential financial and political burden resulting from an armed conflict in Europe's East with the loss of life, and in all probability huge flows of refugees to the West, as well as the potential to involve other regional powers with a serious risk of unintended consequences developing.

18
Building a "Consensus for Peace" in Armenia and Azerbaijan

Dennis Sammut

For two decades the Nagorno-Karabakh conflict has defined both the relations between Armenia and Azerbaijan and the political agenda within those countries. Both societies have by and large accepted the war rhetoric in their daily life. Their governments have demanded complete loyalty to their positions on the conflict, leaving little or no room for criticism on these positions. Military rhetoric, the image of the other as the enemy, and the need for patriotism are now part of the national discourse in both countries. This discourse is laced into the school curriculum and is part of the national narrative, reinforced every day by a tightly controlled media. An eerie and disturbing belief in the viability of military solutions, to either maintain the status quo (Armenia) or change it (Azerbaijan), is widespread.

This context provides the background in which, over the last fifteen years, the leaders of the two countries have tried to conduct negotiations with each other in an effort to resolve the conflict. However, the chances of success for these negotiations remain significantly reduced until the trust in military solutions, which has existed for two decades in both Armenia and Azerbaijan, is transformed into a consensus for peace.

A scar on the political landscape

The conflict in Karabakh in 1989–94 has left a mark on the political landscape of both countries, and politicians are often defined by their attitudes to the conflict.

In Armenia, those who fought in the conflict are perceived as heroes. The leaders of Karabakh, particularly the current President Serzh Sargsyan, and the former President Robert Kocharyan, are depicted as the victors. The picture of the two presidents in military fatigues talking to troops is prominently displayed on the web site of the President of Armenia and often in public places. Armenia is constantly described as having emerged from the conflict as the winner, having achieved "all" of its objectives.

Among both government and opposition politicians in Armenia, underlying the discussion on the future is the sense that anything other than the present status quo is somehow less beneficial to their country. No serious politician dare offer an alternative scenario, at least not in public.

In Azerbaijan, the situation is the other way round. Azerbaijan emerged from the conflict as a loser, and the military defeats, as well as the loss of territory and the influx of refugees and IDPs, defined the post-conflict political landscape. The parties which governed Azerbaijan immediately after its independence, following the collapse of the Soviet Union in 1991, are still tainted with the stigma of defeat. The government of Heydar Aliyev, which replaced them, is depicted as having saved the country by negotiating a ceasefire which gave Azerbaijan the chance to regroup and prepare to regain its territory, either through negotiation or, if that failed, through war. The governments of Heydar Aliyev and, since 2003, that of his son Ilham Aliyev, feel that on Karabakh they have occupied the moral high ground. However, this will change if the government is seen to be negotiating a deal on Karabakh which will not deliver on the promise of liberation. Opposition parties see any sign that the government may be ready to compromise in the negotiations on Karabakh as a sign of weakness, and an opportunity to recover the political ground that they lost when Karabakh was lost. Conscious of this, the Azerbaijani government has shown little desire to compromise, and its public statements are inevitably robust.

Government and opposition political elites in both Armenia and Azerbaijan have left themselves little room for manoeuvre and this has been one of the major obstacles to the peace process so far. Both sides have sought refuge in seemingly irreconcilable and maximalist comfort zones, usually articulated around the principles of *territorial integrity* by the Azerbaijani side, and *self determination* by the Armenian side. These approaches are, however, flawed.

For the Armenian government the limitations of the victory in Karabakh have long since become obvious. While Armenia captured territory, it has paid for it with isolation. Much of its limited resources have to be dedicated to the military budget; its dependence on Russia increases rather than decreases, and its economic vulnerability has been exposed by the Georgia–Russia war and the global economic crisis. The efforts to normalise relations with Turkey are an attempt to start addressing these problems, but only a resolution of the Karabakh conflict can address the fundamental problem.

For the Armenian opposition, the dangers of the status quo should also be obvious. For as long as there is a Karabakh conflict, those who are perceived as the victors in the conflict will always have the upper hand. The current authorities could always also justify economic and social problems and blame them on the Karabakh conflict, the Turkish–Azerbaijani blockade and the need to dedicate resources to the military budget, rather than to what the opposition claims to be corruption, mismanagement or bad policies. By defending the status quo the Armenian opposition is therefore narrowing its own chances of ever winning power. One can argue that rather than oppose the peace process, the Armenian opposition would be much better served if seen as part of a national effort for peace, which would create a level playing field and move the political debate to other issues where the government does not have such strong credentials.

Many similar arguments also exist on the Azerbaijani side. Fifteen years after the ceasefire, Azerbaijanis are asking whether the time for Azerbaijan to regroup and regain its lost territory has not been enough. Increased oil revenues and, in tandem, huge increases in military expenditure have increased people's expectations. The government is now under pressure to show results. After the war in Georgia in 2008 the folly of the military option has become all too apparent, even though in public the Azerbaijani government continues to maintain it as an option of last resort. The alternative to war is progress through negotiations, and in this regard the options currently under consideration – the so-called Madrid Principles, or Basic Principles – offer Azerbaijan the best opportunity to regain its territory adjoining Nagorno-Karabakh and to repatriate its refugees and IDPs. The issue of the status of Nagorno-Karabakh itself remains a point of contention. However, this issue can only be resolved through a formula which overrides the contradictory principles of territorial integrity and self-determination. No such formula can emerge, let alone succeed, until there is a much more solid commitment on both sides to make peace work.

For the embattled Azerbaijani opposition, already under considerable pressure because of the heavy-handed approach of the government, the sooner Karabakh stops being the dominant factor in Azerbaijani politics the better. If the opposition is able to present a united front with the government on a peace deal on Karabakh, it can then shift the political debate to other issues and share some of the credit that a peace deal can bring.

One can, therefore, conclude that political conditions exist in both countries for a shift towards a consensus for peace. However, this will require tough political decisions and entails the two governments reaching out, first and foremost, to their internal opposition. This process may take months, if not years, but the sooner it starts the better.

The voice of public opinion

There are lessons to be learnt from other conflict situations. In Northern Ireland, for example, the political distance between Unionists and Republicans was so wide that a consensus for peace was considered all but impossible. Yet, there emerged a strong force of civil society and grass-roots groups who started to demand a rethink of positions, piling up pressure on the politicians to revisit entrenched positions and think the unthinkable. This process took more than decade before it started bearing results.

Their ability to keep the politicians focused on the peace process eventually led to the power sharing-agreement enabling hard-line politicians like the Reverend Ian Paisley and Martin McGuiness to transform themselves into peace doves, jointly heading a unified administration, and actually working together for the good of Northern Ireland.

Some wonder if this Northern Ireland experience is relevant for Nagorno-Karabakh. For a long time the Karabakh peace process has been a top-down process, with only very small groups within the ruling elites in Armenia and Azerbaijan involved in developing policy or strategy around it. With some small exceptions, public engagement with the process was discouraged.

The public debate on Karabakh in both Armenia and Azerbaijan needs to be intensified, and the options that are available must be discussed frankly and honestly. Both governments will have to go through a steep learning curve with regard to how to involve their populations in this process and make them stakeholders of a peace deal.

The role of civil society and media

Civil society and the mass media have an important role to play in this process.

There are important, nuanced differences in the way civil society organisations operate in Armenia and in Azerbaijan; however, in both countries the civil society remains fragile and there is a sense of distrust between government and civil society organisations. On Karabakh, civil society organisations sometimes appear to foreign observers as part of the problem rather than part of the solution, their rhetoric being sometimes much worse than that of the official positions. In this they are just reflecting the unpleasant reality of the current perceptions among the populations at large. This situation will change once there is open debate and options are better understood.

By and large, the media in Armenia and Azerbaijan are instruments of indoctrination. Radio and television operate under very tight government controls. Newspapers, if not controlled by governments, are mouthpieces for political parties. It is only in new media, web based news portals and sites, that one sees some first signs of attempts to go beyond stereotypical positions.

The governments in Armenia and Azerbaijan need to allow more space for proper media debate on the Karabakh conflict and conflict resolution. It is likely that initially, this space will be occupied by radical groups, whose position is more extreme than is that of the government or even the main opposition parties. However, in the right conditions the forces of moderation should emerge and be able to take the debate forward in a more constructive manner.

Embarking on a long and hazardous journey

Many in the region, and indeed beyond, are under the misperception that peace in Karabakh can be achieved in one historic moment, with the stroke of a pen. In fact, this will be a long and hazardous journey. The most that those involved in the current negotiations (facilitated by the OSCE Minsk Group) are hoping for at present is a breakthrough which would see the sides agree on some sort of road map.

If this breakthrough is ever achieved, then building broad political support for its implementation will become even more important. One can expect that there will be those who, for one reason or another, will try to undermine any deal. Again, the example of Northern Ireland is useful. Here, fringe dissident groups, particularly on the Republican side, have sworn to fight on and have been trying to derail the peace process through random acts of violence. However, broad consensus to make the peace process work meant that these groups have been marginalised, and despite their capacity to conduct violent attacks they have not been able to trigger the chain of action and reaction that they had hoped for.

Given the pains of the consequences of the Nagorno-Karabakh conflict – including the tens of thousands of bereaved, the suffering of hundreds of thousands of displaced, and the vehemence of the enemy imagery which has now sunk deep in both Armenian and Azerbaijani societies, especially among the young – any peace process to have a chance to succeed needs to be accompanied by a very intensive and concerted effort to heal the wounds and improve understanding.

It is only by building a broad mass of those who believe that peace is the only way forward for resolving the Karabakh conflict and, indeed, for taking the region to a better qualitative position in the world community, that the catastrophe of war that some are now starting to believe is inevitable can be averted. Building this mass is the main challenge for the region over the next decade.

19

The Karabakh Dilemma: Right to Self-Determination, Imperative of Territorial Integrity, or a Caucasian New Deal?

Frank Engel

At the time of this writing more than 16 years have elapsed since the cease-fire which brought the military conflict around Nagorno-Karabakh to an end. Sixteen years of uncertainty – for the people of Karabakh, for the hundreds of thousands who were displaced by the conflict on both sides, and for Armenia and Azerbaijan. Sixteen years of talks and negotiations, of proposals and counter-proposals, of conferences and colloquia. Sixteen years after the war, the status quo appears like the best option still – because one of the alternatives might well be another war. The first armed conflict between 1992 and 1994 killed around 30,000 persons, both soldiers and civilians. A remake of the Karabakh war could turn out to me more deadly still.

The circumstances suggest that a solution to the Karabakh problem is not in sight. A better formulation would be that a mutually acceptable and agreeable solution is not in sight. Any change to the precarious status quo will inevitably cause the current reality to shift to what one party or the other would find disadvantageous. Karabakh continues its trajectory into the unknown, and the regular front-line skirmishes remind us that this conflict is far from frozen.

There are multiple ways of contemplating the issue of the Karabakh conflict. There is the legalistic approach, used by all sides, but obviously with fundamentally different bases and outlooks, and resulting in deadlock. There is the political approach prolonging (in a mindset of wishful thinking) the years of negotiations, proposals and counter-proposals which have been made in the framework of the Minsk group process. And there is a different approach still: taking stock of the facts as they are (or publicly appear) today and sketching out a perspective beyond the sterile framework of the Karabakh crisis diplomacy. In sum, a "European" approach. This is the one I venture to describe – knowing well that this, too, may remain wishful thinking for a very long time. But had the founding fathers of the European Communities, later the EU, not embarked on just such a daring course, the "Old Continent" would still be at war with itself today.

The arguments for the independence of Karabakh are as well known as those which Azerbaijan uses to plead its cause of territorial integrity. In a nutshell, the problem is the collision of the right to self-determination and the imperative of ensuring territorial integrity.

Because those two notions collide frontally and forcefully in the Karabakh conflict, I have serious doubts whether the current official developments and Madrid Principles will be of any real help in terminating the conflict. Even if Armenia withdrew its troops from surrounding territory (which it should) and even if, after that, Azerbaijani nationals returned to both these territories and Karabakh (which they should of course be able to do), the question is: Do we believe for a minute that a status referendum held in Karabakh in the oppressive atmosphere of today would have any result short of sovereignty as a Karabaghi state? Whether the population of Karabakh is nearly 100 per cent Armenian or 75 per cent Armenian, this Armenian population will not, as things currently stand, accept anything less than the independent Republic of Nagorno-Karabakh. This is what has already happened. And this is precisely what Azerbaijan will not accept.

The post-Soviet space contains a few patches of territory, all nominally fulfilling the Montevideo criteria for recognisable statehood, where the two principles – self-determination and territorial integrity – collide. They do not do this in the same manner. They do not do this with the same intensity. But what Karabakh, Transnistria, Abkhazia and South Ossetia have in common is that they do not want to live as parts of the larger state surrounding them: a state with which they do not share the language, the religion, the history, or any combination of those. Rather, what is wanted is an internationally recognised state, a Member State of the United Nations, which has at its disposal those means of interstate lobbying that the de facto states lack. Their existence is due to a Soviet order which is now long gone. But it cannot be denied. They do exist. They are real. Karabakh is real, Abkhazia is real, Transnistria is real and South Ossetia is real.

After centuries of warfare conducted with a view to conquering additional territories, the modern-day international community came to the conclusion, with the founding of the United Nations, that borders were not to be changed again. Not by force at least and, ideally, not at all. That goes for successor states as well. Any state which was independent and could boast a defined territory in 1945 was covered at least by the principle that its borders were safe for the future. Decolonisation in Africa and elsewhere respected the borders drawn by the colonial powers for fear that any other approach would lead to war again. But did Africa, for instance, live through a half-century of peace after decolonisation took on momentum around 1960? It did not. And one of its persistent problems today is contested borders.

Tightly controlled, often closed borders drawn right through population settlements and politically organised territories. Many new states appeared after the founding of the United Nations. The vast majority of the UN members of today were not members in 1945 – largely because they did not exist then. The UN was founded by 51 states, and now has a membership of 192, a difference of 141 or almost three quarters. Most of the new Member States are former colonies which acceded to independence after the foundation of the UN, and states which resulted from the break-up of larger ones that no longer exist today. The vast majority of those territories were granted the right to exist and to be recognised by the international community. A few were not. And the question is, of course: Why were certain ones treated one way, and others so differently?

The answer to the question most probably resides in the simultaneous invocation of the right to self-determination and the right to territorial integrity. If the latter does not come into the equation, the former is easy to satisfy. No one laid claim to what is now the Democratic Republic of the Congo after Belgium let go of its former colony. No one claimed the Czech Republic or Slovakia after both parts of what was Czechoslovakia agreed to accede to independence and succeed the former UN member, Czechoslovakia. No one else's territorial integrity was at stake here – the matter was sorted by the right to self-determination alone, and borders were not contested. The situation was different in the former Yugoslavia, where much of the warfare of the 1990s must be explained by territorial aspirations conflicting with the republican borders within the former Yugoslavia. And it was different again in parts of the former Soviet Union.

The Soviet specificity affecting Karabakh was that a territory whose population was very predominantly Armenian was included in a non-Armenian Soviet republic – a little like the old Abkhaz polity: a Soviet Republic in its own right until Stalin decided its incorporation into the Georgian SSR. This situation was tolerable to the people as long as they all were Soviet citizens, living in one and the same country, and it became explosive only when the Soviet Union began to disintegrate at the end of the 1980s, with the independence and sovereignty of its constituent republics being openly sought and obtained shortly thereafter.

Armenians in Karabakh faced the prospect of becoming citizens of the Republic of Azerbaijan, which would have a guarded international border with the future independent Republic of Armenia, and which might well decide that the "Armenity" of Karabakh would no longer formally be guaranteed and protected. Had Karabakh originally been included in the Soviet Republic of Armenia, instead of Azerbaijan, history after 1990 would have been different. However, from the very beginning the Soviet state insisted on its inclusion within the SSR of Azerbaijan. Where was the reason or the logic behind this decision? Why was Abkhazia joined to the SSR of Georgia after it had been a constituent republic of the Soviet Union for a decade (albeit only as treaty republic)? Dictatorships do not justify their decisions, and if they do, their reasons are often far from practical. The nefarious effects of such decisions then outlive the dictatorships, as seen in the Caucasus. Sadly, another Caucasian war cannot be totally ruled out at the present juncture. There has been one in 2008, after all, and the Georgian war of that summer proves quite eloquently that rash action can quickly lead to full-blown military confrontation. In the case of Karabakh, one has to bear in mind that there has been a ceasefire, but that the dividing line between Azerbaijani and Armenian–Karabakhi territory remains a front line on which tension remains high, far away from accepted and recognised international borders. One simply does not know how political and military fortunes will develop, especially in Azerbaijan, whose resources today far exceed those it could muster in the early nineties – including for war. One can also have the impression that there is more understanding, internationally, for countries whose official borders have been infringed upon than for those who infringed on them. This was rather evident in 2008, when sympathy for Georgia – even though it may well have been the aggressor – far exceeded that for Russia. During the Karabakh war, Europe and the West were busier contemplating devastation in the Balkans than here in the Caucasus but, since then, public opinion here has grown weary of the eternal military confrontations that surround us. There is a sense that the accepted international order should prevail, and that includes borders as defined by the schoolbook maps. In circumstances like these, it might seem tempting for Azerbaijan, in a quick military move, to retake the territory that was once officially allotted to it. But the Karabakh war of the 1990s has proven that in all likelihood, there will never be a swift victory against Karabakh. Should there be a new war, it would be likely to both draw out in time and cause heavy loss of life. The now-recovering economy of Karabakh would be laid waste again. Renewed warfare is not in the interest of Karabakh and Armenia, certainly – nor in that of Azerbaijan, from an objective viewpoint. Besides, Azerbaijan's economy is based on infrastructure which is in range of Karabakhi artillery.

Given the continued, and continuing, risk of war and the impasse in which the Karabakh problem finds itself, a bolder approach is required. Such an approach by necessity requires reconciliation on a scale not seen in the Caucasus. And Europe might well be a source of inspiration here.

Sixteen years after the Karabakh war, Armenia and Azerbaijan (with Karabakh in between) are still on confrontational terms. The border between Armenia and Azerbaijan is closed in the North, and is made up of a front line in the South. Even if this line is called the "Line of Contact", many of the tangible contacts made there are deadly, and hundreds of soldiers lose their lives there each year. It is one of the most hostile border environments in the world, only surpassed by the border between North and South Korea. But this is not all, since the Turkish-Armenian border, notwithstanding football and real diplomacy, remains closed as well, as it has been since 1993, in Turkish retaliation against the Armenians backing Karabakh in the war.

The scene of Karabakh diplomacy is still filled with preconditions and fundamental opposition. Turkey insists there can be no normalisation of its relations with Armenia, an open border included, as long as no solution to the Karabakh issue is in sight (read: withdrawal of Armenian forces from what is "officially" Azerbaijan). Azerbaijan insists that its border with Armenia could and would be opened once the Karabakh issue is settled. The Karabakhi people will go for nothing less than independence, no matter what international proposals may be made tothem, which position will of course prevent any border openings and perpetuate the front-line reality. Situations like these were the reason why, until 1945, every generation of Europeans had known at least one war. You do not make peace if you are not prepared to move ahead.

Sixteen years after the Karabakh war, no such movement has been made yet. For the purpose of historical comparison: 16 years after World War I, World War II was being prepared in Europe, and broke out five years later.

Sixteen years after World War II, however, in 1961, the Treaty of Rome was reality, the Council of Europe was twelve years old and going strong, and Western Europe, this age-old battlefield, was transforming into a prosperous area of cooperation and economic development. Sixteen years after the ceasefire for Karabakh, people continue to die on the Line of Contact, many Caucasian borders remain closed, another Caucasian war has taken place resulting in the definitive loss of Abkhazia and South Ossetia by Georgia, and there are no edifying signs of major change.

Borders, and therefore states, are often rather arbitrary creations. They are by necessity established on the territory of previously existing political entities, as the geographical frameworks of governance have constantly evolved through history. Often the changes did not occur voluntarily. But can that be an argument in favour of forcible restoration of previous realities in the twenty-first century?

Only very recently have Italy, Slovenia and Croatia been able to make significant progress to settle border disputes that had been around since after World War I. It can safely be assumed that the solution of these disputes has been greatly facilitated by the fact that both Italy and Slovenia are members of the European Union, and that Croatia is set to join soon. In Europe, more precisely within the European Union, borders have largely become irrelevant by now. Minorities are protected, and linguistic, religious and other personal rights are guaranteed, wherever a person may live. In those circumstances, the old Istrian-Triestin-Slovenian-Croatian problem complex has lost its acuteness. In the Caucasus, circumstances remain largely different. It would probably be reasonable to argue that the conflict between the right to self-determination of Karabakh and of the Armenian

Karabakhies, and the right to territorial integrity of Azerbaijan, cannot be solved by according precedence to one of these rights over the other. It can only be solved if borders lose their significance. Or rather, if they change their function fundamentally.

Instead of separating, dividing, breaking up and alienating, borders can be perceived as uniting, bridging, joining together and ultimately healing wounds of the past. This is how we have come to regard them in Europe – most of Europe, finally, after the end of the confrontation between East and West. This is how they must come to be regarded in the Caucasus, if peace, stability and regional cooperation are to prevail over war, confrontation and distrust. This is a most arduous task. But it has been successfully performed elsewhere. Even in the most improbable locations.

There will be no change in the perception of borders if Turkey does not assume its fundamental responsibility. As a country seeking accession to the EU, this responsibility is not the courting of fellow countries of the Turkic nation. It is to establish normal relations with all its neighbouring countries, with open borders, and without preconditions. The border between Turkey and Armenia must be opened, or else it must be made clear to Turkey that the accession negotiations are halted. The same goes for normalisation with the Republic of Cyprus, by the way – and for progress in solving the Cyprus conflict that Turkey can and must initiate with goodwill.

Azerbaijan must recognise that Turkey has obligations of its own, and that they are spelled out above. The challenge for Azerbaijan is to prepare itself for a solution of the Karabakh conflict without Turkish coaching and interference. Karabakh will not come under full Azerbaijani jurisdiction again – just like Abkhazia will not be simply a part of Georgia again. Karabakh and Armenia must recognise that, at the end of the day, independence for Karabakh might be less realistic than joining the Armenian state as an exclave. It would not be the only one in the region.

Nakhitchevan is separated from the mainland of Azerbaijan. Why would it be totally inconceivable that part of the Armenian nation would live separated from the Armenian mainland? After all, Soviet-era state organs of both the SSR Armenia and the SSR Nagorno-Karabakh have demanded that Karabakh be joined to Armenia before Karabakh, faced by resolute refusals by Moscow, resolved to declare independence. Let there be open borders. Let there be normal communications between Baku, Stepanakert, Nakhitchevan and Yerevan. Let there be a perspective of safe return for the hundreds of thousands of displaced persons. And let there be recognition, across the region, that it is not the only one where, in such a future, there would be minorities with rights.

Alternatively, Azerbaijan would have to accept that Nagorno-Karabakh becomes a quasi-federated entity on its soil with highly autonomous powers. Probably, at least for a while, with armed forces of its own included. It is reasonable to assume that for Azerbaijan, this is hardly a more edifying perspective than either Karabakhi independence or federation of the territory with Armenia. But if this were considered preferable by Azerbaijan, then Armenia and Nagorno-Karabakh must be prepared to consider it. Alternatives to the sterility of the Minsk process have to be explored. If progress is to be made, if trust is to be built, if the perspective of a military solution to the current deadlock is to be eliminated once and for all, the Caucasus must embark on a mission of reconciliation no less intensive than that of Europe has been. How else could it be? For the Caucasus is part of Europe and its difficult history. Europe has accepted that a painful history is no pretext and no justification for a painful future. Will the Caucasus come to accept that as well?

20

Learning from Georgia:
A Non-Use-of-Force Treaty
for Nagorno-Karabakh

Otto Luchterhandt

On 13 July 2009, in his speech at the Royal Institute of International Affairs in London, the President of Azerbaijan, Ilham Aliyev, said that his country was prepared to keep the option of solving the Karabakh war through the use of force open: "Unfortunately, I cannot totally rule out a military solution, as we have the total right based on international laws to restore our territorial integrity, which no one can question.... Today Azerbaijan has powerful and modern armed forces that are capable of restoring the country's territorial integrity".[1] Aliyev delivered this speech just three days after the meeting of the OSCE Minsk Group at L'Aquila, Italy. On that occasion, the Co-Chairs of the Group adopted a series of Basic Principles for a peaceful, political solution of the Karabakh question, and recommended the heads of state of Armenia and Azerbaijan use them during their future negotiations.

The decision to put an end to the Karabakh conflict, even by war if necessary, is the official position of Azerbaijan. The country finally agreed on the military doctrine that the Milli Mejlis (the Azerbaijani Parliament) chose to follow on 8 June 2010. This is what was decided: "Following the Republic of Armenia's continual occupation of a part of the territory of the Republic of Azerbaijan, and its refusal, during the efforts to solve the problem in a political way, to leave the area it took possession of, Azerbaijan reserves the right, in accordance with international law, to use any necessary means, including force, to restore its territorial integrity".[2]

---

[1] Transcript of the visit of Ilham Aliyev to Chatham House, "Foreign Policy Challenges for Azerbaijan", 13 July 2009, http://www.chathamhouse.org.uk/files/14383_130709aliyev.pdf (date accessed: 30 November 2010).

[2] http://www.polit.ru/news/2010/06/08/azerdoc.html (date accessed 30 November 2010).

One month later, the Azerbaijani Foreign Minister, Elmar Mammadyarov, justified this position by appealing to the right of all states to self-defence: "Any State in the world, whose regions are occupied by another country, can use force appealing to chapter 7 of the United Nations Charter, article 51 – right of self-defence … . According to the UN Charter, when a country's regions are occupied, you have the right to use force to free them. It is really simple, and simplicity is the reason why the military doctrine has been accepted as it is".[3]

Mammadyarov acknowledged that an "indirect menace" to Armenia was implicit in this statement. In any case, he added that in the Karabakh question "not all the possible diplomatic solutions have been tried. We do believe that, with some political willingness on the part of Armenia, we can create a situation where everybody wins: Armenia, us, and all the other peoples in this region".

The official position of Azerbaijan – to retake the occupied territories, including Nagorno-Karabakh – may be compatible with the constitution of the country, but is definitely not compatible with international law. Azerbaijan wrongly cites the right of self-defence according to article 51 of the UN Charter.

The following considerations will make this point clear, and Azerbaijan's position will be compared to that of Georgia before the "August War" of 2008; conclusions will then be drawn from that experience and applied to the Karabakh conflict.

Azerbaijan's misapprehension: self-defence does not permit a force-based resolution to the Karabakh conflict

The principle of refraining from the use of force applies to Azerbaijan, as well as to Armenia and Nagorno-Karabakh. According to this principle, it is forbidden for a country to pursue its objectives with "threat or use of force". As is generally understood, this refrain represents the basis of modern international law, and the UN Charter therefore made it one of its fundamental principles (article 2, no. 4). The general refraining from force is a peremptory norm (*ius cogens*). As a consequence, according to international law, all international treaties which contravene it are automatically invalid and void (article 53 of the Vienna Convention on the Law of Treaties).[4] However, it is true (and Azerbaijan appeals to this point) that the right of self-defence by a state represents an exception to the general refraining from force. This

---

[3] "Die militärische Option bleibt auf dem Tisch", *Frankfurter Allgemeine Zeitung*, 5 July 2010, p. 6.

[4] Vienna Convention on the Law of Treaties, 23 May 1969: United Nations Treaties Series – UNTS, Vol. 1155, p. 331.

is expressly recognised in article 51, para. 1 of the United Nations Charter: "Nothing in the present Charter shall impair the inherent right of individual or collective self-defence if an armed attack occurs against a member of the United Nations, until the Security Council has taken measures necessary to maintain international peace and security". Azerbaijan can appeal to the right of self-defence only if, and as long as, an "armed attack occurs". The battles for Nagorno-Karabakh have now long passed. Armenian troops concluded what they referred to as "liberation" and what Azerbaijan referred to as "occupation" of territories belonging to Azerbaijan in the spring of 1994. As will be analysed in further depth below, in May 1994 a ceasefire agreement was reached in Bishkek, the capital of Kyrgyzstan. Since then, Armenian forces have launched no further armed attacks.[5]

In international law, or rather in international case law, the extent and intensity of force required for a military intervention to be defined as an "armed attack" in the sense of article 51 of the UN Charter, remains a disputed issue. To make a useful distinction which includes the smallest instances of armed action, the International Court of Justice (ICJ) of the United Nations also fell back on the definition of aggression applied by the UN General Assembly of 1974.[6] It was then declared that an armed attack could also be "the invasion or attack by the armed forces of a state on the territory of another state, or any military occupation, however temporary, resulting from such invasion or attack".

It is therefore correct to talk of an "armed attack" when an enemy occupies the territory of another state. And, as an occupation is an action that endures, it represents a kind of perpetuation of the armed attack. If you follow the Azerbaijani interpretation, the Armenian forces had attacked Azerbaijan in the war for Karabakh at the beginning of the Nineties and the occupation of the Azerbaijani territory represents an "armed attack" against which it has the right to defend itself. The official position of the military doctrine of Azerbaijan can seem, in this light, to rest on a legal basis.

In any case, what the Azerbaijani government is failing to recognise, is that on 11 May 1994 the parties involved in the conflict (Azerbaijan, Nagorno-Karabakh and Armenia) reached, as previously mentioned, a ceasefire agree-

---

[5] It remains an open question whether, according to article 51 of the UN Charter, during the war for Karabakh that took place between 1992 and 1994, the Republic of Armenia launched a real "armed attack" against the Republic of Azerbaijan. In the current context it is not possible to analyse this issue further. However, the legal accuracy of the following considerations is not influenced even of one considers that such attacks took place.

[6] Definition of Aggression, Resolution No. 3314 (XXIX) of the General Assembly of 14 December 1974, Text: UN. General Assembly A/RES/3314 (XXIX) 14 December 1974; UN Yearbook 1974, p. 846.

ment, which became effective on the 12 May 1994.[7] The agreement was based on the Bishkek Protocol, which was concluded on 5 May 1994 in the capital city of Kyrgyzstan, on the occasion of the meeting of the CIS Inter-Parliamentary Assembly. The Protocol was signed by the authorised representatives of the Parliaments of Azerbaijan, Nagorno-Karabakh, and Armenia,[8] and it became effective thanks to the initiative of the Council of the Inter-Parliamentary Assembly and the close cooperation of Russia.[9]

The Ceasefire Agreement was signed between 9 and 11 May. The ministers of defence of the three conflicting sides signed it separately, in their respective capital cities. As scheduled (Point 4), the agreement became effective on 12 May, when the three signed the completely identical documents which were received in Moscow by the mediator, Russia. According to article 12 of the Vienna Convention on the Law of Treaties, this agreement has the same legal value as an international treaty. The fact that the content of the agreement is essentially limited to the ceasefire (Point 1) does not, of course, change the situation. However, compared to the previously negotiated ceasefire, the greatest step forward of the agreement is that the ceasefire should, and does, have a permanent effect.

Furthermore, the contracting parties agreed for a conference of their ministers of defence to take place in Moscow upon Russian invitation. The objectives of the conference would have been the following (Point 2): firstly, to newly establish the lines of separation of troops; secondly, to clear some "urgent military-technical issues"; and thirdly, to agree on the preparation of a deployment of international monitors. As a fourth point, a trilateral "agreement on the cessation of the armed conflict" had to be reached no later than 22 May.

The meeting of the ministers of defence took place in Moscow on 16 and 17 May, the mediator being the Russian Minister of Defence, Pavel Gratschov. Under peremptory pressure by Gratchov, an agreement was reached, but the president of Azerbaijan refused to sign it.[10] However, during another meeting on 26 and 27 July 1994, which ended with a further agreement,[11] the defence ministers of the three conflicting parties clearly agreed that the

---

[7] Russian Text of the Agreement by W. Kazimirov Nikolajewitsch (2009) "Mir Karabachu" [Peace for Karabakh], Moscow, 346–47.

[8] Kazimirov (2009), op. cit., 345–46.

[9] The task of drafting fell to Kazimirov, who at the time, was the Russian representative in the Minsk Group of the OSCE. In December 1993, confidential talks between Azerbaijan, Armenia and Nagorno-Karabakh had taken place in Mariehamn, in the Åland Island Peace Institute, thanks to the initiative of the CIS and Russia. For a detailed explanation of the creation of the Bishkek Protocol see Kazimirov (2009), op. cit., p. 146 ff.

[10] For a detailed report on the "post-Bishkek" negotiations, see Kazimirov (2009), op. cit., p. 146 ff.

[11] Ibid. pp. 167 and 422.

Bishkek Protocol and the obligations resulting from it would be valid until the achievement of a greater political agreement declaring the complete resolution of the conflict. Such an agreement is still pending. What is the relationship between the Bishkek Ceasefire Protocol and Azerbaijan's right to self-defence? The answer is clear: Azerbaijan is bound to respect the ceasefire for the entire duration of the protocol, which is indefinite. Correspondingly, it has to renounce carrying out any military efforts or actions. Consequently, Azerbaijan's theoretic right as a state to self-defence according to article 51 of the UN Charter is, in the specific case of the Karabakh conflict, being superimposed by the Bishkek Ceasefire Protocol, and is therefore limited by the obligation of a ceasefire and of non-resumption of military activities. Azerbaijan can appeal to the full right of self-defence again only when the ceasefire is interrupted by the Armenian side, thus becoming obsolete because of the new "armed attack", as indicated in the article 51 of the UN Charter.

These legal remarks and hypotheses regarding the legal relationship between Azerbaijan's right of self-defence and its obligation to respect the ceasefire are confirmed by the most detailed interpretational rules of the general refraining from force (art. 2 no. 4 UNO-Charter). These rules were set by the United Nations General Assembly on 24 October 1970 in the "Friendly Relations Declaration":[12] "Every state, likewise, has the duty to refrain from the threat or use of force to violate international lines of demarcation, such as armistice lines, established by or pursuant to an international agreement to which it is a party or which it is otherwise bound to respect".[13]

The rule applies perfectly to the case of the Ceasefire Protocol, and therefore also to the current situation of the Karabakh conflict. Since the protocol is a trilateral treaty of international law, the ceasefire lines between the Armenian and the Azerbaijani troops represent "international lines of demarcation", in the sense of the Friendly Relations Declarations of the UN General Assembly.

The Ceasefire Protocol was not rendered obsolete by the occasional skirmishes which resulted in dead and wounded and took place between Azerbaijan and Armenia after it was signed. Until now, on no occasion has it been possible to establish which side fired the first shot or violated the

---

[12] Declaration on Principles of International Law concerning Friendly Relations and Cooperation among States in Accordance with the Charter of the United Nations, Text: UN General Assembly, Resolution 2625 (XXV), http://daccess-dds-ny.un.org/doc/RESOLUTION/GEN/NR0/348/90/IMG/NR034890.pdf?OpenElement (date accessed: 12 February 2011).

[13] Paragraph 5 of the first Principle: "The principle that States shall refrain in their international relations from the threat or use of force against the territorial integrity or political independence of any State, or in any other manner inconsistent with the purposes of the United Nations".

ceasefire. Usually, the conflicting parties accuse each other.[14] Apart from the question of responsibility, it must be noted that since 1994 the Ceasefire Protocol has generally been observed and respected by the parties to the conflict. Until now, sporadic violations of the agreement have not reached an intensity which allows for or requires talk of a resumption or continuation of the war. The incidents can all clearly be qualified below the level of "armed attack" as interpreted by the case law of international tribunals. As the International Court of Justice noted in its decision of 1986 on the *Nicaragua v. United States of America*[15] case, not all border violations which take place with the employment of weapons are to be seen as "armed attacks" without first considering their strength. Furthermore, it is possible to talk of "armed attack" only when "military force is used against another state in a massive and coordinated way".[16]

In conclusion, and to summarise, it must be noted that the political position of Azerbaijan in relation to the Karabakh conflict, that is, that the conflict can be solved by force according to the political discretion of the country, is contrary to international law. This position contradicts the non-use of force in relation to the ceasefire lines agreed in the Treaty. Therefore, Azerbaijan cannot appeal to the right of self-defence as long as the Ceasefire Protocol is valid.

Lessons from the Georgian war of August 2008

It should be highly worrying to Armenia and Nagorno-Karabakh that Azerbaijan ignores the open-endedly valid Bishkek Ceasefire Protocol in having written its legal point of view into its military doctrine. This legal stance, that is, the fact that it retains the right for a solution to the conflict through the use of force, contradicts the Bishkek Protocol and should be deeply worrying for the entire international community. The dangers posed by an irresponsible leadership which ignores the non-use of force rule under an agreement of international law, and which tried to restore its jurisdiction on a separatist region which it claims as its own through the use of a blitzkrieg, should be clear. Indeed, the international community experienced all these things in the dramatic events of 2008 which took place in the South Caucasus.

---

[14] Since Azerbaijan adopted the military doctrine, incidents around the demarcation lines have increased significantly when compared to recent years, which have been largely calm.

[15] Military and Paramilitary Activities in and against Nicaragua (*Nicaragua* v. *United States of America*), ICJ Reports, 1986, 14 (para. 191, 195).

[16] This is the convincing definition of M. Herdegen (2010) "Völkerrecht", 9, München, § 34 Marginal No. 12, p. 255.

The constellations in Georgia in 2008, before it triggered the military conflict with Russia, were exactly arrayed like the one described above. With the
Sochi Agreement, signed on 24 June 1992 by Russia and Georgia, the latter was
obliged to solve the conflict with South Ossetia, which was striving for autonomy and independence, without the use of force and only through political
means. This obligation had been strengthened by further agreements signed
between 1994 and 1996. Despite all this, the Head of State, Mikheil Saakashvili,
had repeatedly declared in public that, if necessary, Georgia was ready to
re-establish its sovereignty and territorial integrity by using force against the
separatist territory. He then carried out a hurried and massive rearmament, the
dimensions of which strikingly contrasted with Georgia's economic competi-
tiveness, which strongly implied that military force would follow verbal threat.
Part of the international community, most notably the United States and other
NATO Member States, not only failed to take a stand against the rearmament,
but even supported and strengthened the Georgian leadership in its irresponsible and dangerous actions by providing significant military support.

The report, made public on 30 September 2009, of the "Independent
International Fact-Finding Mission on the Conflict in Georgia", set up by
the EU, clearly noted that by attacking Tskhinvali (the capital city of South
Ossetia) during the night of 7 and 8 August, Georgia had acted against its
obligation under international law to refrain from the use of force and not
to enact any military solutions in its conflict with South Ossetia.[17]

The experience of the Georgian war is also particularly instructive for
the Karabakh conflict because the leaders of the UN mission in Georgia
(UNOMIG) have tried for years to persuade Georgia to reach an agreement
on the non-use of force, especially with Abkhazia. However, President
Saakashvili has always shied away from this politically and legally significant move. He clearly did not want his political plans and options to be limited by a further, explicit international obligation. Certainly, the previous
agreement on the non-use of force, signed between Russia and Georgia, as
with Abkhazia and South Ossetia, was no guarantee that the idea of solving the conflict in South Ossetia through a military campaign would be
abandoned forever. However, such agreements on refraining from the use
of force would seriously increase the obstacles which stand in the way of a
decision to use force or start a war: breaking such an agreement and aggression contained in such a step would have been obvious to the eyes of the
world. Stronger obstacles for decisions to put political ambitions above international law do at least lower the likelihood of the use of force. This would
lead to more security, stability, and respect of those international laws in
international relations, and this would represent a great progress.

---

[17] Tagliavini Report, Vol. II, September 2009, p. 239 ff., http://www.ceiig.ch/pdf/
IIFFMCG_Volume_II.pdf (date accessed: 25 July 2010).

Lessons for the Karabakh conflict

Those states which find themselves in a political position similar to Georgia's should draw conclusions from the events which led Georgia to war in 2008. These include the war itself and its consequences for both Georgia and the Caucasus in general. The most important lessons which can be learnt from the Georgian war are the following:

1. The military success of an action can never be taken for granted, even in the case of a particularly advantageous position for a blitzkrieg or surprise attack, as with Georgia's starting point in South Ossetia;
2. There is a significant risk that starting a war recklessly may result in losing exactly those objectives which should have been achieved through the military action;
3. The legal and political obstacles created to prevent breaches of international law and launching a war should be strengthened in favour of political predictability and international safety.

As they force the opposing parties to reach their aims by using solely political means, non-use of force agreements are a tried and tested tool of international law capable of creating a situation of greater security. They strengthen political reasoning and prevent the signatories from undertaking military adventures as if they were nothing more than gambles. Non-use of force agreements are advantageous not only for one of the concerned parties, but for both of them and for their neighbouring states as well; such states are usually affected by the consequence of a war, whether due to floods of refugees crossing borders, or by economic and financial losses.

Applying this to the Nagorno-Karabakh conflict, it follows that the first objective of the international community must be to compel the three parties in the conflict – through political and diplomatic pressure – to reach an effective non-use of force agreement. This task is particularly assigned to the three Co-Chairs of the OSCE Minsk Group. Up to this point, it seems that they have not yet completely grasped the significance of non-use of force agreements. Certainly, in the aforementioned document of Basic Principles, written on the occasion of their meeting at L'Aquila, the principles of non-use of force, territorial integrity, equal rights and the right to self-determination have – correctly – been raised to "Basic Principles" of a reasonable compromise for the solution of the Karabakh conflict.[18] However, the simple enumeration of principles, in the style of a preamble, will not have the same

---

[18] "The Basic Principles reflect a reasonable compromise based on the Helsinki Final Act principles of Non-Use of Force, Territorial Integrity, and the Equal Rights and Self-Determination of Peoples" http://www.osce.org/item/38731.html (date accessed: 25 July 2010).

legal meaning as an independent non-use of force agreement. The preamble approach is too abstract, too weak, and is therefore inadequate. Naturally, it cannot have the same legal quality, nor the legal and political strength and effects of a dedicated non-use of force agreement with its mutual obligations for the signatory parties.

The conclusion of an agreement on the non-use of force should take place independently from the major negotiations regarding a solution to the Karabakh conflict. Obligations to renounce the use of force are widespread and rooted in current international law; therefore, at the outset they are ideal for creating and stimulating a basic level of trust between the parties in conflict. In this way they can positively influence the basic conditions for reaching a future compromise.

Concluding a non-use of force treaty on the one hand and individual peace deal components for the Karabakh conflict on the other are not one-to-one interrelated like quid pro quo. Between them no link must exist or be created. Agreements on the non-use of force are an independent basis for the solution of political conflicts, as far as those solutions are intended to be based on trust and should be lasting, sustainable and successful. Considering the background of its military doctrine, Azerbaijan cannot be expected to make proposals for a non-use of force agreement. The initiative must therefore come from Armenia and Nagorno-Karabakh, and its aim must be to convince Azerbaijan to agree to it. The Co-Chairs of the Minsk Group must also be convinced to support the idea, so that they can use their authority to move the conflicting parties to signing a non-use of force treaty.

With such an initiative, Armenia and Nagorno-Karabakh would assume a proactive role in shaping a peaceful solution to the Karabakh conflict.

They would thus reduce the danger of becoming an object of diplomatic and political actions of other nations, to which they might only be able to react in a defensive or even helpless manner.

Conclusion

21
Conclusion: Realistic Scenarios and How to Avoid a War in Nagorno-Karabakh

Michael Kambeck

This volume has covered a diverse set of aspects concerning the Nagorno-Karabakh conflict. Two key conclusions follow. On the one hand, the deplorable and worrying situation between the conflict parties has become, over the past decades, deeply rooted in a negative cycle of distrust and fear. Recently, it has deteriorated further, making measures to avert scenarios of military escalation more urgent than ever. On the other hand, following the title of this book, each author has highlighted neglected potential and exposed new factors. These indicate that, with the necessary political will and attention, escalation can still be averted.

Based on the authors' threat assessments, this final chapter first outlines the status quo, followed by scenarios of war and peace. It then concludes with recommendations on how war in Nagorno-Karabakh and the wider region can be avoided. These recommendations are either taken directly from the authors' contributions to this volume or follow the logic of their arguments and lessons learnt from recent developments.

Inconvenient truths about the status quo

The status quo in and around Nagorno-Karabakh is one of "no war and no peace".[1] For a certain time, such a status may be in the interest of some people. Gurbanov's analysis in this volume describes, from an Azerbaijani point of view, how regimes use the external threat as an argument against internal democratisation and, more generally, to secure their internal power. The status quo in this context can help governments on both sides to put

---

[1] E. Walker (1998) "No Peace, No War in the Caucasus: Secessionist Conflicts in Chechnya, Abkhazia and Nagorno-Karabakh", *Strengthening Democratic Institutions Project, Belfer Center for Science and International Affairs*, Occasional Paper.

democratisation into a waiting room and, in return, the lack of democratisation inhibits progress to resolve the conflict and overcome the status quo. However, at least since the war between Russia and Georgia in August 2008, we know that such a situation can very easily turn into war. As Luchterhandt analyses in detail, the Bishkek Cease Fire Treaty is indefinitely valid under international law and prohibits military action. Nevertheless, many contributors see alarming parallels between the situation today around the Nagorno-Karabakh conflict and that between Georgia and Russia prior to August 2008. Halbach, one of the authors of the EU's assessment of the causes of the Georgian–Russian war,[2] describes these parallels in detail in his contribution to this volume. In particular, he delineates the cycles of provocation and the trust in military tools as a means of politics. He nonetheless concludes that the situation around Nagorno-Karabakh is actually even more alarming, as it is the only one of the so-called frozen or protracted conflicts which is characterised by an absence of international observers and ceasefire monitoring. It must be added that, since he submitted his chapter, the number of ceasefire violations has increased even further.[3] This was the OSCE Minsk Group's key motivation for launching its second attempt[4] to convince the conflicting parties to withdraw snipers from the line of contact, a prerequisite to installing permanent observers, whose security can otherwise not be guaranteed. In the current situation along the line of contact, snipers do not play any significant offensive or defensive role and can be compared to classical cannon fodder. However, while Armenia has publicly welcomed and supported the OSCE Minsk Group initiative,[5] Azerbaijan has refused it

---

[2] IIFFMCG (2009) Report of the Independent International Fact-Finding Mission on the Conflict in Georgia, http://www.ceiig.ch/Index.html (date accessed: 13 June 2011).

[3] For an overview of the most recent incidents, consult the Crisis Watch Database: http://www.crisisgroup.org/en/publication-type/crisiswatch/crisiswatch-database. aspx?CountryIDs={A0E7BED7-BFDE-4C1A-80A3–1315BD08D09C} (date accessed: 13 June 2011).

[4] The first initiative was made by the OSCE Chairperson-in-Office, Greek Foreign Minister Dora Bakoyannis, on 11 May 2009, http://www.osce.org/cio/50901. The second initiative was made by the OSCE Chairperson-in-Office, Lithuanian Foreign Minister Audronius Ažubalis, on 18 March 2011, http://www.osce.org/cio/76156 (date accessed: 13 June 2011).

[5] OSCE (2011) "Statement by H.E. Mr. Edward Nalbandian, Minister of Foreign Affairs of the Republic of Armenia at the 852nd Meeting of the OSCE Permanent Council", Vienna, 3 March 2011, PC.DEL/187/11, http://www.osce.org/pc/76003 (excerpt: "International community, the UN Secretary General, OSCE Minsk Group Co-Chair countries, and different OSCE Chairmanships, including the current Lithuanian, have made proposals on **consolidation of cease-fire** and on **withdrawal of snipers from the Line of Contact, both initiatives supported by Armenia and Nagorno Karabakh**. President of Armenia proposed to reach an agreement

for the second time.[6] The key argument for this refusal is that such a move could fix the status quo for years to come or even indefinitely. In return, this logic means that every few days, some – mostly very young – conscript soldier must die to keep the conflict fragile. As perverse as this may seem, there was no public international condemnation of Azerbaijan's position, and the mediators seem to be prepared to live with:

- the permanent risk of an accidental military escalation, caused by exchanges of fire between snipers,
- the international community's continued total lack of independent information about smaller and potentially larger incidents along the line of contact ("who shot first" questions) and
- the permanent supply of victims, televised by both sides to display the other side's evilness, effectively rendering any trust-building measure futile.

Like many experts who have followed this conflict since the beginning, Sammut concludes that military actions simply remain an accepted political means in the South Caucasus. He argues that trust in military strength is the one thing that seems to unite the two sides. This is reinforced on the Armenian/Karabakhi side by the successful counteroffensives of the early 1990s. The first of these drove the combined Soviet/Azerbaijani forces out of the core of Karabakh between 1991 and 1993.[7] The second responded to a large-scale offensive by Azerbaijan in 1993,[8] which cancelled the first ceasefire loosely in place at the time. In the end, the results were large-scale territorial losses for Azerbaijan and the Armenian/Karabakhi control of the seven districts surrounding mainland Karabakh, the so-called security buffer zone.

---

on non-use of force, which was supported by international community and again rejected by Azerbaijan.") (date accessed: 13 June 2011).

[6] RFERL, "Countdown to Karabakh Conflict Talks in Kazan", 07 June 2011, http://www.rferl.org/content/countdown_to_karabakh_conflict_talks_in_kazan_/24227837.html (excerpt: "Mammadyarov said Armenia also continues to insist on the withdrawal of snipers from the Line of Contact separating Armenian and Azerbaijani armed forces ... It is not snipers, but troops that should be pulled back from the occupied territories.") (date accessed: 13 June 2011).

[7] This began with the Azerbaijani Operation Circle, in which Soviet troops surrounded key villages, allowing Azerbaijani special police forces to enter and commit atrocities, which aimed to change the ethnic nature of the villages. See timeline: April–July 1991.

[8] In August, Russia mediated a temporary ceasefire which held until early November, when Azerbaijan launched a new offensive. Nagorno-Karabakh Armenian forces repelled the attack and advanced into southwest Azerbaijan. See timeline: August 1993–November 1993.

From the same year, 1993, stem the key sources of Azerbaijan's self-perceived legal and moral high-ground, namely the four UN Security Council resolutions on the Karabakh conflict.[9] Under the impression of special reports by the Minsk Group about the heavy losses and open war situation in Karabakh, the Security Council called for an end to the fighting, underlining that "all occupying forces" must withdraw from the territories which they have occupied. While Armenia interprets this as referring also to the Azerbaijani forces in the Shahumyan region of northern NK, the resolutions name territories outside the core of Nagorno-Karabakh now controlled by NK Armenian forces as examples. For Azerbaijan, the four resolutions mean that in the year of traumatic losses, the international community and its highest legal body side-line with their position. The resolutions emphasise the inadmissibility of the use of force for the acquisition of territory, which is what Azerbaijan until today perceives to have happened with the war until 1994. For Azerbaijan, the four resolutions mark the clear legal backing for its position and they are often quoted when there is a need to justify hard-line positions or to draw attention to the unacceptable status quo while pointing the finger at the adversary Armenia/NK.[10] Azerbaijani embassy representatives mention the resolutions wherever possible in public events touching upon the NK conflict.[11] In contradiction with the Minsk Group proposals since the Bishkek ceasefire, Azerbaijan considers the call for a troop withdrawal to be valid for all territories, not only the territories surrounding NK, the so-called buffer zone.[12] For Armenia, the resolutions were at the time directed to both sides. But the stronger argument then and today is the impossibility to

---

[9] For the four UNSC resolutions adopted in 1993, see: UNSC resolution 822 (1993) http://documents-dds-ny.un.org/doc/RESOLUTION/GEN/NR0/700/07/img/NR070007.pdf?OpenElement; UNSC resolution 853 (1993) http://documents-dds-ny.un.org/doc/RESOLUTION/GEN/NR0/700/38/img/NR070038.pdf?OpenElement; UNSC resolution 874 (1993) http://documents-dds-ny.un.org/doc/RESOLUTION/GEN/NR0/700/59/img/NR070059.pdf?OpenElement; UNSC resolution 884 (1993) http://documents-dds-ny.un.org/doc/RESOLUTION/GEN/NR0/700/69/img/NR070069.pdf?OpenElement (date accessed: 19 October 2011).

[10] president.az, "Ilham Aliyev participated in an official reception marking the 20th anniversary of the restoration of state independence of the Republic of Azerbaijan", 17 October 2011 (excerpt: "Azerbaijan's territorial integrity recognized by the international community and the United Nations must be restored. Four UN Security Council resolutions must be implemented unconditionally. The occupying forces must withdraw from our lands.") (Date accessed: 19 October 2011).

[11] Own observation made in Brussels, Berlin, Rome, Paris and London.

[12] president.az, "Speech by President Ilham Aliyev at a ceremony to inaugurate the State Flag Square", 1 September 2010 (excerpt: "Our state flag will be hoisted in Nagorno-Karabakh, Khankandi and Shusha. We must and we are making this day nearer by our work.") (Date accessed: 19 October 2011).

comply with the request for a withdrawal, as a long as there is a visible threat to the (ethnically Armenian) population of NK. While Armenia is arguably more comfortable with the status quo than Azerbaijan, the four UN resolutions underscore the thin ice on which this status is based. For the Armenian side, the one way to achieve a firmer legal status and allow for the (painful) withdrawal of troops – effectively overcoming the four Security Council Resolutions – is a package solution as offered in the Minsk Group's Madrid principles. In this sense, the existence of the four "old" resolutions remind the Armenian side that they have to find a "new" and stronger status. On the other side, for Azerbaijan, those resolutions pose an obstacle in the current negotiations, as they interpret them to offer everything which Azerbaijan has never been offered again in the Minsk Group since 1994. All proposed solutions to the conflict reflect the security of the ethnic Armenian population in NK, and that their right for self-determination is equal with Azerbaijan's right for territorial integrity. It is noteworthy that the four resolutions all called for a lasting ceasefire regime and strongly supported the Minsk Group. While de-facto the four resolutions are today a reminder of the times of heavy fighting and the protracted weaknesses of the status quo since the ceasefire, the Security Council clearly intended them to contribute to peace, not to be an argument against differently formulated proposals by the Minsk Group today. In any case, they are indispensable to understand the viewpoint of Azerbaijan in this conflict then and now.

Not from international law, but from Azerbaijan itself comes a more significant factor weakening the status quo. While both sides have strongly invested in their defence, Azerbaijan's reliance on military means has strongly been bolstered by its disproportionate military acquisitions over the past ten years. Baku has built up a thriving petro-industry which provides for an annual military budget several times that of Armenia and Karabakh.[13] The International Crisis Group describes the ongoing arms race as follows:

> Azerbaijan's official defence spending has risen twenty-fold during the presidency of Ilham Aliyev, with an average annual increase

---

[13] M. Muradova (2011) "Azerbaijan Boosts Defence Production", Central Asia-Caucasus Institute, http://www.cacianalyst.org/?q=node/5482 (excerpt: "On January 14, Azerbaijani President Ilham Aliyev stated that "... Azerbaijan's defence budget in 2011 is 30 per cent higher than the total [annual] budget of Armenia ... we spend US$ three billion only for military expenses". (In October, Azerbaijan adopted a US$ 3.12 billion military budget for 2011, including a 90 per cent hike in military spending in comparison with 2010. "... It means that the difference between the two countries is on a non-comparable level. For the military budget, we can allocate as much [money] as we want, while Armenia will depend only on aid from abroad ...", Aliyev proudly declared at the government meeting.") (date accessed: 13 June 2011).

approximating 50 per cent, from $135million in 2003 to $3.12 billion today. ... Armenia's official defence budget pales in comparison, but Yerevan is also arming. According to its budget, it plans to spend some $390 million on the army in 2011. Some analysts estimate that the total defence figure, counting Nagorno-Karabakh's, is closer to $600 million.[14]

In this context, Markedonov argues that once war has been rejected as a tool for resolving the conflict, it will be possible to discuss other issues. This question has been dealt with most prominently at the level of the OSCE Minsk Group negotiations, but also in public debate, predominantly through public war threats made by President Aliyev and high-ranking Azerbaijani officials. In 2010–11, these threats reached a frequency of approximately every second week.[15] In the following example of a statement by Ilham Aliyev, he considers the war which ended in 1994 to be only the first stage, and apparently expects further stages:

We must be ready to liberate our occupied lands at any time. And I'm completely confident that Azerbaijan is capable of doing so today. We have considerably increased our military power. ... Azerbaijan must make it to the ranks of the developed countries in terms of economic progress, and this is our goal. We are a modern country. This is why the first stage of the war decides nothing. It only proves that the people of Azerbaijan and the Azerbaijani state will never accept this situation and will restore their territorial integrity by any means.[16]

Other representatives of the leadership in Baku are more explicit:

Azerbaijan must attack Yerevan, said Azerbaijan former lead negotiator and presidential adviser Vafa Guluzade Thursday, adding that the attacks must be so severe that Armenia would not be able to "forget it".[17]

[14] International Crisis Group (2011) "Armenia and Azerbaijan Preventing War", *Europe Briefing*, No. 60 Tbilisi/Baku/Yerevan/Istanbul Brussels, 8 February 2011, 5–7, http://www.scribd.com/doc/48420672/Armenia-and-Azerbaijan-Preventing-War-Europe-Briefing-N%C2%B060-Tbilisi-Baku-Yerevan-Istanbul-Brussels-8-February-2011 (date accessed: 13 June 2011).
[15] See also: European Friends of Armenia "Collection of war threat statements by President Ilham Aliyev and other Azerbaijani Officials", http://www.eufoa.org/uploads/AliyevWarThreats.pdf (date accessed: 13 June 2011).
[16] News.az, "Karabakh to remain part of Azerbaijan – Ilham Aliyev", 14 July 2010, http://www.news.az/articles/19078 (date accessed: 29 July 2011).
[17] Asbarez, "Azerbaijan must attack Yerevan, says political expert", 14 July 2011, http://asbarez.com/97048/azerbaijan-must-attack-yerevan-says-political-expert/ (date accessed: 29 July 2011).

Azerbaijan's Defense Minister Safar Abiyev told OSCE Minsk Group co-chairmen that his country is seriously preparing for war against Armenia to "liberate its territories from occupation".[18]

The latter is not the only example where the target audience was by no means the domestic public of Azerbaijan. Considering the damage which such statements do to Azerbaijan's image and credibility, it is difficult to comprehend the strategy behind this. Yet the basic ideas behind these statements are apparently mainstream among the Azerbaijani leadership. Armenia has also responded sporadically to Azerbaijan's war threats. Speaking at a meeting of the Central Office of the Foreign Ministry and the heads of Armenia's diplomatic missions, President Serzh Sargsyan stated:

> Baku is not ready for peace as it's impossible to set peace by advocating a war; to reconcile societies by sowing Armenophobia; build trust by instigating race of arms. Such behaviour demonstrated by Azerbaijan is unacceptable and we will make adequate steps. Be sure – in case of a new military adventure Armenia will again coerce the rival to peace.[19]

The principle of refraining from the use of force applies to Azerbaijan, as well as to Armenia and Nagorno-Karabakh. This principle prohibits countries from pursuing their objectives with "threat or use of force". This prohibition constitutes a basic concept of modern international law and is one of the fundamental principles (Article 2, Nr. 4) of the UN Charter.[20] Numerous declarations and international obligations exclude military actions and threats of war, while constraining the parties in the conflict to reach effective agreements without any use of force. This principle is also embedded in the Helsinki Final Act, to which both Armenia and Azerbaijan are signatories, and which states that: "the participating States will refrain from any acts constituting a threat of force or direct or indirect use of force against another participating State. Likewise they will refrain from any manifestation of force for the purpose of inducing another participating State to

---

[18] Asbarez, "Azerbaijan Preparing for War, Says Defence Minister", 14 February 2011, http://asbarez.com/93413/azerbaijan-preparing-for-war-says-defense-minister/, (date accessed: 29 July 2011).

[19] Mediamax, " 'There is a red line which we'll never cross', the Armenian President states", 30 August 2011, http://www.mediamax.am/en/news/karabakh/2187/ (date accessed 31 August 2011).

[20] See in this volume: O. Luchterhandt (2011) "Learning from Georgia: A non-use-of-force treaty for Nagorno-Karabakh", Chap. 20.

renounce the full exercise of its sovereign rights. Likewise they will also refrain in their mutual relations from any act of reprisal by force".[21]

The Presidents of Armenia, Azerbaijan and Russia reaffirmed their shared commitment to seeking a political solution to the conflict in the "Moscow Declaration" on Regulating the Nagorno-Karabakh Conflict, signed on 2 November 2008. Its stated objective was "establishing regional stability and security in the South Caucasus". The three presidents agreed that the search for a peaceful solution should be accompanied by "legally binding international guarantees of all its aspects and stages." However, by June 2009, President Aliyev had resumed his military rhetoric, stating: "Nagorno-Karabakh is an ancient Azerbaijani land, and we will make every effort to restore Azerbaijan's territorial integrity. We can use political, diplomatic and, if necessary, military means. We do have such a right. International law allows that".[22] Despite the pleas of the international community, Azerbaijan's war threats against Karabakh have increased.[23] In June 2010 EU High Representative Catherine Ashton issued a statement on Nagorno-Karabakh, calling on both sides "to respect the ceasefire, restrain from the use of force or any threat thereof, and continue efforts for the peaceful resolution of the Nagorno-Karabakh conflict".[24] In a 7 June 2011 interview with the Polish "*Nowa Europa Wschodnia*" (New Eastern Europe), the Personal Representative of the OSCE Chairman-in-Office, Andrzej Kasprzyk, called for an end to threats of war.[25]

With a view to such escalation cycles, it is important to understand the status quo against the background of what the people think. This volume contains some unique insights into how the people perceive the conflict. Cooper and Morris present the results of the first-ever comparative opinion poll in Nagorno-Karabakh and Armenia, which was conducted under the supervision of an international polling institute. They describe how deeply

[21] OSCE (1975) Conference on Security and Co-operation in Europe, Final Act, Helsinki, 1 August 1975, http://www.osce.org/mc/39501 (date accessed: 13 June 2011).

[22] Armenialiberty, "Aliyev again Threatens New War for Karabakh", 05 January 2011, http://www.armenialiberty.org/content/article/1599118.html (date accessed: 13 June 2011).

[23] European Friends of Armenia "Collection of war threat statements by President Ilham Aliyev and other Azerbaijani Officials", op. cit.

[24] Europa (2010) "Statement by the spokesperson of High Representative Catherine Ashton on Nagorno-Karabakh", A 110/10, Brussels, 22 June 2010, http://www.consilium.europa.eu/uedocs/cms_data/docs/pressdata/EN/foraff/115451.pdf (date accessed: 13 June 2011).

[25] Asbarez, "OSCE Chairman Rep. Calls for End to War Threats", 7 June 2011, http://asbarez.com/96429/osce-chairman-rep-call-for-end-to-war-threats/?utm_source=feedburner&utm_medium=feed&utm_campaign=Feed%3A+Asbarez+News%29 (date accessed: 13 June 2011).

people in Armenia and in Karabakh distrust Azerbaijan, but also that they do strive for peace and would even support the removal of snipers. This point is surprising, as the above-mentioned logic would dictate that removing parts of your own military is in itself a sign of weakness and a risk, regardless of international guarantees or military analyses. Yet, the poll also shows that the public has not yet been prepared for the return of the seven districts around Karabakh. Yerevan's official position has consistently been that, once a comprehensive peace deal is found, for example on the basis of the Basic Principles proposed by the OSCE Minsk Group, the seven districts will pose no problem.[26] Implicitly this means that they will be returned as part of a comprehensive peace deal. This is in line with the findings of a recent OSCE report,[27] according to which there is no Armenian/Karabakhi settlement programme implemented in those districts. These findings contradict Azerbaijani accusations and but also caused disappointment among some more nationalist parties in Armenia.[28]

Yet, history does play a role and is partially responsible for the troubled status quo. Coulie describes how history has become a burden for the people. Ethnic Armenians have lived side by side with ethnic Turks for hundreds of years, stretching from Baku to Istanbul and beyond. However, especially since the 1915 Ottoman Genocide against the Armenian people,[29] and Stalin's strategic and legally doubtful[30] allocation of the predominantly ethnic Armenian Nagorno-Karabakh to the Soviet Republic of Azerbaijan in 1921,[31] the relationship between the two sides has been based mainly upon traumata. From this perspective, the Karabakh war which ended in 1994 was merely the last

[26] RA Ministry of Foreign Affairs, "The Armenian Foreign Affairs Minister Edward Nalbandian received the OSCE Minsk Group Co-Chairs", press release, 09 June 2011, http://www.mfa.am/en/press-releases/item/2011/06/09/mg_co_chairs/ (date accessed: 13 June 2011).

[27] OSCE (2011a) "Executive Summary of the 'Report of the OSCE Minsk Group Co-Chairs' Field Assessment Mission to the Occupied Territories of Azerbaijan Surrounding Nagorno-Karabakh", 24 March 2011, http://www.osce.org/mg/76209 (date accessed: 13 June 2011).

[28] The strongest negative reaction to the OSCE MG Field Assessment Mission report came from Vahan Hovhannisyan (Dashnaktsutyun party): http://www.panorama.am/en/politics/2011/03/25/hovhannisyan/ (date accessed: 07 July 2011).

[29] There have been numerous publications made on this subject. The Armenian Genocide memorial (www.genocide-museum.am) lists official documentation, states that recognised the Armenian Genocide officially and a number of background facts. Another list of documents can be found here: "*International Affirmations of the Armenian Genocide*", http://www.wbarrow.co.uk/rememberarmenia/pdfs_in_chapters/02a_armenia2_affirmations.pdf (date accessed: 07 July 2011).

[30] Today's international law was of course not yet developed, yet the principle that legal acts must involve the parties concerned and not be concluded without them and against them already existed.

[31] See timeline: July 1921.

dramatic episode of this traumatisation. Cox's eyewitness account in this volume bears witness to some of the disturbing effects this has had. Coulie argues that, while history should not get in the way of future solutions, it does need to be considered when tabling solutions. He argues that the Karabakhi independence movement, the first to appear in the outgoing USSR,[32] sought to overcome the trauma through separation. Yet, in the long run, self-determination should not generate monocultural or monoethnic entities, because the ensuing loss of the richness in human terms would be greater than the political gain. Besides, monoethnic entities would not be likely to gain real peace and stability. There is a strong need for more people-to-people contact and cultural exchange, as between France and Germany after World War II. In this context, Rochtus suggests considering the components of self-determination within a larger national framework, comparable to those implemented by the independence movement of Flanders. Yet Rochtus also recognises the limits of such options, especially since the independence movement in Karabakh was based on the wish to protect the ethnic Armenian majority not only against political, economic and cultural disadvantages, but above all against physical harm exerted by the Azerbaijani parent state. The loss of life and physical health is also key to understanding the traumatised views expressed by people during the large-scale Town Hall Meeting project implemented in 2009 in Armenia, Nagorno-Karabakh and Azerbaijan, as outlined by Poghosyan. The most interesting but also the most worrying result of these is the strong disconnect between the views and arguments of people in Armenia and Karabakh on the one hand and people in Azerbaijan on the other. The meeting records give an indication as to how far this disconnect has grown and how the two sides live in what they perceive as different worlds, with all dangerous implications for the peace process.

The status quo is unsustainable because it promotes mainly two sources of instability:

- an arms race between the conflict parties and
- a growing gap between the people on both sides of the line of contact, their perceived realities, and their fear and hatred of the enemy.

At the same time, the status quo discourages factors of stability, such as large-scale people-to-people contacts and trade. If this situation is prolonged, it will inevitably lead to a new military escalation. This means that the status quo must change to reverse the above-mentioned effects and at least tolerate factors of stability while reducing factors of instability. Otherwise, the status quo will one day be changed by military force.

The two sides often accuse each other of playing with the status quo. Azerbaijan accuses Armenia and Karabakh of prolonging it in hope of

---

[32] See timeline: February 1988.

achieving some sort of stabilisation over time, comparable to the development in the Kosovo case.[33] Meanwhile, Armenia accuses Azerbaijan of putting its official rhetoric into practice, that is, actively preparing to gain control over Karabakh by military force. Thus, Baku uses the time of the precarious status quo to accumulate petrodollars and devote them to military acquisitions. It is difficult to say who in the long run gains more advantages from a prolonged status quo. In fact, both parties have been quite successful in preventing the other from profiting thoroughly from the time factor. Meanwhile, Gurbanov's assumption that the delicate status quo is to some extent strategically, and to some extent psychologically, perpetuated, explains at least some of the actions of the three conflict parties, especially Azerbaijan.

Scenarios of peace

Following the above analysis, one could wonder why no new war has broken out over the last 17 years. Asking analysts, politicians, military experts and other insiders about the rationality of war they tend to produce incoherent answers. But they all have one component in common, irrespective of whether asking in Armenia or in Nagorno-Karabakh, irrespective of whether they are foreign experts, for example from NATO or the EU, or a high-ranking member of the Karabakhi army: the scope of a new war would likely be drastically larger than in 1994 and the final outcome would be uncertain but always horrible. Thus, the key reason as to why military hostilities have so far not resumed is that rationally, war carries much greater risks than does any diplomatic solution. Hence, two different kinds of factors determine the scenarios of peace:

- Peace due to a lack of interest in war, or due to other peace factors outside of the peace negotiations
- Peace factors within the peace negotiations

Peace due to a lack of interest in war or other peace factors outside of the peace negotiations

It may sound trivial, but from an objective point of view only Azerbaijan has an interest in considering military options. In fact, as shown above, Baku is announcing this publicly, and with increasing frequency. By contrast, Armenia and Karabakh have almost nothing to gain from a military

---

[33] President.az, "Speech by Ilham Aliyev at the VII OSCE Summit" (excerpt: "Armenia does not want peace, doesn't want to liberate occupied territories, but wants to keep the status-quo as long as they can and make negotiation process endless", http://en.president.az/articles/1189 (date accessed: 07 July 2011).

confrontation. They would put at risk the security of all that they gained in the war which ended in 1994, as well as all that they have built up in Nagorno-Karabakh. It would make no sense to risk all this for the very few aspirations that remain: Shahumian, a small territory in northern Karabakh controlled by Azerbaijan, and a few other villages where ethnic Armenians constituted the majority[34] before being displaced during the conflict. However, there is virtually no debate in Armenia or Karabakh about seeking to regain control over these places. Their names mainly appear in discussions about the fate of displaced ethnic Armenians, who often remain overshadowed by the displaced ethnic Azeris, for whom Azerbaijan organises international "recognition" campaigns.[35] Thus, the only plausible reason for the Armenian side to start a war could be preventive strikes, following credible intelligence suggesting that Azerbaijani strikes are imminent. Although this argument does sometimes make it into the public debate, it has never been seriously considered or supported in any official statement. It remains confined to small and more radical political forces.

In comparison, Azerbaijan has very concrete goals – goals about which the government in Baku has been making public bellicose promises for many years, effectively putting itself under pressure to deliver. Many times, President Ilham Aliyev has promised in public that Azerbaijan will never tolerate any form of independence for Nagorno-Karabakh, adding that if the "occupying troops" of the "aggressor" do not withdraw, Azerbaijan will resort to the military option.[36] While this does not yet entail his choosing that option, it demonstrates the interest. Formulated positively: The likelihood of war between the two countries is slightly reduced by the fact that not both but only one of the two has genuine strategic interests in starting hostilities.

War is also against the interests of the other players in the South Caucasus. Russia's efforts in the Minsk Group negotiations go well beyond showcasing. The Russian president has clearly invested political capital, even at the expense of domestic criticisms of weakness, as in the aftermath of the failed

---

[34] As part of the Soviet Autonomous Oblast of Nagorno-Karabakh, a small territory east of Martuni, some small villages west of Tartar, the former ethnic Armenian enclave of Getashen (Az. Çaykənd) and above all the entire Shahumian region in the north of Karabakh could be named. Besides, Azerbaijan controls the Armenian village of Artsvashen, an enclave situated north of Lake Sevan.

[35] The European Azerbaijan Society (TEAS), "Azerbaijani IDPs call upon the EU to speed their return", 18 March 2011, https://teas.eu/news/2011–03–18/azerbaijani-idps-call-upon-eu-speed-their-return (date accessed: 11 July 2011).

APA, "Conference on Nagorno Karabakh conflict held at European Parliament", 19 April 2011, http://en.apa.az/news.php?id=145346, (date accessed: 11 July 2011).

[36] Original quotes from President Aliyev, cf. European Friends of Armenia "Collection of war threat statements by President Ilham Aliyev and other Azerbaijani Officials", op. cit.

Kazan summit.[37] Besides, the much-reported-upon Russian military base in Gyumri, recently prolonged until 2044, has a mere 3500 soldiers, while, as Markedonov describes, in the same week that its contract was prolonged, Russia also struck a surprisingly friendly deal with Azerbaijan over their common border.[38] This means that Russia is genuinely trying to maintain good relations with both countries and is seeking a peace deal in the framework of the Minsk Group. That said, Russia also sells arms to both sides and in doing so is sometimes perceived to shift the balance towards one side or the other. However, an outbreak of war would ruin the income of the war parties, putting an end to their acquisitions in the medium term. Moreover, Russia has invested heavily in infrastructure and service companies in the South Caucasus, especially in Armenia.[39] At the time of making those investments, almost no other investors were willing to take the risks: investing was highly speculative and mainly politically motivated. But, today, those companies are sending considerable profits back home to Moscow, adding another reason why Russia has an interest in avoiding war.

Neighbouring Turkey and Georgia share a similar lack of interest in a new Karabakh war, as it would affect their own infrastructure projects, most notably the BTC pipeline,[40] but it also would be problematic for their fundamental economic and political stability. Georgia is still recovering from the war with Russia in 2008. The prospect of a large influx of refugees on its southern border, where already today a large ethnic Armenian minority and an ethnic Azeri minority live, would strongly compromise their interests of stable political and economic development. Turkey's role is less clear: it

---

[37] Radio Free Europe / Radio Liberty (RFE/RL), "Russia's Medvedev 'Frustrated' With Karabakh Impasse", 27 June 2011, http://www.rferl.org/content/russia_medvedev_frustrated_karabakh_impasse/24248417.html (date accessed: 08 July 2011).

[38] See Markedonov in this volume. More sources: RTT News, "Deal to Extend Russian Military Base in Armenia Comes into Force", 07 July 2011, http://www.rttnews.com/Content/GeneralNews.aspx?Id=1660226&SM=1 (date accessed: 11 July 2011).

Kremlin.ru, "Ratification of agreement on state border between Russia and Azerbaijan", 27 June 2011, http://eng.kremlin.ru/acts/2476 (date accessed: 11 July 2011).

[39] H. Khachatrian (2006) "Russian Investments in Armenia: Their Economic Background and Possible Political Impact", Central Asia-Caucasus Institute, 13 December 2006.

RFERL, "Russian Energy Giants to Invest in Armenian Utilities", 17 June 2011, http://www.rferl.org/content/russian_energy_giants_to_invest_in_armenian_utilities/24238600.html (dateaccessed: 11 July 2011).

[40] The Environmental Audit Committee, "Regional Conflicts and BTC Pipeline: Concerns over ECGD's due diligence", http://bankwatch.org/documents/EAC_BTC_Conflict_26.8.08.pdf (date accessed: 08 July 2011).

sides with its "brother nation" Azerbaijan,[41] but it has no interest in further destabilising its socio-economically weakest regions in Eastern Anatolia and fears that Kurdish separatists might use the conflict to improve their own status. The prospect of a large-scale regional war with inevitable international interventions would also bear a number of risks, as nobody could predict whose troops would finally end up where. Besides, oil-rich Azerbaijan would transform from a strong business partner into a source of refugees, against Turkish interests. Iran, as the third neighbour, has a difficult relationship with Azerbaijan, since Iran views the strong ethnic Azeri minority in northern Iran, which makes up almost a quarter of the Iranian population, as a destabilising factor.[42] Furthermore, a military confrontation on its northern border, with the possible deployment of Western troops, would be seen as a serious challenge to Iranian national security. Azerbaijan, on the other hand, cooperates strongly with Israel to acquire military equipment, and if Israel should ever intervene militarily against the nuclear programme in Iran, they will require Azerbaijan for logistical help.

The external major powers, the EU and the United States, have always had a strong interest in peace and stability. Semneby and Tannock describe how the EU has designed its entire Eastern Partnership to promote peace and stability. The United States is no less keen on those goals but, as Giragosian outlines, places a stronger focus on strategic goals, such as energy transit routes, air corridors and political relations with Russia. Clearly, the prospect of having to cope with incalculable humanitarian aid or deploying peacekeeping forces in the South Caucasus motivates all EU and US decision makers to contribute actively to a peace settlement.

Overall, this results in a situation in which almost no player can see advantages in war scenarios, and the only one threatening to go on the offensive, Azerbaijan, also faces considerable rational deterrents. Azerbaijan is proud of its vast military acquisitions,[43] yet Baku also knows that a war would likely destroy all the wealth it has built up. Strategic sites of the oil and gas

[41] President.az, "Ilham Aliyev and President of Turkey Abdullah Gul had press conference", 16 August 2011, http://en.president.az/articles/605 (excerpt: "We co-operate and interact in all other fields as brothers and friends. This is our strategic line. I recall the saying of the great leader Mustafa Kamal Ataturk. He said: the Sorrow of Azerbaijan is our Sorrow; the Joy of Azerbaijan is our Joy. The national leader of the Azerbaijani people Heydar Aliyev said: Turkey and Azerbaijan are one nation and two states.") (date accessed 18 August 2011).

[42] S. Cornell (2004) "Iranian Azerbaijan: A Brewing Hotspot", presented at Symposium on "Human Rights and Ethnicity in Iran", 22 November 2004, Stockholm, http://www.azeri.dk/en/articles/Iranian_azerbaijan.html (date accessed: 8 July 2011).

[43] Reuters, "Azerbaijan leader warns of army buildup at huge parade", 26 June 2011, http://ca.reuters.com/article/topNews/idCATRE75P0LD20110626 (date accessed: 8 July 2011).

industry would be Armenia's first retaliation targets, especially the most important pipelines, the routes of which cross Azerbaijan towards Georgia, just a few kilometres north of the mountains of Nagorno-Karabakh. It has long been known that the rocket and ordnance potential of the combined Armenian and Karabakhi forces includes ballistic missiles, among them the type R-17 (NATO name SS-1 Scud B).[44] Potential petro-industry targets on the shores of Baku are just within their 300 km range. Potential targets further to the southwest, along the coastline between Danizkanary, Qobustan and Alat, are in more comfortable reach. Besides, both the Armenian and the Karabakhi armies have upgraded those missiles in range and precision and also acquired an undisclosed number of more modern retaliation missiles.[45] Thus, the governments on both sides of the Line of Contact know that rationally, they would have to fear fundamental losses. Those losses would have the strong potential of leading to a change of political power domestically, as Armenia and Azerbaijan share the common experience of falling governments triggered by developments in the Nagorno-Karabakh conflict.[46]

Finally, there are at least three other factors that dissuade Azerbaijan from launching hostilities in the near future:

- The Eurovision Song Contest, to be held in Baku in May 2012;
- Presidential elections in Azerbaijan in October 2013;
- The Olympic Winter Games, to be held in Sochi in February 2014.

While it is arguably a weak deterrent, the Eurovision song contest will be a rare opportunity for Baku to present itself internationally as a modern and thriving country. An outbreak of war prior to this event would make it impossible to host. Even if a war were somehow contained or if it came shortly after the event, it would entirely counter the contest's positive communication effect.

While the democracies in Eastern Europe are all more or less defective and still in the making, the nature of the regime in Baku is arguably comparable

---

[44] S. Minasyan (2010) "Nagorno-Karabakh after two decades of conflict: Is prolongation of the status quo inevitable?", *Caucasus Institute Research Papers*, 52, http://www.caucasusinstitute.org/wp-content/uploads/2011/02/CI_RP_2-eng.pdf (date accessed: 29 July 2011).

[45] Azatutyun.am, "Armenia Confirms Possession of Sophisticated Missiles", 20 December 2010, http://www.azatutyun.am/content/article/2254125.html (date accessed: 12 July 2011).

[46] Power changes in Azerbaijan triggered by the Nakgorno-Karabakh conflict: Ayaz Mutalibov (19 May 1990–6 March 1992); Abülfaz Elçibay (16 June 1992–1 September 1993). Power change in Armenia: Levon Ter-Petrosyan (16 October 1991–3 February 1998). See timeline.

only to that in Minsk (Belarus), as is reflected in EU reports.[47] Hence, it is safe to claim that the presidential elections in 2013 will be won by Ilham Aliyev, unless there is a severe political disturbance. Such a political disturbance could mainly come from a war in Nagorno-Karabakh, in which the most likely development would show that Baku cannot fulfil its repeated promise that reconquering the territory would be very fast and decisively victorious.

According to insiders, the Olympic Games in Sochi were put on the table by Russian President Medvedev during the trilateral summit in the OSCE Minsk Group context on 5 March 2011 in Sochi. Allegedly, Medvedev expressed a strong wish to rule out any regional development which could hamper the Olympic Games. Rumours contend that he even threatened an assertive Russian response in the event of hostilities which could endanger the games. While these remarks, if they were made, were expressed during confidential negotiations and cannot be confirmed, it is safe to assume that Russia has a very clear interest to this end and, whether uttered or not, the potential war parties must be aware of possible effects of this Russian interest.

In any case, the risks rationally outweigh the potential benefits of starting a war. However, it remains to be seen whether the rational approach is applicable, given certain developments, especially in Baku's policy. These will be discussed below, in the section on scenarios of war.

Peace factors within the peace negotiations

The OSCE Minsk Group has led negotiations ever since the 1994 Bishkek ceasefire agreement came into force. Following the war between Georgia and Russia in 2008, and with tensions on the Line of Contact rising since summer 2010, the Minsk Group accelerated and intensified the negotiations. Beyond the Basic Principles for a comprehensive peace deal, the process has for years been synonymous with a peaceful perspective, as opposed to the military option, repeatedly threatened mainly by Azerbaijan. However, negotiations are not a goal in themselves, and Azerbaijan has often complained

---

[47] Europa (2011) European Commission, High Representative of the European Union for Foreign Affairs and Security policy, *"Implementation of the European Neighbourhood Policy in 2010, Country Report: Azerbaijan"* {COM(2011) 303}, http://ec.europa.eu/world/enp/pdf/progress2011/sec_11_640_en.pdf (date accessed: 12 July 2011).

Europa (2011a) Permanent Council, *"EU Statement on Human Rights, Fundamental Freedoms and the Rule of Law in Azerbaijan"*, Vienna, 1 September 2011, http://www.delvie.ec.europa.eu/en/eu_osce/eu_statements/2011/September/PC%20no.878%20-%20EU%20on%20HR%20in%20AEZ.pdf (date accessed: 2 September 2011).

Europa (2011b) EEAS, *"Statement by High Representative Catherine Ashton on Azerbaijan"*, Brussels, 20 May 2011, http://www.consilium.europa.eu/uedocs/cms_data/docs/pressdata/EN/foraff/122137.pdf (date accessed: 29 July 2011).

that Armenia sees the negotiations merely as a means of prolonging the status quo.[48] Over the course of the negotiations, there have been times when first one side was happier with the current draft, and then the other. For instance, during the St Petersburg summit in June 2009, President Aliyev left prematurely and a large-scale shooting incident followed immediately on the Line of Contact. Thereafter, Baku was blocking any progress arguably until the Sochi summit in March 2011, while communicating that they accepted the version of the Minsk Group document presented in December 2009 in Athens. This may seem confusing, but it simply reflects the ups and downs, the preferences and aversions regarding different versions of the Basic Principles. The Armenian side has communicated less about its specific likes and dislikes, but has clearly blocked any version of the Basic Principles which did not entail a free expression of will for the future determination of status for Nagorno-Karabakh. Asked by a radical oppositional newspaper,[49] the Armenian foreign minister made it clear that Armenia does agree to all the points in the latest Minsk Group proposals, as long as they come as a package which implements the Minsk Group Co-Chairs' declarations of L'Aquila and Muskoka.[50] The Kazan summit in June 2011 was supposed to bring the breakthrough. However, when President Aliyev arrived, he presented a list of new demands on issues ranging across the board, most of which the foreign ministers had formerly agreed upon or already had dismissed. The summit ended with a weak declaration about continuing the process.[51] Armenia complained publicly about Azerbaijan's derailing action, but the international community perceived this as the usual finger pointing between war parties. Azerbaijan complained about Armenia in the same way, saying that the peace process never delivers any results. But once the Minsk Group Co-Chairs started reporting back domestically about what happened, the picture became clearer. In Russia, strong new diplomatic attempts were announced, also to safeguard the image of President Medvedev, who faced criticism for alleged

---

[48] President.az, "Speech by Ilham Aliyev at the VII OSCE Summit" (excerpt: "Armenia does not want peace, doesn't want to liberate occupied territories, but wants to keep the status-quo as long as they can and make negotiation process endless", http://en.president.az/articles/1189 (date accessed: 07 July 2011).

[49] RA Ministry of Foreign Affairs, "The Address of the Foreign Affairs Minister Edward Nalbandyan at the Annual Press Conference, Summarizing the Foreign Policy", 14 January 2011, http://www.mfa.am/en/press-conference/item/2011/01/14/nalbandian_summary/ (date accessed: 29 July 2011).

[50] RA Ministry of Foreign Affairs, "Declarations of the OSCE Minsk Group Co-Chairs", 2009–10, http://www.mfa.am/u_files/file/statementseng.pdf (date accessed: 29 July 2011).

[51] Reuters, "Armenia, Azerbaijan blame each other for Karabakh failure", 25 June 2011, http://uk.reuters.com/article/2011/06/25/azerbaijan-armenia-karabakh-idUKANT55197620110625 (date accessed: 29 July 2011).

weakness after the Kazan failure.[52] US Secretary of State Hillary Clinton used her trip to Turkey to demand a renewed attempt to conclude the Armenian-Turkish rapprochement, effectively communicating the government's frustration over Baku's stance.[53] The French Co-Chair, Bernard Fassier, presented the details at the EU's Political and Security Committee meeting in Brussels.[54] One month after Kazan, it was clear to most of the decision-making circles that Baku had deliberately derailed the best chance in years to reach an agreement. Thomas de Waal wrote "Many sources, including ones in Baku, confirm that it was the Azerbaijani side that blocked agreement in Kazan."[55] And in an interview with Hürriyet, Azerbaijani Deputy Prime Minister Hasanov made a shockingly open statement, admitting that "Baku is negotiating with Yerevan solely for the sake of negotiating, as Azerbaijan would be labelled an 'anti-democratic state' if it did not participate in the meetings". He then went on to speculate about Turkey's role in a new war over Karabakh: "We always say that if things keep going this way, we could declare war. We would have liked to see Turkey behind us, but there is international law."[56] While this was perceived as a small shock among experts, there was no public reaction from the international political community to these statements.

That said, the Minsk Group has delivered concrete results in the past. The Minsk Group already assisted in the preparation and implementation of the 1994 Bishkek ceasefire itself, which was not just by chance signed by the Russian Minsk Group Co-Chair, Vladimir Kazimirov, rather than, for instance, by the Russian foreign minister.[57] In recent years, there have been

---

[52] Itar-tass, "Russian president disappointed with the results of the Kazan summit on Nagorno Karabakh conflict settlement", 27 June 2011, http://www.itar-tass.com/en/c142/173888_print.html (date accessed: 29 July 2011).

[53] *Hurriyet Daily News*, "US asks for action from Turkey for reconciliation", 24 July 2011, http://www.hurriyetdailynews.com/n.php?n=us-asks-for-action-from-turkey-for-reconciliation-2011–07–24 (date accessed: 29 July 2011).

[54] According to several participants to the first PSC after the Kazan summit in June 2011, Ambassador Fassier confirmed Aliyev's presentation of a long list of last minute amendments while Armenia accepted the texts formerly agreed between the Azerbaijani and Armenian Foreign Ministers, under Russian and Minsk Group mediation. However, Fassier apparently stopped short of explicitly and directly blaming Azerbaijan for the failure of the summit, retaining the neutral communication style of the MG Co-Chairs.

[55] RFERL, "Can the 'Medvedev Moment' Be Saved for Karabakh?", 28 July 2011, http://www.rferl.org/content/medvedev_moment_saved_nagorno_karabakh_kazan/24279692.html (date accessed: 29 July 2011).

[56] *Hurriyet Daily News*, "Azerbaijan backs Turkey over Cyprus but fears Karabakh impact, says Azeri deputy PM", 21 July 2011, http://www.hurriyetdailynews.com/n.php?n=azerbaijan-backs-turkey-over-cyprus-but-fears-karabakh-impact-says-azeri-deputy-pm-2011–07–21 (date accessed: 29 July 2011).

[57] Formally, the main negotiator was the Russian Federation as MG Co-Chair, while the MG sidelined the process – comparable to today's trilateral summit format.

other achievements: Firstly, the Moscow declaration, the first document bearing the signature of the presidents of independent Azerbaijan and Armenia. The declaration excludes the use of force in solving the Nagorno-Karabakh conflict.[58] However, upon his arrival in Baku, President Aliyev contradicted the words of the declaration by making it clear that it does not deprive Baku of its right to use military force to regain control over Karabakh.[59] Secondly, there have been a number of smaller achievements, such as the exchange of prisoners, an OSCE study on the situation in the seven districts surrounding Karabakh, visits by the Co-Chairs even to Karabakh and crossing the Line of Contact, and so forth. These were all small signs of peace- and confidence-building, with the OSCE study confirming that there is no Armenian settlement programme in the seven districts,[60] countering repeated allegations from Azerbaijan to this effect. Thirdly, there was the March 2011 Sochi agreement on an exchange of prisoners (again) and on OSCE Minsk Group-led investigations into each incident on the Line of Contact.[61] Armenia has publicly welcomed such investigations. No public reaction has come from Azerbaijan. Lastly, but not least, the OSCE has repeatedly suggested the removal of snipers along the Line of Contact, allowing the deployment of international observers. This was accepted by Yerevan[62] but rejected by Baku.[63]

[58] RFERL, " 'Moscow Declaration' A Victory for Armenia", 03 November 2008, http://www.rferl.org/content/Moscow_Declaration_A_Victory_For_Armenia/1337592.html (date accessed: 29 July 2011).

[59] Azernews, "President discloses key elements of Garabagh paper", 03 December 2008, http://www.azernews.az/en/Nation/9099-President_discloses_key_elements_of_Garabagh_paper (date accessed: 29 July 2011).

[60] This question is important for the credibility of Armenia, which stated that it would return those districts as part of a comprehensive peace deal. The key conclusion was that the number of people residing in those districts has not changed between 2005 and 2010 and that no infrastructure has been created to make the few ethnic Armenian settlements permanent. It furthermore concluded that the few people residing there are mainly ethnic Armenian refugees from the pogroms in Azerbaijan, who mostly have no valid passports. Source: OSCE, Executive Summary of the "Report of the OSCE Minsk Group Co-Chairs' Field Assessment Mission to the Occupied Territories of Azerbaijan Surrounding Nagorno-Karabakh", http://www.osce.org/mg/76209 (date accessed 29 July 2011).

[61] Azatutyun, "Armenian, Azeri Leaders Pledge to Seek Peaceful Karabakh Settlement", 07 March 2011, http://www.azatutyun.am/content/article/2330373.html (date accessed: 29 July 2011).

[62] OSCE (2011) "Statement by H.E. Mr. Edward Nalbandian, Minister of Foreign Affairs of the Republic of Armenia at the 852nd Meeting of the OSCE Permanent Council", op. cit.

[63] Azerbaijan never publicly rejected the proposal, but it is clear that Armenia accepted it and it was then never implemented. In an attempt to bring about any kind of movement on this issue, the OSCE chairman in office, Azubalis, coming back

To summarise, currently, the key party complaining about the lack of progress in the Minsk Group negotiations, namely Azerbaijan, is also the key party obstructing those very negotiations. This encompasses the negotiations over the Basic Principles, but also any other potential paths towards peace. Whatever the future will bring to these negotiations, there will never be a concrete result as long as such obstructions do not trigger any international reaction or concrete negative consequence. At the same time, the negotiations have brought about results which are less visible, but nevertheless very significant. Armenia has publicly confirmed that the seven districts surrounding Nagorno-Karabakh will be returned, as part of a comprehensive peace deal including all the provisions mentioned in the L'Aquila declaration.[64] Meanwhile, the OSCE report has shown that this is matched with reality, in that there actually is no settlement programme in those districts.[65] These are results which Azerbaijan should not underestimate. No military option could bring about those results with any comparable likelihood. Azerbaijan has accepted various versions of the Basic Principles, albeit only those which leave loopholes concerning the process after the districts around Nagorno-Karabakh are returned. But the biggest problem for Armenia is the lack of reliability of its negotiation partner and doubts as to whether Azerbaijan is at all interested in progress through negotiation. Most bluntly, in 2011 the Azerbaijani deputy prime minister informed Turkish journalists that Azerbaijan is simply negotiating for show.[66] In order to become meaningful, the process urgently requires more trust. But developments since 2009 do not leave much room for the emergence of this trust from anywhere.

---

from a trip to Baku, suggested in Yerevan that the Armenian/Karabakhi side unilaterally remove their snipers. This only makes sense if Azubalis received a rejection from Baku to a bilateral removal. Cf. News.az, "OSCE calls for withdrawal of snipers from Azeri-Armenian front line", 18 March 2011, http://news.az/articles/armenia/33166 (date accessed: 29 July 2011). Panarmenian, "OSCE CiO urges Baku to withdraw snipers from Karabakh conflict zone", 14 March 2011, http://www.panarmenian.net/eng/world/news/64065/ (date accessed: 29 July 2011).

[64] The White House, "Joint Statement on the Nagorno-Karabakh Conflict by U.S. President Obama, Russian President Medvedev, and French President Sarkozy at the L'Aquila Summit of the Eight, July 10, 2009", http://www.whitehouse.gov/the_press_office/Joint-Statement-on-the-Nagorno-Karabakh-Conflict/ (date accessed: 29 July 2011).

[65] OSCE (2011) "Executive Summary of the 'Report of the OSCE Minsk Group Co-Chairs' Field Assessment Mission to the Occupied Territories of Azerbaijan Surrounding Nagorno-Karabakh", op. cit.

[66] *Hurriyet Daily News*, "Azerbaijan backs Turkey over Cyprus but fears Karabakh impact, says Azeri deputy PM", 21 July 2011 (excerpt: "Baku is negotiating with Yerevan solely for the sake of negotiating, as Azerbaijan would be labelled an 'anti-democratic state' if it did not participate in the meetings."), op. cit.

Scenarios of war

As stated above, rationally, no party has an interest in war. However, there is a certain degree of irrationality in Azerbaijan's actions, which is well reflected in the public war threats made by Azerbaijani state officials. Despite the factors mentioned above, which speak against Azerbaijan's interest in starting a war, Azerbaijan's military rhetoric has grown significantly. The examples given earlier, and many others,[67] demonstrate a certain irrationality behind Azerbaijan's external policies. Azerbaijan obviously tolerates or even actively promotes escalation and accepts the direct damage to its image and credibility in the eyes of the international community. If the war threats were only intended for a domestic audience, why then were they made, for instance, during an international press conference with the Minsk Group Co-Chairing Ambassadors or during a visit in Turkey?[68]

If, for argument's sake, one were to assume a strategic strike by Azerbaijan, it would have to include at least the following two cornerstones in its strategy.. First, it would have to ensure that the international community reacts as slowly and incoherently as possible. For this, the timing has to coincide with other prominent international developments absorbing political and media attention, such as the recent crisis in Libya and the "Arab Spring" in general, but also a holiday season. Furthermore, any war – even the most strategic one – would be presented as a war by accident. Otherwise, the international community's reaction and condemnation would come too quickly for Baku to achieve irreversible results on the ground. The second mind-map would centre around an attack's achievable results, which need to justify the foreseeable severe retaliations. It is not possible to predict exactly which scenario would unfold, since there are too many unknown factors, such as: the success rate of an initial attack, the success rate of the counter-attack, the geographic shifts of the Line of Contact, other regional players' reactions, and the international reaction. But we can assume two families of scenarios.

The first one envisages a very short confrontation restricted to a small geographic scope. This would require the presence of strong factors containing the violence shortly after its start. This containment could originate from both war parties achieving certain goals. If only one side achieved some of its goals, it would be very difficult to contain the use of force quickly. Alternatively, the containment could come from external forces, including painful political sanctions. While theoretically possible, all such developments seem unlikely to happen soon after an outbreak of a new

---

[67] European Friends of Armenia "Collection of war threat statements by President Ilham Aliyev and other Azerbaijani Officials", op. cit.
[68] *Hurriyet Daily News*, "Azerbaijan backs Turkey over Cyprus but fears Karabakh impact, says Azeri deputy PM", 21 July 2011, op. cit.

war. Achieving goals on both sides, which would allow both parties to save face, is unlikely given the Karabakhi defensive positions and the offensive equipment acquired by Azerbaijan. Moreover, it would bring little change to today's status quo. Besides, the expected heavy retaliation would not justify abandoning the use of force quickly in exchange for some smaller territorial gains. By definition, containment by external political or military forces takes time and is, therefore, also unlikely to pre-empt a larger escalation.

The second family of scenarios, a long and grave military confrontation, is therefore more likely. It comprises those scenarios in which Azerbaijan attempts to regain control over the whole of Nagorno-Karabakh. This can only be achieved either through the complete annihilation of the entire NK defence, and consequently causing a worst-case humanitarian crisis, or by cutting off the supply routes from Armenia into Karabakh. The former is not only difficult to imagine, it is also almost impossible to achieve in this mountainous and well-defended area. Besides, it would also be counterproductive, since merely attempting such dramatic action would certainly trigger a strong reaction from other players in the region, which in turn would almost certainly prevent leaving control over the territory to Azerbaijan unchallenged. The second alternative, cutting off the supply routes, is therefore rationally more likely. But cutting off supply routes is only achievable if either the whole territory of Karabakh is already under Azerbaijani control, which is unlikely with supply routes still intact, or if the cut-off comes from the rear, meaning from the Northwest and from Nakhichevan combined.[69] Arguably, the south of Armenia is very well defended, too, and crossing it from Nakhichevan would be quite a challenge. But it may not be as well defended as Karabakh itself. Again, it would not be serious to claim to predict accurately the further development of such scenarios, because the same uncertainty factors mentioned above apply. But what is certain and common in all these scenarios is that it is inconceivable that any of them could unfold without drawn-out fighting, very heavy losses on all sides, and the involvement of other regional players.

The involvement of Nakhichevan would hardly be possible without Turkey playing a role. In fact, even today, Turkey has facilitated the Azerbaijani rearmament of Nakhichevan through its tiny land-link to the Azerbaijani enclave. Anyway, it is difficult to imagine a long war between Armenia and Azerbaijan, including retaliation against both capitals, Baku and Yerevan, without Turkey and also Russia becoming involved. As Collective Security Treaty Organisation (CSTO) Secretary General Nikolay Bordyuzha formulated it: "I can cite Russian President Dmitry Medvedev, who said it one year ago in Yerevan during the informal CSTO summit. President Medvedev said Armenia is Russia's ally in the CSTO with all its consequences. I think

---

[69] See maps in the back of this book.

everything is said with that statement concerning alliance relations and mutual duties."[70] This means that the Russian president and the CSTO secretary general would feel obliged to aid Armenia in the eventuality of an attack by Azerbaijan. This can be explained by the CSTO's desire to be taken seriously and to deter any country from attacking its members. But it can also be explained by Russia's determination to prevent a shift of influence in the South Caucasus to the benefit of Turkey or Azerbaijan. For a more detailed analysis of Russia's stance, see Markedonov's contribution to this volume. As mentioned above, it is fair to say that, despite Russia's commitments to Armenia in the event of a war, it is currently not a partisan player.

Thus, while more precise developments and concrete outcomes cannot be predicted accurately, if war breaks out there is a very high likelihood of a long duration of hostilities, with unprecedented numbers of victims and destruction. Furthermore, a geographic spread of the conflict would be very likely in any of the escalation scenarios.

Ten recommendations to avoid a war in NK

At many times during this conflict, the road to peace has seemed impossible. Irrespective of developments in the nearer future, this conflict will linger for years to come. If developments continue to be negative, it will be a question of *when*, not *whether* some form of military escalation occurs. But there is no reason why Armenia and Azerbaijan should not manage what other countries have managed, some of whom were at war for centuries. The recipes for peace are always the same, and they start with confidence-building measures. While peace has always been rewarding for those who make it, a new war in Karabakh would be a dangerous gamble with unpredictable outcomes. The only certainty would be the ensuing humanitarian crises, which would likely reach dimensions yet unknown to the South Caucasus. But all this can be avoided. Moreover, the benefits of peace would not only outweigh the political, human and economic costs of war, but they would also outweigh the costs of the currently fragile no-peace-no-war status quo.

Following the analysis above, there are recommendations to avoid war in the short term and to achieve peace in the medium-term:

1. **Obstructions in the negotiation process need to become more transparent.** The OSCE Minsk Group constantly faces refusals of seemingly balanced proposals, last-minute obstructions, and even the

---

[70] Panorama.am, "Nikolay Bordyuzha: Armenia is Russia's ally in CSTO with all its consequences", 06 July 2011, http://www.panorama.am/en/politics/2011/07/06/bordyuja/ (date accessed: 08 July 2011) CSTO=Collective Security Treaty Organisation, cf. List of terms, English translation of the quotation corrected by adding articles.

non-implementation of agreed steps, such as the Sochi agreement. At present, neither side needs to fear any consequences of such obstructions. Statements of the Minsk Group Co-Chairs and their ambassadors are profoundly impartial, although this interpretation of impartiality means that even clearly obstructive steps are covered in silence. The entire international community follows suit and generally refrains from any statement which in their eyes might hamper the mediation. Such silence is effectively a *partial* response, in that it favours the obstructing power. The international community must begin to publicly reward compromise and trust-building and publicly denounce obstruction. Otherwise, it will continue to allow the obstructive powers to dismantle the peace-building process. In fact, every obstruction which is met with silence is an invitation to more obstruction. This would weaken all actors and institutions seeking to resolve the conflict, first and foremost the OSCE itself.

2. **The Minsk Group must change its approach of low-communication.** Currently, only the OSCE Minsk Group possesses an international mandate to negotiate between the conflict parties. Therefore, as the key mediator, the Minsk Group may not always be in a good position to name and shame one of the sides for obstructing the process. The whole term *obstruction* may be a political judgement. However, the Minsk Group is the only source for certain information. This information is vital for the correct assessment of the decisions by the international community. The Minsk Group must at least bring transparency into factual and procedural developments of this conflict. Halbach points out that sometimes even the texts of Minsk Group declarations differ in their translations, causing more uncertainty. Rumours, sometimes deliberately spread by politically interested parties, dominate the debate about the mediation. As Cooper and Morris have shown, at least in Armenia and Karabakh, the public currently does not understand the extent and value of the Minsk Group's profound work. This is because they do not know enough about it. Concretely, the OSCE should launch a dedicated Minsk Group website which lists all procedural and factual information, such as the Minsk Group statements, the dates and rough descriptions of proposals submitted and the overall responses of the two conflict parties and, ultimately, a calendar with past and planned high-level meetings.[71] If the OSCE does not communicate facts about the efforts it undertakes in this conflict,

---

[71] One concrete example: even with extensive research it is currently difficult to find public sources about when the OSCE submitted proposals for a ceasefire consolidation and the removal of snipers from the Line of Contact. While the positive response to this proposal by Armenia can, with some research, be found in the press, the negative response of Azerbaijan was publicly not very clear (cf. note 6). Why should it be *partial* or *undiplomatic* to state the procedural information publicly that the OSCE made such a proposal, which was accepted by one and declined by the other side?

the public in the countries concerned cannot appreciate their work and will not be prepared for eventual solutions. Besides, communicating at least such factual or procedural information will contribute to the above-mentioned transparency and strengthen the constructiveness of the parties involved and with that the OSCE itself.

3. **The Minsk Group should not be reformed to include more obstructive elements in its negotiation format.** Both sides have complaints concerning the format of negotiations. Armenia complains that one of the conflict parties, that is, Nagorno-Karabakh, is excluded from the negotiations. Azerbaijan often suspects that France or Russia favour Armenian positions. Yet, so far, these points have never been a reason for the lack of results. Armenia has provided the biggest push to date, effectively accepting the return of the seven districts around Nagorno-Karabakh as part of a comprehensive peace deal with all points of the l'Acquila declaration. Azerbaijan, however, still does not accept that the people of Nagorno-Karabakh cannot be forced into the realm of Azerbaijan. Instead, the people of Karabakh need to overcome their traumata, everything which, over decades, they learnt to associate with the *Azerbaijani state,* in a genuine and legally binding plebiscite. Other negotiating formats would not be able to reap different or better results for Azerbaijan because, whoever negotiates, the results must also take into account the population of Nagorno-Karabakh. Theoretically, a new UN format might involve new states, some of which may be more Azerbaijan-friendly, but the results of such negotiations could not reach conclusions which can actually be implemented unless they were very similar to those proposed by the Minsk Group. A different idea sometimes discussed is the direct representation of the EU, replacing France. This, however, would add differing opinions, slower reaction times and more complicated internal consultations. In fact, the reason why Russia has hosted a series of presidential summits, prepared by the Co-Chairing ambassadors, already follows a lesson learnt in the past: while such a high diplomatic level is necessary to reach real conclusions, one cannot wait for the French, US and Russian presidents to find free slots in their agendas and meet with the presidents of Armenia and Azerbaijan. If the risk of reforming the negotiation format is taken, it should make the process more efficient and effective, not less.

4. **Azerbaijan should stop its war threats and genuinely try to negotiate peace.** The current format of negotiations is criticised mainly by Azerbaijan for its lack of effectiveness. And yet, as elaborated above, Azerbaijan is the main blocking force and even publicly states it is negotiating mainly to please the international community.[72] Accompanied with repeated war threats, the negotiations cannot result in the courageous

---

[72] *Hurriyet Daily News*, "Azerbaijan backs Turkey over Cyprus but fears Karabakh impact, says Azeri deputy PM", 21 July 2011, op. cit.

Armenian concessions for which Azerbaijan may hope. Azerbaijan must, therefore, opt for a single strategy: war or peace. Pursuing both simultaneously will only result in a snail-pace escalation towards war, with all its negative consequences. Besides, even with the usage of huge PR budgets, the image of Azerbaijan as a source of aggression derives from its war threats and would be dominant once a war breaks out.

5. **In the short term, agreed confidence-building measures need to be implemented.** First and foremost, this counts for the Sochi agreement to investigate incidents along the Line of Contact. The OSCE must implement a transparent format for these investigations, effectively ensuring that all sides will co-operate fully or face public condemnation if they do not. Such investigations will, in themselves, deter new incidents. The circle of allegation and counter-allegation, complete with televised pictures of predominantly young victims and their families, must be broken. The same is valid for stopping the ongoing threat of force, which is not only against existing agreements between the conflict parties but also against international law.

6. **A ceasefire consolidation treaty needs to be signed and implemented.** Luchterhandt has outlined a concrete and balanced legal proposal in more detail in this volume. Markedonov even suggests that the international community should force the parties into a new treaty, banning the use of force. Whatever its concrete format, the treaty should be restricted to overcoming those few points which currently make the outbreak of war all too likely. In particular, these are: the presence of snipers along the Line of Contact; the absence of international observers; and the repeated threat of force, mainly from Azerbaijan. Azerbaijan could use this treaty to demonstrate its commitment to the peace negotiations. As the implementation – the implementation, not just the signing and ratification – of such a treaty would offer a genuine improvement of the security landscape around Nagorno-Karabakh, Armenia should offer a genuine quid pro quo. Whichever country launches this initiative will score valuable points, as it demonstrates a genuine commitment to peace. At worst, such an initiative would demonstrate which party is constructive, and which is obstructive.

7. **The EU needs to enact a comprehensive arms embargo against all conflict parties.** This embargo must also be binding for associated countries. As Halbach and Sammut outline, one key cause of escalation is the ongoing arms race, combined with a certain reliance on military means. It is inconceivable why the EU is trying so hard to support peace and prosperity in the region while no arms embargo exists. Should a war really break out, European politicians will have to answer very uncomfortable questions regarding exports from the EU itself, but also from associated countries. While the embargo would not in itself stop the arms race, it would make acquisitions more expensive and slower, for both sides.

Besides, it would demonstrate that the EU has the will and capacity to take concrete measures.

8. **The EU needs to propose concrete incentives for peace.** Several authors in this volume described the EU's positive effect, both real and potential, on the democratic and prosperous development of the South Caucasus. The EU should boost this stance by conditioning key programmes aimed at furthering the negotiations and implementing existing agreements. Here, the various authors offer their own specific recommendations. Hovhannisyan argues that the EU should use its bilateral relations with Armenia and Azerbaijan to help ensure that the projects of reform, state-building and consolidation of the rule of law remain active. Halbach describes how strongly the EU supports democracy and socio-economic development in all "frozen conflict" areas, except for Nagorno-Karabakh. Brok focuses on pushing both parties to act in accordance with international law. Poghosyan's approach suggests working more intensively directly with the people. Tannock suggests prioritising those ENPI tools which have a cross-country dimension. He adds that the EU should consider sending a civilian observation mission into the conflict zone. Until it sends observers on the ground, the EU cannot answer the notorious "who shot first" question. This could also facilitate the negotiation of a comprehensive peace deal, because one of the key obstacles is which countries would provide the observers and troops to safeguard the peace deal. At present, the EU is clearly the international player best positioned to promote democracy and prosperity in the region. The arrivals of the EU's Eastern Partnership Programme and the new Association Agreement negotiations have strengthened this role very much. To this end, the EU is currently under-exploiting its potential to link those programmes to the conflict resolution. Besides, the EU should draw up, at least nominally, a cross-border investment plan, which would act as an incentive for the people and provide a visible alternative to both the status quo and war.

9. **The EU needs to publish concrete disincentives for war.** With the EU's current position, none of the war parties have to fear a strong reaction in the case of a new war, except a condemnation of "excessive use of force". The EU is so neutral that it so far always calls upon "both sides", even when it is known that only one side is responsible. Paradoxically, this false understanding of neutrality actually favours the more obstructive force. It encourages obstruction and must, therefore, be changed. Only then will the EU regain its credibility in this process. The EU must also agree upon and communicate the outlines of concrete disincentives for war. This is also necessary to reduce the reaction time following the potential outbreak of war. Currently the EU's stance again resembles that before the Georgian–Russian war in 2008, when it reacted too slowly to all expert warnings and did not prepare in an effective way. A public

outline of painful disincentives would reduce the likelihood of war and, with that, the likelihood of having to implement these disincentives. This should happen at the level of a Foreign Affairs Council meeting. The EU possesses an arsenal of very painful measures, without having to move a single soldier. This includes political isolation, total or partial trade embargos, travel bans, and freezing bank accounts. Arguably, the EU's most powerful tool would be the threat of recognition or non-recognition of Nagorno-Karabakh, depending on who is held responsible for an outbreak of war. In diplomatic language, this could be reduced to: "The initiation of hostilities and their origin would have a direct effect on the EU's position on the status of Nagorno-Karabakh". Such steps, especially if formulated as a package, would be a serious and effective deterrent for war and make war less likely.

10. **Both sides must recognise that time plays against their interests.** None of the authors of this book expressed contentment with the status quo. The status quo is in nobody's favour. Both parties have been quite successful in preventing the other from profiting thoroughly from the time factor. This is also clearly visible from citizen's opinions expressed during the town hall meeting project in Azerbaijan, Armenia and Nagorno-Karabakh, as described by Poghosyan. The biggest weakness of Armenia – its economic situation as a landlocked country with two closed borders – becomes more and more relevant as the economic difference between Armenia and Azerbaijan continues to grow with time. The biggest weakness of Azerbaijan also is exacerbated with time: the de facto existence of a state which governs the people of Nagorno-Karabakh in a more democratic and efficient way than Azerbaijan ever has, and which has all the time needed to prepare the mountainous area militarily for defence against all sorts of possible attack scenarios. Armenia and Azerbaijan could attract significantly more foreign investment, or achieve higher prices for domestic assets, if investors would not have to factor in the risk of a war. If the conflict were resolved, both countries would have more political options in their foreign relations, becoming meaningful regional players. They would also become stronger partners to their various strategic and economic allies. The entire region would benefit from more trade and more economic certainty. The entire international community would almost certainly provide substantial investment plans, if that was the missing element to come to a resolution of the conflict. The permanent risk of war burdens the psyche of the people, drives some parts of the population into migration – especially in Armenia – and with time increases the distrust into their own governments – especially in Azerbaijan. The ongoing *costs of non-resolution* can barely be overestimated. Therefore, both sides should rationally seek a quick breakthrough on the Basic Principles, followed by implementing the roadmap outlined there.

If all or many of those steps were taken together, or at least initiated quickly, the likelihood of an outbreak of war would be reduced significantly. Even initiating those measures, the implementation of which does not require the consent or co-operation of the conflict parties, would make a real difference. The contributors to this book have elaborated so much background and so many aspects of this conflict that it may easily remind of the Gordian Knot. However, all the authors actually unanimously agree on one point: This potential war in the most eastern part of Europe is clearly avoidable. And since it can be avoided, it should be.

Bibliography

Books

F. Adanir and B. Bonwetsch (eds) (2005) *Osmanismus, Nationalismus und der Kaukasus* (Kaukasusstudien, Band 9, Wiesbaden).

H. Avetisyan, M. Aghajanyan, L. Andriasyan, A. Arshakyan, H. Asryan, G. Boyakhchyan, A. Eghiazaryan, G. Isagulyan, A. Melkonyan, S. Minasyan, N. Panosyan, V. Sargsyan and R. Safrastyan (eds) (2009) *The Republic of Nagorno-Karabakh: A Process of State Building at the Crossroad of Centuries* (Yerevan: IPR).

B. Berberoglu (ed.) (1995) *The National Question: Nationalism, Ethnic Conflict, and Self-Determination in the 20th Century* (Philadelphia: Temple University Press).

Z. Brzezinski, Z.K. Brzezinski, P. Sullivan (1996) *Russia and the Commonwealth of Independent States: Documents, Data, and Analysis* (Washington, D.C.: Center for Strategic and International Studies, M.E. Sharpe).

B. Buzan, O. Waever, J. de Wilde (1998) *Security: A New Framework for Analysis* (Boulder: Lynne Rienner Publishers).

L. Chorbajian (2001) *The Making of Nagorno-Karabagh: From Secession to Republic* (London: Palgrave).

L. Chorbajian, P. Donabedian, C. Mutafian (1994) *The Caucasian Knot: The History and Geo-politics of Nagorno-Kharabagh* (London: Zed Books).

J. K. Cooley (2000) *Unholy Wars: Afghanistan, America and International Terrorism: New Edition* (London, Sterling, Virginia: Pluto Press).

B. Coppieters (ed.) (1996) *Contested Borders in the Caucasus* (Brussels: VUB Brussels University Press).

C. Cox and J. Eibner (2003) *Ethnic Cleansing in Progress: War in Nagorno-Karabakh* (New Malden, Surrey: Christian Solidarity International).

C. Cox, J. Eibner. and E. Bonnèr (1993) *Ethnic Cleansing in Progress: War in Nagorno Karabakh* (Binz: Institute for Religious Minorities in the Islamic World).

R. A. Dahl (1989) *Democracy and its Critics* (New Haven: Yale University Press).

T. Darieva and W. Kaschuba (eds) (2007) *Representations on the Margins of Europe. Politics and Identities in the Baltic and South Caucasian States* (Frankfurt/New York: Campus).

T. de Waal (2003) *Black Garden: Armenia and Azerbaijan through Peace and War* (New York University Press).

T. de Waal (2009) *The Karabakh Trap, Dangers and Dilemna of the Nagorny Karabakh Conflict* (London: Conciliation Resources).

T. de Waal (2010) *The Caucasus: An Introduction* (Oxford University Press).

R. Dember and R.K. Goldman (1992) *Bloodshed in the Caucasus: Escalation of the Armed Conflict in Nagorno-Karabakh* (New York: Helsinki Watch).

P. Donabedian and C. Mutafian (1991) *Artsakh: histoire du Karabakh* (Paris: Sevig Press).

A. Fikret and B. Bonwetsch (ed.) (2005) *Osmanismus, Nationalismus und der Kaukasus* (Wiesbaden).

R.H. Ginsberg (2001) *The European Union in International Politics* (USA: Rowman & Littlefield).

J. Gottmann (1952) *La politique des Etats et leur géographie* (Paris : Armand Collin).

A. Hug (ed.) (2011) *Spotlight on Armenia* (London: The Foreign Policy Centre).

ICHD (International Centre for Human Development) (2010) *The Resolution of the Nagorno-Karabakh Issue: What Societies Say: Discussion results of Armenians and Azerbaijanis at the Parallel Town Hall Meetings: Comparative analysis of the THM outputs* (Yerevan: ICHD).

P. Jaward (2006) *Europe's New Neighborhood on the Verge of War: What role for the EU in Georgia* (Frankfurt: Peace Research Institute).

F. Judo and G. Geudens (ed.) (2006) *Internationale betrekkingen en federalisme, Staatsrechtconferentie 2005* (Gent: Vlaamse Juristenvereniging).

S.J. Kaufman (2001) *Modern Hatreds. The Symbolic Politics of Ethnic War* (Ithaca/London: Cornell University Press).

Y. Kalyuzhnova and D. Lynch (eds) (2000) *The Euro-Asian World: A Period of Transition* (London: Macmillan Press).

V. Kronenberger and J. Wouters (eds) (2004) *The European Union and Conflict Prevention: Policy and Legal Aspects* (The Hague: T.M.C. Asser Press).

D.M. Lang (1981) *The Armenians: A People in Exile* (London: George Allen Unwin).

O. Luchterhandt (1993a) *Nagorny Karabakh's Right to State Independence According to International Law* (Boston: Armenian Rights Council).

O. Luchterhandt (1993b) *Das Recht Berg-Karabachs auf staatliche Unabhängigkeit aus völkerrechtlicher Sicht* (Archiv des Völkerrechts, Bd. 31).

D. Lynch (ed.) (2003) *The South Caucasus: A Challenge for the EU* (Paris: Challiot Paper no. 65, ISS-EU).

A.L. Manutscharjan (2009) *Der Berg-Karabach-Konflikt nach der Unabhängigkeit des Kosovo* (Bonn: Zentrum für Integrationsforschung, Diskussionspapier).

A. Martirosyan (2011) *EU and Nagorno-Karabakh: Rhetoric Versus Reality?* (Germany: Lambert Academic Publishing).

D. E. Miller and L. Touryan-Miller (2003) *Armenia: Portraits of Survival and Hope* (Berkeley, Los Angeles, London: University of California Press).

D. Raic (2002) *Statehood and the Law of Self-Determination* (The Hague: Kluwer Law International).

F. Ratzel (1987) *Politische Geographie (oder die Geographie der Staaten des Verkehres und des Kriegs – ed. 1902)* (Munich: Oldenbourg).

V. A. Shnirelman (2001) *The Value of the Past: Myths, Identity and Politics in Transcaucasia* (Osaka: National Museum of Ethnology).

V. Soghomonyan (ed.) (2010) *Lösungsansätze für Berg-Karabach/Arzach. Selbstbestimmung und der Weg zur Anerkennung* (Baden-Baden: Nomos).

E.J. Stewart (2006) *The European Union and Conflict Prevention: Policy Evolution and Outcome* (Berlin: LIT Verlag Münster).

E.J. Stewart (2007) *EU Conflict Management in the South Caucasus: A Preliminary Analysis* (The British Academy, Specialist Group EthnoPolitics: Nottingham).

E.J. Stewart (2008) *The EU as an Actor in Conflict Resolution: Out of its Depth?* (University of Bath: United Kingdom).

R.G. Suny (ed.) (1983) *Transcaucasia, Nationalism and Social Change: Essays in the History of Armenia, Azerbaijan, and Georgia* (Ann Arbor: University of Michigan Press).

R.G. Suny (1993) *Looking toward Ararat: Armenia in Modern History* (Bloomington: Indiana University Press).

R.G. Suny (1994) *The Making of the Georgian Nation* (Bloomington: Indiana University Press).

T. Swietochowski (1985) *Russian Azerbaijan 1905–1920: The Shaping of National Identity in a Muslim Community* (Cambridge: Cambridge University Press).

N. Tocci (2008) *Who is a Normative Foreign Policy Actor? The European Union and its Global Partners* (Brussels: Centre for European Policy Studies (CEPS).
Ch. J. Walker (ed.) (1991) *Armenia and Karabagh: the Struggle for Unity* (London: Minority Rights Group Reports).
A. Yunusov (2007) *Azerbaijan in the Early 21st Century: Conflicts and Potential Threats* [Azerbaijan v nachale 21-go Veka: konflikty I potentsial'nye ugrozy] (Baku: Adyloglu edition).

Articles in journals/publications and books

"1979 USSR Census/Itogi Vsesoiuznoi perepisi naseleniia 1979 goda", *Minneapolis: East View Publications*, http://www.eastview.com/research-collections/product_view.asp?sku=RC000057&Russia/Russian/.
"1989 USSR Census/Itogi Vsesoiuznoy perepisi naseleniia 1989 goda", *Minneapolis: East View Publication*, http://www.eastview.com/research-collections/product_view.asp?sku=IE00030&Russia/Russian/.
Conciliation resources, *Nagorny-Karabakh: Chronology*, http://www.c-r.org/our-work/accord/nagorny-karabakh/chronology.php.
"Military and Paramilitary Activities in and against Nicaragua" (*Nicaragua v. United States of America*), *ICJ Reports*, 1986, 14. Available at http://www.icj-cij.org/docket/index.php?sum=367&code=nus&p1=3&p2=3&case=70&k=66&p3=5
S. Abasov (2010) "Turkey's Gul visits Azerbaijan: A case of sound and fury?", *Eurasia Insight*, 17 August.
V. Adam (2005) "Umdeutung der Geschichte im Zeichen des Nationalismus seit dem Ende der SU: das Beispiel Aserbaidschan", in F. Adanir and B. Bonwetsch (eds) *Osmanismus, Nationalismus und der Kaukasus* (Kaukasusstudien, Band 9, Wiesbaden).
A. Alizada (2010) "Negotiation without (due) representation", Caucasus Edition. *Journal of Conflict Transformation*, 15 August.
A. Ayunts (2010) "Madrid principles: basis for conflict settlement or war?", Caucasus Edition. *Journal of Conflict Transformation*, 15 August.
C. Blandy (2008) "Azerbaijan: is war over Nagorny Karabakh a realistic option? Advanced research and assessment group", *Defence Academy of the United Kingdom*, Caucasus Series 08/17, 12.
M. Çelikpala (2010) "Turkey and the Caucasus: transition from reactive foreign policy to proactive rhythmic diplomacy", *International Relations*, Spring, Vol. 7, No. 25.
S. Charap and A. Peterson (2010) "Reimagining Azerbaijan. Building an Azerbaijan policy based on today's strategic realities", *Center for American Progress*, August.
Chatham House (2009) "Foreign policy challenges for Azerbaijan", 13 July, http://www.chathamhouse.org/sites/default/files/14383_130709aliyev.pdf
S.E. Cornell (2004) "Iranian Azerbaijan: a brewing hotspot", presented at symposium on "Human Rights and Ethnicity in Iran", 22 November (Stockholm), http://www.azeri.dk/en/articles/Iranian_azerbaijan.html.
T. de Waal (2009) "The Karabakh trap: dangers and dilemmas of the Nagorny Karabakh conflict", *Conciliation Resources*, http://www.c-r.org/our-work/caucasus/documents/Karabakh_Trap_FINAL.pdf.
T. de Waal (2010) "Remaking the Nagorno-Karabakh peace process", *Survival: Global Politics and Strategy*, Vol. 52, No. 4.
V.I. Dyatlov (2005) "New diasporas of the Post-Soviet Epoch: prerequisites and mechanisms of formation" [Novye diaspory postsovetskoy epohi: prichiny i mehanizmy

formirovaniya], in В.И. Дятлов, С.А. Панарин and М.Я. Рожанский (2005) *Байкальская Сибирь: из чего складывается стабильность* [Baikal Siberia: What is Stability Constituted Of] (Иркутск: Наталис), 95–137.

S. Freizer (2006) "Responding to South Caucasus conflicts in the European neighborhood", *European Parliament, Committee on Foreign Affairs, Hearing on the South Caucasus*, Brussels.

L. Fuller (2009) "Is the Karabakh peace process in jeopardy?", *Eurasianet-Eurasia Insight*, March.

P. Gamaghelyan (2010) "Literature matters", Caucasus Edition. *Journal of Conflict Transformation*, July.

R. Garagozov (2010) "Towards conflict transformation through the transformation of narratives (preliminary considerations)", Caucasus Edition. *Journal of Conflict Transformation*, August.

S. Ghazaryan, U.E. Franke, N. Koenig, J. Münch, S. Rothenpieler (2010) "Armed conflicts in Europe's greater neighbourhood", *Towards a Safer Europe* (European Values Network, Prague).

P.A. Goble (1992) "Coping with the Nagorno-Karabakh crisis", *The Fletcher Forum of World Affairs*, Vol. 16, No. 2.

M. Herdegen (2010) "Völkerrecht", § 34, *Marginal* , No. 12 (München).

R.H. Hewsen (1972, 1973) "The Meliks of Eastern Armenia", *Revue des Etudes Arméniennes*, N.S. 9 (1972), 285–329 and N.S. 10.

R. Hovhannisyan (1988) "Nationalist ferment in Armenia", *Freedom at Issue*, No. 105.

Institute of Political Research (2009) "Karabakh conflict: 15 Years of neither war nor peace situation", *15 Questions and Answers*, Yerevan, 12 May.

International Crisis Group (2005) "Nagorno-Karabakh: A plan for peace", *Europe Report*, No. 167.

International Crisis Group (2009) "Nagorno-Karabakh: getting to a breakthrough", *Europe Briefing* No. 55, Baku/Yerevan/Tbilisi/Brussels, October.

International Crisis Group (2011), "Armenia and Azerbaijan: preventing war", *Europe Briefing* No. 60, Tbilisi/Baku/Yerevan/Istanbul/Brussels, 8 February.

Y. Kalyuzhnova and D. Lynch (2000) "Euro-Asian conflicts and peace-keeping dilemmas", in Y. Kalyuzhnova and D. Lynch (eds) *The Euro-Asian World: A Period of Transition* (London: Macmillan Press).

V. Kazimirov (2008) "Is there a way out of the Karabakh deadlock?", *Russia in Global Affairs*, Vol. 6, No.1.

H. Khachatrian (2006) "Russian investments in Armenia: their economic background and possible political impact", *Central Asia-Caucasus Institute*, 13 December.

M.H. Kohrs (2005) "Geschichte als politisches Argument. Der "Historikerstreit" um Berg-Karabach", in A. Fikret and B. Bonwetsch (eds) *Osmanismus, Nationalismus und der Kaukasus* (Wiesbaden).

Ch. Kolter (2011) "Chronologie", in Parlamentarische Gruppe Schweiz–Armenien (ed.), *Berg- Karabach: Geopolitische, völkerrechtliche und menschenrechtliche Aspekte eines Konfliktes* (Merkur Druck AG, Langenthal).

O. Krikorian (2010) "Twitter diplomacy. Can new media help break the Armenia-Azerbaijan information blockade?", *Transitions Online*, February.

D.D. Laitin and R.G. Suny (1999) "Karabakh: thinking a way out", *Middle East Policy* 7, No. 1, October.

O. Luchterhandt (2010) "Das Ausscheiden Berg-Karabachs aus Aserbeidschan durch Ausübung des vom sowjetischen Staatsrecht gewährten Selbstbestimmungsrechts" , in V. Soghomonyan (ed.) *Lösungsansätze für Berg-Karabach/Arzach. Selbstbestimmung und der Weg zur Anerkennung* (Baden-Baden).

D. Lynch (2003) "A regional insecurity dynamic", in D. Lynch (ed.) *The South Caucasus: A Challenge for the EU*, Challiot Paper, No. 65 (ISS-EU, Paris).

G. Maisuradze (2009) "Time turned back: on the use of history in Georgia", *Caucasus Analytical Digest*, No. 8.

C.B. Maloney (2005) "Commemorating the 17th anniversary of the Nagorno-Karabakh freedom movement", *Congressional Record Proceedings and Debates of the 109th Congress*, First Session, Vol. 151, part 2.

S. Markedonov (2009) "Russia's internal South Caucasus: the role and importance of Caucasus societies for Russia", *Caucasus Analytical Digest*, No. 4.

S. Markedonov (2009) "The big Caucasus: consequences of five day war", *Threats and Political Prospects*, Athens, Xenophon Papers, No. 7.

H. Marutyan (2007) "Iconography of historical memory and Armenian national identity at the end of the 1980s", in T. Darieva and W. Kaschuba (eds) *Representations on the Margins of Europe. Politics and Identities in the Baltic and South Caucasian States* (Frankfurt/New York: Campus).

N. Milanova (2003) "The territory-identity nexus in the conflict over Nagorno Karabakh: implications for OSCE peace efforts", *Human Rights Without Frontiers International*, No. 2 (ECMI: Flensburg), p. 3.

S. Minasyan (2009) "Armenia's attitude towards its past: history and politics", *Caucasus Analytical Digest*, No. 08.

S. Minasyan (2010) "Nagorno-Karabakh after two decades of conflict: is prolongation of the status quo inevitable?", *Caucasus Institute Research Papers*, No. 2, August.

M. Mooradian and D. Druckman (1999) "Hurting stalemate or mediation? The conflict over Nagorno-Karabakh, 1990–95", *Journal of Peace Research*, Vol. 36, No. 6.

M. Muradova (2010) "Stalement in Karabakh peace talks", *CACI (Central Asia and Caucasus Institute) Analyst*, 18 August.

M. Muradova (2011) "Azerbaijan boosts defence production", *CACI (Central Asia and Caucasus Institute) Analyst*, 19 January.

G. Novikova (2010) "Implications of the Russian-Georgian war in the Nagorno-Karabakh conflict: limited maneuverability", Caucasus Edition. *Journal of Conflict Transformation*, 15 August.

A. Poghosyan (2010) "EU's current and possible role in the Nagorno-Karabakh conflict resolution process", Caucasus Edition. *Journal of Conflict Transformation*, 15 August.

D. Rochtus (2009) "Kruitvat Nagorno-Kaukasus: Wordt Nagorno-Karabach volgend strijdtoneel?", *Internationale Spectator*, Vol. 2 (Translation: "Powder-barrel Caucasus: Will Nagorno-Karabakh become the next battle-place?").

V. Rouvinski and M. Matsuo (2003) "Clash of myths", *Journal of International Development and Cooperation*, No. 9.

F. Shafiev (2007) "Ethnic myths and perceptions as a hurdle to conflict settlement. The Armenian-Azerbaijani Case", *The Caucasus & Globalization*, No. 2.

V. Socor (2010) "Russian military power advancing in the Black Sea-South Caucasus region", *Jamestown Foundation Eurasia Daily Monitor*, Vol. 7, No. 157.

G. Usher (1999) "The fate of small nations: The Karabakh conflict ten years later", *Middle East Report*, No. 213.

R. Van Dijck (1996) "Divided we stand: regionalism, federalism and minority rights in Belgium", *Res Publica*, No. 12.

J. Velaers (2006) "In foro interno, in foro externo: de international bevoegd-heden van gemeenschappen en gewesten", in F. Judo and G. Geudens (eds), *Internationale betrekkingen en federalisme, Staatsrechtconferentie 2005* (Gent: Vlaamse Juristenvereniging).

E. Walker (1998) "No peace, no war in the caucasus: secessionist conflicts in Chechnya, Abkhazia and Nagorno-Karabakh", *Strengthening Democratic Institutions Project, Belfer Center for Science and International Affairs*, Occasional Paper.

C. Welt (2010) "The thawing of a frozen conflict: the internal security dilemma and the 2004 prelude to the Russo-Georgian War", *Europe-Asia Studies*.

P.R. Williams and F. Jannotti Pecci (2004) "Earned sovereignty: bridging the gap between sovereignty and self-determination", *Stanford Journal of International Law*, Vol. 40, No. 1.

A. Zverev (1996) "Ethnic conflicts in the Caucasus 1988–1994", in B. Coppieters (ed.) *Contested Borders in the Caucasus* (Brussels: VUB Brussels University Press).

Articles in newspapers or online

"Armenia and Turkey sign peace deal", *Financial Times*, 10 October 2009, http://www.ft.com/cms/s/0/381c000a-b5c0–11de-9c58–00144feab49a.html#axzz1c4wtnruj.

"Armenia suspends normalisation of ties with Turkey", *BBC*, 22 April 2010, http://news.bbc.co.uk/2/hi/8636800.stm.

"Azerbaijan 'flattened' sacred Armenian site", *The Independent*, 30 May 2006, http://www.independent.co.uk/news/world/europe/azerbaijan-flattened-sacred-arme-nian-site-480272.html.

"Azerbaijan: Islamic party sets up body for Karabakh", *BBC Monitoring Global Newsline Former Soviet Union Political File*, 2 August 2010.

"Azerbaijan promises Nagorno-Karabakh vast autonomy", *Interfax*, 19 May 2005.

"Die militärische Option bleibt auf dem Tisch", *Frankfurter Allgemeine Zeitung*, 5 July 2010.

"Gladstone on Armenia: he cannot find words to describe the guilt of the Turks", *The New York Times*, 26 June 1896.

"Karabakh people want Armenia to withdraw from peace talks", *BBC Monitoring Global Newsline Former Soviet Union Political File*, 29 July 2010 (Public Television of Armenia, Yerevan, in Armenian 1600 gmt 29 July).

"Opposition official notes Armenian foreign policy change after deal with Russia", *BBC Monitoring Global Newsline Former Soviet Union Political file*, 24 August 2010.

A. Postma (1997) "Vlaanderen is Nederlands natuurlijke bondgenoot", *De Standaard* (Translated: "Flanders is the natural ally of The Netherlands").

Articles on websites: News' websites

"A military doctrine is adopted in Azerbaijan" [V Azerbaijane prinyata voennaya doc-trina], *Polit.ru*, 8 June 2010, http://www.polit.ru/news/2010/06/08/azerdoc.html.

"Aliyev again threatens new war for Karabakh", *Armenialiberty*, 5 January 2011, http://www.armenialiberty.org/content/article/1599118.html.

"Andrew is only one of the many friends of Azerbaijan", *London Evening Standard: Londoner's Diary*, http://londonersdiary.standard.co.uk/2011/03/andrew-is-only-one-of-the-many-friends-of-azerbaijan.html.

"Armenia confirms possession of sophisticated missiles", *Azatutyun.am*, 20 December 2010, http://www.azatutyun.am/content/article/2254125.html.

"Armenia, Azerbaijan blame each other for Karabakh failure", *Reuters*, 25 June 2011, http://uk.reuters.com/article/2011/06/25/azerbaijan-armenia-karabakh-idU-KANT55197620110625.

"Armenian, Azerbaijani clashes continue in Karabakh", *Radio Free Europe/Radio Liberty*, 22 June 2010, http://www.rferl.org/content/Armenian_Azerbaijani_Clashes_Continue_In_Karabakh/2078581.html.

"Armenian, Azeri leaders pledge to seek peaceful Karabakh settlement", *Azatutyun. am*, 7 March 2011, http://www.azatutyun.am/content/article/2330373.html.

"Armenian opposition party concerned about new deal with Russia", *Radio Free Europe/Radio Liberty*, 24 August 2010.

"Armenia to host Russian military base for 49 years", *Panorama.am*, 5 August 2010, http://www.panorama.am/en/politics/2010/08/05/baxdasaryan-security/.

"Azerbaijan announces another surge in defense spending", *Radio Free Europe/Radio Liberty*, 13 October 2010, http://www.azatutyun.am/content/article/2189711. html.

"Azerbaijan backs Turkey over Cyprus but fears Karabakh impact, says Azeri deputy PM", *Hurriyet Daily News*, 21 July 2011, http://www.hurriyetdailynews.com/n. php?n=azerbaijan-backs-turkey-over-cyprus-but-fears-karabakh-impact-says-azeri-deputy-pm-2011–07-21.

"Azerbaijani IDPs call upon the EU to speed their return", *TEAS*, 18 March 2011, https://teas.eu/news/2011–03-18/azerbaijani-idps-call-upon-eu-speed-their-return.

"Azerbaijan leader warns of army buildup at huge parade", *Reuters*, 26 June 2011, http://ca.reuters.com/article/topNews/idCATRE75P0LD20110626.

"Azerbaijan must attack Yerevan, says political expert", *Asbarez*, 14 July 2011, http://asbarez.com/97048/azerbaijan-must-attack-yerevan-says-political-expert/.

"Azerbaijan preparing for war, Says Defence Minister", *Asbarez*, 14 February 2011, http://asbarez.com/93413/azerbaijan-preparing-for-war-says-defense-minister/.

"Azerbaijan recognized the fact of clash and victims in Nagorno-Karabakh" [Azerbaijan priznal fact boevogo stolknoveniya v Nagornom Karabakhe I nalichiye zhertv], *The Caucasian Knot* [Kavkazskiy Uzell], 19 June 2010, http://www.kavkaz-uzel.ru/articles/170417/.

"Azerbaijan: referendum to abolish presidential term limits sparks criticism of Baku", *Eurasianet*, 28 January 2009, http://www.eurasianet.org/departments/insight/articles/eav022909a.shtml.

"Azerbaijan says Karabakh talks last chance for deal", *Radio Free Europe/Radio Liberty*, 21 November 2009, http://www.rferl.org/content/Azerbaijan_Says_Karabakh_Talks_Last_Chance_For_Deal/1884135.html.

"Azerbaijani side kills 20-year-old Armenian soldier after exchange of POWs", *News. am*, 18 March 2011, http://news.am/eng/news/51842.html.

"Britain's Prince Andrew under fire over the company he keeps", *Radio Free Europe/Radio Liberty*, 10 March 2011, http://www.rferl.org/content/british_prince_andrew_under_fire/2333914.html.

"British Ambassador to Armenia: we try to establish dialogue in region through media, NGOs", *Panarmenian.net*, 9 March 2011, http://www.panarmenian.net/eng/society/news/63600/British_Ambassador_to_Armenia_we_try_to_establish_dialogue_in_region_through_media_NGOs.

"Can the 'Medvedev moment' be saved for Karabakh?", *Radio Free Europe/Radio Liberty* 28 July 2011, http://www.rferl.org/content/medvedev_moment_saved_nagorno_karabakh_kazan/24279692.html.

"Conference on Nagorno Karabakh conflict held at European Parliament", *APA*, 19 April 2011, http://en.apa.az/news.php?id=145346.

"Countdown to Karabakh conflict talks in Kazan", *Radio Free Europe/Radio Liberty*, 7 June 2011, http://www.rferl.org/content/countdown_to_karabakh_conflict_talks_in_kazan_/24227837.html.

"Deal to extend russian military base in Armenia comes into Force", *RTT News*, 7 July 2011, http://www.rttnews.com/Content/GeneralNews.aspx?Id=1660226&SM=1.

"EU ready to financially support Nagorno-Karabakh settlement", Commissioner Fule's interview with RFE/RL's Armenian Service, *Azatutyun*, Prague, 22 June 2011, http://www.azatutyun.am/content/article/24273170.html.

"Experts from Yerevan and Baku consider the Iranian and Turkish attempts to help the Karabakh conflict resolution as not serious" [Experty v Yerevane I v Baku schitayut popytki Irana I Turtsii pomoch' v reshenii karabakhskogo kobflikta neser'eznymi], *The Caucasian Knot* [Kavkazskiy Uzell], 30 April 2010, http://www.kavkaz-uzel.ru/articles/168296/.

"Foreign Investments in Azerbaijan grow 25.5% in April", *News.az*, 21 May 2010, http://www.news.az/articles/15951.

"Full text of the Protocols' project of military base between Moscow and Yerevan", *News of Armenia [Novosti Armenii]*, 17 August 2010, http://news.am/rus/news/28027.html.

"Karabakh to remain part of Azerbaijan – Ilham Aliyev", *News.az*, 14 July 2010, http://www.news.az/articles/19078.

"'Moscow declaration' a victory for Armenia", *Radio Free Europe/Radio Liberty*, 3 November 2008, http://www.rferl.org/content/Moscow_Declaration_A_Victory_For_Armenia/1337592.html.

"Nagorno-Karabakh: timeline of the long road to peace", *Radio Free Europe/Radio Liberty*, 10 February 2006, http://www.rferl.org/content/article/1065626.html.

"Nikolay Bordyuzha: Armenia is Russia's ally in CSTO with all its consequences", *Panorama.am*, 6 July 2011, http://www.panorama.am/en/politics/2011/07/06/bordyuja/.

"OSCE calls for withdrawal of snipers from Azeri-Armenian front line", *News.az*, 18 March 2011, http://news.az/articles/armenia/33166.

"OSCE Chairman Rep. Calls for end to war threats", *Asbarez*, 7 June 2011, http://asbarez.com/96429/osce-chairman-rep-call-for-end-to-war-threats/?utm_source=feedburner&utm_medium=feed&utm_campaign=Feed%3A+Asbarez+%28Asbarez+News%29.

"OSCE CiO urges Baku to withdraw snipers from Karabakh conflict zone", *Panarmenian. net*, 14 March 2011, http://www.panarmenian.net/eng/world/news/64065/.

"Present-day Armenia located in ancient Azerbaijani lands – Ilham Aliyev", *News.Az*, 16 October 2010.

"President discloses key elements of Garabagh paper", *Azernews*, 3 December 2008, http://www.azernews.az/en/Nation/9099-President_discloses_key_elements_of_Garabagh_paper.

"RF recognized its support territorial integrity of Azerbaijan" [RF podtverdila podderzhku territorial'noi tselostnosti Azerbaijana], http://www.rian.ru/politics/20100524/237860555.html.

"Russia has Lion's share in investments in Armenia: Russian trade representative. Yerevan", *Arka News Agency*, 17 September 2008, www.arka.am/eng/economy/2008/09/17/11200.html.

"Russia's Medvedev 'frustrated' with Karabakh impasse", *Radio Free Europe/Radio Liberty* 27 June 2011, http://www.rferl.org/content/russia_medvedev_frustrated_karabakh_impasse/24248417.html.

"Russian energy giants to invest in Armenian utilities", 17 June 2011, http://www.rferl.org/content/russian_energy_giants_to_invest_in_armenian_utilities/24238600.html.

"Russian president disappointed with the results of the Kazan summit on Nagorno Karabakh conflict settlement", *Itar-tass*, 27 June 2011, http://www.itar-tass.com/en/c142/173888_print.html.

"Russian troops in Armenia set for mission upgrade", *Radio Free Europe/Radio Liberty*, 31 July 2010.

"The Armenia's MFA promulgated the Armenian-Turkish protocols: the full versions [MID Armenii obnarodoval Armyano-Turetskiye Protokoly: polnye versii]", *News of Armenia (Novosti Armenii)*, 31 Augusr 2009, http://news.am/ru/news/3438.html.

"The Black Sea brought Russia and Turkey together" [Chernoe more cblizilo Posiyu I Turtsiyu], 16 May 2009, http://www.dni.ru/economy/2009/5/16/166399.html.

"The Nagorno-Karabakh Ministry of Defense: on the Azerbaijani military post incident took place [Ministerstvo oborony Nagornogo Karabakha: na postu VS Azerbaijana proizohhel intsident s primineniem oruzhiya], *The Caucasian knot [Kavkazskiy Uzel]*", 21 January 2010, http://karabakh.kavkaz-uzel.ru/articles/164575/.

"Theoretically placement of Turkish military bases 'possible in Nakhchivan'", *News. Az*, 24 August 2010, http://www.news.az/articles/21523.

"There is a red line which we'll never cross", the Armenian president states', *Mediamax*, 30 August 2011, http://www.mediamax.am/en/news/karabakh/2187/.

"US asks for action from Turkey for reconciliation", *Hurriyet Daily News*, 24 July 2011, http://www.hurriyetdailynews.com/n.php?n=us-asks-for-action-from-turkey-for-reconciliation-2011-07-24.

"Vahan Hovhannisyan: lack of resettlement program makes Azerbaijan be cynical", *Panorama.am*, 25 March 2011, http://www.panorama.am/en/politics/2011/03/25/hovhannisyan/.

E. Danielyan "Armenia and Karabakh encouraged by UN court ruling on Kosovo", www.day.az, 22 July 2010, http://www.jamestown.org/programs/edm/single/?tx_ttnews%5Btt_news%5D=36679&tx_ttnews%5BbackPid%5D=484&no_cache=1.

M. Muradova "Azerbaijan, Armenia, Russia using faith to find Karabakh peace", *Eurasia Net*, 28 April 2010, http://www.eurasianet.org/node/60948.

M. Robinson, "Karabakh clashes risk escalation – EU envoy", *Reuters*, 8 September 2010, http://uk.reuters.com/article/2010/09/08/azerbaijan-armenia-idUKLDE6870BK20100908.

Other websites

Conference on Security and Co-operation in Europe, final act, Helsinki, 1 August 1975, http://www.osce.org/mc/39501.

Council of the European Union (2004) *2590th Council meeting – general affairs and external relations*, Press Release, 14 June, C/04/195, http://europa.eu/rapid/press

ReleasesAction.do?reference=PRES/04/195&format=HTML&aged=0&lg=et&guiLanguage=en.

Council of the European Union (2008) *Declaration by the presidency on behalf of the EU on the escalation of tension between Georgia and Russia*, Brussels, 6 May, PESC/08/59, http://europa.eu/rapid/pressReleasesAction.do?reference=PESC/08/59&format=HTML&aged=0&language=EN&guiLanguage=en.

Council of the European Union (2008) *Declaration by the Presidency on behalf of the European Union on Georgia*, Brussels, 21 April, PESC/08/52, http://europa.eu/rapid/pressReleasesAction.do?reference=PESC/08/52&format=HTML&aged=1&language=EN&guiLanguage=en.

Council of the European Union (2008) *HR Javier Solana on the situation in Abkhazia and South Ossetia*, Brussels, 11 July, S250/08, http://www.consilium.europa.eu/uedocs/cms_data/docs/pressdata/en/declarations/101791.pdf.

Council of the European Union (2009) *Joint declaration of the Prague Eastern Partnership Summit*, 8435/09 (Presse 78), Brussels, 7 May, http://www.europarl.europa.eu/meetdocs/2009_2014/documents/depa/dv/200/200909/20090930_04en.pdf.

Council of the European Union (2009) *Presidency report to the European Council on the European External Action Service*, 23 October, 14930/09, http://register.consilium.europa.eu/pdf/en/09/st14/st14930.en09.pdf.

Council of the European Union (2011) *New EU Special Representative for the South Caucasus and the crisis in Georgia*, Brussels, 26 August, http://www.consilium.europa.eu/uedocs/cms_Data/docs/pressdata/EN/foraff/124436.pdf.

Council of the European Union (2006), *Mission statement of Peter Semneby, EU Special Representative for the South Caucasus*, 20 February, http://eeas.europa.eu/policies/eu-special-representatives/former-special-representatives/pdf/peter_semneby.pdf

Delegation of the European Union to Georgia, Political & economic relations, http://eeas.europa.eu/delegations/georgia/eu_georgia/political_relations/index_en.htm.

Europa.eu

Europa (2010) *EU launches negotiations on association agreements with Armenia, Azerbaijan and Georgia*, Press Release, 15 July, IP/10/955, http://europa.eu/rapid/pressReleasesAction.do?reference=IP/10/955&format=HTML&aged=0&language=EN&guiLanguage=en.

Europa (2010) *Statement by the spokesperson of high representative Catherine Ashton on Nagorno-Karabakh*, A 110/10, Brussels, 22 June, http://www.consilium.europa.eu/uedocs/cms_data/docs/pressdata/EN/foraff/115451.pdf.

European Council (2010) *Remarks by Herman Van Rompuy at the OSCE Summit*, Astana, 1 December, PCE 288/10, http://www.consilium.europa.eu/uedocs/cms_Data/docs/pressdata/en/ec/118111.pdf.

European Parliament (2001) *EU relations with South Caucasus*, resolution on the communication from the Commission to the Council and the European Parliament on the European Union's relations with the South Caucasus, under the partnership and cooperation agreements, 28 February, http://www.europarl.europa.eu/sides/getDoc.do?pubRef=-//EP//TEXT+TA+P5-TA-2002-0085+0+DOC+XML+V0//EN.

European Parliament (2007) *EU-Armenia parliamentary cooperation committee ninth meeting*, Final statement and recommendations, Brussels, 29–30 January, http://www.europarl.europa.eu/meetdocs/2004_2009/documents/re/651/651470/651470en.pdf

European Parliament (2007) *Strengthening the European Neighbourhood Policy*, Strasbourg, 15 November, A6-0414/2007, http://www.europarl.europa.eu/sides/getDoc.do?type=TA&reference=P6-TA-2007-0538&language=EN.

European Parliament (2008) *A more effective EU policy for the South Caucasus: from promises to actions*, Strasbourg, 17 January, A6–0516/2007, http://www.europarl. europa.eu/sides/getDoc.do?type=TA&reference=P6-TA-2008–0016&language=EN.

European Parliament (2008) *Declaration on the situation in Georgia*, Brussels, 5 June, P6 TA(2008)0253, http://www.europarl.europa.eu/sides/getDoc. do?type=TA&reference=P6-TA-2008–0253&language=EN.

European Parliament (2008) *EU-Russia Summit of 26–27 June 2008*, Strasbourg, 19 June, P6_TA(2008)0309, http://www.europarl.europa.eu/sides/getDoc. do?type=TA&reference=P6-TA-2008–0309&language=EN.

European Parliament (2009) *EP-EU-Armenia parliamentary cooperation committee tenth meeting*, Final statement and recommendations, Yerevan, 7–8 April, http://www. europarl.europa.eu/meetdocs/2009_2014/documents/dsca/dv/dsca20091006_04/ dsca20091006_04en.pdf.

European Parliament (2010) *Motion for a European Parliament resolution on the need for an EU Strategy for the Southern Caucasus*, 23 April, http://www.europarl.europa.eu/ sides/getDoc.do?pubRef=-//EP//TEXT+REPORT+A7–2010-0123+0+DOC+XML+V0// EN&language=EN.

European Parliament (2010) *The need for an EU strategy for the South Caucasus*, Strasbourg, 20 May, A7–0123/2010, http://www.europarl.europa.eu/sides/getDoc. do?pubRef=-//EP//TEXT+TA+P7-TA-2010–0193+0+DOC+XML+V0//EN.

European Union (2010) *Statement by high representative Catherine Ashton on Nagorno Karabakh*, A 84/10, Brussels, 21 May, http://www.consilium.europa.eu/uedocs/ cmsUpload/114603.pdf .

European Union (2010) *Statement by HR Catherine Ashton on Nagorno-Karabakh*, A 110/10, Brussels, 22 June, http://www.consilium.europa.eu/uedocs/cms_Data/ docs/pressdata/EN/foraff/115451.pdf.

European Union (2011) *Statement by high representative Catherine Ashton on Azerbaijan*, A 194/1, Brussels, 20 May, http://www.consilium.europa.eu/uedocs/cms_data/ docs/pressdata/EN/foraff/122137.pdf.

European Union External Action (2008) *Report on the implementation of the European Security Strategy: providing security in a changing world*, Brussels, 11 December, http:// www.eu-un.europa.eu/documents/en/081211_EU%20Security%20Strategy.pdf.

European Union External Action, *Eastern Partnership*, http://ec.europa.eu/external_ relations/eastern/index_en.htm.

Executive Summary of the "Report of the OSCE Minsk Group Co-Chairs' field assessment mission to the occupied territories of Azerbaijan surrounding Nagorno-Karabakh", 24 March 2011, http://www.osce.org/mg/76209.

Joint declaration of the European Union and the republics of Armenia, Azerbaijan and Georgia, Europe – press release, 22 June 1999, http://europa.eu/rapid/pressReleasesAction.do?reference=PRES/99/202&format=HTML&aged=1&language=EN& guiLanguage=en.

Permanent Council (2011) *EU statement on human rights, fundamental freedoms and the rule of law in Azerbaijan*, Vienna, 1 September, http://www.delvie.ec.europa.eu/en/ eu_osce/eu_statements/2011/September/PC%20no.878%20-%20EU%20on%20 HR%20in%20AEZ.pdf.

OSCE.org

Joint statement by the heads of delegation of the Minsk Group Co-Chair countries, OSCE – Press Release, 17 July 2010, http://www.osce.org/press/72085.

OSCE Minsk Group draft, "Comprehensive agreement on the resolution of the Nagorno-Karabakh conflict", Argument II, point 2, July 1997.

"Report of the OSCE Minsk Group Co-Chairs' field assessment mission to the occupied territories of Azerbaijan Surrounding Nagorno-Karabakh", http://www.osce.org/mg/76209.

Statement by H.E. Mr. Edward Nalbandian, minister of foreign affairs of the Republic of Armenia at the 852nd meeting of the OSCE permanent council, Vienna, 3 March, 2011, PC.DEL/187/11, http://www.osce.org/pc/76003.

Statement by the OSCE Minsk Group Co-Chair countries, l'Aquila, 10 July 2009, http://www.osce.org/item/51152.

Statement by the OSCE Minsk Group Co-Chair countries, L'Aquila, Italy, 10 July 2009, http://www.osce.org/item/51152.

Others

"2010 Agreement in Russia and Azerbaijan legalized the borders between each other" [Rossiya I Azerbaijan uzakonili granitsu mezhdu soboi], 3 September 2010, http://www.rtkorr.com/news/2010/09/03/168737.new?ref=rss.

CA&CC Press, resolution of the European Parliament on Nagorno-Karabakh, 11 March 1999, http://www.ca-c.org/dataeng/books/book-1/12.appendix-20.shtml.

ComRes EuroPoll survey among MEPS about Nagorno-Karabakh , August 2010, http://www.eufoa.org/uploads/Documents/documents/European%20Friends%20of%20Armenia%20Europoll%20Report%20Sept2010%282%29.pdf.

D.C. Blair, "Annual threat assessment of the US Intelligence Community for the senate select committee on intelligence", 2 February 2010, http://www.dni.gov/testimonies/20100202_testimony.pdf.

European Friends of Armenia, "Collection of war threat statements by president Ilham Aliyev and other Azerbaijani Officials", http://www.eufoa.org/uploads/AliyevWarThreats.pdf.

Human Rights Watch (1997) Response to Armenian government letter on the town of Khojaly, Nagorno-Karabakh, 23 March, http://www.hrw.org/en/news/1997/03/23/response-armenian-government-letter-town-khojaly-nagorno-karabakh.

Independent International Fact-Finding Mission on the conflict in Georgia, September 2009, http://www.ceiig.ch/Report.html.

International affirmations of the Armenian genocide, http://www.wbarrow.co.uk/rememberarmenia/pdfs_in_chapters/02a_armenia2_affirmations.pdf.

Kremlin.ru, "Dmitry Medvedev, President of Armenia Serzh Sargsyan, and President of Azerbaijan Ilham Aliyev discussed future possibilities for reaching a settlement of the Nagorno-Karabakh conflict", 27 October 2010, http://eng.kremlin.ru/news/1206.

Kremlin.ru, "Ratification of agreement on state border between Russia and Azerbaijan", 27 June 2011, http://eng.kremlin.ru/acts/2476.

President.az, "Ilham Aliyev and President of Turkey Abdullah Gul had press conference", 16 August 2011, http://en.president.az/articles/605.

President.az, "Speech by Ilham Aliyev at the VII OSCE Summit", http://en.president.az/articles/1189.

RA Ministry of Foreign Affairs (2005) Statement in Armenian National Assembly hearings on resolution of the Nagorno-Karabakh Issue, 29 March, http://www.mfa.am/en/speeches/item/2005/03/29/vo/.

RA Ministry of Foreign Affairs (2010) Declarations of the OSCE Minsk Group Co-Chairs, 2009–2010, http://www.mfa.am/u_files/file/statementseng.pdf.

RA Ministry of Foreign Affairs (2011) The address of the foreign affairs minister Edward Nalbandyan at the annual press conference, summarizing the foreign policy, 14 January, http://www.mfa.am/en/press-conference/item/2011/01/14/nalbandian_summary/.

RA Ministry of Foreign Affairs (2011) The Armenian foreign affairs minister Edward Nalbandian received the OSCE Minsk Group Co-Chairs, press release, 09 June, http://www.mfa.am/en/press-releases/item/2011/06/09/mg_co_chairs/.

Statement by the presidency on behalf of the European Union at the OSCE Permanent Council on "presidential elections" in Abkhazia, Georgia, 12 December 2009, Vienna, 17 December 2009, http://www.se2009.eu/fr/reunions_actualites/2009/12/18/eu_statement_in_the_osce_on_presidential_elections_in_abkhazia_georgia_12_december_2009.html.

Tagliavini-Report, Vol. II, September 2009, p. 239 ff., http://www.ceiig.ch/pdf/IIFFMCG_Volume_II.pdf.

The British Alumni Association of Armenia, official website, http://www.baa.am/membership/list.php.

The Environmental Audit Committee, "Regional conflicts and BTC pipeline: concerns over ECGD's due diligence", http://bankwatch.org/documents/EAC_BTC_Conflict_26.8.08.pdf.

The European Azerbaijan Society, Azerbaijan and the UK – "The special relationship", external public communication, https://teas.eu/sites/default/files/UKAZ.pdf.

The Freedom House (2011) Nations in transit 2001, http://www.freedomhouse.org/images/File/nit/2011/NIT-2011-Release_Booklet.pdf.

The HALO Trust, "Nagorno Karabakh", http://www.halotrust.org/operational_areas/caucaus_balkans/nagorno_karabakh/problem.aspx.

The White House (2009) Joint statement on the Nagorno-Karabakh conflict by U.S. President Obama, Russian President Medvedev, and French President Sarkozy at the L'Aquila summit of the eight, July 10, http://www.whitehouse.gov/the_press_office/Joint-Statement-on-the-Nagorno-Karabakh-Conflict/.

The White House (2010) G8 Summit: Joint statement on the Nagorno-Karabakh conflict by Dmitry Medvedev, President of the Russian Federation, Barack Obama, President of The United States of America, and Nicolas Sarkozy, President of the French Republic, Muskoka, 26 June, http://www.whitehouse.gov/the-press-office/g8-summit-joint-statement-nagorno-karabakh-conflict-dmitry-medvedev-president-russi.

The White House (2011) Joint statement on the Nagorno-Karabakh conflict by Dmitry Medvedev, President of the Russian Federation, Barack Obama, President of the United States of America, and Nicolas Sarkozy, President of the French Republic at the Deauville Summit of the Eight, 26 May, http://www.whitehouse.gov/the-press-office/2011/05/26/joint-statement-nagorno-karabakh-conflict-dmitry-medvedev-president-russ.

UK parliament (1992) Hansard of the House of Lords Debate "Armenia and Nagorno-Karabakh", 15 December, vol. 541, http://hansard.millbanksystems.com/lords/1992/dec/15/armenia-and-nagorno-karabakh.

UN Embassy in Azerbaijan, official website, http://ukinazerbaijan.fco.gov.uk/en/about-us/working-with-azerbaijan1/funding-opportunities/020-CPP.

UN General Assembly (1970) Declaration on principles of International Law concerning Friendly Relations and Cooperation among states in accordance with the Charter of the United Nations, Resolution 2625 (XXV), http://daccess-dds-ny.un.org/doc/RESOLUTION/GEN/NR0/348/90/IMG/NR034890.pdf?OpenElement.

Official documents

Commission of the European Communities (2001) *Country strategy paper 2002–2006 and National Indicative Programme 2002–2003 – Republic of Armenia*, 27 December, http://eeas.europa.eu/armenia/csp/02_06_en.pdf.

Commission of the European Communities (2003) *Communication from the commission to the Council and the European Parliament "Wider Europe – neighbourhood: a new framework for relations with our Eastern and Southern neighbours"*, Com(2003)104 final, Brussels, 11 March, http://ec.europa.eu/world/enp/pdf/com03_104_en.pdf.

Commission of the European Communities (2004) *European Neighbourhood Policy*, Strategy Paper, Brussels, 12 May, COM(2004) 373 final.

Commission of the European Communities (2005) *European Neighbourhood Policy, Country Report, Armenia*, Commission Staff Working Paper, 2 March.

Council of the European Union (2010) *Council decision extending the mandate of the European Union Special Representative in South Caucasus*, 2010/109/CFSP, 22 February, Brussels.

ENPI Armenia Country Strategy Paper, 2007–2013.

European Commission (2010) *Progress Report Azerbaijan*, Commission staff working document, Brussels, 12 May, SEC(2010) 519, http://ec.europa.eu/world/enp/pdf/progress2010/sec10_519_en.pdf.

European Commission, High Representative of the European Union for Foreign Affairs and Security Policy (2011) "Implementation of the European Neighbourhood Policy in 2010, Country report: Armenia", Brussels, 25 May, http://ec.europa.eu/world/enp/pdf/progress2011/sec_11_639_en.pdf.

European Commission, High Representative of the European Union for Foreign Affairs and Security policy (2011) "Implementation of the European Neighbourhood Policy in 2010", Country report: Azerbaijan, Brussels, 25 May, http://ec.europa.eu/world/enp/pdf/progress2011/sec_11_640_en.pdf.

European Commission, High Representative of the European Union for Foreign Affairs and Security Policy (2011) "Implementation of the European Neighbourhood Policy in 2010, Country report: Georgia", Brussels, 25 May, http://ec.europa.eu/world/enp/pdf/progress2011/sec_11_649_en.pdf.

European Council (2003) *A secure Europe in a better world*, European Security Strategy, Brussels, 12 December.

European Neighbourhood and Partnership Instrument, Armenia: Country Strategy Paper 2007–2013, http://ec.europa.eu/world/enp/pdf/country/enpi_csp_armenia_en.pdf.

European Neighbourhood Policy, EU/Armenia Action Plan (2006) http://ec.europa.eu/world/enp/pdf/action_plans/armenia_enp_ap_final_en.pdf.

European Neighbourhood Policy, EU/Azerbaijan Action Plan (2006) http://ec.europa.eu/world/enp/pdf/action_plans/azerbaijan_enp_ap_final_en.pdf.

Gharabagh. Documents of Armenian Art (Documenti di Architettura Armena Series) (1988), Polytechnique and the Armenian Academy of Sciences, Milan, OEMME Edizioni.

Independent International Fact-Finding Mission on the Conflict in Georgia, Report Volume II, September 2009.

Official Journal of the European Communities (1988) *Joint resolution replacing Docs. B2- 538 and 587 88 – On the situation in Soviet Armenia*, No. C 94/117, July.

Official Journal of the European Communities (1988) *Troubles in Armenia: Joint resolution replacing Docs. B2–39, 47 and 67/88 – On recent events in Soviet Armenia*, No. C 94/117, 11 April.

Official Journal of the European Communities (1989) *Joint resolution replacing Docs. B2- 1262, 1296 and 1304/88 – On repression in Soviet Armenia*, No. C 12/146, 16 January.

Official Journal of the European Communities (1990) *Joint resolution replacing Docs. B3- 137, 139, 145, 156, 157 and 162/90 – On the situation in Armenia*, No. C 38/81, 19 February.

Official Journal of the European Communities (1990) *Joint resolution replacing Docs. B3- 137, 139, 145, 156, 157 and 162/90 – On the situation in Armenia*, No. C 38/82, 19 February.

Official Journal of the European Communities (1990) *Resolution on the situation in Armenia*, Doc. B3–556/90, No. C 96/260–261, 17 April.

Official Journal of the European Communities (1993) *Republics of former Soviet Union – East-West relations in Europe*, (a) B3–0540, 0551, 0554, 0565, 0605 and 0606/93, No. C 176/173, 28 June.

Official Journal of the European Communities (1993) *Resolution on Armenia*, Resolution B3–0049/93, No. C 42/165, 15 February.

Official Journal of the European Communities (2001) *Treaty of Nice amending the Treaty of the European Union, the treaties establishing the European Communities and certain related acts*, 10 March, 2001/C 80/01, http://eur-lex.europa.eu/en/treaties/dat/12001C/pdf/12001C_EN.pdf.

Official Journal of the European Communities (2004) *European Parliament resolution on EU policy towards South Caucasus*, P5_TA (2004)0122, No. C 98 E/197, 23 April.

Official Journal of the European Union (2003) *Extending and amending the mandate of the Special Representative of the European Union for the South Caucasus*, Council Joint Action 2003/872/CFSP, 8 December, http://www.consilium.europa.eu/uedocs/cmsUpload/L326–13.12.2003.pdf.

Official Journal of the European Union (2004) *Treaty establishing a Constitution for Europe*, C 310 Vol. 47, 16 December, available at http://eur-lex.europa.eu/JOHtml.do?uri=OJ:C:2004:310:SOM:en:HTML

Official Journal of the European Union (2007) *Treaty of Lisbon amending the Treaty on European Union and the Treaty establishing the European Community*, signed at Lisbon, 2007/C 306/01, 17 December, http://eur-lex.europa.eu/JOHtml.do?uri=OJ:C:2007:306:SOM:EN:HTML.

Official Journal of the European Union (2010) *Council Decision 2010/109/CFSP extending the mandate of the European Union Special Representative for the South Caucasus*, L. 46/16, 23 February.

Official Journal of the European Union (2010) *Extending the mandate of the European Union Special Representative in South Caucasus*, Council Decision 2010/109/CFSP, 22 February, http://eur-lex.europa.eu/LexUriServ/LexUriServ.do?uri=OJ:L:2010:046:0016:0019:EN:PDF.

Russian Text of the Agreement by W. Kazimirov Nikolajewitsch (2009) "Mir Karabachu" [Peace for Karabakh], Moscow.

United Nations (1969) *Vienna convention on the Law of Treaties*, 23 May, UNTS, Vol.1155, 331.

United Nations (1974) *Definition of aggression*, Resolution Nr. 3314 (XXIX) of the General Assembly, UN Yearbook, 14 December, A/RES/3314 (XXIX).

Index

Printed and bound in Great Britain by
CPI Antony Rowe, Chippenham and Eastbourne